THE WAR DIARY OF THE
EMPEROR FREDERICK III (1870-1871)

FREDERICK WILLIAM
Crown Prince of Prussia, afterward the Emperor Frederick III.
Published for the first time by permission of H.M. Emperor William II.

THE WAR DIARY OF THE EMPEROR FREDERICK III
1870-1871

TRANSLATED AND EDITED
by
A. R. ALLINSON, M.A.

Fully Illustrated

GREENWOOD PRESS, PUBLISHERS
WESTPORT, CONNECTICUT

Originally published in 1926
by Frederick A. Stokes Company, New York

First Greenwood Reprinting 1971

Library of Congress Catalogue Card Number 77-114529

SBN 8371-4824-3

Printed in the United States of America

FOREWORD

DURING his last visit to this country, on the occasion of the Jubilee celebrations of 1887, the Crown Prince of Germany (afterwards the Emperor Frederick III) deposited for safekeeping at Windsor Castle three boxes of papers, amongst them being the original MSS. of his Diary of the War of 1870–71. The Prince's own record of this in his own handwriting runs as follows :
"*Windsor Castle*, 18*th July*, 1887.—With the consent of Her Majesty the Queen of Great Britain and Ireland, Empress of India, I have here to-day handed over to the safekeeping of Dr. Muther (Librarian of Windsor Castle) three wooden boxes, bound with iron, my own personal property. The said boxes were in my presence placed in a secret, fireproof chamber under the state staircase of Windsor Castle, on which occasion only Dr. Muther and the Keeper of the said Castle, along with my lackey Lüdtke, were present. . . ."
The reason for this rather strange procedure—the delivery of the intimate papers of the German heir to the Throne into the care of a foreign State—is in part explained in an entry made by the Empress Frederick (Crown Princess of England) in her private Diary :
" He (the Crown Prince) unfortunately could not consider them in safe custody in Berlin, and, as he believed he might perhaps be sent the next winter on a journey to a foreign country, he regarded his papers as being in a better place of concealment under Mamma's care than in our house in Berlin."
The tacit reference is no doubt to Prince Bismarck, the more or less avowed enemy of the Crown Prince and his English Consort and their political party generally.
The year following, after the Emperor's death (June 15, 1888), and in connection with the unsealing and inspection of his father's literary remains ordered by a decree of the Emperor William II (the now " ex-Kaiser "), the widowed Empress had the three boxes returned to her from Windsor, and after repeated examinations of the contents by Ministers of the Crown appointed for the purpose, a selection from the

papers was deposited in the Domestic Archives at Berlin, including the four successive recensions of the War Diary.

. . . . . .

Years before this, however, access to the manuscript War Diary had been obtained by a protégé of the Crown Prince's, Professor Heinrich Geffcken, under the following circumstances, as stated by himself :—The late Emperor Frederick, whose contemporary he had been as a student at Bonn, and who had subsequently shown him repeated favours, had in February 1873 invited him (at that time Professor of Constitutional History at Strasburg) to visit him at Wiesbaden, where the Prince was taking a cure, and had there handed him for his inspection a Diary concerning the events of the War of 1870–71. With the Prince's permission he had taken this with him to Carlsbad, returning it to the lender in about three weeks' time.

Eventually, in August 1888, after his patron's death, he prepared for the press a number of extracts—running to something less than twenty pages and mainly of political interest, and these appeared in the October number of the *Deutsche Rundschau* of that year. Geffcken was put on his trial for high treason, though the prosecution was soon abandoned, while Bismarck seized the opportunity to write a Report to the Emperor, in which he denied or questioned the accuracy of a number of the assertions of the Diary and took occasion to make a venomous attack on the author, and generally to belittle the memory of the late Sovereign. " Begotten of hate and born of passion, it (the Chancellor's Report) does not belie its origin. It was meant to expose and disparage the Crown Prince's liberal English political views."

The only result was a resounding scandal and much embittered controversy, in the course of which the publication of the Diary *in extenso* was loudly called for. But this demand it was impossible to satisfy, the author having left explicit written instructions that the work was not to be made public till after the lapse of fifty years from the date of its final completion. This period has now expired, and 1926 has seen the publication in Germany of the complete Diary, printed from the last and fullest of the successive recensions of the text, under the editorship of the distinguished scholar and *littérateur*, Dr. H. O. Meisner.

. . . .

These successive recensions are four in number :

(A) A series of entries in the Crown Prince's own hand in two red leather note-books (a gift, as noted by himself in the first volume, from the English Queen), evidently made at the time or immediately after the events described; these run from July 26, 1870, the date of leaving home, to March 17, 1871, when the writer was back again in Berlin; the entries are continuous, but from the nature of the case brief.

(B) 1. A version written in the Prince's own hand on large quarto sheets of paper, beginning July 26, 1870, and ending March 14, 1871, the date of arrival back on German soil, with superscription, " Diary during the War 1870." Evidently not the first draft, but a copy made with chemical ink from an original now no longer existing.

2. The same version in another hand on single sheets of silver paper written on one side only; again apparently a copy made with chemical ink; bound in red leather with gilt edges; with note in the author's own hand at the beginning: " Duplicate of my daily entries for the Crown Princess."

(C) Shows the work in a much more advanced stage; a transcript made by Krug, at that time Groom of the Chambers to the Prince, on folio sheets written on one side only; copiously corrected throughout by the Crown Prince and occasionally by other hands. Including considerable additions by the author, it already amounts to 366 folio pages as against the 245 quarto pages of (B); a note in the Crown Prince's hand on the cardboard box containing the MS. reads, " First Revision of the Diary." The large increase in bulk is mainly due to the inclusion of material from the correspondence with the Crown Princess.

(D) The last and final revision followed in the text as now printed and published; another fair copy in Krug's handwriting from the Crown Prince's original copy of (C), but revised by a number of other persons and with large additions in the author's hand, chiefly relating to military details, but involving no changes of definite importance; the length has now increased to 761 folio pages. Finally completed, in all probability, in the course of the year 1872.

. . . . .

The style and general temper of the Diary are eminently characteristic of its author—manly, direct, straightforward and unassuming. Little attempt is made after literary polish, and anything like fine writing is conspicuous by its absence. In places sentences are clumsily put together and the phraseology awkward and inelegant; but the meaning is always clear, the facts succinctly and effectively marshalled and the writer's views and personal opinions expressed in forcible and unmistakable language. The general impression produced throughout on the reader's mind is that of a man of a powerful and well-balanced intellect, a kindly and sympathetic nature, and an affectionate, if at times a rather sentimental, temperament. Again and again, in strong contrast to Bismarck's brutal attitude, as revealed in Dr. Busch's "Life," towards the beaten French, the Crown Prince's expressions of sympathy and commiseration, albeit not unmixed with contempt, for the vanquished foe stand out agreeably.

. . . .

As especially noteworthy features may be singled out: the author's descriptions of the battles of Weissenburg and of Wörth (August 4 and 6, 1870), at both of which he was in command; that of the battle of Sedan (September 1, 1870), at which he was present, and his narrative of the interview after the French *débâcle* between Napoleon III and King William; intimate side-lights on the characters of Bismarck and von Moltke; incidents of the long-protracted siege of Paris; details of the negotiations for an Armistice, and later for Peace—Jules Favre, Thiers and Count Bismarck; particulars of the ceremonial Proclamation of "Emperor and Empire" in the *Salle des Glaces* of the Palace of Versailles and of the highly dramatic discussion on the evening before that event between the King, the Crown Prince and Count Bismarck; and finally the account of the entry of the German troops into the French capital.

. . . .

No doubt, apart from these and the like "purple patches," the Diary is not without its *longueurs;* but as a whole the book forms a valuable and fascinating contribution to our knowledge of a momentous period of history as mirrored in the mind of an eye-witness, and one pre-eminently in a position to observe and judge events accurately and dispassionately from the inside.

A. R. ALLINSON.

Hampstead.

CONTENTS

	PAGE
FOREWORD	v
DIARY—JULY 11, 1870, TO JULY 17, 1871	
PREFACE	1
TEXT	3
APPENDIX	341
INDEX	343
MAP OF THE SCENE OF WAR	*at end*

ILLUSTRATIONS

FREDERICK WILLIAM, CROWN PRINCE OF PRUSSIA (AFTERWARDS THE EMPEROR FREDERICK III)		*Frontispiece*
THE CROWN PRINCE AT THE BATTLE OF WÖRTH	*Facing page*	32
VICTORIA, CROWN PRINCESS OF PRUSSIA (AFTERWARDS THE EMPRESS FREDERICK)	,, ,,	62
NAPOLEON III, EMPEROR OF THE FRENCH	,, ,,	98
EUGÉNIE, EMPRESS OF THE FRENCH	,, ,,	128
VILLA "LES OMBRAGES," RESIDENCE OF THE CROWN PRINCE AT VERSAILLES	,, ,,	140
BISMARCK AT VERSAILLES	,, ,,	170
FRIEDRICH KARL, PRINCE OF PRUSSIA	,, ,,	192
LUDWIG II, KING OF BAVARIA	,, ,,	210
GENERAL BLUMENTHAL	,, ,,	224
FRIEDRICH I, GRAND DUKE OF BADEN	,, ,,	250
WILLIAM I, GERMAN EMPEROR, KING OF PRUSSIA	,, ,,	268
JULES FAVRE	,, ,,	282
LÉON GAMBETTA	,, ,,	298
ADOLPHE THIERS	,, ,,	314
MOLTKE BEFORE PARIS	,, ,,	330

THE daily impressions received during the campaign of 1870, 1871 and only cursorily jotted down in my Diary under stress of military duties I have supplemented and completed since my subsequent return home by extracts from the correspondence regularly maintained between my wife and myself.

On principle, however, I was firmly resolved to set down only my actual, personal experiences and feelings from day to day; consequently no improvement or alteration has been made under the influence of later events.

Thus my Diary is a contribution to the history of that great and memorable War, containing also much information, hardly to be found elsewhere, throwing light on events of which the outside world takes a view differing widely from the reality. Similarly, the character of prominent personages will often wear another aspect than that in which the present age and History represent it.

But revelations of this kind are not for contemporaries to know; I therefore direct that no one else but my wife and my grown-up children is to examine my Diary till the year 1922 is ended. After that there is nothing to hinder its publication.

MY DIARY DURING THE CAMPAIGN OF 1870, 1871 AGAINST FRANCE

From the moment when, in the early days of July, the claim of the Hereditary Prince Leopold of Hohenzollern had roused feelings of lively excitement among the French and speeches of a tone hostile to Prussia were heard in the French Chamber, as well on the part of Deputies as of Ministers, the general situation in Europe, hitherto entirely peaceful and inoffensive, had quite suddenly assumed a critical aspect. I had in consequence gone repeatedly from Potsdam to Berlin to visit the Foreign Office in search of enlightenment from the representative, Acting Privy Councillor von Thile, of Count Bismarck, then absent in the country at Varzin. At the same time, despite the language held by the French, I could not think that France was seriously contemplating a breach with us, still less that a war was at our very doors.

As a rule our interviews took place in the garden of the Ministerial building, where, besides Herr von Thile, I also met Colonel von Stiehle, who represented the Chief of the General Staff, General of Infantry von Moltke. While the political and military aspects were by turns under discussion, the Spanish Ambassador (Don J. de Rascou) would be patrolling the side paths, hoping for information,— which, however, could not be afforded him, as obviously Prussia had nothing to do with the family concerns of the Hohenzollerns.

11th July.—The news from France assumes an exceedingly menacing character; to-day Herr von Thile took a very grave view of the situation, and could hardly, in these difficult circumstances, rest content to have to rely on telegraphic correspondence between the Royal Court at Ems, the residence of Count Bismarck in Lower Pomerania and that of the Prince of Hohenzollern at Sigmaringen, and only in this way receive his instructions. It was now urged on all sides that the Hereditary Prince should repudiate his undertaking to mount the Spanish throne; but no one knew where he was, for, thinking no ill, he had undertaken a holiday tour in the Alps.

No less embarrassing to the French Embassy was this aggravation of difficulties, for the Secretary, M. le Sourd (the Ambassador accredited to the North German Confederation, Count Benedetti, was at Ems), has, in presence of the Austrian Chargé d'affaires (Baron von Münch-Bellinghausen), expressed his intention of leaving Berlin, on the grounds that there is nobody there with whom he can discuss affairs, and, into the bargain, he receives no replies to questions asked. Colonel von Stiehle, on the contrary, was very optimistic, convinced that, if it did come to war, we should beat the French.

I had to-day to tell my wife explicitly that things were taking a serious turn,—information I had till now refrained from giving her, seeing that barely four weeks had elapsed since the birth of our daughter (the Princess Sophie) on June 14.

12th July.—To-day Count Bismarck announced that, in view of the menacing condition of things, he proposed to come to Berlin,—a sure sign we are begirt with perils. The news from Paris makes it appear no longer an improbability that the French may actually effect an inroad with unmobilized troops into German territory. This and other less disquieting information I received at the house of Second Lieutenant Count zu Dohna-Schlodien of the 1st Dragoon Guards regiment as I held his infant daughter at the font.

The French Ambassador, M. Benedetti, has been staying for some days now at Bad Ems and seems to be in frequent personal communication with His Majesty. Here in Berlin Prince Gortschakoff, Russian Imperial Chancellor, and Prince Heinrich VII of Reuss have arrived.

13th July.—I had a conversation of some length with Count Bismarck, who late last night received news that the Hereditary Prince of Hohenzollern renounced his claims to the Spanish throne, by which step he regards peace as assured; he is persuaded, therefore, he may very soon be able to return to Varzin. He gave me the impression of being taken completely unawares by the sudden and threatening turn of affairs in France.

After that, came Count Gortschakoff to see me; he considers peace to be in any case assured, notwithstanding tidings that have just reached him to the effect that France is not yet satisfied by the mere fact of the Hereditary Prince's renunciation, but requires guarantees from Prussia that no other Hohenzollern shall ever go to Spain as king; he thinks we must wait and see if this is so, and in that case consider what attitude we should adopt in view of such a demand; but he still believes that even this point may find its solution. Our behaviour in the whole matter, no less than the course pursued by the Hereditary Prince, and finally the temper of our Press, filled him, he declared, with such admiration that he would fain take measures to make the Cabinets of the Great European Powers cognizant of the facts.

From Paris I heard how a few days ago the Emperor Napoleon said to one of his former Ministers,—a truth indeed that everybody must realize,—that at the present moment Spanish concerns are practically unimportant, inasmuch as the question really at issue is the struggle for preponderance of power as between France and Prussia. If this is authentic, we should be fully justified in concluding that France is resolved on war at any price.

Some of the French papers criticize the policy of the French Cabinet, while Ollivier's organs, on the contrary, say that, apart from the Hohenzollern renunciation, the further concession must be made by Prussia to surrender Mainz absolutely to the South Germans, to break off their military relations with Prussia, and finally to carry out the stipulations of Article V of the Peace of Prague relative to North Schleswig.

14*th July.*—To-day hopes of maintaining peace again vanish, for the French demands indicated by Prince Gortschakoff have actually been sent through M. Benedetti to our King, who of course instantly rejected them and, recognizing the whole infamy of France, leaves Ems to-morrow, to await the conclusion of matters at Berlin. We must therefore make up our minds for the worst!

15*th July.*—Count Bismarck informed me that in the afternoon, accompanied by the Minister of War and General von Moltke, he was going to Brandenburg to see the King, immediately to lay before His Majesty the seriousness of the situation and bring about a definite decision without delay. I joined the party. On the way Count Bismarck explained to us in clear, earnest and dignified language, without any of those jests and gibes he is usually so fond of, his views of our relations with France, so that I now realized quite plainly that by this time any concession for the sake of peace was become impossible. The strength and condition of the French Army he and General von Moltke painted as being in reality far less imposing than was hitherto imagined, making our prospects more favourable than has been supposed.

Arrived at Brandenburg, we found the King surrounded by an excited throng; at every station from Ems to here he had met with the most encouraging signs of enthusiasm in view of the probability of war. He was not a little surprised at our coming, but after listening to Count Bismarck's discourse on the return journey, he could raise no serious objections against the urgency of an imperative order of mobilization.

When we arrived at the provisional Potsdam Station at Berlin, Herr von Thile whispered in my ear that war had already been declared in Paris by Ollivier; at that same moment, in the waiting-room, the telegraphic summary of Ollivier's speech was handed to His Majesty, leaving no possibility of further doubt that war was decided on. I had to read the telegram aloud, whereupon the King said to Count Bismarck, Generals von Roon and von Moltke that now the VIIth and VIIIth Army Corps must be mobilized, for without a doubt in four-and-twenty hours the French would appear before Mainz. But I pressed His Majesty to order the immediate mobilization of the whole Army, Landwehr and Fleet, as under the circumstances no time was to be lost. The King acquiesced and, without moving from the waiting-room, gave the order for mobilization, and there and then I announced the news to the public waiting on the platform.

The King embraced me with the deepest emotion; we both felt we must prepare ourselves for a contest involving the most sacred rights and privileges, perhaps the very existence, of the Fatherland, a battle that must be fought out with streams of the noblest blood of our People ! Thereupon the King, and I with him, drove off. The crowd stood shoulder to shoulder all the way from the station to the Royal Palace, uttering one unbroken storm of cheers that gave witness to their enthusiasm for the coming struggle.

Before the Palace, so dense was the crowd that it was with difficulty we reached the terrace, itself thronged with officers. The cheers were never-ending. Again and again the King had to show himself, whereupon the whole assembled multitude with one voice sang the " Heil dir im Siegerkranz," and then " Die Wacht am Rhein." The latter the

King only recognized when I drew his attention to it; at this moment all felt what a solemnity of meaning underlay the words.

16*th July.*—I had again passed the night at the "New Palace" at Potsdam, and felt bound next morning to communicate to my wife frankly and freely the whole state of affairs; then I returned to Berlin to witness the preparations for the march to the front.

His Majesty does not wish to decide just yet upon the highest commands and the distribution of posts on the General Staff; but it seems that three great Armies are to be organized, one of which, made up of the South German contingents, will be put under my command,—undoubtedly the most onerous of responsibilities, with these troops so ill-disposed towards us and quite untrained in our school, to have to fight so efficient an adversary, one, moreover, long since prepared against this War, who will certainly invade South Germany long before those States are likely to be ready with their mobilization.

The North German Reichstag is convoked for July 19th.

17*th July. Sunday.*—At the Potsdam Garrison Church we sang "Ein' feste Burg"; Divisionsprediger Strauss preached an impressive sermon. Afterwards in Berlin I attended a Council of War at the Palace, at which His Majesty showed himself more compliant than yesterday. It was noteworthy how no one would speak right out when the question came up as to Prince Friedrich Karl and his appointment to a high command, until His Majesty in some excitement insisted on an expression of opinion, and then how all were unanimous that the Prince should lead that Army (the IInd Army as it is entitled) which the King would accompany and so be on the spot to exercise special control.

To me were assigned all South German troops, together with the XIth Prussian Army Corps, which the Commander of the 20th Division, Lieutenant-General von Bose, is to receive, with the prospect also of getting the Vth Army Corps I am so attached to (to which under Steinmetz I owed my first victories of Nachod, Skalitz and Schweinschädel, in the Bohemian campaign).

My request to have Major-General von Stosch again as Chief of the General Staff or as Quartermaster-General could not be granted, as he is absolutely indispensable as Intendant-General of the Army. On this I begged for my old and trusty friend Lieutenant-General von Blumenthal, Commander of the 14th Division as Chief of Staff, and Colonel von Gottberg, Chief of the General Staff of the IXth Army Corps as Quartermaster-General.

The enthusiasm for the War is positively indescribable; in view of the perilous situation of the Country every party predilection is ignored. There is a rush to join the colours, every man is eager to share the fight, and even in South Germany the population is so fired with a unanimous zeal for this War that Princes and Cabinets will find it impossible to stem the current, much as they might wish to. Even from America come the most encouraging telegrams, cheering on the King for the coming struggle! One may truly say that, in face of the wanton provocation of France, all Germany has risen like one man; it will very surely re-establish her unity.

18th July.—Wherever I appear, masses of excited sympathizers crowd about me; never before have I seen such genuine unaffected devotion to a great cause as was manifested during these three days; in fact this temper of mind is far and away more marked than it was at the outbreak of the Austrian War of 1866.

19th July.—To-day the ceremonial opening of the North German Reichstag by His Majesty took place in the White Hall. The Deputies had attended in numbers never before equalled, and gave evidence of unanimous enthusiasm during the reading of the really fine and dignified speech, free from any sort of controversial matter, which was delivered by the King in a voice trembling with emotion.

The official declaration of war was to-day presented by the Secretary of Legation, Le Sourd, to Count Bismarck; it would seem to abound in foolish phrases. In a few days the French Embassy quits Berlin. Colonel Stoffel goes to-day, it having been made pretty clear to him that his further presence here is undesirable.

In company with the King I went for the anniversary of the death of Queen Luise to Charlottenburg, where we prayed for some time and with very anxious hearts beside the coffin of the grandparents. On leaving, I said to my father that a struggle begun under such auspices must be won. I hope to God I have foretold right!

My official nomination to the supreme command of the IIIrd Army, which is to consist of the Vth and XIth Prussian, both Bavarian Army Corps, together with the

Württemberg and Baden Divisions, I received to-day; I must start without any delay for South Germany, to make acquaintance with my new subordinates.

I shall soon be parted from wife and children. To-day, at any rate, we had a peaceful afternoon together.

20th July.—I went to see General von Moltke, to discuss things with him, as also to glean information from the Offices of the General Staff about the South Germans. General von Moltke thinks I should not go to South Germany yet.

After that, I went to see Count Bismarck, who advised me, at once and *en clair*, to telegraph, by way of personal announcement, to the South German Princes the news of my coming arrival, as the impression produced would be excellent; so far as practicable, he said I should certainly visit those Courts. We went together to His Majesty, and Count Bismarck gave his views. I sent off my telegram there and then.

In France the temper of the country would seem to be against the War, while that of the troops is by no means so chauvinistic as it originally was said to be.

From the Hanover district highly treasonable expressions are to be heard; we must keep a watchful eye on that Province.

England seems to be pushing forward preparations for war, but meantime has entrusted her Ambassador here (Lord Augustus Loftus) with the duty of representing the French Embassy.

21st July.—Duke Ernst of Saxe-Coburg arrived in Berlin, having travelled day and night from Fiume, where the War news reached him, and asks for employment as Commander of a Reserve Army Corps, or, supposing a flanking force were established in the Elbe dukedoms, for command of the troops assigned that duty, or else the command of an important Cavalry Reserve Corps attached to one of the main Armies. Should none of these demands be fulfilled, he desires active duties on my Staff.

22nd July.—My mother arrived early this morning from Coblenz, greatly moved by the enthusiastic temper shown on the Rhine.

My Staff comes together little by little; as in 1866, the offices are installed in my Palace.

Most of the German Princes are arriving to offer their services to the King and express their devotion to the common good of the Fatherland.

23rd July.—To-day I spent quietly at the "New Palace" with my dear ones, my thoughts a little distracted from the alarmingly serious situation in which we stand by the preparations for the baptism of my engaging little daughter Sophie, which is appointed for to-morrow.

Troop trains are running night and day, all the usual passenger services being cancelled.

24th July.—To-day, on the birthday of my dear daughter Charlotte, our youngest daughter, Sophie Dorothea Ulrika Alice, was baptized with the traditional ceremonial and the utmost display of the customary pomp and parade. The King was too deeply affected to hold the child himself, and my mother undertook the office. The Kings of Bavaria and Württemberg I had invited to be godfathers in view of their proven friendliness as our allies, and seeing I am appointed leader of their troops. Among the company, arrayed in gala dress, reigned a feeling of gravity and gloom; I took this opportunity to make my farewells to all my guests, so that in the main this baptismal festival bore more the character of a good-bye party than anything else. Which of us will come back?—that was the thought of everyone who accompanies us on the great venture; but that in the end we shall win the day, even though the beginning may well be marked by losses, of this everybody is convinced. In many ways I deplore the fact that it has fallen to my lot to command the South Germans, an Army little to be depended on. I am fully determined to utilize it as a reserve force, which will be called upon to act mainly on the flank of the Army of the centre, for I shall hardly be in a position to carry out any great enterprises.

25th July.—I went to-day with my wife to pay a quiet visit to the grave of my son Sigismund [1] to take the Holy Sacrament.

In the afternoon I learned at Berlin that I must start to-morrow, the 26th July, at an early hour, if I am to visit Munich, Stuttgart and Karlsruhe before the marshalling of my Army is completed. Unexpected as this news was, I was bound to find time to communicate it to my parents and at the same moment to bid them farewell!

I had given orders that the Vth and XIth Army Corps should occupy close lines of cantonments about Landau and Germersheim for the defence of our position on the Klingbach

---

[1] The third son of the Crown Prince, born Sept. 15, 1864, died June 18, 1866; interred in the Friedenskirche at Potsdam.

and that Lieutenant-General von Kirchbach should immediately assume command of them. Should the enemy pass the Rhine at Strasburg, the XIth Army Corps is to cross the river at Germersheim to reinforce the Baden forces at Oos under the supreme command of Lieutenant-General von Werder. If, however, the French take the offensive on the left bank of the Rhine, Württembergers and Badeners are to march by way of the Maxau and Germersheim on the Klingbach, where, supposing the Bavarians are not yet ready for action, the IVth Army Corps will, if need be, serve as support.

26th July.—To-day I left wife and children, and at half-past five in the morning drove away from the "New Palace." The thought of sharing the same pang of parting with all my married fellow-countrymen faring to the front gave me some sort of composure in this terrible hour. As my wife and I had agreed that, whenever my departure was settled, we would bid one another no formal farewell, I had told her nothing yesterday of my start being suddenly fixed for this morning and so spared her the actual final good-bye before the War by giving her no explicit reason for my leaving at such an early hour. Only when I was already on the way did my little daughter Viktoria, who saw me off sobbing and crying and would *not* let me go, convey a line or two from me that told her how things stood. My children, on the contrary, knew that I was bound for the scene of action, —but I must not let my thoughts dwell on those moments.

At Grossbeeren—perhaps a good omen—I took train and travelled by way of Leipzig, where authorities and inhabitants gave me a very cordial welcome, to Munich, Stuttgart and Karlsruhe, to announce myself and my appointment personally to the South German Princes, whose troops I am to command together with the Vth and XIth Army Corps. A military train, which carried the 2nd battalion of the Silesian Fusilier regiment No. 38—old comrades of my Silesian Army of 1866—brought us in broiling hot weather, and after an extremely tedious journey, to Bamberg. At Wittenberg I saw the works for the repair of the fortifications, which had been carried to the fullest completion with all possible speed; God grant the necessity may never arise for defending ourselves there! At Altenburg I found the Ducal family assembled on the platform. At every Saxon, and later every Bavarian station, we were received with enthusiastic cheers, while special Committees entertained the men, exhausted by the oppressive heat. Frequently I was personally acclaimed as "The Generalissimo of the South German host!" Who would ever before have dreamed that Bavarians and Saxons would greet a Prussian Prince with tumultuous hurrahs specially emphasizing the Unification of our Country.

At the station, telegrams announced the advance of the French forces against the frontier of the Palatinate; the telegraphist's limbs were shaking with excitement, and he could not comprehend how the news failed to fill us with consternation and how we could calmly proceed on our way to Munich.

27th July.—Soon after sunrise I arrived at Nuremberg, the place I love so well, where the assembled multitude welcomed me almost as if I were in a Prussian town; and so it went on everywhere,—at Ingolstadt, where I addressed the Officers' Corps of the garrison assembled at the railway station, and all the way to Moosburg, whither King Ludwig had come to greet me.

I find him strikingly altered; his good looks have largely vanished, he has lost his front teeth, looks pale and has something nervous and agitated in his way of speaking, so that he never waits to hear the answer to his own question, but while his interlocutor is speaking is putting fresh questions relating to other matters. He appears to me to be heart and soul in the business, and to be eagerly following the national bent. His swift decision to sign the order for mobilization presented to him by the War Minister, Lieutenant-General von Pranckh, without the cognizance of the Minister for Foreign Affairs, Count Bray, is universally commended.

At the railway station at Munich there awaited me all the Royal Princes, the Staff and Guard of Honour of the Infantry and Cavalry, as well as an extraordinarily large number of the public, whose cheers gave me a tumultuous and enthusiastic welcome. Queen Marie was awaiting me in the "Trier" apartments assigned to me; she looks well and dear as ever, and displayed a touching and friendly cordiality. Duke Friedrich zu Schleswig-Holstein, to my utter surprise, I found here, and that as a just appointed Bavarian General. He seems to me, pending the definite settlement of the German question, to be desirous of substituting for his erstwhile attitude of reserve a certain inclination to change sides; however, he refuses to don a Prussian uniform, but prefers to take his part in the War as a Bavarian soldier, later on to complete his reconciliation with us. Meantime he has addressed an open letter to his people, in which he informs them of his sentiments. But for the immediate present he goes back home again to put his household affairs in order.

Count Usedom and Prince Chlodwig Hohenlohe I was delighted to find of the party. The latter has no doubt of Austria adopting an attitude of absolute neutrality, but cannot come to any very clear conception of the views of a Cabinet under the direction of Beust, which of course is bound to pay proper regard to Hungary and German Austria. Count Andrassy he does not look upon as the friend of Germany he has hitherto passed for. Bavaria's present attitude he thinks admits of no doubt; albeit at the time the loan was under consideration there was a moment when the Committee [1] had spoken in far from patriotic terms; fortunately, however, he said, in full session the National party had won the day and the mischievous Ultramontane faction was outvoted.

Dinner *en famille* with music, but in an anxious mood on the part of the high dignitaries, preceded a gala performance at the Theatre, at which "Wallenstein's Lager" with Prologue was admirably performed. At our entrance and exit, as well as at different other opportunities, we were greeted in a full house with tumultuous applause by the public. The King thought that Schiller in his writings largely expressed democratic tendencies, and believes that for this reason the erection of the monument to him in Berlin will not be popular. He asked me whether it was still customary in the Prussian Army for every soldier to take his doxy on service with him!

At two in the morning I pursued my journey to Stuttgart, after another cheery tea in the Queen's apartments had ended the day. As I took train a letter from the King was handed me, in which, as Count Bray had already intimated, he expressed his heartfelt desire to see one day a triumphant Peace assure the independence of Bavaria.

28th July.—Early this morning I reached Ulm; here I was met by the newly-appointed Commandant of the fortress built by him, Lieutenant-General von Prittwitz, who, for all his seventy-five years, looked like a young man, fresh, hale and hearty, and could not speak too highly of the good relations existing between himself and the Bavarians and

---

[1] To which the Second Chamber had referred the demand of the Government for the granting an extraordinary credit of five to six million florins.

Württembergers. Even in Württemberg I was everywhere accorded the warmest of welcomes in the way of addresses and cheers.

At Stuttgart the King (Karl I) met me on the platform, surrounded by Princes, Generals and a Guard of Honour. My announcement he received with a stiff, formal politeness, then took me in his carriage and drove with me through a cheering, shouting crowd to visit Queen Olga. My Aunt [1] was in a friendly and gentle vein, yet I thought her looking pale and ill; she had me breakfast with her at once, after which the King, who is beginning to get grey, conducted me to my room. Here he talked a great deal about his "Kingly duties," and how one must know Württemberg thoroughly to judge it aright, for it was by no means so democratic as was usually supposed; but indeed the Constitution of the State, now of long standing (dating from 1819), had introduced many elements that made bad blood and had corrupted the Press; still he hoped, he said, that after the War these defects might be remedied. He concluded with the remark that he must get to his work, for he knew from long experience what his office implied, as he had first mounted the throne when forty years of age.

The War Minister, Lieutenant-General von Suckow, talks like a veritable fire-eater, is full of zeal and ardour for this great national endeavour and is a man wholly devoted to his office, who lashes in appropriate terms any whose behaviour has not been clean and straightforward. Minister von Varnbüler expressed himself very patriotically—in which sentiments I encouraged him—and set forth how not only had he all along been convinced that in the event of a French attack Germany would be one in defence of the Fatherland, but that he had, in the year 1867 at the railway station here, actually assured the Emperor Napoleon of this. The Minister asked me confidentially to use my influence that, as Prince Luitpold of Bavaria was in evidence at the Royal Headquarters, so on the part of Württemberg an Envoy might be received,—to which end he recommended Prince Wilhelm of Württemberg, General von Baumbach, for the present in command of the local Division, or else the Ambassador von Spitzemberg in Berlin, while the latter could be given another status as Major in the Landwehr. Only yesterday did the French Chancellor of Legation in this country, Delongraye, leave Stuttgart, while the Württemberg Envoy, who, as it

---

[1] Queen Olga was a daughter of the Tsar Nicholas I, husband of the Princess Charlotte of Prussia, paternal aunt, therefore, of the Crown Prince.

happens, is Varnbüler's son (!), has followed suit and quitted Paris.

A dinner in *campagne tenue*, as the invitation read, together with a drive to the " Villa Berg " with both their Majesties, concluded my stay. At my departure the crowd was still greater than in the morning and the cheering never-ending; in truth these South Germans gave me just as warm a welcome as we are accustomed to receive in our old Provinces. I felt almost embarrassed in presence of the King, who sat beside me in the carriage, for it was manifest these compliments were paid not to him, but to me as representative of the Power that had undertaken the solution of the German question,—a task the dynasty of Württemberg could hardly be accounted competent to carry through.

Several unknown individuals handed me uncommonly fine bouquets for my wife, one of which actually displayed the North German colours figured in dark pansies. Such demonstrations at such a time mean something, for they are in no way artificial; that is why I attach such importance to them, albeit I am well aware what a weight of responsibility this attitude of the German people lays on us for the future, when once, with God's help, an honourable, lasting peace has been attained.

I found Prince Gortschakoff here, the Russian Imperial Chancellor and Foreign Minister, who had been recalled to St. Petersburg, but whom the transport of troops prevented from going further. Our conversation, as may be supposed, was concerned with the state of affairs politically,—Austria's neutrality, the probable attitude of Denmark and Italy, the future of the South German States, and what else was of immediate interest. He believes that Austria will not depart from her neutrality, on the maintenance of which Russia keeps a watchful eye. It is sought, it seems to me, to induce Denmark to adopt an attitude of strict neutrality. Of Italy nothing definite was known; she would appear to have little money and small inclination to intervene for France. As to the future of the South Germans, Prince Gortschakoff pointed out to me how it would be wise to respect minor peculiarities of these States, as, for example, not to interfere with foreign Embassies accredited to them,—a thing I deemed quite natural, while I added further that, after such a war as the present, Germany would need an altogether different form of representation than had heretofore been customary in the North German Confederation. Moreover, I insisted that a closer military connection of the several German contingents with one another would be absolutely essential.

Count Zeppelin, of the Württemberg General Staff, who with three Baden officers and dragoons undertook a daring reconnaissance from Lauterburg, found on the 24th of the month the Sulzbach only lightly invested, got as far as Niederbronn, but was then surprised at Schirrlenhof, where he was just baiting his horses. For himself, he escaped with no little difficulty, while Lieutenant Winsloe fell and the rest were taken prisoners. So far then there seem to be no concentrations *en masse* in that section of the Lautertal. That the French are not even yet attacking is very remarkable; for the last two days their onslaught was hourly expected, and had already been notified several times in false telegrams. This unreadiness of the enemy points to miscalculations, which will surely give Napoleon bitter food for reflection, but over which every German is exultant.

In the evening I travelled to Karlsruhe, as always hitherto, welcomed at every railway station in a fashion betokening lively hope and confidence. The meeting with my sister and brother-in-law [1] was deeply moving, what with a brilliant gathering of officers, the Guard of Honour, and the enthusiastic public. My sister had already gone with her children to Heidelberg, as alarming rumours made their further stay at Karlsruhe appear dangerous; but now I was come, nothing stood in the way of their remaining at that place, to the great delight of the inhabitants; it was really touching to hear how all felt for the present truly relieved and actually in safety.

29th July.—I employed to-day in visiting the fully armed fortress of Rastatt, the Officers' Corps of which welcomed me enthusiastically. The fortress, its garrison reinforced by our Pomeranian regiment No. 34, gives the impression of being entirely defensible.

Genial hours with my brother and sister, my niece Marie [2] and her husband, Prince Wilhelm of Baden, who joins my headquarters, and Prince Herrmann Hohenlohe-Langenburg, who will undertake the volunteer nursing of the sick here, distracted us for the moment from the anxieties of the present. Our thoughts were mainly occupied with the question how we should henceforth contrive to direct the noble enthusiasm of the nation into right channels, and in what manner, after Peace had been fought for and won, we should endeavour to restore what has too long been allowed

---

[1] Only daughter of King William I, the Princess Luise, was wife of the Grand Duke Frederick I of Baden.

[2] Princess Maria Romanovska, daughter of Duke Maximilian of Leuchtenburg, a son-in-law of the Tsar Nicholas I.

to lapse, and whether a redoubled effort would prove effectual in completing a liberal and enlightened re-edification of Germany.

Active zeal distinguishes the inhabitants in nursing the sick and wounded; the Palace of the Grand Duchess Sophie is already completely equipped as a Depot.

30th July.—With a heavy heart I parted from my sister and her husband and left Karlsruhe, my mind stirred by the news that the French were advancing by way of Hüningen (northwards of Bâle) as well as on the confines of the Palatinate. The just completed Karlsruhe–Mannheim line I utilized as far as Lussheim, passing Wiesenthal and Waghäusel![1] On the way I visited a Bavarian infantry and cavalry bivouac, taking this opportunity to make acquaintance with the Bavarian soldier. True, the Prussian point of view must be entirely abandoned, for here everything is quite different from what it is with us; clumsiness of build and startling corpulence prevail even in the younger class of levies. Still the soldier shows quite a smart bearing, only he does not seem accustomed to be addressed by superiors. The way of picketing the horses in bivouac wastes an enormous amount of room. The men greeted me as if I were one of their own countrymen in a fashion I have never before found outside Prussia, but indeed I can never again look upon Bavarians and Württembergers as foreigners. Would that this outburst of ardent attachment to my person might find its confirmation in an early victory! Men's minds could not be better attuned for all that has yet to be done.

My headquarters I have fixed at Spires, close to the noble Cathedral, which contains the tombs of seven German Emperors. In the most amiable way President von Pfeufer and consort received me in their house. Only Lieutenant-General von Blumenthal, together with my personal A.D.C.'s and First Lieutenant von Viebahn, having accompanied me, my Staff was to wait for me here. We were not a little surprised not to find the latter, but only late at night, after a fifty hours' journey, did they put in an appearance, famished. A like fate befell the Duke of Coburg, the Hereditary Grand Duke of Weimar, the Hereditary Prince of Hohenzollern and Prince Wilhelm of Württemberg.

My first walk took me to the Cathedral; I could not but have a lively recollection of the occasion, in the year 1861,

---

[1] It was at these two places that, on June 21 and 22, 1849, the Baden insurgents were defeated by contingents of the Prince, later King William, of Prussia.

when I and my wife witnessed here the first meeting of the Prince of Wales with his future bride.[1]

In the afternoon I inspected the little fortress of Germersheim, which is fully armed; its Commandant, General Butz, gave me the impression of being a man of energy. Here I unexpectedly came upon Lieutenant-General von Bose, General in Command of the XIth Army Corps, who with his assembled Staff was on the march in the direction of Landau.

Starting from Germersheim, I made a reconnaissance of the ground along the Klingbach, with the object of finding positions for my Army in case the enemy should attack me there, and discovered some highly favourable points. On the same occasion I came upon sundry detached cantonments of the XIth Army Corps and encountered the Duke and the Hereditary Prince of Saxe-Meiningen.

The Palatinate looks like one great garden of flowers and fruit, albeit this year the whole countryside is crying out for rain. " Fröhlich Pfalz—Gott erhalt's ! " (Joyous and gay —God keep it aye) is the chosen motto of the Country; may it be saved from War's ravages !

Of the French plans still nothing is known for certain; so we begin to think they are entrenching themselves in the hills, there to wait our attack.

I issued to-day the first General Army Order to the forces united under my supreme command.

Headquarters: Spires, 31st July, Sunday.—At divine service, in the Evangelical church, an extraordinarily ugly building erected subsequently to the horrors of the French devastations in the baroque style of architecture, the authorities had assembled in full force. With deep emotion we sang, " Ein feste Burg " and " In allen meinen Taten."

Late yesterday evening I received a telegram from General von Moltke to the effect that His Majesty deemed it desirable that, as soon as the Württembergers and Badeners were arrived, I should at once move forward southwards on the left bank of the Rhine, to prevent the bridge at Lauterburg being broken and to ensure the effectual protection of South Germany.

But I do not consider we are yet in a condition to carry out such an undertaking, as my Army is not yet assembled, even the transport trains are lacking, and I accordingly sent an answer in that sense.

The inhabitants, now the Prussians are on the spot, feel safe again, and together with the whole population of the

---

[1] Princess Alexandra, eldest daughter of the Prince (1863 King) Christian (IX) of Denmark.

Palatinate, and all South Germans, regard the immediate future in a temper of enthusiasm and confidence. Indeed we may say without presumption that at this moment the " Mainlinie "[1] no longer exists.

In the afternoon I joined my sister, her sister-in-law and their children in the noble Park of Schwetzingen; its avenues offered welcome shade in the broiling heat; the Castle itself is fitted up as a Military Hospital.

Headquarters: Spires, 1st August.—Was expecting by to-day to receive orders from the Royal Headquarters; but as the Staff seems unlikely to reach Mainz before to-morrow, this is hardly probable.

Again to-day Bavarian troops continued to march through here. The complete difference of uniform from ours, and above all the similarity of the Artillery to the French, is so striking that the question has already been raised whether some badge, as, for instance, a brassard, such as we wore in 1864, should not be introduced as a distinguishing mark. However, such an expedient has its disadvantages; the enemy could only too easily utilize such a simple means of recognition utterly to delude their opponent and work his ruin; so I felt bound to declare against it.

With the Duke of Saxe-Coburg and Sir Robert Morier, just arrived from England, I had in front of the Dom under shady lindens a long, suggestive and to me very heartening talk. Gustav Freytag[2] has arrived, to accompany us as Chronicler of the campaign, and soon I hope yet to see Baron von Roggenbach with us.

Thanks to the French dilatoriness, the German Armies are quite ready for battle; so it may well happen that, for all the French sabre-rattling and all their age-long preparation against a sudden onslaught, *we* shall be the aggressors. Who could ever have thought it?

News from home we have none whatever; I have only received two letters, both at once, from my wife. We have every reason to conjecture that the King left Berlin yesterday evening, so that now operations must begin at once. What a stirring moment must this departure have been!

Lord Granville would seem to be abandoning not his one-sided sympathy with Napoleon, but his marked predilection for caution.[3] The revelations which we have made

[1] Line of demarcation between North and South Germany.
[2] Freytag, Gustav, novelist, historian and poet, 1816–1895; born at Kreuzburg, Silesia.
[3] The policy of the English Foreign Minister, only since the 6th July in charge of affairs, was, as a matter of fact, characterized by vacillation and weakness.

public [1] as to Benedetti's designs must make an impression on all the world (be their origin what they choose to think) and can only redound to our advantage.

Belgium's neutrality might enable us to gain the momentary advantage that France is prevented from attacking us on that side, while, on the other hand, if England were our ally, her troops, staying in Belgium, would have been of little benefit to us.

Mr. Cartwright, Member of Parliament for Oxford, was presented to me; he gives the impression of being a clever man, has travelled widely and in particular knows Germany and Italy thoroughly. Before he reached my headquarters, he was taken for a spy and narrowly escaped being clapped in prison! In his opinion there are many of the wiser heads in Italy who promise themselves the winning of Rome as Italian capital rather by a *rapprochement* with France than from a good understanding with us; [2] yet this does not justify us in presuming that this will therefore actually happen.

It grows more and more probable that in the end I shall engage the French at Weissenburg, while Prince Friedrich Karl, pressing on to the south-west on Kaiserslautern, could attack the enemy on the flank. Thus then we stand at the beginning of a historical world crisis! I am not despondent, but yet the gravity of the situation makes my heart tremble in view of the battles we shall have to fight, the starting-point of which will be an immediate irruption from positions in the hills. A premonition tells me that with the end of this War a respite must intervene of slaughter and bloodshed. But the point now is to carry out my chosen motto: " With God, fearlessly and undauntedly to go forward ! " All with one accord are animated by this sentiment.

Late this evening it was reported that the French were making a sudden move northwards from Strasburg, so that eventually no force at all worth considering faced me; I shall not, therefore, be called upon to fight so soon as expected. Still, all this is not really clear yet. At Saarbrücken yesterday our VIIth and VIIIth Army Corps were compelled by the enemy's preponderance of force to evacuate the place. That we were not obliged to do this much sooner, indeed immediately on the declaration of war, is noteworthy enough; as

[1] On July 25 *The Times*, the material being supplied by Bismarck, published an outline of a Prusso-French offensive alliance drafted in Benedetti's handwriting in August 1866, the fourth Article of which bound Prussia to support the French in the conquest of Belgium.

[2] As a fact, the victory of the German arms at Sedan was to help the Italians in getting their capital, just as Königgrätz brought them Venetia.

it is, Prince Friedrich Karl and General Steinmetz will just be obediently following the enemy's lead.

My headquarters is become congested with men and vehicles to such an extent that there was nothing left to be done but grade it in two sections. To the first belong all actually employed on necessary services, officers therefore of the General Staff and A.D.C.'s; to the second all the rest, including the numerous Princes. Naturally under these circumstances, it was impracticable for all of us to assemble in one room and at one table. By this time the Duke of Coburg was so friendly disposed as to adopt sundry hungry souls and provide for them.

Headquarters: Spires, 2nd August.—The order came to-day to organize the concentration of my whole Army in view of the commencement of operations from Landau. The Bavarian IInd Army Corps (von Hartmann) is to push forward from Bergzabern on Weissenburg, our Vth Army Corps to come up in support, the XIth Army Corps to do the like more to the South in the direction of the Bienwald, while Lieutenant-General von Werder, to whom I have confided the command of the Baden and Württemberg troops, is to advance to the Lauter. The Ist and VIth Army Corps are already on the march to reinforce the Main Army, as, thanks be to God, it appears that Austria will remain inactive, so that only my old-time Army Corps, the Pomeranian, stays behind to safeguard the frontiers, supported by Landwehr and Mecklenburgers. The Bavarians, so they say, are fairly well ready, for they now lack only some 1000 Reservists, together with transport wagons and hospital necessaries.

Besides the correspondent of *The Times*, Mr. Russell, another reporter for the *Daily News*, Mr. Skinner, will go with us. In addition to these, other journalists, who every day turn up by dozens, will not be received officially. First Lieutenant von Verdy arrived, sent here by General von Moltke; also Dr. Appia from Geneva put in an appearance at my quarters.

Headquarters: Landau, 3rd August.—Full of gratitude I took my leave, after enjoying a last bathe in the Rhine, from the amiable family of the Pfeufers, to march to Landau. The armed fortress stands so low and so closely surrounded by neighbouring heights that I could not defend it, for its bombardment could be nothing more than just an amusement for the enemy; Landau, in fact, can only be regarded as a *place de moment* and is entirely out of date.

In the afternoon I paid a visit to my old comrades in arms of 1866 with the Vth Army Corps at their bivouac, where men and officers gave me a rousing welcome. The Vth Army Corps will again, not a doubt of it, do first-rate service, but let us hope with lighter losses than in '66. The bivouac of the XIth Army Corps I could only inspect cursorily, but came upon Lieutenant-General von Bose in his encampment.

In all probability we shall have an engagement to-morrow, for I am bound to acquire the certainty as to whether the news that Weissenburg is evacuated by the French, so that the river Lauter can be crossed, is accurate. If our prospects turn out as we hope, and I put the enemy to flight, I can in that case carry out a flanking movement so as to join forces with Prince Friedrich Karl in the direction of Saargemünd, or Saaralben. The stifling weather continues, greatly hindering the movement of troops, especially in the case of the infantry. In this beautiful Palatinate country, which, alas! is still vainly thirsting for rain, it is particularly hot.

The Quartermasters of the VIth Army Corps have already arrived, so now from to-morrow on I can count on the Silesians, whom Lieutenant-General Count Wilhelm zu Stolberg follows with the 2nd Cavalry Division, as a reinforcement to my troops.

How hard it will be to-day, this 3rd August, on the King, instead of, as he had hoped, unveiling the statue of his father,[1] to find himself on the march to the front.

Action of Weissenburg

Headquarters: Schweighofen, at the Pastor's house, 4th August.—A victory over the French under my own eyes! God be praised, our very first encounter with the enemy was a success, for our men's confidence is already much enhanced, while the foe has now got a clear conception of the strength of the Germans they have wantonly challenged. What a lucky thing, too, that we won the day in conjunction with the Bavarians and were able this day to establish ourselves in possession of the historical Weissenburg lines.[2]

In accordance with my dispositions previously issued, I wished to-day, 4th August, to cross the Lauter with the vanguard of my troops, and to this end to march through the Bienwald by four roads, but for to-day expected only a skirmish between outposts, inasmuch as the reports so far

---

[1] In the Berlin Lustgarten.
[2] Earthworks familiar from the experience of previous wars on both sides of the town of Weissenburg.

come in announced that Weissenburg itself was not occupied, but that entrenchments had been thrown up on the surrounding heights. I had left Landau at four in the morning, had proceeded as far as Bergzabern, and there, just as I was getting to horse, came the report that overnight French troops had entered Weissenburg and the gates had been barricaded. In heavy rain I accompanied the march of the Bavarian Division forming the advance guard under Count Bothmer till close upon Weissenburg, and there, as the first shells began to fall, took up my post of observation on the high ground eastwards of the village of Schweigen. It was already a quarter past nine when a lively fire of sharpshooters broke out, in which two Bavarian batteries joined in, whose shells soon set fire to houses in the town, whereupon I despatched Major von Hahnke to gather information as to how the engagement was going. Next I sent Captain Lenke to Lieutenant-General von Bothmer, for it was said the Bavarians had already pushed on into the town. The former reported that an interchange of shots was being maintained with the apparently weak garrison, and that the Bavarians hesitated about a serious onslaught; that against us were two enemy batteries in action, behind which three infantry battalions, two more batteries and weak contingents of cavalry were drawn up. A little later Captain von Viebahn confirmed this information. Captain Lenke reported that a serious attack was not to be looked for until Count Bothmer was sure of support from the Prussian columns. This course was the right one; in particular it turned out that the old enceinte consisting of wall and moat of that old-time fortress was still complete, and even the gates were barricaded, though on no part of the works were guns actually in position. I had accordingly already given repeated orders that the infantry action should develop only by degrees, so as to wait for the arrival of the Vth Army Corps, which presently, exactly at the hour counted on, viz. ten o'clock, reached the Lauter, eastwards of Altenstadt, with its advance guard. Major Dresow had brought them my order to hurry on the advance, seeing the IInd Bavarian Army Corps was already in action—news that was greeted on all sides with hurrahs. Lieutenant-General von Sandrart at once advanced with the 9th Division across the Lauter by St. Remy, and had shots fired, without seeing the enemy, in order to apprise the Bavarians of his arrival. Dresow thereupon issued similar orders to the XIth Army Corps, so that the heads of that force were brought into position to surround the enemy's right flank.

Major-General von Bothmer was sent with the 17th Infantry brigade against the village of Altenstadt; there a hot engagement ensued for half an hour, which ended in the capture of the Weissenburg railway-station by the Ist battalion of the 58th Regiment of Infantry, and in which the battalion commander, Major von Gronefeld, the colours in his hand, met a hero's death. Short as was the action at this point, it nevertheless involved considerable losses, especially in officers. From Altenstadt the 58th Infantry Regiment and the 5th Jägers, reinforced by the Silesian Infantry Regiment No. 47, pushed on the attack and arrived presently before the walls of Weissenburg, after the Bavarians had little by little drawn near the enceinte.

Meantime the French had mounted batteries on the Geissberg against the advancing columns of the Vth and XIth Army Corps; at the same moment we seemed to catch the sound of infantry fire, when the peculiar rattling noise preceding the detonation led us to suspect mitrailleuses. I sent Lieutenant von Gustedt of the Hussar Guards regiment to the near neighbourhood of the field of action to ascertain exactly whether cavalry could be at all employed against this artillery, but he declared that these guns were posted behind walls in which loopholes had been contrived, and that infantry, too, were in occupation of the position, so that only a systematic attack by unmounted men was practicable. It was past midday when the XIth Army Corps, marching on the thunder of the guns, advanced on the Geissberg from the south-east under the fire of its guns and took it; thus the artillery of the Vth Army Corps, already brought up, could operate with more effect, while the 41st Infantry Brigade set about the attack from Schleithal. Meanwhile Major-General von Voigts-Rhetz with a part of the 18th Brigade and the 59th Infantry Brigade began to storm the Geissberg from the north, so that the enemy was forced to retire his right wing, in order to offer as concentrated a resistance as possible to our oncoming columns. The castle of "Geissberg" as well as a farmhouse lying lower down the hill served him as a base from which a murderous fire was kept up on our men.

There followed an infantry action, no less instructive than interesting, while the King's Own Grenadier Regiment, acting in conjunction with the 4th Posen Infantry Regiment No. 59, had to clamber up the steep slopes of the Geissberg. Taking advantage of every dip in the very broken surface of the hillside, our gallant infantrymen won more and more ground, till at last they had come so close to the farm buildings just mentioned that the necessary reinforcements must needs be waited for. I am rejoiced to be able to say that our fellows behaved just as they always did on peace-time manœuvres—an observation confirmed quite unreservedly by our Bavarian comrades, and which is certainly as high commendation for the men as it is for our fighting system! The extent and strong position of the Geissberg farm premises, and the gardens and walls belonging to them, afforded the French, who made a gallant stand, a favourable position for defence; but when battalions of the XIth Army Corps actually surrounded the enemy's right flank, resistance was no longer possible, and a white flag over the Geissberg castle showed our men that the enemy surrendered themselves prisoners. In this way a whole enemy battalion fell into our hands, while the rest of the infantry, seized with panic, had already dashed down the southern slope of the hill and escaped. About the same hour I had again sent Lieutenant von Gustedt forward, this time for the purpose of getting information as to the entry of our men into Weissenburg. Though it was now close on one o'clock, the Bavarian infantrymen still lay at a considerable distance from the enceinte in vineyards and gardens, directing their fire at the town, from which came single detached shots; guns were asked for to batter in the Landauer gate of the town, which could not be opened in any other way, and these I at once ordered up. Simultaneously the Bavarian Aide-de-Camp, Baron von Stauffenberg, was despatched to General von Hartmann with urgent instructions to take Weissenburg now without loss of time. The rain had stopped at last, and the sun broke through the clouds. When our artillery had shot down the gate, a large detachment of Bavarian infantry dashed into the town, while the Prussian battalions forced their way in by the southern gate; on this, street fighting began at different points with Turkos and infantrymen of the 74th of the line, till eventually the whole garrison was made prisoners of war. Thereupon a never-ending succession of hurrahs could be heard from the triumphant Bavarians.

After yet another short but ineffectual attack on the Geissberg had been attempted by the French, a movement mainly concerned with securing his own retreat, and our artillery had said a word to the retiring enemy, the French disappeared altogether from the field of battle.

The day was ours: no sooner across the frontier than we had put the enemy to flight and thereby won a strong position, together with the command of the roads and railways leading to Strasburg. Adding up the number of troops brought into action on our side, the total strength will amount to two Divisions, for by no means all regiments of my Army Corps came under fire. The enemy's strength would seem to come to one Division, and this was probably only the vanguard of stronger masses which still remained in the rear. We had, therefore, such was our good fortune, by no means lost our time and are the first since 1815 to have once again beaten the French! To the gallant regiments and their leaders belong the honours of the day, a six hours' battle with an evenly matched foe, inferior in numbers it is true, and having some of them only come up in the night, but having the advantage of the ground enormously in their favour. Without exaggeration we can say that every single man is deeply impressed by the seriousness and importance of this War, and the fighting spirit is even more ardently manifested than it was four years ago; hence the consciousness of having won this victory over the enemy is important beyond words.

The suspense during the hours of the fight was, needless to say, intense, though I had a good view of the field of battle and was thus enabled to give the necessary orders according to the progress of events. When the engagement was over, as I rode over the field of battle, I experienced emotions of quite another sort, for wherever I showed myself even for a moment, the most enthusiastic cries of triumph greeted me from officers and men. I saw dying and severely wounded men spring up by sheer force of will to let me see the joy they felt; many were just able to wave a maimed hand in token of greeting as I passed. From the windows of the houses fitted up as hospitals, from field ambulances, from the dressing-stations, invariably came the same expression of intense delight to see the struggle for our just right beginning so well. Every band struck up the "Heil dir im Siegerkranz," and the massed battalions to which I rode up, to congratulate them in the King's name, would never let me get a word out for their vociferous hurrahs. My welcome from the King's Own Regiment was especially moving, for with this gallant regiment it has become almost a matter of routine to be present at my victories as a shining example of steady courage and devotion. I found the same thing on the Geissberg, and while men and officers crowded round me and I was asking for particulars, there was brought to me the flag of the Fusilier battalion shot clean through the pole; with it in his hand the Ensign had instantly been shot down, then Lieutenant Siemon shared the same fate, whereupon Major von Kaisenberg took the flag, but fell severely wounded, till at last Sergeant Förster, dashing ahead of the storming party, reached the summit with the colours. It cannot be described with what an expression of conscious pride the witnesses of such gallantry narrated the incident; I could but press to my lips that banner of victory so gloriously borne.

Close by on the southern slope of the hill mentioned lay two encampments formed of *tentes d'abri*, which had been abandoned with all equipments, together with the still untouched midday meal, rations and fodder and everything. The First Silesian Jägers No. 5 had taken a gun—an achievement due to Captain von Schwemler's company, and in particular to Sergeant-Major Meyer and Jäger Hausknecht. It was a strange coincidence that I came to see this trophy just when the massed battalion had been mustered, while immediately opposite it stood the crowd of enemy prisoners. The French were made aware of my presence by the cheers of the Jägers; the French officers saluted me courteously and I spoke a few civil words in praise of their gallantry.

The dark side of a day of battle quickly became apparent in all its sad significance, for we had had a notably large number of losses in officers as well as in men, whose eagerness to come at the enemy induced them only too often to neglect the needful rules of prudence. Of the King's Grenadier regiment, as also of the 58th Infantry regiment, the half of the body of officers is disabled, in the former indeed all the Staff officers. Major von Kaisenberg, who had before this won the order " Pour le Mérite " at the battle of Skalitz, lay severely wounded in the upper part of the body in a ditch close to the castle of Geissberg; from the distance he gave me a smile, his face deathly pale, but beaming with joy. I sprang from my horse and asked how he felt; he would say nothing about this, but had words only for his congratulations, and presently exclaimed : " What matters my wound, if it means such a triumph for such a King ! " I embraced him, one I shall never see again in this life ! Count Waldersee, Commander of the 5th Jäger battalion, lies at Altenstadt fatally wounded with a shot through the lungs; he must have fully realized his danger, for directly he saw me come in, he began to speak of what was to become of his children. Major von Unruh, of the King's Grenadiers, who had already greatly distinguished himself in 1866, had been shot in the foot and had at once had the ball extracted in the castle of Geissberg; when I came there, he was already walking about again and showed me the bullet, which, praise God ! had done him no serious injury. The rooms and stables fitted up as dressing-stations in the buildings in the Geissberg were, of course, of a very indifferent sort. Here lay the body of the French General of Division, Douai, whose little dog crouched near him; his Adjutant, wounded by his side, a fine, well-set-up man, told me how the General, standing in the mitrailleuse battery, was hit by a well-aimed shot from our artillery, a fact I immediately communicated to our artillerymen, the more so as a mitrailleuse had been dismounted by our fire very soon after the beginning of the action. A crowd of terribly voluble French surgeons accosted me, all speaking at once, complaining they had neither the necessary bandages nor instruments, that even up here they had been fired on, although they had hoisted a white flag. With this, they pointed to a sort of pocket-handkerchief, which I could barely make out from the farm-yard. Of the Geneva Convention they professed to know practically nothing whatever and wore no armlets with the red cross, but had eventually twisted their handkerchiefs round their arms, after their attention had been drawn to the absence of the appointed badge. "Procurez-nous notre bagage," cried the surgeons, "car du moment que la déroute et la débandade ont commencé, elles ont pris la fuite dans le direction de Wissenbourg!" (Get us our baggage, for from the instant the defeat and rout began, they took to flight in the direction of Weissenburg.) This naïve utterance regarding the nature of the retreat gave us a welcome corroboration of the disorganized condition in which the enemy had quitted the field of battle. The wounded lay mostly at Altenstadt, but very inadequately provided for, there being in particular a great lack of fresh water. The native population appears ready and willing to help, while compassionate Sisters also from the neighbourhood have hastened up to succour the sufferers.

The Bavarian troops, the greater part of whom I came upon already in bivouac, greeted me with much enthusiasm, and I addressed some words of grateful commendation to them. They have had no heavy losses; their training is very different from what we demand, so that their system of fighting ought not to be regarded with our eyes; still they have done their duty to-day and carried out the task, not an easy one, of taking Weissenburg fortress, so soon as our Prussian troops gave the good example. The Turkos opposed to them proved themselves veritable savages, for they shot wounded men and shammed dead, to open fire again afterwards from behind; so the German soldiers will give them no quarter henceforth. Citizens of the town have fired from the houses, a fact already, it appears, deposed to on oath, and several arrests have been made in consequence. We have on our side made 600 unwounded prisoners, the Bavarians 400, including 12 to 20 officers. The enemy's loss exceeds ours by a considerable number.

My headquarters I installed not far from the town at Schweighofen, in the house of the very amiable Catholic curé, Schaefer by name. French prisoners, whom I saw here, and whose bearing was polite and pleasing, told me, when I declared they had fought well: " Ah! mais vos soldats prussiens se battent admirablement!" (Oh! but your Prussian soldiers fight admirably!) They were fairly well informed as to our system of service, and condemned in it the cruelty of compelling married men to take the field. I cannot deny that, in the calm of the curé's house, once orders had been duly issued and I could enjoy a little quiet, I was overwhelmed with grief at the thought of our losses of to-day.

Headquarters: Sulz, 5th August.—An oppressively sultry wind was blowing, only cooled late in the evening by a thunderstorm, when to-day I set out on the march to France. The landscape in the foot-hills is beautiful; the villages wear a prosperous look, but are deserted by their inhabitants, terrified by silly rumours of German cannibalism. We had to go over a part of yesterday's battle-field, the description of which I pass over, because the cruel sight, every time I behold it afresh, grows more and more abhorrent to me, and took the direction of Hagenauer and Hochwald, with the object of reconnoitring the ground to the east of the Vosges. Once I have crossed that chain, I can get in touch with the IInd Army Corps; meantime as a preliminary, Prince Friedrich Karl and I, each for himself, must undertake the difficult passage. Everywhere we came upon traces of the hurried French retreat, for a mass of weapons, munitions and other objects they had thrown away bestrewed the roads. A sad sight was the dead body of a civilian with a gaping shot wound through the forehead, lying far from the battle-field in the ditch by the roadside. Many French soldiers have borrowed civilian clothes, to enable them to escape unrecognized. On the march I came upon the XIth Army Corps; an extraordinarily large number of men had fallen out of the ranks exhausted, for which the new boots, only just given out, must bear much of the blame. General von Kirchbach leads the van with his Army Corps, the Vth, but, to nurse his wound, in a carriage; when to-day I showed him the telegram in which my wife expresses her sympathy, he wept with joy. The cavalry follows on the heels of the enemy, while Lieutenant-General von Werder, to whom I entrusted the leadership of the Württemberg and Baden Divisions, has so far encountered no opposition.

I established my headquarters at a place called Sulz, after Lieutenant Count Rothkirch of the 2nd Hessian Bodyguards regiment had reported the spot unoccupied by the enemy and the neighbourhood safe. The small château, built in the Louis Quatorze style, belongs now to a wealthy Jew; not far from here the two Countesses Tascher [1] own a country house. My brother-in-law, the Grand Duke of Baden, in company with his brother, Prince Karl, took me by surprise here and did me the pleasure of staying for the night in one of my apartments. Baron F. von Roggenbach joined my headquarters as Major of Baden Landwehr. More and more unwounded prisoners are being brought in, their number already amounting to the thousand; as a result of the first engagement since the outbreak of hostilities we may well call this a high figure. A telegraph book discovered at the railway-station here gives a great deal of important information as to the enemy's intentions, but above all indicates how ill prepared the French were for the opening of hostilities in organization and the massing and maintenance of troops. These telegrams lead us to conjecture that the French Army is concentrating its main force before Metz.

Reconnaissances show that on the heights westwards of, and therefore behind, Wörth lie great French bivouacs to a strength of something like three Divisions, while railway trains are still bringing up continual reinforcements. The situation of Wörth is much stronger and more hilly than that of Weissenburg, for the steep sides of the valley of the Sauerbach, a stream hardly fordable by infantry and which is bordered by wide, swampy meadows, form a particularly defensible position. Frontally only an artillery engagement can be fought; on the wings the forest facilitates a possible attack, while the diminished volume of the Sauerbach at Eberbach (the enemy's right wing) might also give assistance. Under such circumstances I shall, of course, neither attack nor try to storm Marshal MacMahon's position, so particularly well adapted for defence as it is, but rather by outflanking the wings to force the enemy to withdraw them—a manœuvre easy to carry out seeing my whole Army Corps lies in a half-circle in front of my headquarters, part in

---

[1] Daughters of Count Louis Tascher de la Pagerie, Senator and Lord Chamberlain of the Empress Eugénie's household. One of them, the Countess Stéphanie, was a correspondent of the Crown Prince's parents. The family was related to the Bonapartes through the Empress Josephine, mother of Hortense.

bivouac, part in cantonments. True I am in constant apprehension lest, considering the fighting spirit of the Vth Army Corps, the smallest accident may bring on a pitched battle, so upsetting my well-laid plans.

Battle of Wörth

Headquarters : Sulz, 6th August.—I have to-day completely defeated Marshal MacMahon, putting his troops to utter and disorderly retreat. So far as it has been possible to ascertain, his whole Corps was engaged, reinforced by Failly and Canrobert as well as by troops from Grenoble, approximately a force of 80,000 men against me, who brought 100,000 men into the fighting line.[1] The engagement, which, alas ! again cost us a very great number of officers and men, deserves the title of a veritable battle, in which the greater part of my Army fought. Generals von Kirchbach and von Bose are the heroes of the day; unfortunately the latter was seriously wounded. My ever-victorious comrades of the Vth Army Corps were again, as usual, well to the front. The XIth Army Corps, in this its baptism of fire, has proved its gallantry, and was vigorously supported by the Württemberg Division under the command of Lieutenant-General von Obernitz. The Bavarian troops were terribly slow, so that I was obliged to say the strongest things to them before, at last, they advanced and attacked properly. The Baden troops came little under fire, as they formed my own special reserve.

The native population has been talking ever since yesterday evening, with every sign of unfeigned anxiety for their goods and chattels, of a great battle fixed for to-day.

Quite early in the morning we had already heard brisk firing, and gathered from it that probably the enemy were making a demonstration against the troops of the Vth and XIth Army Corps in course of changing their bivouacs. Reports stated that from earliest daybreak outpost skirmishes had been going on. A battalion was then sent forward to

[1] These alleged reinforcements are a mistake of the German High Command based on statements made by prisoners. MacMahon, apart from his own Corps, the chief command of which he retained himself, had the Infantry Division Conseil-Dumesnil of the 7th Corps from Mühlhausen, together with the 2nd Reserve Cavalry Division, Vicomte de Bonnemains. In consequence of this error as to the contingents brought into action by MacMahon, the number given in the text is too high—the German total also is put too high. In the course of the battle only 64,000 infantry and 430 cavalry participated. At the Crown Prince's disposal there were in all 76,000 infantry and 5,750 cavalry.

support the outposts of the Vth Army Corps in the direction of Wörth, and were fired on, while in the case of the IInd Bavarian Army Corps, Lieutenant-General von Hartmann, a brisk engagement developed. In consequence of this the Vth Army Corps had gradually moved its artillery eastwards of Wörth and so afforded relief to the Bavarians, so that eventually, after an obstinate fight, the Division Count Bothmer was pushed forward as far as Neweiler. The enemy, however, seemed to contemplate no further efforts; in particular after the brisk firing no offensive movements had ensued, and a part of our troops had already found it possible to bivouac.

Directly I learnt of this state of affairs, I ordered the Vth Army Corps not to offer battle, and to avoid whatever might precipitate a new engagement, because I was unwilling, before the concentration of all my forces, to provoke a pitched battle, especially on such unfavourable ground. The Vth Army Corps sent on this order of mine to the Bavarian Division, Count Bothmer, who was still in action, and who interpreted it in the sense that they too should cease fighting, and accordingly retreated in the direction of Langensulzbach. At this moment it seemed to me at Sulz that no more fighting was going on in any quarter, and as we could hear no firing, we all supposed that no further action would occur to-day. My brother-in-law, the Grand Duke of Baden, left us in consequence and travelled back to Germany.

Towards twelve o'clock began a heavy cannonade, which quickly increased in violence; so I had my horse saddled and galloped for the firing to make personal inquiry on the spot as to the course of events. A large proportion of my Staff followed only later. After a dark, rainy morning the weather was beginning to clear up.

On the way I was met by hurrying orderlies, who were to bring up ammunition carriers. The gun-fire grew more and more intense, so that a battle appeared to me no longer doubtful. On the way also I received another proof of this, inasmuch as Captain of Horse von der Lancken, who had been sent on ahead by order of General von Kirchbach to report, told me that the advance guard brigade, the 20th of the Vth Army Corps, under von Walther, was actually involved in the fighting, and that to break away was no longer practicable; he declared, moreover, he was bound to ask for reinforcements for both his wings, for in spite of the capture of the town of Wörth, the position of the Vth Army Corps might be endangered. On this, I let him know that

THE CROWN PRINCE AT WÖRTH.
Lithograph from a Painting by Camphausen.

THE EMPEROR FREDERICK III.

on his right wing General von der Tann and on his left General von Bose would intervene.

I immediately despatched Lieutenant Count Harrach to the XIth Army Corps with orders, as rapidly as possible to make every effort to retire by way of Elsasshausen and past the Niederwald on Fröschweiler. This order found General von Bose already on the march in the appointed direction, for he had on his own initiative moved off towards the thunder of the guns. To Lieutenant-General von Werder I gave the order to follow up the XIth Army Corps with his Württemberg Division, advancing on Gunstett and crossing the Sauer, while the Baden Division was to remain behind in reserve. To the Ist Bavarian Army Corps under von der Tann I sent Major von Freyberg with the order, while leaving one Division in the rear as reserve, to march off with all possible speed in order to push in between the right wing of General von Kirchbach by Wörth and the left wing of General von Hartmann by Langensulzbach.

The Bavarian Captain von Xylander carried the order to General von Hartmann to take such action on the left flank of the enemy as to enable the IInd Bavarian Army Corps to take position westwards of the Sauer, consequently behind the French wing and facing Reichshofen. Lieutenant-General von Kirchbach I made acquainted through Captain von Sommerfeld with the order I had just given, on which the former reported to me that according to statements made by prisoners the whole of MacMahon's Army was opposed to us; that the engagement had gone favourably for us and that twice already brigades of the 10th Division had repulsed a hostile attack on Wörth; that at that moment one brigade was crossing the Sauer, to seize the neighbouring heights, so that only one remained in reserve. The main attack, however, he would only execute when the reinforcements on the wings had arrived. Lieutenant-General von der Tann soon after this had a personal meeting with Lieutenant-General von Kirchbach to discuss the necessary dispositions.

It was about two o'clock that the battle raged with especial fury. Lieutenant-General von Bose had at once sent Lieutenant-General von Schachtmeyer's Division into action, followed immediately by the Division von Gersdorff, and attacked Elsasshausen, while the French held the strong position of Fröschweiler and the heights near it with the utmost tenacity and conspicuous bravery. Wörth and Elsasshausen were now the main points about which the struggle raged; the town itself of Wörth was as good as in possession of the Vth Army Corps, as also the thickly planted vineyards to the north of that place. At this crisis the Bavarians again afforded little help; I therefore sent Lieutenant von Gustedt to Lieutenant-General von der Tann, to bring him as fast as possible to the support of the Vth Army Corps. The first-named came upon the Ist Bavarian near Görsdorf and was witness how Tann, who rode at its head, gave the requisite orders; from where I stood I could still perceive no sign of going into the battle line, so I despatched Major Dresow to the Ist Bavarian Army Corps with the order to bring all available forces at last into action; more particularly as on the part of Lieutenant-General von Hartmann again no effective movement was to be noted. The latter, as observed just above, had withdrawn the Division Bothmer in the direction of Langensulzbach; by this movement the enemy had been encouraged to concentrate his whole force (which, moreover, was being all the time increased by the continual arrival of troop trains) on Wörth, now that he found his flanks no longer threatened. By this time Kirchbach had convinced himself of the considerable reinforcement of the enemy's front of attack, but was unwilling to allow Marshal MacMahon time to complete his deployment, and, encouraged by the advance begun from the south by the XIth Army Corps, had decided on the attack on Elsasshausen–Fröschweiler. At once the 20th Brigade, von Walther (37th and 50th regiments of the line), followed by the 19th Brigade, von Henning (6th and 46th of the line), had been ordered forward in the direction of Elsasshausen–Fröschweiler; but as the enemy's resistance was a very gallant one, the 9th Division also, under Lieutenant-General von Sandrart, had to be brought up, so that soon the whole Vth Army Corps was in action. Again the Bavarian IInd Army Corps gave little helpful support to the extreme right wing, inasmuch as Lieutenant-General von Hartmann, in order to relieve Division Count Bothmer, which had already that morning been under fire and over-strained, had ordered forward the Division Walther—a movement which required a long time to execute, with the result that only the brigade Schleich was available. To the Württembergers, who were nearing Gunstett, I sent, not later than two o'clock, Prince William of Württemberg, accompanied by Lieutenant von Stülpnagel, with the order to despatch the cavalry and infantry with all possible speed by way of Eberbach against the enemy's line of retreat by Reichshofen; meantime I urged von der Tann most earnestly to drive the enemy out of the vineyards and out of Fröschweiler.

THE EMPEROR FREDERICK III.

Little by little we gained ground as the battle progressed. The unceasing din of cannon and musketry re-echoed loudly in the hills, while the sun had now broken through the clouds. Already numerous convoys of prisoners were passing the spot where I stood, and the Duke of Coburg, who spoke with many of them, had discovered a regimental commander among them, as also the correspondents of the *Gaulois* and the *Figaro*. Many would have it Napoleon and his son were present. The volunteer stretcher-bearers attached to my headquarters, under the orders of Baron von dem Knesebeck-Tylsen, I could see carrying out their heavy and melancholy duties calmly and effectively. Colonel von Stosch, Commander of the Ist Lower Silesian Infantry regiment No. 46, was borne from the field not far from me. A sight I shall never forget was that of a rifleman shot through the mouth, who was carried by on a stretcher directly under my eyes, and kept briskly waving his hand to me as long as ever he could see me, as he was unable to speak.

The Ist Silesian Dragoon regiment No. 4 now rode up, without my having given them any definite order; by Major Mischke I sent directions to their Commander, Colonel von Schenck, to ride through Wörth followed by his Division, an order the whole regiment received with cheers. The men of the XIth Army Corps had been obliged to attack and take a wood before they could climb the steep slopes by Elsasshausen under the most furious fire from the enemy's artillery and mitrailleuses, and had had to make use of causeways just constructed across the extremely swampy banks of the Sauerbach. Luckily General von Bose was more and more surrounding the enemy's right wing, which rested on the village, by this time in flames; moreover, Lieutenant-General von Werder, carrying out my orders admirably, now began to cause MacMahon serious anxiety about his rear. I could clearly recognize that little by little the French right wing was being retired— a movement the enemy carried out with exemplary skill, while his left wing held its ground against the Bavarians with the utmost tenacity. Several times over I saw French advances pushed forward with the greatest impetuosity, in which Zouaves leapt about with incredible agility; yet our gallant fellows repelled every attack successfully. During these hostile attempts the battle generally had come to a standstill, especially round Fröschweiler, where from the eastwards the Vth Army Corps still continued to attack indefatigably, the more so as sundry reports gave me to understand that the troops held a difficult position, and support, particularly on the right flank, was much to be desired.

By Captain of Horse von Mutius I sent orders to the Ist Bavarian Army Corps at once to cross the Sauerbach and to engage the enemy on the right wing of the Vth Army Corps. Besides this, I demanded that any officer of rank, who in view of this order of mine was not advancing as promptly as might be, should be reported to me. Lieutenant-General von Kirchbach I informed of the state of matters at the moment, letting him know how already the enemy's line of retreat by Reichshofen was threatened by the Württembergers, while General von der Tann might at any instant be in action on his right flank. Lieutenant Count Seckendorf, who had been sent to the Vth Army Corps, brought me a message from Lieutenant-General von Kirchbach to the effect that the situation of his Army Corps gave him no anxiety.

The Bavarians were making very little progress, especially as the Turkos concealed in the vineyards maintained a well-aimed fire, which our men could not return in like measure, while enemy mitrailleuses directed their fire on the columns. I had already seen several Bavarian detachments leaping very nimbly down the hill slopes in the greatest disorder, while the unpleasant reports regarding the impossibility of bringing these troops forward kept pouring in. At last my patience gave out and I called out very loudly to Major von Freyberg, Bavarian Military Representative at Berlin: " Ride to your countrymen by Fröschweiler and tell them the Crown Prince of Prussia orders them in the name of their King now at last to engage the enemy properly and drive them back; everywhere we see our troops advancing victoriously; they alone came to a standstill in face of the foe ! " It was a hard saying, but true, and a word of this sort at a grave crisis is not without effect; some while after an energetic advance was at last made.

About the same time the 2nd Württemberg Brigade, von Starkloff, very opportunely got in touch with my extreme left wing from Eberbach, just as several French cavalry brigades made a sudden attempt to throw themselves on our artillery. However, the artillery stood their ground, and with their fire once more inflicted notable losses on the enemy, finding in the calm courage of our infantry the most efficacious help and support. Simultaneously at the western issue from Elsasshausen, men of both corps, Colonel von Stein, Chief of the General Staff of the XIth Army Corps leading them in person, had quickly united, so as to open an annihilating fire on the enemy squadrons, resulting in the disorderly flight of this body of cavalry.

Little by little the thunder of the guns began to fall silent, as I received from the mouth of Lieutenant-General von Kirchbach the announcement he could now say that for to-day he had really and truly sent Marshal MacMahon about his business. The Bavarian fire still continued; yet this fighting had at any rate this advantage, that the French remained over-long in this part of the field and were forced to leave behind a host of prisoners in our hands. Suddenly there broke out again and again a brisk fusillade; we supposed it to indicate a new push on the part of the enemy, till the news came that the Bavarians were celebrating the victory in the prescribed way by letting off salvoes of jubilation.

The French then were actually on the run; they were beaten and we were the victors! MacMahon's tough resistance, his practical skill, fighting for a gradual withdrawal, were well worthy of admiration—but he relinquished the battle-field to me and I had vanquished him. I may say this much in the literal sense of the word, for throughout the action I was able from the different standpoints I took up to see quite well the movements of my troops and their gallant behaviour, issue the necessary orders, and into the bargain be readily found. Lieutenant-General von Blumenthal and Colonel von Gottberg seconded me with conspicuous clear-headedness, coolness and intelligence, so that this day of itself confirmed once more—if still necessary—my old admiration and unlimited confidence in the former, and won the latter my fullest appreciation. To my officers of the General Staff, Major von Hahnke above all, as likewise to the Adjutants and A.D.C.'s, I can give unqualified praise and express my entire satisfaction, for in the rendering of intelligent reports, in the right interpretation of orders and their carrying out, one and all have proved themselves thoroughly serviceable and dependable. Many of them were previously all but unknown to me, Weissenburg and Wörth had rapidly brought us together.

It was half-past four of the afternoon before I could telegraph the news of the victory to His Majesty the King, which was then in the same way communicated to my wife and the Kings and Princes. At the same hour the firing entirely ceased, and in a moment a deep stillness reigned, as though nothing had happened, while the lovely summer's evening spread its mantle over hill and plain.

I gave the needful orders for the pursuit of the flying enemy, who were retreating on Bitsch by way of Reichshofen.

Next I rode over the battle-field, beginning from our left wing, that is to say, in the neighbourhood of Elsasshausen, and then taking the line by way of Fröschweiler to Wörth. To begin with, a Pioneer Company had to be called up with all haste to build a temporary pontoon bridge, under direction of First Lieutenant von Kleist of the Engineers, over the Sauer, which was not to be crossed otherwise. A quite wonderful effect was produced by a fire that first broke out at the topmost summit of the church-steeple of Fröschweiler, and, while the fight was still in progress, had given us the impression of its being gilded by the beams of the evening sun.

One must be familiar with the sight of battle-fields and of the look of troops that have just been in action to form any conception of the appearance of the bloody field of Wörth; to describe it is impossible. The losses on both sides were very heavy, many a contingent had lost half its officers, numerous regimental and battalion commanders had been killed and wounded, no single regiment had come off without very sensible losses. General von Bose was twice wounded, especially by a shot in the heel that actually threatened his life; his son, who was also his A.D.C., was seriously wounded by his father's side. Colonel von Bothmer, only on the outbreak of the War appointed to the command of the 17th Infantry Brigade, having up to that moment served under me as Commander of the 6th Pomeranian regiment, was saved from death only by his watch, albeit carried from the field severely wounded; the bent and crumpled watch was pointed out to me on the ground. Very wisely Colonel von Stein had taken over the command of the XIth Army Corps, acting for the Commanding General who had been carried to Wörth immediately after receiving a second wound. Lieutenant-General von Kirchbach was able to-day, despite his wound at Weissenburg, to command, if only from his carriage, his gallant Army Corps, seconded in this with the greatest activity and judgment by the Chief of his General Staff, Colonel von der Esch. When I encountered the first-named, we fell into each other's arms; as ever, my meeting with the Vth Army Corps was so affecting that I was moved to tears. Generals, officers, men—all dashed up to me, the bands struck up "Heil dir im Siegerkranz" and the Hohenfriedberg March, and the hurrahs of the brave fellows drowned any possibility of my expressing my gratitude, which to-day more than ever stirred me to the bottom of my heart.

Lieutenant-General von Sandrart, also Colonel von Voigts-Rhetz, I greeted before the front of the King's Grenadier regiment. These old war veterans acquitted themselves not less well to-day than in all my earlier successes. When I came to the 3rd Posen Infantry regiment No. 58, Lieutenant Baron was presented to me, who stormed Weissenburg, colours in hand, after his Battalion Commander had fallen. Every man was filled with well-justified pride to have won this most important victory over the French. No less enthusiastic was the crowd of wounded men who lay about us; so far as their shattered limbs and their sufferings allowed, all waved to me or tried to make some sign of greeting, and if only by a radiant look, gave me to understand that they claimed their share in the glory of the day. Enthusiasm such as this is proof enough of the spirit with which our People in Arms has entered on this struggle. The happiness of having won the victory speaks no less eloquently in the dimming eye of the fallen than in the loud jubilations of the survivors. I heard never a complaint from our men, but everywhere found a most touching resignation and an admirable patience, which years ago I had come to recognize as a characteristic of our nation.

Many regiments of the XIth Army Corps I saw to-day actually for the first time, especially those of the Thuringian States and several from Hesse. I congratulated them on the successes of the new confederate army and the baptism of fire it had so bravely confronted, this in view of thirty guns taken and six mitrailleuses, of which a proportion is to be credited to this Army Corps. Many a " Hoch " burst from the ranks of these brave fellows, among whom the Thuringians similarly greeted the Dukes of Saxe-Coburg and Saxe-Meiningen. My nephew, the Hereditary Prince Bernhard of Meiningen, has proved to-day that Prussian blood flows in his veins.[1] The XIth Army Corps had likewise to bewail serious losses, and the great number of the fallen about Elsasshausen and in the neighbourhood of the captured guns showed how hard the fighting had been there. I shall never forget the sight of Lieutenant-General von Blumenthal's nephew, who, severely wounded and pale from loss of blood, gave me a smile; while close

[1] His father, Duke Georg zu Saxe-Meiningen, was by his first marriage husband of the Princess Charlotte, daughter of Prince Albrecht of Prussia.

by, all round him were crowding up in their curiosity to see the mitrailleuses, and get acquainted for once at close quarters with these much-belauded bullet-squirts. The artillerymen merely made bad jokes about this new-fangled innovation in their arm, the effect of which, however, is unmistakably deadly within the narrow limits of their zone of fire.

Not far from the burning village of Fröschweiler, Lieutenant Augustin (of the 3rd Hessian Infantry regiment No. 83) brought me a captured French eagle. I was really rejoiced to see this new addition to our old friends in the Potsdam garrison church, but could not, in spite of repeated and urgent inquiries, get any accurate information from anyone as to how this trophy was taken; it appears that Bavarians and Prussians both lay claim to the exploit. The capture of a second eagle has also been notified to me.

It was only to-day I made a first acquaintance with the Württemberg troops, but for this surely no moment and no place could be more fitting than the evening of a day of victory like this. They gave me cheers, which next minute were repeated among the Bavarian Ist Army Corps, already bivouacking not far from Fröschweiler, still burning fiercely in several places. I was glad to be able to say some appreciative words to them in recognition of the final, decisive attack at the finish of the battle. I was most heartily rejoiced that the South Germans were able to bear so real a part in this glorious day, for now is the cement found that will bind together the widely different portions of the German forces united under my supreme command. An event of the sort must mean something; it is a historical fact, the consequences of which are bound to be of immense and far-reaching importance—if only we make a serious endeavour not to suffer such a moment to pass without profiting by it!

The losses of the French must be extraordinarily heavy;[1] the dead lay in heaps, and the red cloth of their uniform showed up wherever the eye fell. Six thousand unwounded prisoners have already been reported to me, including Regimental and Battalion Commanders, and over a hundred other officers. Among them I came upon a Colonel of Cuirassiers, who must have recognized me by my star, for he instantly gave me my proper title: " Ah, monseigneur, quelle défaite, quel malheur; j'ai la honte d'être prisonnier,

---

[1] The French losses, including the missing, amounted in round numbers to 770 officers and 20,540 men; amongst these in prisoners 200 officers and 9,000 men.

nous avons tout perdu ! " [1] I tried to comfort him by saying : " Vous avez tort de dire d'avoir perdu tout, car, après vous être battus comme des braves soldats, vous n'avez pas perdu l'honneur." [2] To this he replied : " Ah, merci, vous me faites du bien en me traitant de la sorte ! " [3] I had him give me the address of those belonging to him so as to send news to the family. Later I came on a great number of other officers in like plight, to whom I spoke to the same effect, commending their gallantry, and adding that we would endeavour to alleviate their lot as far as possible. "Ah, ça est-ce qu'on va nous laisser nos épées et sommes-nous prisonniers sur parole ? " [4] was the reply of one of the foremost, whereupon I assured them they would be treated as officers who had fought with honour. " Ah, mais néanmoins on m'a arraché mon révolver," [5] one of them observed at this. " Comment va le maréchal ? " [6] others cried; I answered that rumours spoke of him as wounded, while only the death of his Chief of Staff, Colson, was definitely reported, and General of Division Raoult severely wounded. Others again praised the bravery of our soldiers. I impressed upon our escort parties to see to it that no affronts were put upon the prisoners, and this the men promised me. Wherever these details met me, endless hurrahs broke out; on one such occasion I saw a crowd of French prisoners wave their caps and heard their cheers !

In the village of Fröschweiler, where the church, along with several farm-buildings, was blazing fiercely, I found the French General of Division Raoult severely wounded in the thigh, lying in a small peasant's house. He was very friendly and ready to talk, but would accept none of my offers of help, saying he was quite comfortable on the bed and his friend standing at his side would take every care of him and even share his captivity with him, and had already sent news to his family of his hopeless condition, for so he considered it. I sought to comfort him, but he said he felt no fear at all at thought of his end; for he had lived as a soldier, and so he knew how to die like one, and God would surely be merciful to a brave warrior.

[1] " Ah, your Highness, what a defeat, what a calamity; I am disgraced, I am a prisoner, we have lost all ! "
[2] " You are wrong in saying you have lost all, for, after fighting like gallant soldiers, you have not lost your honour."
[3] " Ah, thank you, you do me good by speaking to me like that."
[4] " Ah, that means they are going to leave us our swords and that we are prisoners on parole ? "
[5] " Ah, but, for all that, they snatched my revolver from me."
[6] " How goes it with the Marshal ? "

A château of the Counts Türckheim with garden was fitted up in the village of that name as a hospital and dressing-station and had been deserted by its inmates; while the battle was raging the Countess with her people had sought refuge in the cellar; later on, when the fight was over, to devote herself to the care of the wounded. Close by the château the fire was so fierce that the heat was unbearable, though it was still hopeless to think of extinguishing the flames while our men were all hurrying up and down in search of water and such-like camp requisites. Loud jubilation and triumphant joy on every face, and near by the dimming eyes of the dying, amongst whom the grinning masks of the Turkos made a hideous impression.

The evening was spent partly in issuing orders, partly in collecting information in view of drawing up the report of the battle to His Majesty. A talk with Herr von Roggenbach afforded me a welcome distraction after the intense emotions of the day, which leave me nothing else to say save : " God was with us, His be the honour ! "

Late at night came the news of a victory won by Lieutenant-General von Goeben near Saarbrücken (battle of Spicheren). So with that Army too the War has opened prosperously. Undoubtedly the French will be already disconcerted by our successes, and an impression in our favour cannot fail to follow among the Great Powers.

Headquarters : Sulz, 7th August.—To-day I gave my troops a rest and time to restore things to order.

All day long wounded and prisoners were being brought in here, so that the town is already overcrowded. The Pioneers with great handiness and rapidity knocked up three great sheds near the railway station buildings, in which it remained cool in spite of the heat. The slightly wounded were at once sent on to Weissenburg and Landau by the railway, which is again restored to working order. The men told me that in 1866 at Königgrätz the fire was not anything like so fierce and sustained as yesterday; the Zouaves' shooting is very good, but, speaking generally, the French infantryman fires too soon and often aims too high; of Turkos and Zouaves they took little account, and thought that, brave as these are, they would be a match for them. The helmet has often proved of good service, as it has minimized the effects of the astonishingly large number of head wounds. Many instances were cited of the Turkos' villainy, especially their shooting wounded men, and their way of first shamming dead and then behind backs firing at our men. The mitrailleuse has made no great impression, whereas the captured French officers spoke very highly of our artillery. The temper of prisoners was strangely embittered against Mac-Mahon, whom they blamed for bad leadership, called him " un cochon " (a pig), while they designated the Emperor as " une vieille femme " (an old woman) !

The correspondents of the *Gaulois* and the *Figaro*, who had been taken prisoner yesterday on the church tower of Wörth, were brought before me. Both stated they were opponents of Ollivier, had written against him and were not at all favourably disposed to the War, and declared they knew very well it was not we who had instigated it.

It was only to-day I got a clear idea of the fact that the Bavarian Corps von Hartmann, acting quite in accordance with my intention, had moved out from Lembach· and engaged the enemy's left rear flank, and so materially contributed to bring about the fate I hoped to prepare for MacMahon by the envelopment of his left wing by Generals von Bose and Werder.

Our losses will certainly exceed the number of 3,000, though so far nothing can be said definitely, as the reports are self-contradictory and it has not yet been possible to state the total even approximately.[1] But undoubtedly we need a rapid repair of strength, for already, it seems, lieutenants are commanding battalions. Our officers are too brave and go too recklessly ahead of their men; this is especially true of the Vth Corps, that has proved itself so splendid, whereas we may perhaps say for the XIth, in the case of the newly enrolled regiments, that a further stimulus might be required.

The French must have suffered fearfully; two Cuirassier regiments, for instance, have been absolutely wiped out.

The news of a victory won by Lieutenant-General von Goeben at Saarbrücken filled all hearts with delight and was for the wounded, to whom I communicated it in all quarters, highly inspiriting. It is of great importance that the Ist and IInd Armies have now moved forward, as I must first cross the Vosges before I can get in touch again with the two forces, and to do this will have to divide up my Army in separate columns.

A Comte de Leusse, Maire of this arrondissement and Deputy, asked for assistance for two thousand wounded French, who are like to perish of hunger and sickness in his château of Reichshofen. He had lodged MacMahon for almost a week, made reconnaissances with him, had been near him for the greater part of the battle and had witnessed the rout, " qui

---

[1] In reality 489 officers and 10,153 men.

n'était pas une fuite, mais une défaite," [1] he said. He dreaded famine in a few days if my Army stayed longer, as the French had consumed everything. Another fortnight would be needed before the Commissariat would be ready with their measures for providing supplies. This confirms me more than ever in the conviction that we have brought the French to a pretty pass. Moreover, all reports point to the fact that the main Army has not yet been marshalled and despatched, that we forestalled them at Weissenburg and Wörth and that people in France were very imperfectly informed of our position and advance—all this being part of the fanfaronade with which they have wantonly provoked the War at the first possible opportunity! Yesterday during the engagement train after train was despatched to Wörth, each carrying loads of from sixty to a hundred men, who without any definite leadership were sent into the firing-line; it is said too that MacMahon would have chosen to defer the fight till to-day.

I have given the order for to morrow, the 8th, for my whole Army to move forward in four columns to the banks of the Saar. It appears to me of the first importance to reach that river on the 12th at different points to be indicated more precisely later, to which end, wherever the enemy is encountered, he must be instantly attacked and driven back before he finds it possible to reinforce.

The different columns will often be separated by very high and difficult hills, so that mutual support will hardly be practicable; however, in all cases where this can in any sort be offered, it must be given; on this account it is of the first necessity that the several columns marching in one another's vicinity should keep in touch.

In principle the provisioning is carried out by a system of requisitions, but at the same time each man must carry with him a standing ration for three days to prevent any difficulties about food arising in the sparsely populated mountain chain; in especial transport trains and columns must follow on one or two days' march behind their Army Corps, and under no circumstances should be pushed into the mountain defiles before these have been passed by the troops. The great distances make it impossible for me to arrange any regular receipt of orders; still I expect to receive reports, so far as at all feasible, of the doings of the several Corps, as also supposing one of them cannot reach quite punctually the appointed points on the Saar.

---

[1] Which was not a rout, but a defeat.

THE EMPEROR FREDERICK III.

Headquarters: Merxweiler, 8th August.—The advance to the Vosges was began to-day in streaming rain; I went as far as Merxweiler, which lies on the railway, where a friendly and highly intelligent ironmaster, who spoke German, entertained me. A terribly sad sight was that of the fallen, who were just being buried, and whose stiffened features and limbs still revealed the last convulsive spasm in which death surprised them. A larger grave near Gunstett had just been filled in, and a simple, roughly carpentered cross erected over it by comrades of the fallen, against which were piled muskets to form a rude pyramid. This simple monument had something strangely touching about it.

Everywhere wounded men of both armies lay in the villages, while the less seriously hurt were already to be seen on their way to the eastward depôts. Some French officers, amongst them the Commander of the 36th regiment of the line, asked me: "Êtes-vous le Prince Charles?" (Are you Prince Charles?), whereupon I told them that my uncle was with the King; they took me, of course, as everybody does, for my cousin.[1]

At Moosbrunn I found several Prussian wounded, among them being officers, who were doing fairly well. But as they were entirely without medical assistance, though a wonderfully elegant party of French orderly nurses was supposed to be at work in their neighbourhood, I left the auxiliary physician at my headquarters to remain with them until one of Dr. Appia's numerous assistants came to take charge.

Here too I found Major Hicksch along with a number of men of the 2nd Thuringian Infantry regiment No. 32, who had soundly beaten a Cuirassier regiment and a body of enemy Uhlans, whose clumsy leaders had brought them first into vineyards, then into the streets of the village! Their equipment, of splendid material and workmanship—cuirasses, helmets, sabres, saddles, tschapkas and lances—lay about in heaps, the mere sight of which proved how appalling had been the enemy's losses here and made me shudder. The fallen had only just been buried, while the dead horses all lay about still and were already beginning to poison the air. A fellow, originally from Weimar, whom my mother had had taught gardening in England, accosted me, waving a Turko Guide's flag he had looted, and told me his adventures in the drollest fashion. The French Cuirassiers who had been taken prisoners for their part declared they had properly served out their officers for their bad leadership, having simply shot them. In addition to all the other horrors of war and

---

[1] Prince Friedrich Karl, son of Prince Karl.

battle-field, such stories as this, and from the vanquished to the victors!

Fortunately the smiling landscape of the foothills distracted our thoughts a little from these dismal pictures. We encountered a detachment of the Ist Hessian Hussar regiment No. 13. Not only had they been present at the above-mentioned annihilation of French Cuirassiers, but had themselves taken part in the cavalry mêlée, in which the small, nimble fellows slashed down the heavily-built giant Cuirassiers from their horses, without themselves suffering any losses of importance. Very naïve and natural the way these fine representatives of " New Prussia " descanted on their baptism of fire.

I received telegrams of congratulation from my mother, the Queen-Mother of Bavaria,[1] the Kings of Bavaria and Saxony, the Grand Duke of Mecklenburg-Schwerin, as well as from various towns and public bodies. We for our part can only telegraph at rare intervals and must always be prepared for a delay of some days in the transmission of intelligence.

At Gunstedt I met the Swiss physician Dr. Appia, one of the originators of the Geneva Convention, with a numerous retinue of doctors; he expressed the lively interest he took in my victories and willingly placed his own and his companions' services at my disposal. We need them badly, for so numerous are the wounded that, despite the daily increasing number of volunteer surgeons and charitable Sisters, the nursing staff is proving altogether insufficient. The battle-field of Wörth is over a mile in extent, and as brushwood, vineyards and gardens cover a part of it, it is unfortunately unavoidable that, in spite of diligent search, too many sufferers have not even yet been found. Besides which, in the large vineyard close by Wörth, Turkos have established themselves, who fire on every single stretcher-bearer approaching the spot. Lastly, it must be known that the French pay no heed to the white armlet, wear no such badges themselves and have issued no official announcement to their Army of their acceptance of the Geneva Convention. Naturally our men are greatly embittered in consequence, but are more especially furious with the Turkos, because these practise vile, knavish tricks and shoot wounded men; no quarter, therefore, is now given to any such ruffians. Alas! too, many civilians have been caught carrying arms and, so it is asserted, committing atrocities. They have been shot

[1] The widowed Queen of Bavaria was a daughter, Marie, of Prince William (the elder) of Prussia.

at sight. An officer of Zouaves, who was taken prisoner yesterday, was very anxious to send news to his relations, but as he *could not write*, was obliged to dictate his letter. It is hard to understand how a people that employs such men in its service as just described can believe itself called upon to introduce " liberté et civilisation " (freedom and civilization) into Germany.

Headquarters : Obermodern, 9th August.—In streaming rain our march led us through beautiful woodland country, the fertile plains and hills of lovely Elsass. Again and again was noticeable the German look which the population in their prosperous towns and villages has preserved; they much resemble the peasants of the Black Forest. Here nobody understands French, for it is only in the last twenty years that language has been taught in the schools. The natives came forward with a simple, honest naïveté and were prodigiously curious to see me, " because, as they said, he will yet be ours." The women in particular were attracted by the cross (of the Order of the Black Eagle) which I wear; they would not believe me when I told them I was nearly forty and had six children living. Wherever the population is Evangelical, they meet us in a friendly spirit and soon lay aside their fear of the Germans; where, on the other hand, the Catholic priests had worked upon the minds of their coreligionists, one instantly felt the difference. The larger landowners and more important officials are mostly pure Frenchmen, but received us politely and without constraint. It is very noteworthy that the Catholics in Elsass have for a long time past been talking to the effect that this year would yet see a war with Germany, and after the inevitable defeat of the Germans the struggle would at once resolve itself into one against the Protestants in particular. I should not take notice of such-like expressions of opinion had they not been daily repeated on all sides. My quarters were at the house of a friendly Evangelical Pastor, Haan by name, who dilated on the utter disorder in which the flying troops had been passing through here the day before yesterday from as early as six o'clock in the morning. Generally small bands of from half a dozen to a dozen men would come by, many of whom threw away their weapons and tore off their epaulets. Although he and his family speak only German and do not deny the German descent of the community, yet he and his still designated themselves French. He appears to me to belong to the reasonable type of cleric, called down blessings on my House and myself and longed ardently and sincerely for the conclusion of the War; Peace, Peace, he said, was here the unanimous cry, and universal the hatred of the War, for the outbreak of which everyone knew we Germans were in no wise to blame.

Since the 2nd of August we have had no news from Berlin. The more welcome, therefore, sundry Karlsruhe supplements which a Bavarian officer passing through brought with him, and from which we learned that the battle of the 6th at Saarbrücken had been a bloody one; further, that in Paris a state of siege had already been decreed. Strange to say, the results of the battles that have gone badly for the French are openly avowed to the public by announcements from the Empress, this after a Ministerial proclamation had only a short while before denied the first alarming reports. In all quarters the population of Paris is warned to keep calm, for, as would seem to have been said in so many words, " every act of disorder at the present moment is equivalent to victories of the Prussians over the French." This is indeed beginning early, and will give the pernicious instigators of the War serious cause for reflection, only the more so as Emperor and Empress willed it so! The latter, and Ollivier too, should look at battle-fields and hospitals to know by the witness of their own eyes the horrors they have conjured up by their reckless folly.

My headquarters, already overcrowded, is further augmented by the addition of the Hereditary Grand Duke of Mecklenburg-Strelitz, together with A.D.C.'s, the correspondent of *The Times*, Mr. Russell, to whom Lord Ronald Leveson-Gower, in spite of our repeated intimation that there was no room for him with us, attaches himself in a sporting spirit—he demands board and lodging for himself and his horses, but has not so far applied himself to anybody in particular; in addition, Mr. Skinner, correspondent for the *Daily News*, and Mr. Landels, draughtsman for *The Times*.

The church clock here strikes exactly like the one in the Great Quadrangle at Windsor, giving me such a pleasant, home-like feeling! I think, as I hear, how our successes will be of great benefit as affecting English feeling; it grieves me to hear how strongly England's attitude on the question of War contraband is resented in Germany, and particularly in Prussia, though really the legislation of that Island kingdom must be studied to enable me to judge fairly of her conduct.

To-morrow the IInd Division at last moves off over the Saar on the march to the Moselle; so now Prince Friedrich Karl will surely have a great battle before him. We, for our part, have for to-morrow to undertake a long, difficult march through the Vosges, the troops moving forward in separate

THE EMPEROR FREDERICK III.   49

columns; it is to be hoped we shall not be seriously delayed by the mountain fortresses.

In MacMahon's travelling carriage was an accurate survey of the Vosges with notes as to all lines of communication and so on, which, of course, comes in extremely useful for us. The find included many other important papers. In the French officers' tents are discovered a host of toilet paraphernalia, delicacies of all sorts, copies of plays, as well as articles of female dress, including crinolines rolled up in a bundle. The Commandant of Strasburg, General Ducrot, one of the most rabid of Chauvinists, who always talked like a very firebrand of the coming War with Germany, escaped by the closest shave being taken prisoner at Wörth; packed amongst his luggage he had two sets of ladies' clothes.

All this while fresh convoys of prisoners keep coming in, usually a hundred or thereabouts at a time, so that the number of the French losses in the last two days will reach a total of quite 20,000 men. Our own casualties come to a figure considerably above the first estimates, and we shall certainly have over 8,000 dead and wounded.

Since August 7 we have been without news from home; indeed so far it is only from the King and the town of Görlitz I have received telegrams referring to the great victory at Wörth. The latter circumstance I account for by the fact that the news of Weissenburg, as relating to the first victory gained, made more impression on men's minds than that of the second success reported immediately after the other. But Wörth is a victory of historical significance, for, apart from its importance as a military triumph, it is notable for the French having been beaten for the first time since 1815 in a pitched battle. How wonderful that of all others it was given to me, who could never have looked for such a thing, to go straight into action in the first line.

Headquarters : Petersbach, on the western slope of the Vosges, 10th, 11th and 12th August.—Thus the Vosges are already as good as crossed, and connection being now established with the IInd Army Corps, united action of the whole German forces, with the exception of two Prussian Divisions,[1] can now be taken. My old Pomeranian Army Corps has received marching orders; already we outnumber the French by something like 100,000 men.

The health of the troops is still surprisingly good; the

[1] As a matter of fact, only *one* Prussian Division, the 17th (XVIth Corps), was held back, to cover Schleswig-Holstein.

cooling of the air has had a good share in this, though I hope the rain that has now set in may not continue.

On the 10th August we marched in the best sort of weather for surmounting steep mountain tracks—turn and turn about sunshine and rain—and following directly on the heels of the Vth Army Corps, by way of the small fortress of Lützelstein, otherwise La Petite Pierre, to the village of Petersbach. Here I at once took advantage of some hours of leisure to take time by the forelock and set down clearly in writing what terms, supposing it comes to negotiations for peace, should be considered and approved. Again I had an opportunity to discuss things exhaustively with the amiable Freytag; he still preserves in the field his old vein of humour and his artless, unaffected originality; he is a very congenial companion to me, one who puts up with everything and diligently watches events.

The retreating French would seem to have marched through here in somewhat better order, but still in much confusion. The Cuirassiers were mostly on foot; many Alsatian soldiers quitted their detachments and made their way back home; the officers could no longer enforce obedience! They are furious with MacMahon and call him by the most abominable and abusive names; indeed they might very well shoot him next time they come across him, seeing they can only explain his bad leadership as being the result of bribery with Prussian gold. At the camp of Châlons, Gardes Mobiles have already mutinied and been accordingly disarmed, while Canrobert has refused to receive any more drafts of such riff-raff. Even supposing this to be only half true, still it is amazing enough. In front of the neat, two-storey houses of a well-to-do peasant at which I have taken up my quarters, Generals Failly and Ducrot would appear to have had an outrageous and loud-voiced quarrel with one another. Failly was reproached with having refused, out of ill-will to MacMahon, to let his Divisions attack, still fresh though they were; in any case his troops, some part in close formation, marched off at the head of the fugitives. It is thought a stand will be made on the Saar.

The population here is purely German and staunchly Protestant; they understand French only a little, and in every peasant's house hang pictures of Luther and the great Reformers, variously represented. In my host's sitting-room are to be found, beside bibles, Thiers' *Histoire du Consulat et de l'Empire*, Lamartine's *Girondins* and sundry scientific works. Once the people had got over their first alarm and timidity, they thawed and conversed very intelligently. Our host and his wife were remarkably well versed in the latest politics; they knew precisely the circumstances of Prince Leopold von Hohenzollern's candidature to the Spanish throne, and declared openly that on receipt of the news of the Prince's renunciation of his claim everybody had rejoiced at the assured prospect of peace. So much the more were they startled by the War, the natural outcome of which would be the union of Alsace with us. They said French fugitives on their way through here had related how they had never yet had to do with soldiers like the Prussians and victory for the French was no longer to be thought of.

At last the Field Post, as also the Field Telegraph, have succeeded in delivering our belated letters and telegrams, so that to-day I received my wife's congratulations on the victory of Wörth. The fixing up of the wires proceeds with much judgment and the most active zeal, but has to encounter many difficulties, for it constantly happens that our own columns on the march, thinking they have come upon enemy material, do all the damage they can. The native population seldom ventures on the like, dreading the heavy penalties threatened. My batman Winckelstein arrived on the 12th after a dangerous seven days' journey with five letters from my wife—the first home news since the 3rd August, including, therefore, the first intelligence as to the impression produced by my victory in Berlin. The lively interest and sympathy expressed by all classes in unpremeditated and quite unaffected language moved me to tears, for I am not even yet master of my feelings when I think of these successes, but above all when I recall our losses. No man is a soldier and nothing else, or can help in hours of remembrance, with all overflowing thankfulness to Him who governs the strife, to give free vent to his natural human feelings.

With every day the high import of the victories we owe to our brave officers and soldiers comes out more clearly, while on Paris and France generally they are bound to have a terribly depressing effect. Napoleon's first communication about the progress of events is already to be read in the daily press, but he puts our strength at Wörth at something like 40,000 men too high, and the French, on the other hand, at some 30,000 too low.

A French provincial paper brought us from Paris gives the list of names of a new Ministry [1] and its proclamation on taking office; so Ollivier with his blood-guiltiness retires into private life and can gloat at his leisure over the mis-

---

[1] Palikao, 10th August.

fortunes and misery and death of those whom, in his overweening arrogance, he drove to their ruin. Judging by the names, it is the old " régime personnel " come back again. Moreover, all classes of those liable to serve, including the younger men hitherto counted under military age, are called to the colours, to fight as untrained or half-trained soldiers. It must have come to a pretty pass when such measures are resorted to. From the leading articles of the *Gaulois, Figaro* and *Rappel* of the 8th August we learned particulars of the disorders that broke out in Paris in consequence of the withholding of the truth respecting Weissenburg and Wörth. Of the former victory no word was said for twenty-four hours, while concerning the latter only muffled rumours circulated, after great demonstrations had first taken place in celebration of a supposed victory. One paper already contained a translation of my field report to His Majesty of the 4th August, as well as one of the King's telegrams to my mother, with a note to the effect " que ' Fritz ' est le diminutif allemand du nom de Frédéric ! (that Fritz is the German diminutive of the name Frederick). Paris was declared in a state of siege, and the Corps Législatif convoked (for the 9th August) ! All this already, after merely a few Corps of an Army such as this have been defeated.

I received a notification from Count Bismarck to forbid the " conscription," proclaimed by the French, but forbidden by our King, in those parts of the country already occupied, and in every way to prevent its being carried out.

Of politics I have been in entire ignorance since the 26th July, and the same is the case with the diplomats accompanying me, amongst others Count Solms,[1] who has good sources of information in France, and though not possessed of a particularly strong head for politics, still understands his business very well, and can be of use, once he has adequate instructions to go upon. We are curious to know if really, as is said, Austria has concluded a treaty of neutrality with Italy, or whether, as other reports declare, Count Beust deplores having had to surrender to the strong tide of popular sentiment and keep the peace, while all the time he is for war with us—which is all the more annoying to him, " at a time when," as they say, " Count Bismarck subventions the Austrian Press ! "

Duke Friedrich zu Schleswig-Holstein-Augustenburg announces his coming here.

[1] Eberhard Count Solms-Sonnenwalde had been up to the outbreak of War First Secretary of the Embassy of the North German Bund in Paris.

Headquarters: Saarburg, 13th August.—We are lodged at the Préfet's in his official residence, and as he has remained on the spot himself, requisitions, heavy as they must be, are at any rate made by rule and order, and so press less hardly on the inhabitants. Two French Corps have already marched through here, and on top of them both our Prussian, so that the little place has much to bear. Unfortunately some detached bodies of troops passing through the town have broken into wine-cellars; no doubt their thirst on that hot day was very distressing.

At last I received to-day some political intelligence from the Royal headquarters, which sounds decidedly favourable and encouraging for us, while France's prospects daily suffer heavier blows.

In England we have gained consideration from the fact that we agreed at once to the demand coming from them to give a new declaration of guarantee in regard to Belgian neutrality. Russia will not move, Austria and Italy will undertake no hostile action, while Denmark is stringently watched to see that France does not attempt anything in the way of " moral suasion " on her. God be praised, the influence of my victory is already bringing about a change of feeling in our favour throughout Europe; may this temper continue!

The Prince Imperial, it would seem, has already arrived in England! I pity this poor child sincerely. The Princes of the House of Orleans ask to be admitted to the French Army,[1] to come to the help of their hard-pressed fatherland; from their point of view I cannot but find it right and noble, but for Napoleon it will mean serious embarrassments, for, once the Orleans are in France and are in a position to take an active part in the struggle, they will soon gain ground and undoubtedly use every endeavour either to prolong the War, or else, after it is ended, as soon as possible to provoke a new one.

From the latest reports of scouts it appears more and more as if the French intend to make no stand at Metz, but to march on Châlons and only await us there, or as a last resource before Paris itself. Lunéville has already been occupied by my forces; I have had the keys of the town transmitted to me; very shortly my cavalrymen will appear before Nancy.

Our losses from Weissenburg and Wörth we must reckon at 12,000 men, those of the French at twice as many at the least.

[1] Also the then head of the House of Bourbon, Comte Chambord, made a similar request.

Napoleon with his much-betrumpeted victory of Saarbrücken has made himself supremely ridiculous; to entertain " Loulou " three Divisions were necessary and for " Loulou's " entertainment had to put to flight six Prussian Companies, and then the worthless little town had still to be bombarded and burnt!

Headquarters: Blâmont, 14th August.—God bless my dear boy Heinrich, who to-day completes his eighth year, and preserve him to us, that with his brothers he may one day help complete Germany's task in time of peace, for which at this present time it is my duty to do bloody work; this separation from him is very hard to bear. First Lieutenant von Winterfeld, Commander of my Silesian Dragoon regiment, breakfasted with me and helped me to celebrate the day.

We had a hot day's march, but at the end found a very friendly reception from the Maire, an old Artillery officer and Orleanist. With his old mother-in-law, an original, was staying a grandniece of our late friend Bacourt.

One of the older non-commissioned officers of the Infantry escort of my staff marched with a map of France in his hand, and always knew precisely where he was—surely an eloquent token of the level of education now reached even in the lowest classes of our people.

A rumour has been going about that, following outrageously stormy debates in the Corps Législatif, Marshal Bazaine has superseded Napoleon as Generalissimo of the French Army.

On our ride to-day we could plainly hear the sound of the guns bombarding Pfalzburg, where the Artillery of the VIth Army Corps is endeavouring to force that not insignificant stronghold to capitulate; the result will be, the town reduced to ashes, but the fortress untaken.

Our meals were eaten in the open air, in the courtyard of the Seminary of what was once a Monastery and is now a Hospital. Its inmates, and above all the inhabitants of the town, were exceedingly curious to see us dine to music. An ecclesiastic I conversed with confused Hohenzollern and Hohenlohe, and was greatly surprised at our being able to speak French; he also confirmed the universal desire for peace.

The population of all this neighbourhood speaks gratefully of the benefits it owes to Napoleon III, but all believe the last days of the Empire are come; it is all one to them whether the Orleans or the Republic take its place, if only peace be ensured.

The German language stops short here; hence arise the

most unheard-of misunderstandings between our soldiers and the inhabitants, particularly where refreshments are concerned. Unfortunately, if our fellows cannot make themselves understood, they help themselves and soon break in the doors, especially of the wine-cellars. I am fully alive to the mischievous effect of such incidents and endeavour to check them as far as may be, but I shall find no adequate remedy short of stern punishments. Otherwise the folks are gradually recovering from their first terror of us as cannibals, a fear artificially fostered by our enemies. Indeed they laugh at their own delusion, but are in the main inclined to attribute their good treatment at our hands simply and solely to the fact that we are taking over the country as our own, and therefore desire betimes to make ourselves popular. Even our host is convinced this is the right way to look at it.

Lord Adare, correspondent of the *Daily Telegraph*, has arrived, accompanied by an English surgeon who wants to pursue professional studies, but I find myself in an embarrassing position with regard to them, particularly as being foreigners, because, apart from the increase in the number of guests at headquarters, into the bargain, a strongly-worded order has just come from His Majesty prohibiting the admission of any more correspondents from foreign papers; besides which we are specifically warned against Lord Adare, as the representative of a hostilely disposed journal. To the latter, therefore, who does not know a word of German, I am compelled to hand a pass for home.

I begin to believe that we may yet perhaps be able to keep the harvest festival at home, for I can *not* imagine things can go on much longer here. Just four weeks ago to-day we learned of the Hereditary Prince Leopold of Hohenzollern's renunciation of the Spanish throne and heaved a sigh of relief because the danger of war was averted; to-day we are already victors and on the march into France.

Headquarters: Lunéville, 15th August.—An old fortress of the days of Vauban, Marsal by name, has to-day surrendered without loss of time to the Bavarians, whereby 250 prisoners and some fifty guns, together with a large number of muskets, fell into our hands. At Pfalzburg things went exactly as I expected; the French Commandant there has held out very stubbornly and courageously, refusing absolutely to capitulate.

A hot ride brought us to the former capital of Lorraine, well known amongst other things through the ill-omened Peace of 1801. I had expected more of it; the castle reminds one of Fontainebleau, the gardens and grounds of the Park of Versailles; now the vast rooms have been utilized partly as warehouses, partly as official residences, so that only a few ornate inscriptions of Louis XV's and Stanislas Leszczynski's recall the old-time splendour, traces of which are also to be seen in a nobly laid-out garden with avenues of limes and elms, statues and parterres.

The Maire, a former dentist in the service of the Grand Duchess Hélène of Russia, and sundry prominent officials begged for indulgence towards the town, already drained dry by previous perquisitions, as the Préfet had taken his departure. On a closer search, however, we discovered a considerable stock of provisions still here, which will come in useful for the troops. All barracks and military buildings were still so crammed with articles of equipment of all sorts as to show from this alone the haste with which the garrison of the town, four Cuirassier regiments strong, had abandoned the place. Plans of the camp at Châlons and many important documents thus fell into our hands.

Here in Lunéville great dejection and anxiety prevailed because just those Cavalry regiments forming the customary garrison are amongst those almost wiped out at Wörth, and no one of the numerous families of the officers have so far received tidings of the fate of those belonging to them. We were therefore the first to give the poor wretches any information; we have just learned too, from the questions they asked after six different Commanders, that the Cavalry Division must have consisted of more than four Cuirassier regiments; five Colonels are missing, while the sixth escaped here wounded.

Here too a bitter feeling found expression over the War, though no doubt this is in part a consequence of the heavy burdens that are for ever being laid on the community.

Now it is said that Steinmetz, in conjunction with the 18th Division attacking from the South, has won a victory,[1] in the neighbourhood of Metz, though we know nothing as yet of a more precise nature; may the news prove authentic, for the effect will be as staggering on Paris in its present excited condition as on the Corps Législatif, where Napoleon's military incapacity no less than his other defects of character are already a topic of discussion. To-day is actually Napoleon day (the Emperor's birthday), the day on which the French proposed to march into Berlin!

For to-morrow, 10th August, I have provisionally fixed a

---

[1] The action at Colombey-Nouilly fought by the advance guard of the VIIth Corps.

THE EMPEROR FREDERICK III. 57

day's rest for the men, as is urgently necessary for our fellows after the forced marches over the Vosges and the days of rain. Only the Bavarian IInd Corps has had my orders to go forward as far as Nancy, to go into cantonments there and push on its advance guard to Toul and Saint Vincent, of which places the first would seem to be only weakly occupied. The bridges at Pont-Saint-Vincent and Frouard are not destroyed, albeit the railways have been rendered unusable.

The peaceful citizens of Lunéville speak of the great dejection of spirits that had taken possession of all the French troops marching through the place. The country-folk declare openly that they were cheated on the occasion of the *plébiscite*, as it was officially set out that every man voting " yes " was helping to the maintenance of peace.[1] After the experience gained hereabouts, however, a repetition of such an appeal to the voters would lead to a precisely opposite result.

It is still prodigiously difficult to get together accurate details of events at the battle of Wörth; marching as we do in several columns increases the difficulties of intercommunication, not to speak of the fact that so many gallant witnesses are no longer with us.

Headquarters: Lu éville, 16th August.—To-day I received a letter from His Majesty, writing on the 15th August from Herny, which confirms yesterday's rumours of a sanguinary action fought by the Ist Army near Metz. By what it says the French carried their wounded inside the fortifications, while we retired into our bivouacs, but only after the enemy had been well trounced at all points. No doubt the French will talk of a victory, inasmuch as they got back again within the walls. Still it looks more and more as if the French Army is not concentrating about Metz, but is already in full retreat on Châlons.[2] But why? Metz is the chief place of arms in all France.

Strange to say, His Majesty only received my reports on Weissenburg and Wörth on the 14th August. As the King goes to-day to Pont-à-Mousson, I will announce my arrival there to-morrow, and to that end to-day, when we are having

---

[1] The *plébiscite* of the 8th May had declared by an overwhelming majority for a Napoleonic hereditary Empire. In a proclamation that accompanied the decree ordering the *plébiscite* we read : " By depositing an affirmative vote in the urn you will be exorcising the threats of revolution and establishing order and freedom on a firm basis."

[2] This view, that the French Army was already in retreat over the Moselle, was shared also by Moltke and Prince Friedrich Karl.

a day's rest here, I propose to go in the evening to Nancy, so as to be able to start away again first thing in the morning.

For several days now we have been anxious to secure early possession of Pont-à-Mousson and so command that important point for the passage of the Moselle, and even now, to-day, the Royal headquarters may be established there; thus, supposing no serious stand is made about Metz, we can march on the Verdun–Châlons line. I fail to grasp the motives actuating the French.

Headquarters : Nancy, 17th August.—On the road yesterday I spoke to Lieutenant-General von Kirchbach and his Staff, Lieutenant-General von Schmidt and Colonel von Schön, and made known everywhere the contents of the King's letter relating to the engagement of the 14th August.

When I arrived here late in the evening, I found a Bavarian guard of honour with several bands of music waiting for me, as well as Lieutenant-General von Hartmann, who is quartered in the same hotel as myself; after that I saw the Préfet, the Maire, etc., commiserating them on their situation in guarded phrases.

On the point of starting for Pont-à-Mousson, one of my despatch-riders, who had been sent on there, arrives with the announcement that the IIIrd and Xth Army Corps had yesterday, in a sanguinary action before Metz (battle of Vionville Mars-la-Tour), engaged the greater part of the French Army, including the French guards. The IIIrd Army Corps suffered considerable losses, but we remained masters of the field of battle, from which the enemy withdrew in good order. To-day, as early as half-past three in the morning, the King has taken the road to attack the enemy, so that the decisive battle is expected to-day.[1] Of course I could not go there now, but at the very least I might stop where I was, well out of range of my Army, as a mere onlooker, and I believe I have done my duty in exercising this self-denial. Captain Lenke was forthwith despatched to the scene of action, to bring me information or possible orders.

I spent the whole day in feverish excitement, for it is a hard task to sit still when only a few miles away the King and our own people are fighting. But seeing my forces are distant over two days' march from Metz, I cannot, relying on uncorroborated news such as this, concentrate them on that point, especially as some days ago I received an intimation I should not be moved thither so soon as this,

---

[1] The King appeared on the battle-field at six o'clock in the morning, but, as we know, no general engagement followed that day.

because by themselves the Ist and IInd Army Corps already outnumber the French. To-day I await the news whether I am to direct my march westwards, or else, more or less a right-about turn, shall have to take the direction to the north, in order, within the next few days at latest, to join action with the other Armies. In the first case I cause the French constant anxiety for the safety of their flank, and if they *are* beaten and drawn off, I can bring them into great straits in the Châlons neighbourhood. In the latter, I should either reinforce Prince Friedrich Karl, or else have to intervene in such a way that, should he suffer a set-back, I could help him out of his difficulties. It still remains a matter of surprise to me that, in accordance with the dispositions of the Princes, as known up to now, the IInd Army has come to be to the southward of Metz or even by this time to the west of that fortress, so that it would have to attack the enemy, standing more or less with his back to Paris. God help us as hitherto, but what sacrifices in men shall we be called upon to make! I shall remain at least another twenty-four hours at Nancy, to await further developments, while my troops quietly continue their march.

Here in Nancy extraordinary depression prevails, for while on the one hand famine is making itself felt, on the other the troops daily marching through the town are bound to make ever fresh demands on the community, already heavily taxed to supply the needs of the French in completion of their preparations to go to the front. It is hardly credible, but we hear fresh confirmation of the fact every day, in what an utterly unprepared state, especially in the matter of commissariat, the French have been plunged into this War. The calling up of the Gardes Mobiles and the younger men capable of bearing arms, all young folks, therefore, who have never been trained, rouses much weeping and wailing in the country, for naturally such a body of troops, whose leaders are just as inexperienced as their men, is simply food for powder. One's heart might well be wrung at the thought of this, if one were for adopting the purely human point of view—yet of what avail is that? we *must* beat the French, and cannot possibly rest till we have secured the certainty that they will not again disturb the peace of Europe.

The Orleanists are much more numerously represented in this neighbourhood than I supposed; the population looks upon that family as being no gluttons for war.

No letters since 7th August; this time the blame lies with the Bavarian post, which pays all honour to the example of the Thurn and Taxis administration of hideous memory. It is really unheard of, and everybody is loud in complaints over it.

To distract my mind I took a stroll through this pretty town. By elegant ornamentation cleverly applied to the existing buildings of the sixteenth and seventeenth centuries, they have added modern embellishments to these old houses. The principal squares are laid out with rare good taste and give the erstwhile capital of the rulers of Burgundy–Lorraine a really imposing appearance. The Place Stanislas and the Place Carrière are perfect models of ornamental pleasure grounds, to which the luxuriant greenery of the neighbouring Park affords a fascinating background. As a contrast, the tombs of the Princes of Lorraine, apart from a few statues, point only to the iconoclastic fury of the Revolution, following on which the Restoration of 1817 only added the most utterly tasteless adornments.

I visited Madame de Gonneville, a sister of our true friend Herr von Bacourt, who died here, as also their daughter the Marquise de Mirabeau, and afterwards went on to the Mother-House of the charitable Sisters of St. Charles, in which my mother always takes a lively interest, and whose Superiors had already been to see me to depict to me the distress of the poor of the place and beg for indulgence towards the city.

Only after the news had gone about of a sanguinary victory having been won before Metz and the wires had then been suddenly interrupted, it was reported late in the evening by Captain Lenke that no battle had taken place to-day, but one would probably be fought to-morrow.

Headquarters: Nancy, 18th August.—On the suspense of yesterday followed late at night the announcement of a sanguinary action fought on the 16th about Metz by the gallant IIIrd Army Corps, in which we took two eagles, six guns and 3,000 prisoners; further, that yesterday the contemplated attack could not be carried out, but would for certain take place to-morrow.

Our men have already occupied the enemy's southern line of retreat from Metz to Châlons, so the engagement fixed for to-day should be more concerned with the northern. If it goes in our favour, then we may hope to entangle the hostile army in those parts in very serious difficulties, for again yesterday I received the order to pursue my march on Paris, without troubling my head about occurrences at Metz.

General Failly with two Divisions would seem to have marched off to Lyons or actually to Strasburg; consequently the French Army of the Rhine must be weakened and diminished even more than it already was by losses in action. For the rest I can *not* in any way account for this—as little as I am able to realize the motives actuating the French General Staff. It would appear that as early as from the day before yesterday the French Guards have been in the field against us. Probably our IInd Army is to-day pursuing the enemy to bring him to a stand.

I have made my Army acquainted with events at Metz, adding further that according to current rumours the Camp of Châlons is still strongly held, while a new Army is being formed at Paris, so that we might soon again encounter fighting forces of the enemy. On these grounds I have earnestly warned the several Army Corps marching in the first line always to push out their advance guard from a half to a whole day's march ahead and reconnoitre the ground in front with cavalry. The first-named, therefore, must always bivouac, while the troops marching behind take up close cantonments. The IInd Bavarian Corps covers my right, the XIth Corps my left flank, and while I withdraw the 4th Cavalry Division behind the first line of the Army, the 2nd Division will move laterally on the left wing and reconnoitre the ground to the south.

Furthermore, I have given orders to take care that, if an advance guard is seriously threatened by the enemy, it must immediately halt and take stand in order that the main body marching behind can make ready for action; it is above all desirable that the advance guards should undertake no serious offensive operations, in order that the Army covering on the march an extent of something near eight miles may get time to concentrate. I have given stringent orders that the columns keep touch with one another and send news of all incidents, also by relays informing me immediately of any occurrences of importance.

The 4th Cavalry Division, which is already scouting out as far as Ligny, reports, this information agreeing with confidential news from Police Lieutenant Hoppe at Bâle, that considerable enemy forces are gathering about Châlons, where MacMahon has gone and where Napoleon arrived on the 17th August. From Toul a considerable amount of artillery material seems to have been despatched to Paris.

I have just learned the names of my many intimate friends who fell on the 16th August. Colonel von Auerswald is reported dead, Count Reinhold Finkenstein appears to have been wounded and taken prisoner, Counts Wesdehlen and Westarp, von Kleist, Prince Henry XVII of Reuss dead! It is appalling; even though the squares were scattered, the success does not lessen the total of losses of distinguished men.

I had sent Major von Hahnke and Captain of Horse von der Lancken to the Royal headquarters in order to secure news more quickly than yesterday; nevertheless the whole day passed without tidings; only Captain O'Danne, tutor to Prince Wilhelm, who returned after a seven days' journey from Berlin, declared he had heard of an engagement, but we could nowhere catch the sound of guns. Before Toul the IVth Army Corps had undertaken a fruitless assault, which cost the 93rd regiment a number of wounded, who were brought in here to-day. The population looks on this as a French victory, and was evidently in a great state of excitement, which all day long I had the pleasure of watching, dense crowds, among them many men in blouses, filling the street before my hotel. It was mostly people belonging to the working classes, who, being out of work, wander about the town and stare at us with unprepossessing faces. The whole day was passed in painful suspense, only relieved by the arrival of my despatch-rider Hanstein with long-expected letters from home, and in particular, from wife and children.

Headquarters: Nancy, 19th August.—At five in the morning Major von Hahnke returned from the battle-field at Metz. A hot, sanguinary engagement, in which more or less all Army Corps participated, was fought from one o'clock in the afternoon till evening after dark under the eyes of His Majesty. Towards evening quite unexpectedly an immensely powerful French battery came into action, which produced something like a panic among the VIIth and VIIIth Army Corps until the strongest enemy position was taken by my old Pomeranian Army Corps, and this decided the battle. Thereupon we waited till to-day to continue the struggle, and in view of this the King stayed in bivouac on the battle-field.

In the midst of constant suspense and excitement, which never ceased all to-day, came letters from my wife and relatives of the 9th to the 13th August, considerably raising my spirits and distracting my thoughts, for at any rate an odd half-hour, from the battle-fields.

Please God, a momentous turn has been taken in the whole campaign, even though results of the engagements round Metz will not just as yet bring about the final decision between war and peace. For, if the French preparations are as extensive as the newspapers declare, it is only to be expected the enemy will make a show of coming on with all his forces

THE EMPRESS FREDERICK.

and again offer battle. Would it not also be possible that the Great Powers may make a move and ideas of a Conference be brought on the tapis, while we, weakened by the sacrifices of men we have suffered, might in spite of repeated victories find it difficult to counter such efforts to any extent worth attention? Such and the like thoughts rack my brains, especially after a communication from Bismarck brought me yesterday by Count Solms; in the end I tried to ward them off by telling myself how often all calculations are confounded by the actual course of events. It grieves me to think how the King with his seventy-four years is in bivouac and I cannot be with him, to share his thoughts and anxieties. But I cannot leave my Army actually engaged in an advance. Prince Ludwig zu Hessen and his Division would seem to have fought a very pretty action yesterday; the engagement appears to have been less bloody than that on the 16th, in which, as His Majesty has said himself, the gallant IIIrd Army Corps suffered such enormous losses as have seldom been known in a campaign. As yet we can give no names of the fallen, so many said to be dead are alive, men who have lost limbs are reported as lightly wounded, etc., or even have come back to the colours, but it is certain that, when once we get back home, the Fatherland will be drowned in tears. An extraordinary amount of praise has been lavished on me, far more than I deserve. But is it not a strange thing that I, who much preferred to earn recognition in works of peace, am called upon to win such blood-stained laurels? In time to come may the peaceful part of my efforts be all the more beneficent. Even from England come tokens of appreciation for my victories, a thing that pleases me infinitely. Thus, for instance, Lord Granville, in a private letter to my wife, has strongly repudiated the notion that his policy was guided by sympathy for France. Another day of dreadful suspense; I could not and ought not to leave here, yet I was irresistibly drawn to join the King. Part of the forenoon I spent with Prince Ernst of Coburg, in the open air, for our excited mood made any sort of indoor employment impossible. At last, late in the evening, arrived Captain Lenke: to-day nothing had happened, and we could only conclude that the French had had enough and that for the present the fighting round Metz is at a standstill.

Yesterday's battle was, especially for the Guards Corps, frightfully bloody; these had to make a frontal attack on strongly occupied heights, on which were villages specially fortified for defence, and, so it seems, were not properly supported by the King of Saxony's troops.

Headquarters : Vaucouleurs, 20th August.—The last moment permitting me to stay longer at Nancy having expired to-day, I turned out quite early in the morning, and accompanied by General von Blumenthal, set off for the Royal headquarters at Pont-à-Mousson. A ride of four miles in the Moselle valley! It seemed to me as if we might commit to the stream a greeting for the dear home-land.

The King I found well, thank God, but quite cut up by the frightful losses, the total of which cannot be estimated with anything like certainty, but which threaten to approach the twenty thousand. Our meeting moved him deeply. The first thing I said to him, after we had embraced, was that I still deemed my prophecy made over the coffin of the grandparents was a true one—that a thing begun under such auspices must succeed. The King did not absolutely reject the idea, but dwelt again and again upon the sacrifices already made; then he recounted the whole course of the battle of the 18th, to which, it seems, he means to give the name of "Gravelotte." The advance of the Guards Corps seems to have been premature and over-reckless; in particular, the attack of the Ist Guards Infantry brigade under Major-General von Kessel would appear to have been made quite against the principles of the Bornstedt Field at Potsdam, maxims actually practised a thousand times over by him and even laid down in writing. Moreover, the view is held here to-day that the village of Saint-Privat captured by the Guards might have been taken with much less loss of men, if the Saxons had not been so dilatory in their advance on our left wing for the attack on Sainte-Marie aux Chênes. Towards evening the King thought the battle was ended, when, to everybody's surprise, the famous "retraite offensive" the French are so fond of was undertaken from a steep hill-side of such a nature that successive storeys, so to speak, of cannon and mitrailleuse fire, masked by entrenchments, poured down a veritable hail of shot and shell, bringing the advance of the VIIth and VIIIth Army Corps to a standstill and causing their ranks to waver and fall back. The King was close by and, as once before at Königgrätz, had seen sundry shells fall round him, so that General von Roon warned him of his danger, and then, despatching peremptory orders to the Westphalians and Rhinelanders, had striven to restore order. My old Pomeranian Army Corps, which had only just completed a sixteen hours' march, was now ordered forward, and, steady as on manœuvres, climbed the steep hill-side, which the enemy then evacuated—and the day was decided in our favour. The King believed that a new battle must be expected on the 19th, and was therefore unwilling to return to headquarters at Pont-à-Mousson, preferring to bivouac in the open air rather than be separated from his troops. A farm-house, however, was eventually found that had not been burnt down or turned into a hospital, and there the King had slept the night on a bed brought in from a hospital. God be praised He has given my beloved father such vigour, and that all these excessive bodily and mental strains affect him only lightly.

Among my more intimate acquaintances, His Majesty mentioned the names of a number as certainly killed, and others as seriously wounded. My dear friend Jasmund of the East Prussian Fusilier regiment No. 33 is reported dead, but others say they saw him still unhurt in the evening, so I may still hope he is alive. The IIIrd Army Corps is shrunk to one-half, single regiments appear to have lost 1,400 men. At last I left off making any more inquiries at all, dreading to hear of more losses among my friends.

The King presented me with the Iron Cross of the 2nd Class for Weissenburg and of the 1st for Wörth, adding, I was the first who had ever received this special distinction. Naturally I at once begged His Majesty to do the like for General von Blumenthal, as it was not possible for me to wear this Order before this man who had done such distinguished service had received it. He willingly acquiesced in my request and himself informed the General of its bestowal. After that I attended a short Council of War, at which Generals von Moltke and von Roon appeared, and then paid a visit to the Minister Count Bismarck, in whose ante-room lay his eldest son Herbert, badly wounded in the leg at Mars-la-Tour, as the battle of the 16th August is named.

All goes well to-day; General von Moltke remains always entirely unperturbed, confident, clear-headed and firmly resolved to move forward on the main objective—Paris; in a word, he is the complete veteran in all points! Count Bismarck I found moderate-minded and speaking, I should say, very reasonably, his views clear and decisive on all points, calmly and coldly watching events, and in no way unduly sanguine in consequence of our successes so far. Our demands, if it comes to peace negotiations, are: Surrender of Alsace, once a German province, and the payment of all War expenses. On the part of the Great Powers no proposals for peace have as yet been submitted to us. Very soon the needful reliefs for the Army will have arrived; we shall then set out on the march westwards and probably deliver the decisive battle at Châlons. Men's minds are much embittered against General von

Steinmetz; he is looked upon as more self-opinionated than ever and seems to have sacrificed many lives by his want of judgment.

I had likewise the pleasure to-day of seeing Lieutenant-General von Stosch, who was appointed for the duration of the War Commissary-General of the Army. I learned from him that his brother of the Ist Lower Silesian Infantry regiment No. 46, who was wounded at Wörth, had succumbed to his injuries, and furthermore, that on the evening of the 18th August he had repeatedly found opportunities of intervening actively in re-establishing order in the VIIth and VIIIth Army Corps.

About midday I rode back to Nancy, and after a short rest there, set out on my journey of five miles, as it is counted, to Vaucouleurs. Yet it cost us almost twice as much time as was needful because the roads hereabouts are extraordinarily steep, so that one never comes to the end of scrambling up hill and down dale. But, over and above this, the transport convoys delayed us considerably just as it was getting dark. Though, speaking generally, these were better ordered than in 1866, and efforts were made to carry out my order to " keep always to the right," still such a mass of carts must always be an unwieldy body. But a directly mischievous effect was brought about by sundry wagon loads of volunteer ambulance men and canteen carts, which, not aware of my orders, kept plunging into every gap that offered, causing disorder and entirely obstructing my way.

The last look at Nancy offered us a really noble panorama, and the landscape we rode through wore an agreeable aspect, though the woods to our German eyes were more like a plantation of saplings than a forest; everywhere I noticed the fields bore remarkably poor crops, in particular the oats were terribly bad. Everybody is complaining of a bad harvest and the sure prospect of scarcity in the winter, as the War is already sweeping up the small supplies available. Only late in the evening did we reach my quarters in the Pastor's house at Vaucouleurs, quite benumbed by the icy wind that had suddenly risen.

Headquarters: Vaucouleurs, 21st August.—To-day we have a day's rest here at Vaucouleurs. The name awakens in every one of us recollections of Schiller's *Maid of Orleans*, for only three miles away lies Jeanne d'Arc's birthplace, Domrémy-la-Pucelle. But of pious reverence for the memory of that heroine, unique in her way, at the very spot where the Chevalier Baudricourt equipped her and took the field with her—actually the first step in the liberation of her country—no heed is taken. The castle of the Baudricourts is now a mere heap of ruins and the Gothic chapel, in which Joan prayed for long weeks before she revealed herself, a wine-cellar! The friendly Curé of the place, at whose house I lay, told us how the interest manifested in Joan's birth-place by the Allies who marched through Domrémy in the year 1814 first called French attention to the place, with the result that since those days the cottage of the family, which still exists, can boast of the special protection of the State.

The country-folk show us angry faces on our first appearance among them, but after a few hours grow accustomed to the enemy, and presently, when we get into talk with them, they thaw and become quite friendly; in their naïveté they ask absurd questions, speak with little enthusiasm of their Government, and often seem to lay the blame on it of having begun the War. In the towns there occur almost daily outbreaks of indignation against Napoleon, united with unconcealed anxiety at the social upheaval, especially where no troops are stationed and the workmen are idle. One notices how few signs of civilization are to be found in the country parts. The longing for peace is decidedly stronger than the desire for war. But in view of all the dangers a hostile invasion involves for France, the national movements are more keenly watched than would have been conceivable under other conditions with such a system of government as that of Napoleon. The language of *The Times* article of the 9th August I think excellent and very gratifying; it is to be hoped we may soon read the like on the carnage before Metz. Napoleon will find these expressions of opinion little to his taste.

The rest here after the excitements and bustle at Nancy is doing me endless good; in particular my little room gives on to the garden and affords a pretty view over the open valley.

Vitry appears to be held by volunteers in motley garb, for our Cavalry patrols were fired upon by men out of uniform.

Duke Friedrich zu Schleswig-Holstein-Augustenburg has arrived here.

Headquarters: Vaucouleurs, 22nd August.—To-morrow I shall continue my forward march, which leads us through Champagne; it is to be hoped the wine of that district is not going to check us in the same way it did the troops that marched through here in 1814.

It seems that the republican movement at Bordeaux and

Lyons, as also a Garibaldian one of a like sort at Nice, is spreading and that larger bodies of French troops will have to remain in those places, which can only be to our advantage.

To-day I reviewed my Dragoon regiment together with the Ist Posen Infantry regiment No. 18 and a battalion of the 4th Lower Silesian Infantry regiment No. 51, as their cantonments lay quite close to here. By half-past five in the morning I had already had the Silesian Fusilier regiment No. 18, told off for the investment of Toul, march past before me, and was delighted with the excellent show it made. Later on, I got together all my Generals in command at my quarters, in order to communicate to them certain points of view relating to the behaviour of officers and men in action; also I had to give them exact directions for the next day's march, inasmuch as my columns, in order to surround Châlons on the south, will be obliged to move at rather wide intervals between them, while the Crown Prince of Saxony, with a detachment made up of the IVth Guards Corps and the XIIth (Saxon) Corps, is to threaten the camp there more from the eastwards.

At this interview with the Generals had also appeared Prince Albrecht (Senior), with whom Prince Albert of Saxe-Altenburg, a Russian Hussar officer, serves as Aide-de-Camp. Whatever the IIIrd Army Corps includes in its ranks in the way of princely dignitaries came to-day to visit me—with the consequence that everybody except me enjoyed the day's rest.

Four of my officers, First Lieutenant Hartmann, Major von Hahnke, Captain of Horse von der Lancken and Lieutenant von Gustedt, had gone to Tours, but came back again with the news that the capitulation was all but signed when the Commandant, to the surprise of the inhabitants and officers, turned refractory and renewed the cannonade.

Only to-day I learned for the first time how Duke Georg of Saxe-Meiningen, as well as his son, the Hereditary Prince Bernhard, had been in the hottest fire at Wörth, and that the former, by his judgment and his brilliant personal reconnaissances, had rendered important service to the Gersdorff Division. Prince Bernhard, owing to the heavy losses in officers, has at present become substitute Brigade Adjutant. To my great satisfaction very high praise has been accorded to the judgment and general behaviour of the Prince of Wied, who appears to be carrying out all duties of a useful and able Adjutant on the Staff of the XIth Army Corps.

Alas! more and more reports come in of our losses before Metz; so murderous was the battle on the 18th August that the French for their part speak of it as " une boucherie." Should the Great Powers see fit to form a League to try for a lasting, honourable, speedy Peace, they ought, as the very first thing, to put an end to such slaughter in the name of Christianity and human civilization. But how can an Emperor Napoleon, an Empress Eugénie, an Ollivier and a Gramont calmly tolerate this butchery, while at the same time before the world they have the effrontery to prate of the dissemination of civilization?

Of Jasmund's fate still nothing is to be learned, which makes me hope the news of his death is not true, for indeed in him I suffer an infinite loss. I have few such true and faithful friends by my side, and I am convinced that in the future he will often yet be useful to me.

Headquarters: Ligny, 23rd August.—I was just mounting when a perfect downpour of rain began, which only left off towards midday, as we approached our new headquarters, the little town of Ligny. Here King Frederick William III spent two days in the year 1814, while the name recalls the battle of 1815, in which Blücher was defeated by Napoleon on the 19th June. The country was as bad as the weather. The soil is terribly heavy, and may well be fertile in other years. A picturesquely situated mediæval castle is the one and only thing worth looking at.

On top of its old keep I came upon a whole gathering of Englishmen. Lord Ronald Leveson-Gower has not since the 6th August even yet made approaches to a single one of my officers, makes no inquiries and troubles his head about nothing whatsoever, and in spite of repeated suggestions that he should make himself useful in some way, for instance in tending the sick, cannot be roused out of his unexampled apathy. It is really a pity for him that he should be just the one disturbing element in our numerous company. Mr. Russell (*Times*) and Mr. Skinner (*Daily News*), on the contrary, are agreeable and amiable persons, full of the utmost zeal to investigate every detail. Lord Adare, now provided with a Royal authorization, announces his return here, this time direct from Karlsruhe; I have drawn his attention, however, to the blockade of Strasburg, for God knows I have no room for any more lookers-on, important as it is at the moment to have numbers of Englishmen at headquarters.

It all holds good as to marching on Paris, that is, first of all on Châlons, while Prince Friedrich Karl (whom the newspapers are already belauding as a Bayard " sans peur et sans reproche ") with seven Army Corps remains to keep Bazaine shut up in Metz. Under these circumstances General von Steinmetz becomes his subordinate. I own I should be surprised to see this turn out well, for already the old lion of Skalitz would seem to have behaved so outrageously that only His Majesty's personal intervention prevailed to maintain the necessary authority. General von Steinmetz seems wishful to play at being a sort of little despot without there being any reason for it. It is a pity he is growing old, for, set on the right track, he does the right thing—that is how I read his character. But it is no light task to be set in authority over him.

The scheme being organized for the defence of the country (they talk here of " franc-tireurs ") must be opposed with all possible earnestness.

We are lodged in the one-time travelling quarters of Stanislas Leszczynski, dating from the days when this exiled Polish Prince and father-in-law of Louis XV, whose memory is still remarkably vivid hereabouts, was Duke of Lorraine. Our host, an elderly, invalid gentleman, has in his house a rich display of ornamentations and reliefs, reminiscent of the Heidelberg style of decoration, while, except for these, everything lies as neglected as in some enchanted palace.

Duke Friedrich zu Schleswig-Holstein will find himself in a difficult situation, now the letter he wrote to Colonel du Plat on his leaving for the Army has been made public through the newspapers. The fact that he still, even under existing circumstances, persists in his claims makes a bad impression in higher circles. The Bavarian uniform granted him as Major-General of the Bavarian Army makes him distrusted by the Prussians; the Bavarians accord him the coldest of welcome.

It was only to-day the letters from Berlin of the 14th August arrived per field post. My wife is going to Homburg with the object of establishing a model hospital there and inspecting those on the Rhine, which are in a sad state. In Berlin and Potsdam all her endeavours and offers of help in the matter of tending the sick were contemptuously rejected !

Headquarters : Ligny, 24th August.—General von Moltke writes that in all probability Marshal MacMahon is marching off to the north-east, leaving me quite free to continue my advance on Paris, or else to march northwards in pursuit of the enemy. I immediately decided to strike out to the north, to be done with the adversary there before I go on to the capital.

This forenoon the Ist Bavarian Army Corps, General von der Tann, marched through here, a force I saw again for the first time since Wörth. The men were repeatedly urged by their mounted officers to cry out " Vivat hoch " on the march past, till I found it out and forbade it.

Subsequently we enjoyed the pleasure of greeting the King here on his way through the town to his new headquarters at Bar-le-Duc, giving my Staff their first opportunity of paying their respects to His Majesty. He was once more, to the delight of all of us, brisk and blithe, and in a more cheerful mood altogether than on the 20th, making us feel really light-hearted. As we sat at table, suddenly came the quite unexpected news that the camp of Châlons was evacuated and the French marching off northward to Reims. We cannot see clearly as yet what this means, for either it is a general retreat on Paris for a fresh series of butcheries before the gates of the capital, or else Marshal MacMahon is for trying to release Marshal Bazaine from Metz. In the latter case the Crown Prince of Saxony and I would take him on the flank.

The attitude of the Great Powers, now that our successes are more and more conspicuous, grows more favourable to us; this is certainly encouraging, but no less certainly significant, for, if things had gone the other way, they would with one accord have fallen upon us. Otherwise no essential change in policy has manifested itself, except that Austria is more inclined to move.

General von Stosch spent some time with me, and was a real refreshment to me. He will now, in his capacity as Commissary-General, be put very much on his mettle, as we are moving into the Champagne country, which must be absolutely drained dry.

To-day the first Iron Crosses were delivered to me for distribution; luckily now the proper appreciation of the circumstances prevails and my right as Commander-in-Chief of my Army to bestow this decoration in His Majesty's absence has been recognized. General von Blumenthal, Colonel von Gottberg, Major von Hahnke, Captain Lenke, Captain von Viebahn, Captain of Horse von der Lancken and Lieutenant von Gustedt are the first to whom I handed this glorious badge of honour. Major von Hahnke was so overcome as I gave him the Cross he nearly fainted; all had tears of joy in their eyes when they found themselves in possession of the decoration, which we had been used hardly ever to see save in pictures of warriors of earlier days. To-morrow we deliver the Crosses to the different contingents, and I look forward with joyous anticipation to the shouts of jubilation that will ring out on that occasion.

Headquarters: Ligny, 25th August.—By orders from the Royal headquarters our day's rest is not to be till the 27th, and to-morrow we must definitely undertake marches with the object of concentrating on the Changy-Possesse-Givry line.

In the night I had a sudden attack of catarrh of the bowels and was forced to see to myself; nevertheless I attended the celebration of the King of Bavaria's birthday, which consisted in the Bavarian battalion in garrison here turning out, giving three cheers for their King and then offering up a silent prayer.

Still we know nothing certain as to the direction of the French march out of Châlons; possibly they are entrenching themselves about Reims. However, the native inhabitants, who little by little grow more talkative, make out that the main defence is organizing at Paris, where already the Bois de Boulogne has been cleared of trees. A sad pity for the pretty park! The language of the native press strikes a unique note, for one and all they represent all the encounters with us up to now as successes. The wounded feelings of the nation express themselves in hostility towards those who brought about the War, and would fain take this opportunity to be rid of the Emperor, in order to substitute another form of government.

The Duc d'Aumale in a public document commends as worthy of imitation the action of the citizens of Wörth in firing on our soldiers from windows and holes and corners!

Headquarters: Revigny aux Vaches, 26th August.—During the night came the news from the Royal headquarters that it grows more and more likely Marshal MacMahon marched away from Reims on the 23rd to seek reliefs from Metz, in which case he would reach Vouziers on the 25th.

To-day in pouring rain I changed my headquarters to Revigny aux Vaches, though I was not yet fully recovered from my chill. On the way through Bar-le-Duc I paid a visit to His Majesty and found General von Moltke at that moment with the King and in no little excitement, because a well-founded expectation had suddenly arisen of cutting off Marshal MacMahon, who was contemplating the attempt to get reliefs from Metz, somewhere about Mezières or Sedan, and throwing him back on the Belgian frontier. This corroborates the French march to the north from Châlons, but it is not now directed, as was supposed, towards Laon or Reims, but passes between the above-named fortresses and the frontier, squeezing through, so to speak. What a foolhardy undertaking! None but an enemy knowing precisely our strength and our line of march could carry out such a scheme. On receiving this news I at once make a right turn with my Army and move to the north [1] on the line Busancy–Le Chêne–Attigny, hoping, in conjunction with the Crown Prince of Saxony, to block the Frenchmen's road. General von Moltke even thinks to set a mouse-trap for them and be able to make prisoner the enemy's Army. I cannot let *my* hopes soar so high as all that. But if we come up with them, I too believe we shall beat Marshal MacMahon and force him back.

At His Majesty's quarters a letter that had fallen into our hands from the Marquis de Galliffet, one of the Emperor Napoleon's intimate friends, was read out, in which he says that people must clearly realize that the abdication of the Emperor is the only way out of the calamities so far experienced; after that will follow a quite brief régime under the Prince Imperial as Regent, which in turn must open the door for a Republic. The writer wishes that, in view of the lack of leaders for this form of government, the Monarchists should rather take over the management of affairs, or else, the other way round, that in case of a Monarchy Republicans should undertake the task. So that is already the language held by the Imperial favourite! In conclusion Galliffet declares further that the Gardes Mobiles were good for nothing at all, they possessed no sense of patriotism and were badly armed.

To the King, who looked well, though his features still betrayed how his nerves had been racked in the last few days, I was able to communicate extracts from a number of letters just received from England proving how persistent is the satisfaction felt in that country over our successes, and the anger with which Lord Granville repudiated the scandalous stories circulated against him. A pity these letters cannot be made public; nothing could be better adapted to enlighten my countrymen as to English sentiments than the dignified, unassuming expression of genuine sympathy which many from private individuals contain. The King added that England for the moment was showing herself more accommodating, but deplored the laws which legalized the exportation of arms by private manufacturers. I am quite chagrined by the misunderstanding between ourselves and England; especially does the tone of our press daily supply fresh food, if I am to

---

[1] A decision come to on the Crown Prince's own initiative, not under instructions from Moltke, who had rather given the IIIrd Army Corps a free hand to pursue the march on Paris.

say the truth, for the notion that the English neutrality is doing great injury to Germany. Then the revelation of Benedetti's hankering after Belgium is harming us at present in England, for the immediate result of the alarm caused by those documents was the thought that, without previous encouragement on the part of the Prussian Minister, a Benedetti would not have allowed himself to use such language. God grant these misunderstandings may prove to be only of a temporary nature!

My headquarters are established in a cheerful country house, where we take to-morrow's day of rest; so I shall be able to look after myself and get rid of my chill the sooner.

Headquarters: Revigny aux Vaches, 27th August.—To-day was a rest day, and I just spent it in bed. All the reports that reach us from our 4th Cavalry Division, always indefatigable and well posted, confirm General von Moltke's conjectures of yesterday; General von Blumenthal is of the same conviction and expresses it so clearly and positively I find him really to blame, for it is actually only a matter of presumption, and I cannot myself think it possible an adversary of Marshal MacMahon's sort should commit such gross blunders.

The concentration of my troops is ordered for to-day, and we are making ready for the decisive battle within the next few days—an engagement that will be fought, it may be, by Verdun. The Crown Prince of Saxony, who will be yet further reinforced by sundry Corps from before Metz, will have work to do directly, after which it will be my task to fall upon the enemy's rear and flanks. If we win the battle and actually drive the French over the Belgian frontier, either an incalculable complication will result or a quick ending of the War.

The troops will have to make very heavy marches, and for this reason I gave orders to allow them everything possible in the way of lightening the labour.

I have instructed my Commanding Generals, while informing them of the general progress of hostilities, to regard these as the leading considerations influencing operations: that not only is the enemy to be pursued and forced to fall back on Grand-Pré, but his retreat on Vouziers must likewise be cut off; consequently that first and foremost the Cavalry Divisions will come into action. Further, that these French troops form, as far as may be, the right lateral detachment of an enemy force marching on Busancy, so that it would be just *my* Army that would have to attack the French main body. In that case the Vth Army Corps, taking up a favourable position with its advance guard, should detain the enemy until the remaining Corps come up to its support. If, however, the contingent of the Crown Prince of Saxony hears the sound of guns, the enemy must be thrown back upon Grand-Pré or Vouziers.

Headquarters : Sainte-Menehould, 28th August.—At half-past five in the morning came the notification from main headquarters that Marshal MacMahon is halted at Vouziers, his cavalry about Beaumont and Busancy, in which direction I and the Crown Prince of Saxony have to continue our march.

In the evening at half-past eight a change of orders again from the Royal headquarters, substantiating the evacuation of Vouziers and the retreat to the northwards, yet giving no definite indication of the direction, whether Le Chêne or Rethel. Both Bavarian Army Corps are to stand by to support the Crown Prince of Saxony at Champigneulle and Grand-Pré; I am to advance on Vouziers and further to the west, as also to send off a Cavalry Division towards Reims. The VIth Army Corps has direct orders from the Royal headquarters to move to Linarville and Vienne-le-Château.

I changed my headquarters to Sainte-Menehould, the place where Louis XVI and Marie Antoinette were first recognized on their flight from Paris, and to which our troops marched up for the cannonade of Valmy in the year 1792. To-day I feel better, but I still drive as a matter of precaution, particularly as it is raining heavily again.

We can only explain to ourselves these to-and-fro marches of the French by the supposition either that Marshal Mac-Mahon is uncertain of the direction of our march, or else is making for Metz, and has pushed on merely lateral covering forces in the direction of Vouziers and Sainte-Menehould. Shots appear to have been noted in the distance, but I have heard none myself.

The arming of the inhabitants of this neighbourhood has already assumed greater proportions, compelling us to take energetic steps to enforce the surrender of all weapons. Single shots are fired, generally in a cunning, cowardly fashion, on patrols, so that nothing else is left us to do but to adopt retaliatory measures by burning down the house from which the shots came, or else by help of the lash and forced contributions. It is horrible, but, to prevent greater mischief, unavoidable, and is consistent with our proclamation of martial law. Fortunately the infliction of such stern penalties does not lie with me, but with the Commanding Generals.

I received the Maire and a numerous deputation from the town and spoke to them as considerately and civilly as possible. Soon afterwards the roof of my house caught fire, just as Duke Ernst was with me; we thought at first it was some sort of treacherous prank of the inmates, till it came out a fire had been incautiously kindled by the servants to dry sundry articles drenched by the rain.

All indications point to the possibility of a battle tomorrow, supposing the enemy, whose first line has already reached the neighbourhood of Busancy or Beaumont, if he has not by this time actually made a yet further advance, is really continuing his march to Metz. But I am apprehensive that, being informed of our forward march, he may proceed no further, but under cover of one Division or so turn right-about and march back on Laon.

Headquarters: Senuc, 29th August.—Half an hour after midnight comes a communication from the Royal headquarters to the effect that the appearance of a strong force of hostile infantry at Bar, near Busancy, points to the conclusion that the enemy is for making an attempt to raise the blockade of Metz.

The order was given to set out at one o'clock in the morning, marching to the right. On the road we saw to our left the historical heights of Valmy. We had no easy position to-day, for on the narrow roads we fell in with the columns of the Vth Army Corps, followed by the Württembergers keeping no sort of order. Their baggage-wagons were driven so much one on top of the other that I was obliged to put the drivers under arrest for punishment. It touched me to see with what beaming looks the men of the Vth Army Corps greeted me the moment they recognized my face, and with what enthusiasm they received my announcement as to our next intentions. Reports of the most contradictory kind kept coming in regarding the enemy's position and movements, till just as I reached our quarters for to-day, the village of Senuc, General von Moltke most unexpectedly met me, bringing me the Job's tidings that the enemy had slipped his head out of the noose and was marching off to the north-west. He was so persuaded of the truth of this report that he had already despatched orders direct to the VIth Army Corps to change their line of march and go in pursuit of Marshal MacMahon. It were enough to drive one mad, should the enemy slip away and escape. Directly after this my cavalry—I had sent them far on ahead—reported that enemy infantry had occupied a wood quite a short way off, on which, of course, I sent out a reconnaissance party to the place, as such near neighbours to my headquarters were anything but welcome.

We conjecture that the enemy has got wind of our advance and is therefore abandoning his intention of reaching a hand to Bazaine at Metz; consequently, especially if he still means to attempt something before Paris, he will make his first stand at Laon. We found some distraction from our chagrin in a letter that had been captured from a French officer of rank to a confidential friend. Written in a good style, indicating a man of good education, it gives us an unexpected insight into the faults and deficiencies prevailing in the French Army, which must be past belief. Thus he declares that Marshal MacMahon's dispositions were good for nothing; that he had never yet been able to bring his Corps up to its proper strength and is badly in want of guns; that the French artillery is no use against ours. Discipline, he says, is utterly relaxed, for which " les troupes orientales " are largely responsible. Everybody, it seems, pilfers, officers of the Staff not excepted; the author had, first his saddlery, and then his horse, his own property, stolen. The Generals are criticized in the severest terms; the Emperor's conduct at Metz after the battle of Wörth (called Reichshofen by the French) is described as inexcusable because he did not have the advance of my Army arrested. Nowadays the Emperor Napoleon, he avers, follows the Army about, devoid of all consideration, and nothing but a burden to it, and himself in a mood of utter discouragement. Of Marshal Bazaine, he adds, nothing is known; he can only have ammunition for a single engagement, as fresh supplies are not forthcoming, and so on. The writer then goes on to speak as a practised strategist and tactician, and ends up with the startling Latin phrase: " Quem deus vult perdere, prius dementat " (Whom the god is for destroying, he first drives mad)! These utterances are more or less true, but surely accord little with the fanfaronade of the French daily press.

In the middle of our perusal comes Captain of Horse von Mutius with the report that the enemy had not marched away at all, but had been sighted in the direction of Beaumont, this necessitating yet another change of orders. Luckily we are still on the move forward.

At Senuc, an old-fashioned, comfortable little country house belonging to the Maire, M. de Boullenois, whose wife is of the de Recourt family, we found an extremely friendly welcome. The eighty-year-old mother is lying here in the house with a broken leg; she received me very pleasantly, talked at length of the present condition of affairs, but would not admit that France had desired the War. My star and the cross " Pour le Mérite " interested the old lady; I had to tell her a great deal about my wife and children as well as about our country life at Bornstedt. At parting, she begged me earnestly to send her compliments to my wife, whom she admired as an excellent good mother, housekeeper and farmer's wife. The life and domestic habits of this wealthy family of the old minor nobility of the French provinces afford an attractive picture of the often quoted " vie de château," taking the phrase in its simple meaning. The other inmates of the house often spoke of their aversion to the War, without in the least disregarding the blame attaching to their own country, particularly as the Maire is an old soldier and friend of Marshal Canrobert's. From the terrace there was a lovely view over the smiling valley of the Aisne, where we saw no signs of the devastations of war.

Hourly almost arrived further confirmations of the news that the enemy had been seen about Beaumont or Stonne; so there is every prospect of coming up with him to-morrow.

Headquarters: Saint-Pierremont, at the Presbytery, 30th August.—In the middle of the night came a message from main headquarters that all reports are unanimous in saying that in the forenoon of the 30th the hostile Army will be in full force between Beaumont and Le Chêne, or possibly to the south of that line. The Crown Prince of Saxony's contingent moved forward at ten o'clock, following the line Beauclair–Fosse in the direction of Beaumont. My Army is to advance with the right wing on Beaumont by way of Busancy, while two Army Corps hold themselves in readiness for the possible support of the Crown Prince; the remaining Corps are thereupon to take the direction more towards Le Chêne; Grand-Pré I am to occupy.

To-day we have at last discovered MacMahon's whereabouts, attacked and soundly beaten him. True, of my Army only regiments of the Ist Bavarian Army Corps, von der Tann, actually took part in the main action at Beaumont, the heaviest share in which the Crown Prince of Saxony had to bear, facing the centre and left wing of the enemy; but my appearance with five Divisions of Infantry and the Cavalry Division of Prince Albrecht (Senior) before the French right wing compelled the enemy to evacuate before our eyes his altogether excellent position at this point. This was the more welcome to me, as otherwise I should have been obliged to storm it to-morrow. The advance of the Crown Prince's contingent, and more particularly the winning of the disputed ground on the part of our artillery, I was able to observe minutely.

The enemy opposed to me fired upon us from the steep heights of Senuc, paying particular attention to my cavalry with their mitrailleuses, yet without hitting a single man, whereas our artillery at once inflicted losses on the enemy, which we were well able to verify in subsequent advances we made to the very spot, the dead and wounded having been left lying where they fell. At the time the Vth Army Corps was making ready for a hotter fire on the enemy, the XIth Army Corps had already appeared at Senuc, having, on the report of the 6th Cavalry Division that the French were evacuating Le Chêne and retreating in the direction of Beaumont, at once changed its own direction and along with the 4th Cavalry Division marched at once straight for the roar of the guns. The obvious danger threatening the French right wing, together with the simultaneous advance of the Prince's contingent, was the reason why the French evacuated the steep rocky crag of Senuc, which might have been defended like a fortress. Directly it was at all possible we mounted to the heights just abandoned by the enemy and watched his subsequent retirement to the north-west, the direction of which led us to conjecture his making eventually for Sedan or Mezières. But why he goes so close up to the Belgian frontier is still incomprehensible to me.

By this time we thought it was all over for the day, when suddenly at Mouzon and several other places, encompassed by ravines and wooded flats, an excessively hot gunfire broke out, mingled with the rattle of musketry fire. At this point our IVth Army Corps, in conjunction with the Royal Saxon troops, was involved till late in the evening in an obstinately contested engagement, in which eleven cannon were captured and 3,000 prisoners taken. As it was getting dark the enemy set up a perfectly fiendish din of mitrailleuse and gun-fire; this must doubtless have been the rear-guard action of the French crossing the bridge of Mouzon, if it were not, as usual, their final " retraite offensive " again, directly they are forced to retreat in all seriousness.

The fight will certainly be continued to-morrow, but I am inclined to think that already as to-day's result all hopes of the enemy for relief from Metz and any sort of union with Marshal Bazaine are frustrated. A great battle ought to be at hand; the time is now ripe to set the mouse-trap for the enemy in proximity to the frontier fortresses.

The Saxons appear to have won great advantages at Beaumont; indeed it is actually stated that General von der Tann fell upon the enemy in camp, who fled, abandoning everything in such haste that their baggage, all the tents along with the midday meal still cooking over the fires, as well as three pieces of cannon fell into our hands.

When this forenoon I came up with the Vth Army Corps, I had just torn a hole in my cloak. To get the damage quickly repaired, I called up a Company tailor from the ranks of the Westphalian Fusilier regiment No. 37, who carried out his stitching job there and then to the general amusement, while I had the regiment march past before me.

Lieutenant Count Hohenthal of the Uhlan regiment of Guards reported to me with a detachment under him on the battle-field; since yesterday, when he had succeeded in taking prisoner an enemy officer of the General Staff carrying important maps and papers, he had been separated from his regiment.

Before I reached Saint-Pierremont, I had to ride in the dusk through the bivouac of the XIth Army Corps. It was a downright hard ride on account of the extremely awkward and steep roads, and it was only late in the evening I reached our headquarters, established in the Curé's little presbytery-house. Saint-Pierremont is a quite poor, dirty hamlet, at which the French had already for many days past been behaving themselves so ill that by force of contrast we seemed to the inhabitants quite domesticated creatures; they could not speak badly enough of the insubordination of their own fellow-countrymen.

Headquarters: Chémery, 31st August, 1870.—At half-past two in the morning comes a message from the Royal headquarters to the effect that, the enemy having given ground at all points yesterday, the advance was to be continued at an early hour to-day, in order to squeeze the enemy together into the narrowest possible space between the Meuse and the Belgian frontier. The Crown Prince of Saxony's contingent is to push on with two Army Corps to the right bank of the river so as to prevent a retirement of the French left wing to the eastward. The IVth Army Corps is posted to the north of Beaumont, the Guards Corps to the south of that place, the XIIth at Létonne. I am to move against the enemy's front and right wing, and to take up the strongest possible artillery positions on this bank of the Meuse, to harass the French columns encamping on the level ground by Mouzon. Should the enemy trespass over the Belgian border without being disarmed, we have to pursue him forthwith. Accordingly I immediately issued orders at three in the morning that the enemy we beat yesterday is first thing in the morning to-day to be pursued further, right up to the Meuse, and wherever he comes to a halt, to be energetically attacked. As to-day my columns are compelled to march more or less separated from each other, I have sent all the Princes attached to my headquarters to join them, so as to learn exactly the state of things and at the same time be in immediate touch with the Crown Prince of Saxony. The day was magnificent and favoured the reconnaissance we had already undertaken at an early hour over yesterday's battle-fields. It has come to no regular engagement to-day, only skirmishes having taken place.

By to-day's march on the west bank of the Meuse, which left the fortress of Sedan on our right, we are put in a position, to-morrow, the 1st September, to make a circuit of that stronghold from the west. On my right wing I station both Bavarian Corps to act as support for the Crown Prince, and if he on his part pushes forward on Givonne, we shall in this way attack the enemy from two sides at one and the same time, and either capture or drive him over the Belgian frontier; in the latter case, because of the neutrality of Belgium, he must at once lay down his arms. I acquainted the Crown Prince of Saxony with my dispositions for the 1st September, at the same time recommending him to act in the direction of Givonne. His answer was that he had, in fact, just decided to spare his exhausted troops a day's rest, but in view of the momentous issues I had spoken of, he would for his part also attack the enemy.

The King set off at midday with his whole Headquarter Staff on the way to Vendresse through Donchery, left his carriage and had some regiments of the XIth Army Corps march past before him, taking the opportunity to call up from the ranks the officers and men already decorated with the Iron Cross and bestow some friendly words of praise on them. A host of single prisoners keeps constantly coming in; almost all speak of the position of the French Army as no longer tenable, a view the native population is ready enough to corroborate, complaining loudly of the plundering and thieving committed by their own soldiery, and by way of contrast holding up ours as a good example. Yesterday crowds of unwounded fugitives appear to have passed through the place. The scenes just mentioned are even now being repeated with astonishing frequency, and though it is true the defeated battalions are still in good order when they quit the battle-field, yet in their rear comes sneaking in a quite surprising mass of soldiers, of whom by noon to-day whole hordes had been rounded up as marauders. These again are followed by ever-fresh comrades, who are discovered lurking in hay-lofts, cellars and the like hiding-places. A fellow made prisoner in this fashion, an amazingly filthy Zouave, was brought before the King here at my headquarters and made sundry assertions of a pretty outspoken character. I do not mean to say I look upon these facts as a true standard whereby to measure the temper or condition of the French Army generally, but in any case they are noteworthy.

Thirty guns captured, amongst them a number of mitrailleuses, are notified up to noon to-day as result of yesterday's battle. Our losses are, in comparison with those of the first battles, to be called moderate; moreover, the general state of health still remains very good, contrary to expectation and in spite of the green fruit everywhere and more and more every day stripped from the trees. I too am recovering from my illness and on marches have only driven on three or four occasions; the same is the case with General von Blumenthal—a result ardently desired that I might be able, under these incessant strains of mind and body, to keep well and fit for the decisive day now close at hand.

Late in the evening came news from the Royal headquarters that it grew more and more likely Marshal MacMahon was thinking of retreating on Mezières under cover of night and abandoning his baggage. Instantly I sent orders to the XIth Army Corps, which had already pushed forward an advance guard to the further side of the Meuse and destroyed bridges, as also to the Württemberg Field Division, to set out before sunrise on the march northwards and cross the Meuse, so as to bar the way to the French, or else to deploy and make the attack on the line of the Sedan–Mezières high-road.

Battle of Sedan

Headquarters : Chémery, 1st September.—I left Chémery betimes, at four in the morning, riding past the infantry columns in dense fog, and had no little trouble to prevent the men from cheering, repeating over and over again that to-day it was a question of outwitting the enemy, and consequently any sort of noise could only frustrate our purpose. At Donchery, to the west of Frénois, I climbed a steep hill already located by A.D.C.'s the previous day affording me a most splendid view over the country and enabling me to watch the development of the day's events. I should have loved to follow the march of the two Prussian Army Corps, but felt bound to abandon the wish, because obviously I should meantime have lost all chance of surveillance and the possibility of intervening at the right moment. When the sun rose, we were already close upon the fortress of Sedan, but so wrapped in fog we could see absolutely nothing, let alone distinguish particular objects.

On my right wing, in the direction of Bazeilles, somewhere about six o'clock, cannon opened fire with rapidly increasing intensity; this could only be an engagement with von der Tann's Army Corps. Subsequent reports announced that, after crossing the Meuse by two bridges of boats, and also utilizing a railway bridge, this force had at once advanced to the attack on the village of Bazeilles, to bring the enemy to a stand, and this without waiting for the arrival of the Crown Prince of Saxony. Presently the roar of the guns sounded noticeably more distant, this making me think the enemy had succeeded in breaking through at Bazeilles and that we must stand by to pursue. Lieutenant-General von Blumenthal, however, opined that the French could gain nothing by such an attempt, for we should quickly overtake them and get the opportunity of throwing them back on the Crown Prince of Saxony's contingent.

The engagement in question being now more remote from my look-out station, which only allowed me to observe the march of my own two Prussian Army Corps, there followed some anxious hours of waiting. Not once was it possible to see across to Madelincourt, where the IInd Bavarian Army Corps had established itself on the heights, so that it was only by the nearness or remoteness of the cannon thunder on my right flank we could make any conjecture regarding the progress of events. After some considerable time the noise of firing again came nearer, making it seem probable that by this time the Crown Prince of Saxony had reached the scene of action, the more so as now shots were also being fired from the fortress itself.

Gradually the fog cleared away from the tops of the hills, but lay all the thicker in the valleys and along the course of the river; the morning light was still so faint as to render it quite impossible to make out any object whatever on the heights opposite, thus leaving us in complete uncertainty whether enemy troops occupied them or no.

The XIth Army Corps had already by four in the morning crossed over the massive and only slightly damaged bridge of Donchery to the right bank of the Meuse and stood deployed in close order, reaching almost up to the loop which the river forms at this point. At half-past five the Corps received the order to march off and attack the adversary. The Vth Army Corps was at that hour still occupied in defiling across the bridge of boats that had been built below Donchery, and swerving round in a great circle, took the direction to Vrigny aux Bois. Looking like an elongated gut, the XIth Army Corps, followed by the Vth, moved off by the difficult road leading past Vrigny aux Bois, because the broken bridges made it impossible to get round a considerable bend of the river in any other way. I had ordered the Cavalry Division of Prince Albrecht (Senior) to follow these columns and given similar directions for the 2nd, Count Stolberg.

As some of the leading battalions called a halt, in order, as it seemed, to send out patrols in the direction of the village of Villette or Glaire, we thought we could distinguish a French column, which suddenly stopped short and hastily sent back gallopers to Sedan; but as no attack whatever was delivered by the Prussian Corps, which simply continued their march unhindered, I took it for certain that the French were not expecting us from this quarter. Under these circumstances the fog was everything I could wish for, for the longer it lasted, the less hindrance would my advance meet with. I therefore sent orders—it might be seven o'clock then—by Major von Freyberg and Lieutenant Count Seckendorf that the Division von Walther should march to Remilly to support the Ist Bavarian Army Corps, while the Division Count Bothmer was to take up position against Sedan.

It was already past eight and no signs yet to be seen of enemy troops on the heights about Floing and Saint-Menges, so that I now regarded it as certain we should encounter no resistance there and ordered the horses to be brought round—" Nelusko " was my mount to-day—to go myself to these hills, when at the same instant a sunbeam broke through the fog and I now at last discovered that the whole hill-slope of Floing almost as far as Cazal was thickly occupied by troops of all arms. Once again, therefore, I had to relinquish the idea of going directly under fire with our troops, and was now for the first time absolutely forced to stay and watch further developments from my not really over and above advantageous standpoint. Now too the first shots began to fall—it might be nine o'clock or thereabouts— and things grew lively on the hill-side at Floing. Soon the gun-fire sounded from all sides and even on the far-off right wing the rattle of musketry mingled with the bass of the cannon thunder, leading me to conjecture that the Crown Prince of Saxony was now advancing to the attack. Already about this time General von Blumenthal said to those about him, rubbing his hands in the delightful consciousness of victory: " The evening will end with the hoisting of the white flag ! "

I now sent Major Dresow to General von der Tann and the Crown Prince of Saxony to inform them of my dispositions and the state of things in my Army, as also to explain to them the definite prospect there was in the course of the day of my making connection on my left wing with the latter's contingent.

On a height to my right I could see the King with a numerous suite; he had been led to the spot, eastward of Cheveuges, by Lieutenant Count Seckendorf, who had chanced to meet him. His Majesty sent to tell me that he had given direct orders to the IInd Bavarian Army Corps to station one brigade at Frénois, while another was to take position " à cheval " of the Chémery–Frénois high-road, to the south of the latter place.

The Bavarian Division von Walther about this time crossed the Meuse in rear of von der Tann's Corps, then in action, marched up on his left wing and finally intervened in an extremely fierce engagement which was fought round the villages of Bazeilles and Balan and eventually concluded by driving back the enemy on Sedan.

I ordered Captain von Treuenfels of the Artillery to bring up a Bavarian battery in the river valley to the near neighbourhood of Frénois, which bombarded Sedan with great calm and precision, but at the same time certainly drew the enemy's shell-fire closer to us and our standpoint, the shot continually splashing up the water in a pond at the foot of my hill.

Round Floing and Saint-Menges the engagement was more lively. At that point the 21st Division had come directly into action and had started the battle with artillery fire, while the leading battalions came up alongside a garden surrounded by strong walls on the ridge southward of Saint-Menges and extending to the west of Floing, the infantry following on.

The Vth Army Corps, the Corps Artillery at the head, marched by way of Vrigny aux Bois on Fleigneux, to seek a position on the left wing of the XIth Army Corps enabling it to come in touch with the contingent of the Crown Prince of Saxony. The going, over narrow, extremely hilly roads, had been very heavy, and sections of the Vth Army Corps had actually blocked the way for certain regiments of the XIth Army Corps, which were making all haste to move forward, rendering the latter's advance slow and tedious. The obstinate resistance offered by the enemy brought the action to a standstill, until the artillery of the Vth Army Corps came up southward of Fleigneux in the direction of Illy and forced the French to give up the Saint-Menges position and retire to their main position near Floing and Illy.

After a protracted and very fiercely contested artillery duel, the infantry of the XIth Army Corps, together with the 19th, the wing brigade of the Vth, advanced to the attack under command of Major-General von Henning. The French defended their trenches, which had been dug beforehand, as well as all inequalities in the ground, with no little skill. For all that, our infantry advanced to attack them, throwing out great swarms of sharpshooters, with calm and unshaken courage, till the enemy positions were captured. With extraordinary intrepidity the 3rd heavy battery of the IInd Field Artillery regiment took up position during the action on the extreme right flank of the Division referred to, and did excellent service.

The fashion in which the French fought in the engagement described above did not give me the impression that they had ever intended to hold the position to the last extremity, while at the very beginning of the action I actually saw many separate swarms of sharpshooters and squads of men dash to the rear. Soon after this, it is true, greater masses of infantry, though with little mutual cohesion, but just pressing recklessly forward, advanced to meet our fire; yet the French could not long hold out against our infantry deploying in ever stronger force from the village and a sunk way near it. About Saint-Menges and Fleigneux the artillery action continued without interruption, and without the batteries changing their positions.

My station afforded me an excellent view of the development of the fight, especially in the case of the 21st Division; here an enormous telescope, mounted on a tripod, belonging to the Bavarian Captain von Xylander, proved of very great service to us. From Major von Hahnke, on his return towards midday, I received precise information as to the progress of the fight, especially on my left wing; a shell splinter had wounded him slightly on the back of the head, but he refused to let Surgeon-General Dr. Boeger bandage it till he had given me his very exhaustive report.

I now sent Captain von Sommerfeld to both the Army

Corps in action with the order that, employing all available forces, they should press on in the direction of Illy to Givonne in order to effect a junction with the Guards Corps fighting on the Crown Prince of Saxony's right wing; for inasmuch as Sedan was already shut in on three sides, by this union of the two Armies, the enemy would lose his last loophole of escape to the northward.

The Württemberg Field Division, leaving the 3rd brigade, Von Hügel, behind, and followed by the 3rd Cavalry Division, had somewhere about nine o'clock crossed the bridge at Dom-le-Mesnil, for the purpose of keeping the fortress of Mezières under observation. As soon as this movement was completed, I despatched First Lieutenant von Faber to carry orders to Lieutenant von Obernitz to push on to Donchery, so as to have an available reserve in hand. My own attention I kept all the time fixed on Mezières, although Duke Wilhelm of Mecklenburg-Schwerin was posted not far from that fortress and in the course of the forenoon had sent Major von Schönfels, an officer of his General Staff, to me asking for instructions. Towards midday clouds of dust began to rise in that neighbourhood, and we heard the sound of guns, leading me to think that enemy reinforcements were marching up on my left flank; but it turned out later that Major-General von Hügel had repulsed an ineffectual attempt to make a sortie from Mezières and that in other respects nothing dangerous was to be looked for.

About midday, I should think it was, I saw enemy Chasseurs mounted on greys form up for the attack and ride at us. But instantly the quick fire of our infantry broke out with such deadly effect that but few of the riders could have found their way back again; any who did not fall there and then rode helter-skelter for the village of Floing and the before-mentioned hollow way, that is to say, straight for their own destruction, and disappeared like the rest. Three times over these Chasseurs, part formed up in columns of squadrons, part charging in small troops, attempted to drive our men back, but only single individuals succeeded in riding through our infantry; these latter hardly ever mustered in knots, still less formed squares, but mostly delivered their fire standing firm in the ranks, unshaken by the onsets of the horsemen. Besides these Chasseurs, we were attacked also by Cuirassiers, who, like their comrades, charged down the steep hillside with utter contempt of death in face of our murderous fire, yet, as always, without effect and only themselves suffering sensible losses; still it would seem that more of the Cuirassiers survived than among the

Chasseurs. The highest praise is due to our infantry for their calm, resolute bearing and endurance; most particularly I could note and admire this in the case of the Thuringian regiments and the 19th Infantry brigade, which, alas! lost nearly all its officers.

After the failure of these attacks of the French cavalry, deserving though they were of all honour, the French infantry offered no further resistance, but little by little fell back fighting to the fortress, all the while defending the inequalities of the ground with heavy fire. It might have been about two o'clock when the enemy's left wing abandoned its position directly opposite where I stood, while his right about Illy made a more protracted stand against our Vth Army Corps; there the battle was contested round the upland village and two patches of wood, the enemy making repeated attempts to break through to the Belgian frontier, which, however, miscarried every time before the firmness and unfaltering courage of the gallant Vth Army Corps. Only about three o'clock did the enemy give ground here too, and then withdrew in full retreat through the Bois de la Garenne and west of it to Sedan.

By Captain of Horse von Mutius I sent orders to the 4th Cavalry Division halted at Saint-Menges and also to the 2nd, which had meantime come up to Vrigny aux Bois, to move to the Bouillon–Sedan high-road, in order, by holding the defile of Givonne, to stop any possible attempt of the French to break through to Belgium; and at the same time to keep careful touch with the Guards Corps. From the right flank, from the east therefore and north, the roar of cannon came nearer and nearer; it was evident the Crown Prince of Saxony's contingent was in full contact with my left wing, that every moment we were gaining more ground and our plan was being carried to completion with mathematical precision. Marshal MacMahon was surrounded! The most daring combination had been realized in the most brilliant fashion, the calculations of Generals von Moltke and von Blumenthal had been crowned with the most splendid success, and under the very eyes of our King we were on the way to a new and glorious victory.

Then the Bavarian General Count Bothmer, a member of my Staff, came riding up from the neighbourhood of Frénois, where he had talked with prisoners, with the report that the latter declared in the most emphatic way that Napoleon was at Sedan. Of course we declined to believe this, seeing how often since the commencement of the War we had heard stories of the French Emperor's being present without there being a word of truth in them. Another phrase used by these prisoners struck me as more worthy of remark: "Nous sommes perdus, car vous nous avez cernés!"[1]

Major Dresow returned from his long ride to the Crown Prince of Saxony and reported to me that, apart from the hot engagement of the Bavarians round Bazeilles, which we knew about already, the Guards Corps also, along with its Corps artillery, had been in action near Daigny and Givonne; further, that to the southward, somewhere on the heights of La Moncelle, both Saxon Divisions with their artillery, followed by the Prussian 7th Division, had taken up position, while our 8th Division served as reserve for Lieutenant-General von der Tann, to whom some support had also been afforded by the 2nd Bavarian Army Corps von Hartmann.

From two o'clock or thereabouts a veritable panic began everywhere among the French. Not only about Floing and Saint-Menges, but as far as ever the telescopes could make out, everywhere we saw men of all arms bolting headlong for Sedan; each quarter of an hour increased the number of the fugitives, who in ever denser masses crowded into the steep sunk-ways leading up to the fortress. In the midst of this hurly-burly I remarked a detachment of Guides still mounted and on duty, and evidently on their way to the French High Command, so that I could not help the conjecture that at last the Emperor Napoleon really *was* present. As at Wörth, I saw Zouaves taking prodigious leaps in the air. Infantrymen were already running about unarmed, restless and bewildered; to a soldier's eye the whole scene was a painful and repugnant one, as the utter demoralization of the hostile army became evident and each separate individual betrayed the despair that had seized on all, as they realized that not a chance was left them now to avoid being taken prisoners.

Thus then the German net was drawn closer and closer about Marshal MacMahon, who, in fact, was taken prisoner, though in the wood by Fleugneux the fight was again resumed in a desultory fashion; at that spot an enemy cavalry brigade and single bodies of French troops tried again and again to push through to the Belgian frontier.

I now despatched Captain Lenke to His Majesty to inform him in my name as to the progress of the battle as regards my Army; in particular the repulse of the French attacks and the decisive effect of the great artillery action had to

[1] "We are undone, for you have surrounded us."

be made clear and the position of the batteries given. I took the same opportunity to ask for precise information regarding the state of things on the right wing of the battle, for I was left entirely without news. Captain Lenke brought me about four in the afternoon confirmation of my supposition that we were now in possession of Givonne.

At the same hour the fire began to slacken and little by little ceased altogether. Thereupon came the same peaceful quiet I spoke of on the evening of the battle of Wörth, and which was all the more welcome and refreshing as we had all day long been enduring the greatest suspense, while at the same time exposed without a moment's respite to the fiercest blaze of the sun. The sun beat down to-day as sharply as in the hottest summer's day, and we could not spare one moment to seek for shade. A lovely hilly landscape lay about Sedan, to which the verdant Meuse valley, with the river and its manifold curves in the midst, lent a cheerful aspect in sharpest contrast with the grim seriousness of battle. My Staff was joined to-day by Lieutenant-General von Stosch, now Commissary-General of the Army, Freytag the writer and the painter Bleibtreu, while one after the other nearly all the domestic staff of our household had arrived on the scene.

When I had convinced myself that the battle was really at an end, I rode over to the King, overjoyed at the events of the day; yet His Majesty refused even now really to believe in the reality of our triumph. Only when, soon after my arrival, reports confirming the victory came in from all sides, did the King accept our congratulations and clasped me and also General von Moltke by the hand. As to Napoleon's being at Sedan, nothing further had come to light beyond the information I had already received; the rumour had been discredited at the Royal headquarters also. On the other hand, news was already come of serious losses among the Bavarians, as well as of the death of Colonel von Scherbening, Commander of the Guards Field Artillery regiment; Lieutenant-General von Gersdorff, Commander of the 22nd Division, since the battle of Wörth acting in place of Lieutenant-General von Bose as Commander-in-Chief of the XIth Army Corps, is said to be wounded; of this I had had no definite confirmation, but towards evening the wound was notified as serious. Lieutenant-General von Kirchbach had accordingly taken over the supreme command of both Army Corps.

The Royal Staff, augmented by everybody who had contrived to get admitted, presented the appearance of a

THE EMPEROR FREDERICK III. 91

great crush of people, in which the uniform of the Duke of Manchester and that of the American General Sheridan stood out conspicuously.

His Majesty gave orders to bombard Sedan, and by way of enforcing a speedier capitulation to set the place on fire with incendiary rockets. Accordingly I despatched my A.D.C.'s in all directions to find whatever was to be got of artillery material and have it brought up near the town. However, no great damage was done; the rockets only fired the roof of a magazine on the south front, and it was but a short time before all batteries came into action.

During the interval His Majesty was discussing with Bismarck, Roon and myself, but hardly more than as a joke, an incredible possibility, the question what, granting the Emperor Napoleon really and truly fell into our hands, was to be done with such a prisoner.

Presently, after the bombardment had lasted some time, His Majesty ordered First Lieutenant Bronsart von Schellendorf to ride into Sedan as bearer of a flag of truce to invite the surrender of the fortress. Hardly was he gone before several Bavarian officers reported to me that white flags were floating over the walls of Sedan, that French officers, desirous of negotiating for a capitulation, were on their way, and that it was being repeated everywhere that the Emperor Napoleon was actually in the fortress. The like information was brought in by Captain of Horse von der Lancken of my Staff. His Majesty thereupon announced that he would treat only with the French High Command or a plenipotentiary delegated thereby, but gave orders to stop the bombardment at once.

As dusk was falling and the glare from the burning villages in the neighbourhood lit up the sky, appeared First Lieutenant von Bronsart, back from his mission. He had been at Sedan and had spoken personally with the Emperor Napoleon, who wished to express his readiness to surrender in a letter addressed to His Majesty to be delivered at once by his Aide-de-Camp, General Comte Reille.

The feelings that stirred in each hearer's breast at this announcement may well be imagined. The startling and all-important nature of such an event is obvious. The War had reached its culminating point, the instigator of the crying wrong was in our power. Peace could not now be long delayed.

Nothing perhaps better indicates the mood of mind among those present at this moment than the fact that, after Lieutenant von Bronsart had delivered his message, with one voice those behind us cried out : " Now we all must shout hurrah "; yet so weak was the response to this suggestion that the cheer was a dead failure. The reason of this abortive hurrah I believe was this, that each man felt instinctively how inadequate to such a momentous occasion was a mere outburst of cheering of the sort,—and that is just our German way, not to give way to noisy demonstrations in matters of grave importance. But it may be there was another something contributed to the result, to wit, the circumstance that no one was really clear in his mind whether this capture of the Emperor was a piece of good fortune for us or the reverse. In any case, one and all, we felt as if in a dream.

But now the bearer of the letter was in sight. In all haste the Cavalry Guard of the Staff, supplemented by the men of mine and with arms in hand, was drawn up behind the King; before these all present formed a wide half-circle, with His Majesty and myself at his side standing out alone in front of it. Prince Karl, Prince Luitpold of Bavaria, the Grand Duke of Saxe-Weimar, the Duke of Saxe-Coburg, the Hereditary Grand Dukes of Saxe-Weimar, Mecklenburg-Schwerin and Mecklenburg-Strelitz, Prince Wilhelm of Württemberg, the Hereditary Prince zu Hohenzollern, Duke Friedrich zu Schleswig-Holstein-Augustenburg, together with Count Bismarck, General von Moltke and the War Minister von Roon, stood close behind us. The Grand Duke of Saxe-Weimar endeavoured by shifting his position this way and that to get as near as possible to me.

Then appeared Comte Reille, accompanied by Captain von Winterfeld of the General Staff and a Prussian trumpet. Directly he came in sight of the King, he dismounted, quickly adjusted something about his riding-breeches, and then took off his red cap and strode up to the King, a heavy stick [1] in his hand, eyes downcast, it is true, but yet by no means without some dignity, and with a few words presented Napoleon's letter.

The King opened it and read the brief holograph message it contained :—" Monsieur mon frère, n'ayant pas pu mourir au milieu de mes troupes, il ne me reste qu'à remettre mon épée entre les mains de Votre Majesté. Je suis, de Votre Majesté, le bon frère Napoléon. Sedan, 1 Sept., 1870." [2]

[1] Another authority says a " riding-switch."
[2] " My dear brother, not having been able to die in the midst of my troops, it only remains to me to surrender my sword into Your Majesty's hands. I am, Your Majesty's good brother, Napoleon. Sedan, 1st Sept., 1870."

THE EMPEROR FREDERICK III.

Thereupon the King at once told Comte Reille that, unless the whole French Army laid down their arms, he would enter into no negotiations, but at the same time declared himself ready to give an immediate answer to the Emperor Napoleon's communication.

Then the King proceeded at once to discuss with Count Bismarck, General Moltke and myself the tenor of the missive he proposed to send Napoleon, after which the draft of the letter was immediately dictated to Counsellor of Legation Count Paul Hatzfeldt to be set down in writing. The letter,[1] then written out by the King in his own handwriting, ran thus : " Monsieur mon frère. En regrettant les circonstances dans lesquelles nous nous rencontrons, j'accepte l'épée de Votre Majesté, et je prie de bien vouloir un de Ses officiers, muni de Ses pleins pouvoirs pour traiter des conditions de la capitulation de l'armée qui s'est si bravement battue sous Vos ordres. De mon côté j'ai désigné le Général de Moltke à cet effet. Je suis, de Votre Majesté, le bon frère Guillaume. —Devant Sedan, 1 Septembre, 1870." [2]

When the King set about writing out these lines, it was not easy to see where we were to find the necessary materials. Of course no table was to be found anywhere near. A couple of straw-bottomed chairs fetched from a peasant's cottage were put together to form a sort of stand, my Orderly Officer, Lieutenant von Gustedt, laid his sabretasche across them for a table-top, I produced my writing-paper and eagle signet from my holster, the Grand Duke of Saxe-Weimar supplied pen and ink, and thus our victorious King wrote his reply to the vanquished adversary !

While His Majesty was writing, I could not well help saying a few sympathetic words to Comte Reille, whom I had known well in Paris as long ago as 1867. At that time he was appointed to attend me and had shown himself an amiable man and a gentleman in the best sense of the word.

[1] In the copy in Hatzfeldt's handwriting to be found in the Records (Political Archives of the Foreign Office) in two places the word " vos " has merely been corrected in pencil by Bismarck into " Ses." The concluding words, " à cet effet " and the date " Before Sedan, 1 Sept., 1870," have likewise been added (? by Bismarck) in pencil. The complimentary phrase at the end : " Je suis, de Votre Majesté, le bon frère," and the signature do not appear.

[2] " My dear brother. While regretting the circumstances in which we meet, I accept Your Majesty's sword, and beg you to be so good as [send] one of His officers, provided with His full authority as a plenipotentiary to treat of the conditions of surrender of the Army which has fought so bravely under Your orders. On my side I have appointed General von Moltke to this end. I am, Your Majesty's good brother, William. Before Sedan, 1 September, 1870."

My expressions of interest in himself personally and in the fate of the gallant French Army visibly cheered him, and he begged my leave to send his respects to my wife, who also had made his acquaintance in Paris. My question whether by any chance the little Prince Imperial was also at Sedan he answered in the negative, and I instantly drew the conclusion that the Emperor Napoleon cannot, during these last days at least, have any longer felt altogether safe; for otherwise, once he had taken his boy with him to the War, he would never surely have sent him away.

His Majesty handed the letter he had written to Napoleon to the French General, and the latter returned immediately to Sedan under Prussian escort.

No sooner had Comte Reille turned his back than the King and I threw ourselves into each other's arms, both of us deeply moved; I could not help thinking of the 3rd July, 1866, and our meeting on that day at Königgrätz, and how marvellously God had ordained it that now for the second time we were called upon to witness so great a moment together and set the seal on an event of world-wide importance.

My next congratulations were due to Generals von Moltke and von Blumenthal, whose names have from to-day attained fresh lustre and a new renown, and to whom our Army owes an enduring debt of gratitude.

So ended the battle of Sedan.

His Majesty ordered Count Bismarck and General von Moltke first thing in the morning of 2nd September to begin the negotiations for surrender with the French General whose arrival was to be expected, and both betook themselves for that purpose to Donchery for the night. From the Royal headquarters the order was issued that till further notice all movements of attack were to cease, but on the other hand the troops were to hold themselves ready to repel by force of arms every attempt on the part of the enemy to break through. Should the negotiations entered upon lead to no result, hostilities will be immediately resumed, for which the opening of fire on the heights of Frénois will give the signal.

The King returned to his yesterday's headquarters, I went back for the night to Chémery, but could only move on the high-road slowly and not without many difficulties arising from the congested traffic. At the places we passed through our men, among whom the news of Napoleon's capture was spreading like wild-fire, had placed in the windows all sorts of lights and lamps—any they could hunt up for themselves and others too that the inhabitants were quite ready to supply; others stood about along the wayside hurrahing and waving lights in greeting to us. Nothing was to be heard anywhere but shouts of joy and jubilation, and even the natives of the district were not averse to these demonstrations of triumph, rejoicing openly to be rid of the Emperor. On my arrival at Chémery, which was brightly illuminated, the band of the 3rd Posen Infantry regiment No. 58, which had remained there on guard, struck up "Heil dir im Siegerkranz" just as I had entered my little room, and the noble hymn, "Nun danket alle Gott," whose notes so gripped my heart I could not keep back the tears of pure joy.

In the quiet evening hours how many prayers of thankfulness will be raised by the troops in their bivouacs all over the battle-field to the great Arbiter of Victory!

The War Minister visited me late in the evening to congratulate me on the victory. He had received news that his son with the Guards Artillery was severely wounded and had hurried to his bedside, to find him still alive indeed, but lying in a hopeless condition.

Headquarters : Donchery by Sedan, 2nd September.—As a boy I was often told in my History lessons : " Die Weltgeschichte ist die Weltgericht ! " (The world's History—an epitome of the world's Justice). To-day when I begin to measure the real significance of yesterday, I am able fully to appreciate the profound truth of the words. Yesterday impressions crowded on the mind too fast and with too overwhelming a force for me to be capable of completely grasping their vast import, for indeed our successes surpass the most sanguine expectations. But shall we therefore attain to peace, or will the Empress Regent first protract the War to the bitter end, or, again, will the Emperor in the last resort put us in the way of solving the dilemma? These anxious thoughts ever ran in my head side by side with exultation over the victory we had won.

The King had announced his intention of awaiting from eight o'clock onwards to-day the further developments of the day on the same height from which I had directed the battle yesterday; His Majesty, however, actually appeared at a much later hour, and while I was waiting on the highroad at the foot of the hill, drove up with General von Moltke as his only companion from the direction of Donchery. From him I learned as follows : The negotiations with the French General Wimpffen, who had come out from Sedan, had, to begin with, led to little result, since the General showed no disposition whatever for capitulation and had returned to Sedan for fresh instructions. The whole situation had entered upon a completely new stage from the fact that suddenly at five in the morning the Emperor Napoleon had left Sedan by carriage, accompanied only by his Aide-de-Camp, and had come to a stop in a potato field not far from Donchery, to wait till Count Bismarck and General von Moltke were informed of the fact. Both hurried at once to the spot and offered him the use of their lodging at Donchery, which, however, the Emperor declined; it looks as though he wished to avoid towns altogether, and so preferred to alight at a peasant's cottage.[1] Napoleon then said he had come in person to try to obtain better terms than the laying down of arms we demanded, and proposed withdrawal of the Army bag and baggage into Belgium, where it would be interned; furthermore, he had besought the two to beg an interview for him with the King. The impression all this had produced on Moltke was that the reasons alleged were merely a pretence, while in reality the Emperor Napoleon's life was no longer safe at Sedan, and he was forced after sundry unpleasant incidents to fly from the neighbourhood of his own soldiers. Stories were current how at night bands of soldiers assembled in front of his house with cries of " à bas le cochon " and such-like insults. His household had been exceedingly anxious about getting the carriages and baggage wagons out of Sedan, and they all felt as if a mountain had been lifted from their breast when the news came that these were well out of the fortress. General von Moltke utilized the interval, while a more seemly place of meeting than the peasant's cottage was being arranged at the Château de Bellevue,[2] to hurry to the King and report how matters stood, while Count Bismarck had the gratification meanwhile of entering into conversation with the Emperor.

Our Cuirassiers were ordered out of bivouac to form a guard of honour for Napoleon.

Acting on behalf of His Majesty, Lieutenant von Treskow, here in the open field, presented General von Moltke with the Iron Cross of the First Class, which I pinned on his breast with my own hands.

At last the King appeared, and, on General von Moltke's proposal, gave his order to demand unconditional surrender; the officers, however, were to be put on parole. Should these terms not be accepted, fire was to be opened again at once. General von Moltke returned with this order, which he had himself urgently recommended, with the result that at midday or thereabouts the capitulation was agreed to

---

[1] It was a weaver's house.
[2] A small country house to the north of Frénois.

unconditionally and signed by Generals von Moltke and Wimpffen. The latter complained bitterly on the occasion that, having arrived only two days ago from Algiers, he of all people had the miserable duty thrown on him, yesterday to take over a command, only to ratify to-day the laying down of arms.

Till the news of the signatures having been affixed was personally communicated to the King by General von Moltke, we all waited on the hill above Donchery. Count Bismarck appeared meantime and reported his interview of several hours with the Emperor Napoleon; they had, it appeared, smoking cigars the while, conversed on all possible subjects, politics only excepted. The little house, in and in front of which this meeting took place, ought surely to become famous in history. The Emperor seems to remain entirely passive in face of future events and to wish to leave all decisions to the Government at Paris.

After General von Moltke had publicly announced the enemy's capitulation, the King addressed a few gracious words to the German Princes then present and to the officers; then came breakfast, at which it was debated pro and con as to whether His Majesty ought to see Napoleon, and whether in that case it was better to go to him or to have him come to us. I was now as warmly in favour of a meeting as I had been opposed before the capitulation was concluded to any such step, but was averse to inflicting the humiliation of a summons to our hill-top in full view of the troops, urging rather that the King should ride over to see the Emperor at Bellevue. Then the question arose what place should be chosen for the Imperial prisoner's residence. Many advised Brühl, but I gave the preference to Wilhelmshöhe near Cassel, which His Majesty also favoured. Yet another conference was held with Count Bismarck, General von Moltke and the War Minister von Roon; after that again much valuable time was wasted in doing nothing, the sky threatening rain meantime, till at last we got to horse, the Cavalry Guard of the King's and my own Staff forming our escort.

The ride took us first through Bavarian bivouacs, in which the men, turning out all slovenly and dirty, came crowding up to greet the King, so that I was forced to have Major Mischke ride on ahead just to remind the fellows to behave in a proper and soldier-like manner. In a quarter of an hour we reached the pretty little country-house of Bellevue, where our Body Cuirassiers and Bavarian infantry were on guard. All the Imperial baggage wagons and carriages stood drawn up ready for the road; the French household appeared in their well-known rich liveries, and even the postillions were in gala dress and powder as if for a pleasure trip to the Longjumeau racecourse. All stared curiously, but greeted us politely. Already a great part of our officers of the General Staff was gathered under the walls of the house, while the "maison de l'Empereur" occupied a glass vestibule or veranda that formed the entrance to the main salon. The King and I dismounted, and were received by General Castelnau, who wore a look of dejection. At the door of the vestibule just mentioned appeared the Emperor Napoleon in full uniform, wearing the Star of the Legion of Honour and several minor decorations, and conducted the King into the salon, the glass doors of which I then closed, to take my stand before them, while the Emperor's French entourage stepped down into the garden. Only General Comte Reille and Prince Achille Murat, and later on M. Davillers, one of the Imperial equerries, kept me company. Our talk naturally turned merely on commonplace topics.

The interview between the King and Napoleon opened by His Majesty saying that fate having proved adverse to Napoleon, and the latter having offered him his sword, he was come to ask the Emperor what his views now were. Napoleon left his prospects for the future entirely to the King, to which the other answered that it was with sincere sympathy he saw his adversary before him in such a position, as he was well aware it had been no light thing for Napoleon to decide for War. Napoleon received the remark with warm satisfaction and declared that it was only in deference to public opinion he had decided to take that step. On this His Majesty observed that anyway it was the advisers whom the French Emperor had summoned to his council who brought it about that public opinion took such a direction. The King then asked whether Napoleon had any negotiations of any sort in view; to this the latter said no, adding that as a prisoner he could no longer influence the Government in any way. To the question where exactly the Government was, Napoleon replied, at Paris. His Majesty now offered the Emperor the Royal castle at Wilhelmshöhe near Cassel as a place of residence, an offer the other immediately accepted. Then the King observed that a guard of honour would accompany him to the frontier to secure his personal safety, and this Napoleon accepted with every sign of special gratification, for evidently he no longer feels safe among his own people. Napoleon expressed the belief that he had had Prince Friedrich Karl as his opponent, to which His Majesty replied that I and the Crown Prince of Saxony had been in

NAPOLEON III.
Emperor of the French.

command yesterday. On this Napoleon asked where Prince Friedrich Karl was then. His Majesty answered with marked emphasis: with seven Army Corps before Metz, at which statement the Emperor fell back a pace with every sign of startled amazement; at the same time his face quivered painfully, for it was evidently the first time he had realized that he had not had our whole Army in the field against him. When the King went on to praise the bravery of the French, Napoleon agreed, but with the added remark that his Army lacked the discipline that so highly distinguished ours; the Prussian artillery, he said, was in his opinion at this moment the first in the world, the French troops had found it impossible to stand up against our fire.

The interview may have lasted a good quarter of an hour, after which the King and Napoleon by his side came back into the outer vestibule, where our King's tall, commanding figure looked wonderfully imposing beside the Emperor's short and very thick-set form. When Napoleon saw me he held out his hand to me; copious tears were running down his cheeks, which he kept wiping away with his hand, as he spoke with the utmost gratitude, evident both in words and manner, of how the King had just expressed himself. I told him it was only natural in every case to meet the unfortunate in a spirit of compassion; in answer to my question whether he had been able to get anything of a night's rest, he said that anxiety for his friends amid the miseries of a War had allowed him little sleep. When I then remarked that this War had been of a formidable and very sanguinary character, Napoleon replied, yes, there was no denying that, but it was all the more frightful if one had never wished to have war (" surtout quand on n'a pas voulu la guerre "). After that I said nothing for a moment, because I was loath to make any answer and was greatly surprised to hear such a statement from the mouth of Napoleon, the prime originator of the present War. Presently I asked after the Empress and the Prince Imperial, of whom, however, he had had no news for a week. On his asking how my wife and children were, I could only give him precisely the same answer.

Napoleon begged the King's permission to telegraph in cipher to the Empress, and this was given him; thereupon His Majesty and Napoleon shook hands on parting. I did the like; then the Emperor accompanied our King to the top of the steps, disappearing, however, directly we were in the saddle. The troops shouted hurrah, and we followed our King to the bivouacs of the cheering Army Corps, feeling we had once again in our lives assisted at a historical event, for it must surely mean something noteworthy to have seen the captive Napoleon, at the moment he was about to be carried away to Prussia, standing before our victorious King.

As we left Bellevue, Lieutenant Boyen and Prince Lynar received the unexpected order to attend Napoleon to Cassel, and were given hurried verbal instructions as to their duties; they were both to start on the journey, which was to begin that very day at four o'clock in the direction of Pont-à-Mousson, setting off just as they were on getting off their horses, without so much as waiting for their baggage.

A little later Napoleon had expressed the wish to be allowed to travel by way of Belgium; this was an entirely unexpected complication and involved certain difficulties by reason of the strict neutrality of that country. He was evidently anxious to get away as quickly as possible out of France and from the neighbourhood of his troops. I cannot deny that at this moment I pitied the Emperor and was grieved to think how swift was the punishment that had overtaken him for his insane arrogance; but one's sentiments must always be humane towards the unfortunate, even where reason demands harshness.

Napoleon's entourage, one and all, with the exception of Comte Reille, looked on morosely, and wore the air of being in no way very specially interested; their glittering new uniforms formed a strange contrast with ours, worn threadbare in War service.

The King next rode to the Württembergers' bivouac by way of Donchery and that of the Cavalry Division Count Stolberg. From there we proceeded to the bivouacs of the Vth and XIth Army Corps, beginning at Floing. In the course of the ride I was able to get a really clear conception of what yesterday's battle meant; in particular I now realized the astonishing depth of the dips in the ground and ravines that had impeded the advance of our infantry, but, on the other hand, had proved of extraordinary advantage to the enemy. At Floing I also examined the garden walls which had first of all to be demolished by our persistent artillery fire; these had been loopholed and constituted a regular fortification, while the heaps of dead artillery horses lying about testified to the obstinacy of the struggle. Our fallen had by this time been mostly buried, but we could still hear in the distance the sound of hymns indicating the solemn procession to the graveside. The French corpses still lay for the most part on the battle-field, as also the dead horses, together with heaps of arms and equipment of every kind. This was the first time in the campaign my troops had seen their victorious War Lord; hence the cheering was as hearty as it was moving, for almost the whole force was bivouacking on the spot where yesterday the battle raged the hottest. Again and again great masses of prisoners met us; when one of these gangs was told how the Emperor had just been made prisoner, a Zouave shouted out loud, he hoped they would shoot him (!). Others called out, " Vive la paix ! " and were delighted that they were being taken to Germany. How shameful !

When the King had left the bivouac of my troops, amongst whom unfortunately the 9th Division was not visited, I went on by myself to inspect the 1st Guards regiment, which I saw to-day for the first time in this campaign. It had dwindled to six companies; as many as thirty officers were missing ! Our meeting touched me deeply; a great many seemed overjoyed to see me again. At last I was able to give them greeting and the assurance of her sympathy on the part of my wife. In the cavalry lines I was shocked at sight of the two Dragoon regiments of Guards, since Mars-la-Tour combined into one in consequence of their losses. Here I came upon my little Croatian groom Wenzel Bartek, serving since the previous autumn in the 2nd Dragoon regiment of Guards. His horse had been shot in the belly in the attack and he had only escaped capture by hiding a whole night long in the woods, till he had the chance to find his way back to Prussian troops. The regiment speaks highly of his behaviour.

I rode on next to the 9th Division, and eventually got back home at eleven o'clock at night, tired out and wet through, for the weather had turned to drenching rain. Still I was glad and happy it had been granted me to show His Majesty my gallant fellows with whom I had shared the decisive opening of the campaign, and now this prodigious success, and this on to-day of all days.

Among the captured despatches was one from the French War Minister to Bazaine : " MacMahon is coming with 120,000 men. He will reach Stenay on the 27th. Be ready to march at the first cannon shot when he comes in sight."

Headquarters : Donchery, 3rd September.—Incessant rain in the forenoon gave place later on to the hottest sunshine. To-day begins the disarming of the French. I do not envy our Generals appointed to superintend the business !

Count Bismarck again came to see me shortly before his departure. In the interview with him, at which he openly, more or less outspokenly even, expressed his views as to the future in view of our great success, it came to light that he cherished the design not to give back Alsace, but rather to retain it under German rule for the Bund or for the Empire. The establishment of the Empire itself was only indicated in general outline in our talk; the restoration of the Imperial dignity hardly mentioned. Indeed I noticed that Count Bismarck is only in favour of the plan under certain conditions, and guarded myself accordingly more than ever now against even appearing, at this moment and in the enemy's country, to be desirous of hastening such a consummation, though I am convinced it must come, and will come. Our ambition in Prussia has never been centred on a constant craving for the German Imperial Crown, but all the same the latest development of German history does tend irresistibly to a speedy restoration of " Kaiser und Reich " (Emperor and Empire) by our House, an event which can occur at no more favourable opportunity than at this moment when our King stands at the head of the German host as victor over France on French soil.

I rode in the afternoon to visit the Bavarian Ist Army Corps, to express my recognition of its achievements on the 30th and 31st August, as also on the 1st September, and was received with enthusiasm. Marshal MacMahon's Aide-de-camp, the Marquis d'Aabzac, as son-in-law of Frau von Lazareff, our old acquaintance, came to meet me on the high-road, to obtain permission to remain with the severely wounded Marshal, which, of course, I gladly gave him. He blamed the behaviour of the French troops during the actions of the last few days in the most emphatic terms, said their *élan* was gone and discipline completely relaxed; speaking generally, he maintained that the French Army was now suffering a punishment they had well deserved for keeping their eyes shut to their neighbour's restless activity and refusing to listen to words of warning. I was for going to MacMahon, but d'Aabzac, and other French and Bavarian officers also, spoke most decidedly against the idea, saying the roads were literally cut to pieces and blocked, and that drunkenness had reached such a pitch among the French that some outrage might well be feared.

We find ourselves in a more than peculiar position, having to take over 80,000 men together with 60 Generals and transport them stage by stage to Germany. It is three days' march to the nearest railway station, so that we must detach a great body of troops as escort, and our gigantic success involves likewise its heavy burdens; besides which it is so difficult to obtain the food that will shortly be needful for such a mass of men. For this reason I had despatched Lieutenant von Gustedt to the Commandant of Mezières with the demand that he should send provisions from the stores in that fortress to Sedan for the maintenance of his captive fellow-countrymen; at the same time Lieutenant von Gustedt was to find out if perhaps the capitulation of Mezières was to be received. The latter came to nothing, whereas the question of commissariat was duly settled. My orderly officer was fired upon from the fortress and the staff carrying the flag of truce was hit, whereupon the French officer accompanying him rode forward to stop this scandalous proceeding and subsequently made apologies.

Hardly back home, and after I had had a momentary glimpse from a distance of the melancholy procession of departing prisoners, the French Generals de Failly and Ducrot were announced. In the first instance I had General von Blumenthal deal with them, and only received them myself when I was accurately posted as to what their business was. Both, in fact, wished to travel through Belgium and to be allowed on parole to seek a place of residence in German towns, along with sundry officers and orderlies. Both looked cast down. Of General Failly, who in 1867 in Paris had been in attendance on His Majesty, I inquired if we had fought against each other at Wörth, to which he replied he had only been posted in reserve at Niederbronn. General Ducrot informed me that on the 1st September, immediately after MacMahon had been wounded at half-past seven in the morning, he had taken over the command of the Army, and, anxious about his right wing, had wished to establish a rear support at Illy, the key of the whole position, which would have rendered the debouching of my troops an impossibility. Then suddenly, he said, General Wimpffen had come on the scene, as Napoleon's nominee [1] to the chief command of the whole Army, and had forthwith thrown over all his arrangements, the final result being that the fateful exit was occupied by us. This shows the effects of disunion among leaders. The same tale was told to my suite by the French Aides waiting at the door, with the addition that General Failly, though relieved of his command some time before, had, nevertheless, just remained with his Corps without more ado. General Ducrot inquired after the fate of a cavalry brigade which, following his instructions, must in all probability have sought safety across the Belgian frontier. Both Generals were

[1] A mistake. Wimpffen had received from the Minister of War Palikao plenary powers which, in case of any disablement of MacMahon, transferred the chief command to him.

grateful for the tribute I paid to French bravery, but blamed the behaviour and tactics of their Army on the 1st September, just as d'Aabzac had done before.

The Crown Prince of Saxony came to visit me, accompanied by Major-General von Schlotheim; he was full of praise for the exploits of our troops, but less enthusiastic about the Bavarians; he added that the Generals of the Guards Corps gave him the impression of having hesitated—the same thing again as at Gravelotte—to take upon themselves the responsibility of an impetuous, headlong onset, regardless of consequences.

The Emperor Napoleon only took his departure this morning and drove through Donchery on his way here, to travel by way of Belgium to Aix-la-Chapelle, where he will spend the night. I have proposed Cassel for his place of residence and expressed myself as opposed to Brühl, the locality first suggested, for I look upon a residence on the Rhine as hardly suitable under existing circumstances, also because at Wilhelmshöhe he ought to be less troubled by the public and will there have the enjoyment of the fine, large park for exercise. For the rest he would seem, in the battles two days ago, to have exposed himself really stoutly to our fire. Hardly was he gone when a telegram in cipher from the Empress arrived for him. I immediately sent Count Seckendorff to go after the Emperor with it, affording the former an opportunity to accompany Napoleon as far as Bouillon in Belgium and the privilege of sitting at his table. During his journey through their country the Belgians have displayed great sympathy for Napoleon and the French.

Our losses fortunately proved less than those suffered in the previous battles; indeed only portions of the two Prussian Army Corps came under hot fire, though, on the contrary, the whole of the artillery was everywhere actively engaged, and has had many casualties. Heavy losses fell upon regiments Nos. 6, 46, 93, 94, 83 and the 5th Jäger battalion.

So far then we seem to have progressed. But what will happen now after these magnificent victories and successes? I am convinced the War will be continued all the same, and, thanks to the French system of misrepresentations, the struggle will be protracted in Paris to the bitter end. Then we shall advance before Paris, blockade the city, and when it is eventually taken there still remains the question whether a Government can be found that will be ready to satisfy our demand for the surrender of Alsace, and at the same time be strong enough to do it. How much then yet remains problematical for the future! Still it may be things will be better, and the news of our victory at Sedan is unquestionably a step towards peace. Besides, where are the French to discover the means wherewithal to continue the War after the enormous losses they have suffered?

Headquarters : Attigny, 4th September.—This little decayed place was once one of the capital towns of Charlemagne, and was the scene of the councils and deliberations of different kings; the baptism of Wittekind took place here. The foundations of the church, as also the tower, which shows Romanesque arches, may date from that period. When I was visiting the building, the Curé besought me to spare the church, to which I replied we were no iconoclasts. The universal craving here is for peace, while the Emperor's capture is regarded with indifference; in fact many people are actually rejoiced at it. Only very few are to be found desirous of going on with the struggle to the bitter end, of making a " war to the knife " of it.

To-day my cavalry occupied Reims, out of which 8,000 French marched away, making for Paris. We received the first proclamations announcing Napoleon's capture and the defeat at Sedan. The " Conseil des Ministres " invites the people to keep up their courage, as two fresh Armies are being enrolled and the fortifications put in a state of defence. Ever fresh lies from these incorrigibles, just to gain time.

Four weeks ago we fought at Weissenburg and to-day France is conquered. Yet I cannot rid myself of the thought that the final result does not answer to the just expectations of the German people, because our governing principles will not bring about anything concrete and adequate. I neglect no opportunity of speaking or making my influence felt to open men's eyes, and above all else to forge the German iron while it is still hot; but as I seldom come in close contact with the Royal headquarters, I cannot count on receiving much attention.

Most of my Staff have colds, but without being exactly on the sick list. I am entirely without news of wife and children.

Late this evening, I have just learned that on the 31st August and 1st September sorties were made from Metz, which were driven back by our men with complete success; so we must now be prepared for a decisive catastrophe there. A captured despatch states that Strasburg cannot hold out much longer, which in any case seems probable to intelligent observers. Our successes, unparalleled in rapidity and extent, gratifying as they are, have something almost terrifying about them.

Headquarters: Warmeriville, 5th September.—To-day we have got some idea of the desolate, cold hills of Champagne, though the true " Champagne pouilleuse " lay all the time to our left. The country-folk have made attacks on transport convoys at different places, and again shots appear to have been fired at officers and patrols. Forced contributions will be immediately levied, a punishment indeed that hits them all the harder as these poverty-stricken localities have already been cruelly treated by the French troops.

Here we were quartered in a large cotton factory belonging to the Brothers Harmel, who have done their best, by means of model dwellings, schools, lecture-rooms and many such-like institutions of a benevolent sort, to exercise a paternal and elevating influence over their workmen. All gardens and open spaces are excellently cared for. I examined all the buildings with the greatest thoroughness, an astonished crowd of work-people thronging round, having never expected me to show such an interest. It appears that my visit has raised people's spirits again, depressed by the manifold burdens incidental to billeting. But whether in view of the astonishingly large number of clericals with whom the house swarms, and who have the direction of things in their hands, and the unmistakable signs of the grossest ultramontane bigotry which meets one at every step—statues of the Virgin by dozens, portraits of the Pope and such-like—the aim of the founders can be attained, I cannot say.

I was received here as a guest. Still, as hardly anything certain was known of the true significance of the victory of Sedan, we were obliged to give our hosts particulars in confirmation of the many rumours current—a sufficiently painful duty to me. One heard no word of pity for the Emperor, while Prince Napoleon was spoken of with downright contempt. The longing for peace is very great.

From home we receive constant warnings to beware of hired assassins and covert evil-doers, rumours being rife everywhere of plots and machinations. I give no credence to such stories, nor, even supposing I wished to give heed to them, should I know what to do or what to leave undone, seeing we can hardly forestall the designs of such fanatics in every case. The inhabitants with whom we have thus far come in contact, directly they saw we were human beings like themselves, became amenable and very soon on friendly terms with us.

Headquarters: Reims, 6th September.—To-day I removed my headquarters to the ancient city that was the scene of the French Kings' coronation, and whose Cathedral is one of the most exquisite creations of Gothic architecture. Close beside it stands the former Royal Palace, now the residence of the Archbishop, in which our King has established his headquarters, in the very same rooms in which, in honour of Charles X and his coronation, lilied escutcheons and decorations executed in the most tasteless " Empire style " are still to be seen.

Nothing precise was yet known at the Royal headquarters as to the state of things in Paris and the consequences resulting from the victory of Sedan, though of course rumours of all sorts were in circulation—one, for instance, to the effect that the Parisians had already acclaimed " la déchéance des Bonapartes " (the abdication of the Bonapartes); in fact in the Corps Législatif itself motions of the same tenor would seem to be in contemplation and only postponed for the moment. The population of Reims, among whom the poorest class of factory hands preponderates, is by no means to be counted on as trustworthy; yesterday indeed actual assaults on single soldiers seem to have occurred. The blue blouses, in spite of the rain, were numerously represented in the streets.

My headquarters are at the luxuriously appointed hôtel of the Werlé family—the head of the house is the manager of the famous " Veuve Clicquot,"—where good taste, high-class oil paintings, and a charming, well-kept flower-garden delight the eye. The owners of the house pressed us to drink their native champagne, and I made an exception and did as they wished, as for once we were actually at the place where that wine is made. Otherwise nothing of that sort is drunk at my table. A single exception I did make on the evening of Sedan, when I had champagne served from Napoleon's pavilion at Châlons, which the Oldenburg Dragoon regiment had sent me, to drink to our King's health.

After I had presented myself at the King's quarters came my first visit to the noble Cathedral, the exterior of which reveals a battle between the Romanesque and Gothic taste. The interior recalls Cologne and Halberstadt, and the ancient glass of the windows, in perfect preservation, of the fourteenth century is, next to that I have seen in England, the finest example I have ever come upon of that time-honoured craft; I could not gaze long enough at their beauties. Even more interesting than the Cathedral itself is the old crypt underneath it, and after that the Church of Saint-Remy, situated in the poorest workmen's quarter of the town, entirely of Romanesque origin, where the kings were crowned and where is preserved the sacred vessel from which they were anointed ("La Sainte Ampoule"), now, alas! disfigured with rococo embellishments.

A number of quite cheerful and comfortable-looking clericals conducted us round the churches and streets of the city. Just as we were viewing the great hall, once the scene of the Coronation banquets, a building in the Gothic style, but which is made unsightly by atrocious modern pictures, Louis Schneider brought me a telegram from the King's cabinet, announcing that in Paris the extreme Left had constituted itself a provisional government. Names such as Rochefort, Arago, Crémieux, Jules Favre and Gambetta showed clearly enough what a revolution—a bloodless one, so it seems—had come about. The clerics were profoundly discouraged. "C'est la République rouge qui va tomber sur nous; mais elle ne pourra pas être de longue durée, et puis ce seront les d'Orléans qui obtiendront le pouvoir—tout le monde s'y attend." [1] Such was the first effect of the shock on our French retinue. Still it remains a noteworthy fact that, apart from the longing of the French for peace, a clamorous cry of rage and revenge makes itself heard against this Paris which in its mania for centralization overrides the interests, not to mention the opinions, of the country, without hearing and consulting it. Thus the people make an express distinction between *Frenchmen* and *Parisians*.

Next we made for Saint-Rémy, still hemmed in by the blue-bloused population; the fellows could not understand how we moved about among them so unconcernedly and without escort. "Napoléon n'aurait jamais osé se hazarder ainsi," [2] was a remark I overheard.

During dinner at His Majesty's quarters came messages corroborating previous news, from which it became clear that the populace of the streets, forcing their way into the Chamber of the Corps Législatif, had expelled the parties of the Right and the Centre and then, marching to the Hôtel de Ville, had there promoted the Left to the honours of government. Strangely enough, along with the men named above, Magnin and Trochu appear to remain in the Cabinet.

Madame Werlé had remained behind at her house and learned from me the news from the capital, where her husband is residing as a Deputy; I was sincerely sorry for her, but she bore the pain and distress of the news with exemplary dignity.

[1] It is the Red Republic is coming on us; but it cannot last long, and then it will be the Orleans who will come into power—everybody expects as much.
[2] Napoleon would never have dared to run a risk like that.

Headquarters : Reims, 7th September.—To-day we acquired the certainty that the Republic is once more proclaimed in Paris and the *déchéance*, though not yet publicly notified, is a fact, seeing the disappearance of the Empress—it is believed to Italy or England—is telegraphed. The poor little Prince Imperial appears to be lying ill at Namur; I pity him, the same fate will fall to him as to all the others born heir to the French throne for the last eighty years.

It poured the whole day, and for once I had leisure to think over the latest events. So it has been given to my Army to bring about the great turning-points of this War—after opening the bloody dance with the victories of Weissenburg and Wörth, to show the French Army the true significance of their German adversary, to pave the way for our two other Armies, and finally to achieve the decisive victory at Sedan, at which Napoleon lost his throne and the half of his Army as prisoners. That in this the active intervention of a portion of the Crown Prince of Saxony's contingent gave substantial assistance is a fact to be gratefully acknowledged. Who could ever have believed that my Southern Army, whose motley combination of the most splendid troops of South Germany with regiments of many Provinces only embodied in the Empire four short years ago was hardly likely to awaken any real confidence in anyone, should have held such great deeds in reserve. I thank God that He has let it happen so; but when one has a General like Blumenthal at one's side, and a man like Colonel von Gottberg deals with matters as Quartermaster-in-Chief—he carried out Lieutenant-General von Stosch's ideas, to whom I am indebted for him—one may dare much and do much. The Vth Army Corps I have always been so attached to, under the leadership of General von Kirchbach, forms the kernel of my whole force and carries the Bavarians along with it; indeed they say openly themselves : " If only we are well led, we are good men and gallant in a fight." To my sincere satisfaction I understand that the Bavarian soldiers speak publicly of their confidence in me and seem to be attached to me. The XIth Army Corps is good and again fought splendidly at Sedan. Generals von Bose and von Gersdorff were of the right sort to be at the head of such troops; General von Schachtmeyer too, who commands them now, knows his work excellently well. The Bavarian Lieutenant-General von der Tann is staunch as his sword, but must curb his fiery temper. His colleague, Lieutenant-General von Hartmann, has already seen service with the French in the Napoleonic wars, and for his age still does amazingly good work. Lieutenant-General von Obernitz understands how to spur on the Württembergers, who unfortunately have not yet had an opportunity of attacking as a Division in close order.

Despite all victories and our improved prospects resulting from them, I ask myself every day how the present mangling of each other like wild beasts, contrary to all Christian precepts of virtue and morality that are preached day by day and looked upon as characteristics of our age, can still be possible. But I must *not* let my thoughts rest on these contradictions; otherwise I might almost go mad over it all, seeing that, placed as I am in the midst of the fray, I am bound to be planning ever new ways of destroying my adversaries, all the quicker to make an end of the miseries of war.

But when at last the War is over, will a different spirit from that shown heretofore prevail among the several nations, or will the demoralization nourished on warlike passions grow to yet wider proportions? I build upon the deep seriousness with which our German people entered into the struggle, and which is still preserved, for it was no mood of levity that urged us to the fray, and thus I hope a revulsion of feeling will not fail to appear. But in that case, on the Princes and Governments rests a doubled responsibility to face the questions of the internal development of the independent political as well as of the truly national life. Should the right moment be missed, while the powerful stimulus of the War is gone and nothing of importance has happened, then in the succeeding period of spiritual stagnation will the passions that have been unchained come to the front again and lead to the most lamentable errors. The *Volkszeitung*, in my opinion, writes excellently on this very point; I only wish it were read in influential circles.

The King of Bavaria, by the hand of Adjutant-General Count Rechberg, presented me with his Max Joseph Military Order for my victory at Wörth. I had hardly heard of the existence of this Order, which is only conferred for battles won. As we may imagine, this has been a rare event in Bavaria, so at the present moment nobody in that country possesses the decoration in question.

Freytag, I am sorry to say, leaves us to-day.

Paris papers of the 4th September speak of a great French victory on the 1st at Sedan, which Marshal Bazaine won, falling upon us in the rear. If, after Sedan, such stuff can still be printed, I really do not know where France thinks to discover proof of her boast that she marches at the head of civilization.

Belgium flirts outrageously with the French military

crossing the frontier; such were to be seen even on the 2nd September going over still armed. There are regiments that have marched with arms in their hands through Belgium, who later on, unmolested and actually trailing prisoners with them, were allowed to return to France. It is conjectured from this that the King of the Belgians, a grandson of Louis Philippe, is casting eyes on the French throne—what foolishness! But such conduct surely can hardly be called that of an impartial neutral!

Again fresh intrigues are being hatched against Duke Friedrich zu Schleswig-Holstein, against which, however, I strongly set my face.

Above my bed here hangs a noble picture by Ary Scheffer of the year 1829; it represents the battle of Murten, and the very moment when the whole Swiss host gather for united prayer, while in the foreground Charles the Bold comes riding up, and peering from the gloom, gazes defiantly at the band, on which, at that instant, a beam of light falls. I cannot tell why this painting, every time I look at it, makes me think again and again of the bearing of our Army as compared with that of the overbearing, now captive Cæsar.

Headquarters : Reims, 8th September.—Sunshine at last, but my eyes are full of tears to-day, for private tidings inform me that Jasmund's death is quite certain, for his sergeant-major in a communication to the Chief of Police at Berlin speaks definitely of death and burial. I cannot yet at all realize his loss. I had built such hopes on him for the future, and but few in later days were on such intimate terms with me as he was; a gap has come in the narrow circle of my confidential friends, a gap which, considering my time of life, will never be filled. Many a man may have been more intellectually gifted and of wider cultivation than he, but I know no one who had proved himself more truly devoted and trustworthy throughout many years of faithful service.

Other deaths I hear of are those of Colonel von Brandenstein, Commander of the Magdeburg Fusilier regiment No. 36, and Major von Reinhard of the East Prussian Fusilier regiment No. 33, while I read in the newspapers name after name of acquaintances and of able, promising officers, the fine flower of our youth! The whole country must already be in mourning, yet nothing will bring these lying French criminals to their senses,—indeed it seems as if the powers that be in Paris, who sit there at a safe enough distance from the hardships and horrors of the War, find a positive pleasure in never-ending bloodshed.

More Iron Crosses have come for distribution by me among my forces, and to-day before dinner, which His Majesty took at my quarters, I again decorated several officers of my Staff. All these by carrying orders and by their competent, intelligent reports have given me substantial help towards winning my successes and well deserved this glorious distinction. It moved me to watch the awed surprise followed by tears of delight on the part of the recipients. At my request the King gave the Iron Cross to the Duke of Saxe-Coburg also, as he had already bestowed it on Prince Luitpold of Bavaria, although His Majesty had made it known only a few days before that he did not wish to confer it on the Princes before the conclusion of the campaign. Then, of course, came Prince Karl, the Grand Duke of Saxe-Weimar and a number of Wing Adjutants as recipients of the same honour. Count Bismarck and General von Roon, whose son had succumbed to his wounds, were likewise decorated.

The news from Paris sounds anything but a peaceful note; war to the knife is preached by the papers. However, Count Paul Hatzfeldt, just returned from Brussels, travelled with a number of French newspaper correspondents, who laughed in their sleeve over the idea that " those oxen of Parisians " imagined they could make a stand against us. And all the while these same journalists constantly write in the most bellicose tone !

Headquarters : Château Boursault, by Épernay on the Marne, 9th September.—Slowly I pursued my onward march on Paris, by His Majesty's express orders leaving the Württemberg Division behind provisionally till the arrival of other troops at Reims. Until the XIth Prussian and Ist Bavarian Army Corps, remaining behind at Sedan to guard the prisoners, have joined me again, I dare not with two Army Corps only venture too far towards Paris. Once the Crown Prince of Saxony has taken position on my right flank, we shall be then able to surround Paris and cut off its supplies of water and food.

Just as I was taking my leave of His Majesty to-day the official statistics of the results of Sedan were laid before us. According to these, 82,000 men laid down their arms, besides which 20,000 were taken prisoners during the battle; furthermore, the French loss in dead and wounded can be counted at 20,000 on the lowest estimation; thus in one day alone some 125,000 men were put out of action, to which must be added near upon 600 guns captured. Such figures, as the results of a single day, make one dizzy. The total of arms, horses and ammunition is as yet quite beyond verification; no eagles, however, are to be found, a fact to the credit of the French, as no doubt they burned or hid these. And all this to produce no effect on the Parisian braggarts! How far then do these misguided men actually mean to push things?

Marshal MacMahon has made the statement, which, however, is already contradicted in other quarters, that the French troops have left Paris to go to the Loire country under command of General Trochu, so that no serious resistance will be encountered in the capital. May it prove so!

As hereabouts the franc-tireurs or Gardes Mobiles are already doing more mischief than in the districts we have quitted, I gave orders that to-day Württemberg cavalry should be my escort, and I was pleased to see how well these riders sit their horses, and in what good condition they had them. As usual, when my headquarters gets moving, it rained to-day in torrents; it was under such conditions we passed Épernay, famed for its champagne; a few days ago the knavish inhabitants of the place captured a lieutenant of ours, Count Schmettow, along with a small body of Uhlans. To this hour their subsequent fate remains unascertained. A sharp punishment was at once inflicted in the way of a forced contribution, which has already been paid.

Now the question of peace conditions has once more been raised in many quarters, expressions of opinion are coming from other countries in favour of some modification of our demands. But can one as a German, and in view of the fearful sacrifices of the War, claim a lesser price than the reacquisition of Alsace, formerly a German province; at the same time the decisive word may still remain to be spoken as to the exact delimitation of the frontiers. Since the victory of Sedan hatred and the craving for revenge have, I suppose, taken such a hold on the French that it is useless for us to give any further consideration to any such arguments as the enemy may bring forward in a more or less conciliatory spirit. France is henceforth for all time our natural enemy, who will seek any and every alliance to help them to avenge themselves on us; hence it is our immediate task to weaken France in such a way that she can never again bring the enjoyment of peace into question. Cessions of territory in Alsace facilitate our strategic dispositions, which were rendered immensely more difficult at the outbreak of the present War than they would otherwise have been, and will cause the French no greater distress than the defeats they have suffered have already involved. The separation of Nice and Savoy in order to strengthen France's neighbours at her expense, as, for instance, our *Volkszeitung* suggests, certainly only comes in question as a secondary point, but should be kept well in mind. The firm welding together of German unity, on the contrary, is an urgent and indispensable necessity as a sequel to this struggle, since such a *fait accompli* will inspire the French to pay a proper respect to it, once they have exhausted every effort to hinder its achievement.

Of the Orleans no word is heard at present; the Prince Imperial appears to be in England; the Empress Eugénie seems not to be going to Cassel at all, to avoid being regarded in the light of a fellow-prisoner. Be this as it may, her present place of residence is unknown to us. She seems to have left Paris in no little haste—will she ever set foot there again? I had positively expected she would have mounted horse and put herself at the head of her partisans, preferring to be shot in action to taking flight. But of a certainty she never dreamt that such a consummation of her activities was possible, once she had achieved her passionate desire to make war on us, or at any rate, in her instigation of the struggle with Germany, deemed defeat and exile less conceivable than did the Emperor. She would seem to have saved only what was ready to her hand at the moment. Whether did she really enjoy the years of her life of royalty, or, in spite of the brilliancy and gaiety, did a haunting shadow ever dog her steps? Where now will her fate lead her, seeing Spain too is closed to her? "Alle Schuld rächt sich auf Erden" (All guilt finds its punishment on this earth) —this saying rang constantly in my ears throughout the great day of victory.

My headquarters are at the magnificent Château Boursault, modern, but constructed in the Renaissance style, which the famous Veuve Clicquot built out of her profits from champagne. Her only grand-daughter and heiress, by her marriage to the Comte Chévigné, supplied the wealth; he in return ennobled the house with his title. The youngest generation has already chosen itself a mate among the Dukes of France and gazes from the castle's battlements over the valley of the Marne, bounded by vineyards and nothing but vineyards as far as the eye can reach.

My apartments were once occupied by old Count Chévigné, but he, like the whole family, took to flight. The pictures in his rooms indicate the purely frivolous taste of the French both of former and of more modern times. Elsewhere at

Boursault one finds the ancestral portraits of the aristocratic sons-in-law, together with those of the widow Clicquot, who is to be seen as large as life sitting with her matronly needlework, over the chimney-piece in the billiard-room, her little daughter playing with flowers at her feet. The same is repeated in the painted windows of the village church, behind which a finely wooded plantation surrounds a little hunting-box.

Headquarters : Boursault, 10th and 11th September.—Up here we have fine, fresh air, the very thing to make us full amends for the many town quarters that at last we have left behind.

Several transport columns have been attacked by scattered bands or franc-tireurs, and wounded officers shot by such-like gangs. As Langres and Vaucouleurs seem to be the hotbed of these proceedings, we are sending light columns of Landwehr there. Pfalzburg has no notion of capitulating. Toul is preparing to make a tough defence, and will presently be bombarded by the Grand Duke of Mecklenburg-Schwerin.

Captain von Dresky arrived with letters from my wife at Homburg and other news from home. It is with unfeigned pleasure I learn from various sources that my wife's presence in the hospitals at Homburg, Frankfort and in the Rhine province is properly appreciated, and also that officials and physicians declare they are astonished at the wide range of her knowledge. Certainly I could have looked for nothing else, yet it is with unspeakable satisfaction I hear the facts acknowledged, for it is high time my wife should win the grateful recognition she has long deserved. At this moment she is building a hospital at Homburg at her own expense, in order to see her own special principles brought into operation.

As I understand, my brother-in-law Prince Ludwig zu Hesse received the Iron Cross as having won it by his able generalship before Metz—this to my intense satisfaction. To Surgeon-General Dr. Wilms and Dr. Boeger I presented it with my own hand, to the general delight of all members of my Headquarters Staff. In the case of my personal aides-de-camp, I must hold it over till we have had some experience of things before Paris. The princely members of my Staff, of course, come last of all in order, in other words on the conclusion of the campaign.

Headquarters : Montmirail, 12th, 13th and 14th September.— To-day we quitted the Clicquot halls of splendour, where the galaxy of wax lights had dazzled us with its glitter, to make a longish march up hill and down dale to Montmirail. There a château, built in the sober taste of the Louis XIII period, Vauban, they say, co-operating in the construction, and belonging to the old family of the Rochefoucaults, received me. Many fine old family portraits let into the panelling of the walls indicate that the Revolution raged less furiously perhaps here than elsewhere. Furniture, garden and pleasure-grounds have a genteel, dignified, old-fashioned look, without attempting the luxurious, and are the more pleasing for that very reason. This can hardly be said of the host of sacred pictures and images and other such-like tokens of strong ultramontane leanings that cover all the walls in surprising numbers. The neighbourhood is cheerful and fertile. Half a mile away from the place a pillar, only lately erected, marks the spot from which Napoleon I directed the engagement on the 11th February, 1814, to which that of Château-Thierry was the sequel.

We shall have to stay on here till the 14th September, to see to the march of my Army on Paris and give them the necessary start on the roads leading to the Seine. I may not in any case hurry my move forward, in order to allow the Crown Prince of Saxony time to effect his march northwards on Saint-Denis.

It is very good for all our nerves not to be obliged to be on the march day after day and to be working the while, and that for once a respite has come to the daily excitement that till now wore us out. Lassitude is the natural consequence; I have not for a long time felt in such a need of sleep as during these last few days that have called for less strenuous bodily exertion, while a hearty appetite is another agreeable symptom: my *chef* Schödler succeeds in satisfying it in a positively wonderful way. Days of rest are bound, one would think, to guarantee ample leisure; but as a matter of fact it is just on such days a host of accumulated trifles has to be seen to, but which can never be brought to completion except in parts, so that these bits of business claim absolutely the whole day. I have been at great pains to spare certain hours for getting a breath of fresh air in the park, yet I must freely confess that the reading of newspapers now arriving from home in heaps, albeit quite irregularly, consumed many half-hours. Amongst the rest, we received the first indications of the effect produced by the triumphant news of Sedan; the Berliners must have made a rare hullabaloo.

The present state of things is pure chaos; but we are guarding now against demands pitched in too high a key, for remonstrances would rain upon us from all quarters.

Count Bismarck would be doing a sound, practical thing if now at long last he shelved altogether the wretched North Holstein question; on the other hand, we are endeavouring to make Luxemburg ours, and so once for all from now onwards render the line of advance into France secure. The annexation of Alsace, and perhaps of a part of Lorraine, is surely well earned by the sacrifices Germany has made. I would have these provinces administered separately, simply as Imperial territories, in the name of the Empire, by that time we hope restored, and eventually in that of the Bund, without giving them a dynasty and placing them under any reigning house. An administrative council made up of native-born members, to which Prussian and South German officials would also be admitted, should then take the government in hand during the transition stage from the French to the German political life. The immediate concern is to detach Alsace from the great body corporate of France, yet at the same time to make the country feel that it was becoming a member of another equally great State, and is not condemned to have to make one of the little petty States of Germany. Count Bismarck seems to me to entertain so far no specially wild-cat plans; on the contrary, he expressed himself, while we were still at Reims, in answer to my leading questions, rather cautiously than otherwise.

Italy, where a waiting policy was the order of the day, seems as a result of our victories to be growing more or less aware she may very well attempt in good earnest the solution of the Roman question, seeing no more favourable moment than the present could possibly offer for carrying out this object. If the stroke succeeds, I should be unfeignedly rejoiced.

The Republican régime in Paris will bring the Great Powers to the immediate consideration of the question whether or no it is decided to accord it the same good-will as to that of Napoleon III.

Highly significant of feeling in Germany is the fact that at present numerous addresses are presented to the King dealing with the conditions of peace, and into the bargain with an unconditional refusal to admit interference on the part of foreign meddlers; this will give jealous rivals cause for careful circumspection, and the Great Powers must weigh well what they do, for the Germans would never again be satisfied with a bad Peace.

The French papers we receive are unfortunately at present few and far between, for just now they are specially interesting. They can no longer deny the *fait accompli*, but all the louder and more persistent is the cry for the proposed defence of Paris, to be entrusted to 300,000 men—*people* would be the better word. Two Armies are being organized also at Tours and Lyons, but these are above all else short of artillery, and its substitutes can only be an unsatisfactory patchwork. I shudder to think how so many unlucky Gardes Mobiles and Gardes Nationales must meet our well-drilled, triumphant troops. No doubt a good proportion of them are moved by patriotic enthusiasm, but that does not make them into trained soldiers; rather will they become the useless tools of the obstinate and deluded politicians who sit round a table making resolutions, without ever coming within sight of war, and drive these hordes to the place of slaughter. It is an unheard-of outrage of the powers that be in Paris, this refusal to realize that France is at this moment so completely beaten she can no longer carry on regular warfare. Hearken where you will, everywhere is repeated the same urgent desire for peace, fury against Napoleon, the originator of this calamity, and hatred towards his advisers and abettors, who by falsehood and deceit and bribery enriched themselves at the expense of their country and now, slipping their heads out of the noose, have disappeared.

It seems to me as though our press fails properly to appreciate the decisive part the Corps of my Army took in the victory of Sedan. In particular I have to-day got hold of a translation—it is true a French translation, but the style of which leaves me in no doubt as to its authenticity—of a letter from His Majesty to my mother, in which the Vth and XIth Army Corps are hardly mentioned. I confess I cannot understand it. In this I see plainly enough how at home the old, familiar game is again being played of mentioning my name as seldom as possible, and always giving merely the number of the Armies instead. Other commanders of high rank are invariably indicated by name, which after all is the shortest way, but one that in my case appears to be intentionally avoided.

The French papers call the act of treachery[1] perpetrated at Laon after the place had capitulated, " heroism," and warn " the invaders " that the like will be repeated everywhere.

Mr. Russell, *The Times* correspondent, had vanished some days ago, leaving absolutely no trace behind, till at last, yesterday evening, he reappeared, actually coming from London. He had betaken himself there straight from Sedan, in order to witness the first impression produced by the news of this event, and declares that people had been petrified,

---

[1] Blowing up the powder magazine there.

so to speak, with astonishment. The absence of the Court, he said, from the seat of government, just at this moment, was looked upon with very unfavourable eyes; further, that in Belgium great sympathy prevails for the French, and French prisoners were promenading the streets of Brussels in crowds. Reports were current, he added, that the officers on parole wanted to go to Algeria, to exchange with those on regular service in the forces there, and so enable these to join the new Armies to be enrolled, and thus supply France with a number of trained officers. Many Frenchmen expressed themselves to Mr. Russell to the effect that it was an absurdity, after such prodigious losses in material, to talk of continuing the War. My brother-in-law, the Prince of Wales, had asked him to convey his congratulations to me.

Germans expelled from Paris, who have come direct from there, relate that scarcity of food, unemployment and discontent among the working classes, who wished for peace, prevail in the city. Something of this may well be true, but unfortunately in a besieged town such circumstances can be of little practical effect; however, we have no intention whatever of blockading Paris. In the places occupied by us in this neighbourhood the inhabitants talk with remarkable good sense, and the better educated consider that Paris could not by any possibility meet the demands incidental to a prolonged resistance. Others criticized the orders issued by the gentlemen in Paris, who knew nothing of the distress in the country parts, to barricade and defend every town and village. This came, they maintained, from the absence of any clear preconception of what a sad and sorry plight must inevitably befall the authorities who should so much as make an attempt to resist the enemy in so hopeless a case.

Yesterday a dismounted squadron of Blücher Hussars put to flight a company of franc-tireurs in a skirmish—yet another proof that the French are losing all moral restraint, though no doubt we shall yet meet with many exceptions.

Officers who have been wounded are already returning to their regiments.

Headquarters: Coulommiers, 15th September.—My thoughts to-day dwelt above all else on my family, for on this day six years ago was born my dear little son Sigismund, now gone from us.

Quarters were prepared for me in the same house at which in 1814 my grandfather, and also my father, had stayed. The present owner is the Marquise de Vendresse, an agreeable middle-aged lady, whose apartments are richly adorned with good, old-fashioned drawings. A pretty garden sheltered cows and poultry, refugees from the neighbouring houses. Our horses are stalled in the stables of the gendarmerie, which in France are fitted up with a luxury that with us a rich private proprietor would hardly allow himself.

Newspapers are now coming to hand, hunted out by my cavalrymen of the advance guard. The Republican sheets have assumed a more moderate tone and even speak in praise of the firm discipline enforced with us. Other points discussed are the possibility of an investment of Paris and the question what will happen if the working population has no earnings forthcoming and no provisions either. Finally, one gathers clearly enough from the press the eagerness with which the Government is seeking for alliances, for the mere circumstance that the Ambassadors heretofore accredited pay visits to the Foreign Office, awakens their hopes that the Great Powers might feel warmer sympathy for the Republic than for the Imperial régime.

Roggenbach urges us to use the time to bring about by our influence some system of decentralization in France. Should it come later on to a more protracted occupation of the country, I should deem this no bad idea, but so long as the French think only of revenge and a war to the knife, it is no use beginning anything of the sort.

Deserters, who are now coming in in numbers before Metz, announce that scarcity of provisions has now set in there and already horse-flesh is being eaten. Would this news were true, for in that case there would soon be an end there, and we should secure our Army Corps for free disposal.

Lieutenant-General von Blumenthal is just back from the Royal headquarters at Meaux. There they are looking for a visit from Jules Favre, the present Foreign Minister, whose intention to appear " to offer terms of peace, yet without cession of territory," has been notified by way of Russia. Under these circumstances I shall go to the King to-morrow myself, once again to learn precisely how things stand.

As I was leaving Montmirail this morning, the band played a march, " The Entry into Paris." Should this be taken as a prophetic omen?

Headquarters : Coulommiers, 16*th September*.—In my Army orders of to-day I was already able to indicate the investment of Paris as the next objective. As a preliminary I shall occupy with my Army on the right bank of the Seine the radius between that river and the Marne, and then the section from Choisy-le-Roi by way of Sceaux, Versailles to Noisy.

I rode to His Majesty's quarters at Meaux, but owing to the terribly steep roads and out of consideration for my escort of Uhlans, made only slow work of it; so unfortunately I had not much time to stop, for I must avoid journeys in the dark, as the population is not to be trusted. As everybody is terrified of the " uhlans prussiens " and I don't know what else, my escort inspires satisfactory respect.

At Meaux I learned that a son of Sir Alexander Malet's, having—nobody knows how—been let through by our outposts, had announced himself at Count Bismarck's quarters in search of enlightenment as to our views on the Peace question, and at the same time had inquired whether we should be inclined to discuss things with Jules Favre. To the latter Count Bismarck is by no means ill-disposed; indeed he actually advises the King to receive him, as being all important to hear him and let him speak for himself, so as to get to know the man. Only then can we decide whether serious negotiations are possible with him or no. All this, of course, without ever formally recognizing the Republic. The opinion was also plainly expressed that there is no Peace for us without cession of territory. Favre may be here within the next few days; pray God, a change of mind then is coming on in favour of concluding peace.

England is becoming reconciled, it appears, to the idea of a cession of Alsace; the Tsar Alexander the same; his Minister Gortschakoff less so. The Empress Eugénie would seem to be in England; she was fully bent on staying on at the Tuileries and only left the Palace when the popular pressure grew threatening. She thereupon fled through the galleries of the Louvre and, just as King Louis Philippe did once, mounted a fiacre she came upon in front of the church of Saint-Germain l'Auxerrois. The communications in *The Times* on the days of Sedan are excellent; written in an admirably clear, correct and true fashion. That Mr. Russell went himself to England and wrote a great deal in the train explains how it was possible to publish these so quickly.

It appears the Emperor Napoleon is no less surprised than gratified by his reception and treatment at Wilhelmshöhe by Cassel. How, indeed, could he have expected anything else? We only do ourselves honour by treating him well and suitably. On the journey the attitude of the German public, so General von Boyen tells me, seems to have been tactful on all occasions. The guard detachments of Landwehr on duty at the railway stations seem to have impressed Napoleon by their excellent bearing, and he expressed his admiration in so many words.

Italy is actually on the march to Rome to occupy the city. Urged on by the national sentiment of his people, Victor Emmanuel takes advantage of the opportunity, seizing the favourable moment, that may perhaps never recur; thus at last will the standing abuse of priestly domination in the States of the Church be really made an end of. If Pius IX is wise, he will stay on quietly in Rome, suffer what can be no longer avoided, save at any rate his spiritual office, and join forces with the National Government. For the rest, the Papal States can only benefit by the change and recover their old prosperity, and I should be rejoiced to see Italy once again having us to thank for a great success, one for which her people will be ever grateful.

Austria is suspending her further preparations.

I was present at Count Bismarck's interview with His Majesty, which Prince Karl, without more ado, interrupted with the announcement that he regarded the Château de Ferrières as particularly well adapted for the King's headquarters. This weighty piece of information and his staying on in the room brought the interview to an end.

The newly-appointed Maire of Coulommiers, only three days ago put in office by the Republic, expressed himself to-day in a conversation with the Duke of Saxe-Coburg to the effect that the notion of the Parisians hoping to make a stand was ludicrous; that France was beaten once for all and will have to accept the Peace the victors require of her. From the moment, he said, Napoleon went off to the Army, his position, already all but untenable, was so shaken by Ollivier's appointment that even under favourable circumstances he could not have held out much longer. The Republic, he added, had already been set up some time ago, and this explained why its actual proclamation had fallen so flat.

To-day I received the far from agreeable news that the post containing my letters about Sedan and also about the interview with Napoleon, which left Donchery on the 3rd September, was captured by the French near Verdun. The contents we shall doubtless very soon see printed in the newspapers, but certainly never receive the originals, for the meanness of the French will make them retain this correspondence, whereas I have given orders, in the case of captured French papers, directly we have examined and utilized them, to have them sent on to the addressees. I grieve for the loss, because my letters were written under the very first impression of the great event; possibly the contents in question may afford the French the less inducement for publication as they include no lies.

Headquarters: Chaume, 17th September.—We are now barely six miles distant from Paris but are marching southwards round the city, so that while, on the 19th, my Vth Army Corps, on the extreme left wing, occupies Versailles, the right will extend as far as the neighbourhood of Vincennes.

No longer ago than yesterday the 2nd Cavalry Division, Count Stolberg, was close up to Paris, and at Ablon-sur-Seine their artillery fired on railway trains, bringing them to a halt, whereupon a small infantry detachment leapt from the carriages, but were at once compelled to give way before our shell-fire. All these little successes and occurrences make a powerful and favourable impression on our good fellows, while they are bound to reduce the enemy to a condition of deep depression, knowing us already under the very walls of his capital.

Sections of our first line are constantly coming upon places occupied by enemy posts, whose defenders, however, never offer any serious resistance, but give way at once under the fire of our cavalry. Still this may very well prove otherwise when we reach the Forest of Fontainebleau.

It strikes me as something simply incredible when I find myself issuing orders to station outposts at Versailles and Saint-Cloud.

The Republic carries on without making any great stir, for all the world as if it were just a matter of course; never a word of sympathy for the Emperor, but only exasperation towards his person and the corruption of his extravagant régime.

The noble, fertile land of the old Isle-de-France where we now are smiles a welcome; châteaux and parks succeed each other in picturesque variety and testify to good taste in architecture and the love of flowers. We occupy the empty house of an *avocat*, a man who knew well how to embellish the house he owns with the utmost comfort and cultivate a charming garden. Almost every place is practically deserted, the inhabitants having shut up their houses and fled in terror. The unhappy result, of course, is that the troops billeted there have no other way of getting in but by breaking down doors or windows, naturally causing great damage.

The Grand Duke of Mecklenburg, in command of a Corps made up of his own Division and Prussian regiments, is already on the march for Reims, where he will act as Governor-General of all districts occupied by the Army not forming part of Alsace and Lorraine. His Army Corps is to be known as the IIIrd.

The 5th and 6th Cavalry Divisions have been put under my command.

Headquarters: Corbeil or Saint-Germain-le-Corbeil, 18th September.—The cavalry belonging to my Army and to the Crown Prince of Saxony's contingent have already to-day effected the investment of Paris; to-morrow by the advance of all arms the thing will be an accomplished fact.

To-day captured newspapers give telegrams from Strasburg, in which the French Commandant (Uhrich) describes his situation as critical in the extreme, and at the same time the Prussian fire as very destructive, and ends by admitting that a sortie lately attempted had been unsuccessful. Consequently our prospects of victory there might well seem brighter than before Metz. In Metz, it is true, the complement of horses in the Cavalry is reduced by consumption of horse-flesh, but still, as provender for them is giving out, this disadvantage is not one seriously felt, as no positive famine has yet declared itself; certainly there is nothing definite to be learned about Metz, and it might well be weeks yet before the fortress falls. It must be a wearisome time of waiting for Prince Friedrich Karl to stay tied so long to one spot, while we, for ever on the move forward, have now actually reached Paris.

We are in daily contact with the inhabitants, especially with the country people. The latter make a distinctly favourable impression on me, and deserve a better fate than to be governed by such elements as have now been at the helm for three generations, but in particular by the Bonapartists. The longing for peace is expressed again and again every day, but what help is to be found when here in France even the noblest and wisest are dependent on men who pay heed only to their own private interests, and, using the pretended feeling of the nation as a pretext, demand the continuance of this disastrous war regardless of consequences? In the most naïve fashion the same conversations are now repeated in French villages that we used to have with the peasants in Alsace, who would ask us all sorts of ridiculous questions, finger my star and show themselves just as confiding as the country-folk in our own land.

Again headquarters in an elegant château with flower-gardens and orchards kept up almost in the English style, the property of an ennobled flour-dealer and corn-factor, hard by the Seine. Rhododendrons, Wellingtonias, numbers of evergreen shrubs, thrive here along with luxuriant ivy in most exuberant variety, so that eye and mind found a feast on these fair products of Nature that breathe the deepest peace. In place of the absent proprietor his brother played host in a very amiable fashion. With equal frankness and good sense he spoke of the duties that were to be observed in times of war towards the victors, maintaining that for the owner to stay on the spot was best under the circumstances, and by his presence enable requisitions to be made and paid in an orderly and legal way. His great anxiety was that directly Peace was concluded civil war would break out and the party of the Reds would come to blows with that of the Republic.

Headquarters: Palaiseau, 19th September.—After a cordial parting with our host, we rode along the right bank of the Seine in the direction of Paris, and at Villeneuve-Saint-Georges crossed the river by a bridge of boats. The road, stretching for a mile and a half, is one of the most attractive I have ever seen, for it is bordered by an unbroken succession of country-houses, gardens and parks lying on both sides of the Seine, giving ample witness to the wealth of the Parisians, and recalling English country scenes. Here Prussian soldiers served everywhere as figures in the landscape, for otherwise literally not one single human being was to be seen. The only exception was an oldish lady, who accosted me and informed us she was a fellow-countrywoman, a native of Neustadt on the Dosse, while she related how all the woods round Paris were in flames, and she was convinced the Parisians, among whom she had lived for twenty years, would not endure the approaching investment a fortnight.

All through the ride we kept hearing the roar of cannon, and when, after crossing the bridge of boats, at which point I came upon the 38th Infantry regiment, and was riding through the bivouac of the IInd Division at Orly, I saw shells bursting in the air round about the Park of Sceaux. Thereupon I proceeded at once towards the scene of action, which, so I was informed when I came up with the Vth Army Corps, had been observed as having continued with intermissions for several hours already, and discovered not far from the village of Antony and Croix de Bernis a good point of view from which to observe the further development of events, and to have the opportunity, as circumstances might dictate, forthwith to order up the VIth Army Corps from its bivouac. Mitrailleuse fire alternated with that of the guns and the rattle of musketry, and as the troops hardly shifted their position at all, I gained the impression that the engagement had come to a deadlock. Soon, however, I noticed among the French unmistakable signs that they were preparing to retire, while their left wing was likely to be cut off by certain detachments lying concealed on the southern slope of the chain of hills. After that we had not long to wait till the whole body joined in the retreat on Paris, and our men, manifestly gaining ground, presently occupied the position just before held by the French. Thereupon the firing ceased very quickly, and I presently received reports to the effect that things were going very favourably for us at all points; moreover, that the engagement, the issue of which we had witnessed at three o'clock, had begun as early as daybreak that morning. In fact the 9th Division had been attacked on the march by the French at dawn, so that the Brigade von Voigts-Rhetz had had a hard fight for it; later on, however, they were strongly supported by the intervention of the Bavarians. I could not to-day make out with any clearness who had had most to do with it, whether Prussians or Bavarians; but this much was certain, that both sections had afforded one another mutual assistance, and that, while the Vth Army Corps by my orders was pushing its advance right up to Versailles, the Bavarians in the section allotted them were actually able to occupy an entrenchment with seven abandoned guns in it.

After a ride of eight hours I took up my headquarters at the little town of Palaiseau; a deserted country-house, a delicious little place with park attached, gave just room enough for me and my personal attendants. The population here, as in neighbouring places, had taken to flight, with the result that again to-day the troops seeking billets had found themselves compelled to break in doors to gain an entrance, thereby, of course, involving no little damage to the dwelling-houses.

Versailles had at first proposed to offer resistance, but fortunately the inhabitants and authorities gave up the idea once they were convinced of our strength, and the National Guard accordingly quietly suffered themselves to be disarmed. An effort was made to submit terms of capitulation to me in writing, but this, of course, I declined, deeming it ludicrous to think of treating an open town as if it were a fortress. Then next minute our troops were bidden welcome, because, as the Versailles folks said, they at last found themselves under the protection of a Power that could guard them against a whole host of scoundrelly ragamuffins that had infested the place since the War. For the same reason Sèvres actually asked for men to be billeted there!

A prisoner, a French officer, told us plainly to-day that living in Paris was intolerable, nothing but a rabble being left there, so that already people were shooting each other down. Granting only one-half of this is true, we may still pretty well guess that the enthusiasm for resistance that is proclaimed in the newspapers is, as a matter of fact, non-existent.

Headquarters : Versailles, 20th September.—So now I have taken up my headquarters here at Versailles, being lodged in the official buildings of the Préfecture, an edifice appointed in a style of luxury that passes belief and situated in the Avenue leading directly to the great Palace; from there I can quite easily reach the outposts. As to commissariat, I have given orders to the troops to rely on their own provisioning columns and not on arbitrary requisitions. The General Supervisory Service of Supplies is responsible for the punctual loading up of the food convoys. As a preliminary, provisions in sufficient quantity are lying ready at Versailles for the supply of the Vth Army Corps in cantonments at the place; it is proposed, however, to establish a great magazine to be stocked from the requisitions collected by the detachments of the 2nd, 5th, and 6th Cavalry Divisions told off for that duty. Actual damage to property abandoned here by the inhabitants I have forbidden in the strongest way and threatened severe punishments.

To-day I rode over yesterday's battle-field, the horrid traces of which begin at the closely barricaded houses of Petit-Bicêtre and extend over the whole plateau of Plessis-Piquet as far as Clamart. The newly-dug graves of our men are already in evidence, neat and flower-decked, whereas the burial of the many French dead will have to wait some time yet. To the Bavarians I was able to express my full appreciation of their gallantry, for indeed their achievements are recognized by all Prussians; the Brigade Commander, Colonel Diel, gave substantial help to our Brigade under Von Voigts-Rhetz at a critical moment.

After a visit to the amiable Lieutenant-General von Hartmann at his quarters at Chatenay I went on to the captured entrenchment. During the ride there I was just breakfasting when we were greeted by sundry shells, startling my escort; next moment a shot struck not far from us in a clump of brushwood, while later on, as we were leaving the entrenchment, a shell flew close over our heads. The entrenchment was already reversed and the guns pointed on Paris by Bavarian pioneers. A noble prospect here lay before us; Paris lay directly under our very feet, shining clear in the sunshine with its sea of houses, the richly gilded dome of the Invalides and the numerous forts. To our right, somewhere about Villejuif, we could see a work only just completed, the position of which will surely cause us trouble in the next few days; before we have finished, we shall be obliged to storm this. I cannot conceive what induced the French to evacuate a favourable position such as this, for, supported by a work of this sort, they could give us pause for a length of time. Presumably, once again we have been too quick for them and taken them by surprise.

I am told that in Paris milk is certainly getting scarce, but no lack either of arms or provisions was to be expected. If Paris *could* offer a somewhat longer resistance, what then?

The high-road to Versailles, paved throughout, had been made impassable by cutting down trees, digging trenches and pitfalls and tearing up stones; still it is easy enough to go round or clear away these clumsily contrived obstacles. But it is a pity for the many fine old trees that must doubtless have lined the way.

Late in the afternoon I reached Versailles; the whole population on its feet, but with no very inviting faces, as we rode in.

The Commander of the National Guard, M. de Franchet d'Espéray, nephew of the late wife of General von Luck, behaved with much tact, was circumspect in his whole proceedings, and proved an essential factor in the rapid understanding reached with us. We had played together as children in Berlin, but had not seen each other again since those days; it was therefore a singular thing on both sides to meet again just at this spot and under such circumstances.

We hurried off quickly to the Palace and on to the terrace, where we witnessed a magnificent sunset. To one who immediately before had been treading a battle-field with all its horrors, even a forsaken home of Kings, despite its associations of storm and terror, affords real refreshment. I could not but recall, as I stood there, the fine, warm Sunday in the year 1867 on which the fountains played here in honour of my father and the Tsar Alexander, and we, in company with a host of princely personages, surrounded by an inoffensive throng of onlookers, were the guests of Napoleon and Eugénie,[1] who did the honours with an amiable courtesy that charmed us. How swiftly has the star of that Imperial pair faded! Now Prussian uniforms enliven this superb scene of French pomp and pride!

Headquarters: Versailles, 21st September.—The outposts reported the persistent sound of musketry and cannon inside

[1] On the occasion of the Paris Exhibition.

EUGÉNIE, EMPRESS OF THE FRENCH.
After a painting by Winterhalder.

the Paris enceinte. This does not sound so improbable, as we have heard that as a consequence of our victory of two days ago the Parisian has worked himself up into a veritable panic and that great excitement prevails in the city. It is said, besides, that after the engagement on the 19th the Zouaves had bolted into the city in perfect hordes, and so not a few of them had been there and then shot under suspicion of cowardice.

The entrenchment at Villejuif has been evacuated by the French and occupied by the VIth Army Corps. It is to be hoped we can continue to hold it.

What Jules Favre said or what proposals he made I do not know; the few bits of news I learned about his visit I owe to orderly or other officers, not among the most trustworthy sources of information. It is believed that Count Bismarck has threatened that, supposing the Paris Government does not prove compliant, he will be forced to make further demands for the cession of territory—right up to the line of the Meuse—and promises himself good results from this scare.

I shall have to go to the Royal headquarters one of these days soon, both because under present circumstances my presence there seems to be of some importance, and also for the purpose of personally collecting information, for otherwise, either no communications at all reach me, or only such as are utterly out of date.

The bombardment of Strasburg, now become necessary, distresses me. The maddest part of the whole business is, that desiring to make that town German and gain it over to ourselves, we must first reduce it to ashes to attain our object. But what else is left for the besiegers to do?

An Englishman—refugees he and his family from Paris— who knows Mr. Russell, told me to-day that Paris was fully prepared to make a stand of certainly three months. His tone and bearing impressed me as those of a friend of France, so I answered him with a touch of irony that we had plenty of time to spare and were quite ready for an even longer delay.

Our hours of leisure I devoted to the wounded, who have found accommodation in the " Salon des Glaces " as well as on the ground-floor of the Palace beneath the historical paintings now hidden behind boarding, and, enjoying good air, can easily be moved out of doors to bask in the glorious hot weather. The apartments of Louis XIV remind me vividly of those of King Frederick I in the Schloss at Berlin. I must confess that, as I gazed round these rooms of pomp and splendour in which so much hurt was planned for Germany, and where derision over our internal misery actually finds pictorial representation, I was inspired with a steadfast hope that here in this very place might be celebrated the re-establishment of Emperor and Empire.

Headquarters : Versailles, 22nd September.—I went to-day to the Royal headquarters, established eight miles from here in the Rothschilds' Château of Ferrières. Again the domes of Paris and the sea of houses stretching away to Charenton and Vincennes glittered in the brilliant sunshine, as we rode gulping down the dust raised by my cavalry escort, without which, however, I cannot well travel across country, this out of mere regard for my personal safety. Ferrières may be compared to a chest of drawers standing with its legs in the air. It shows traces of Renaissance style, but in the interior gives the impression of a cabinet of curiosities in the literal sense, equipped, of course, with every possible appurtenance of extravagance and luxury.

The most important news I heard to-day was that the troops of the King of Italy have occupied Rome. So at last the Roman question is done with, and therewith the Italian solved. How often we thought this historical moment was close at hand, only to see it recede again into the far-distant future. The miserable régime of priestly domination is at an end, and once more the triumph of German arms has done the Italians good service. I hope the Pope is wise and far-sighted enough to stay on quietly at Rome and recognize the new order of things, for, should he quit Rome, it is a question if the Papacy can so easily return again to the Eternal City. But it is now rumoured he would fain take refuge in Belgium, nay, steps would seem actually to have been taken in Berlin to offer Fulda to him as a place of residence. God preserve us from ever having these folks settled in our country! That would be the last straw! The occupation of Rome within a few weeks of the publication of the dogma of Infallibility is a strange irony of Fate.

Count Bismarck told me about his meeting with Jules Favre, who first came upon him quite unexpectedly on the high-road, and his subsequent conversation with him in a ruined house; finally, however, he had here at Ferrières two further interviews of a detailed character, which I specially noted down. He is expected back again to-day or to-morrow, so now there are some hopes of peace.

It was still early this morning when I learned from officers how Favre a few days before had come by way of General of Cavalry von Tümpling's headquarters, and had passed the night there to await the arrival from the Royal headquarters

THE EMPEROR FREDERICK III. 131

of the permission he had asked for a meeting with Count Bismarck. Favre seems to have been very courteous, and to have expressed himself as specially grateful for the way he was treated at General von Tümpling's quarters; he left a favourable impression behind him among our officers.

One notices in the present attitude of Austria that Sedan and the Republican régime in Paris have had a strong influence on her policy and brought her preparations to a standstill. Russia indicates her continued friendliness by conferring of the Order of St. George on General von Moltke and a number of German Princes. Italy is holding back. England's sympathies for us are more and more lively among the public.

Ferrières, 23rd *September*, 1870.—I have spent the night here, and first thing next morning took advantage of the glorious day to inspect plantations and park, Lieutenant-General von Stosch accompanying me on the stroll; I was specially pleased with the many evergreens, the arrangement and distribution of which greatly reminded me of Osborne. After the discussion with Generals von Moltke and von Roon at His Majesty's quarters, I returned to Versailles; a short while before had arrived a communication from Jules Favre to the effect that the Ministry could not agree to any of our demands. The poor deluded creatures!

Anyway it was not to be expected that the Parisians would here and now accept our conditions, but Favre's whole bearing and behaviour, his sensible way of speaking and his undertaking to come again left it to be guessed that further negotiations would follow. Even should this opportunity be lost, I am still convinced that we shall not have long to wait for other pourparlers, for conditions in Paris being what they are, no serious, long-continued resistance is to be expected, and then proposals of peace will undoubtedly be made from other quarters also.

In the capital nothing like unanimity is to be found; all parties, all passions are in the wildest ferment. The *esprit de corps* even of the troops of the line is gone. To-day a refugee, a Russian, who had himself witnessed the Paris fight of the 19th, told me how the flower of the troops had come dashing back into the town in the wildest confusion. Placards posted upon the walls signed by Trochu announced publicly next day that the Zouaves had fought badly, and several had accordingly been shot in punishment. Notwithstanding the accumulation of provisions, butter and milk are already dear.

At Lyons it seems the Social Democrats propose to take serious steps in advance and establish a government for themselves as a set-off against that in Paris. In Southern Kabylia discontented tribes are on the move, so that troops, only just arrived at Marseilles from Algeria, had to be sent back there at once.

Some regiments of the VIth Army Corps had had an engagement early this morning by the entrenchment and village of Villejuif; a certain number of severely wounded men were brought in, but otherwise the losses appear to have been only slight. As to the result, I could gather no clear idea, for I could only get in speech with the troops marching back from their station in reserve to their cantonments, and their reports did not agree. The bivouac of the VIth Army Corps has been broken up to-day.

Again we watched a lovely sunset from the uppermost terrace of the Palace, surrounded by Prussian officers and soldiers strolling up and down.

Headquarters: Versailles, 24th September.—The cousins Albrecht and Wilhelm von Mecklenburg paid me a visit. The latter still goes lame from bruises received in the explosion at Laon and uses a stick. He is of opinion that no blame attaches to the Commandant of Laon; it was really an extra crabbed-tempered artillery sergeant was to blame for the treachery. Later arrived, first the Prince of Schwarzburg-Rudolstadt and then the Duke of Saxe-Meiningen to see me.

We received to-day the welcome news that Toul had at last surrendered—a success that is the more important as it makes it possible for direct railway communication with home to be immediately re-established, albeit traffic must stop short at Meaux because of the destruction of viaducts and bridges. The Grand Duke of Mecklenburg-Schwerin will be pleased to have won a success with his men, which honestly I do not grudge him. At Strasburg the siege has now reached the stage of breaching the defences, so its capture cannot well be much longer delayed; unfortunately the storming of the citadel might yet cost much blood.

As to Paris, heavy siege artillery will have to be brought up to harass the city with fire of all sorts. The question is, will the inhabitants endure this patiently? moreover, the strong forts of Mont Valérien, Vincennes and Saint-Didier may yet, by reason of their lofty situation and long-range guns, give us many an uncomfortable hour. Refugees from Paris still keep constantly slipping in one by one; they are unanimous in confirming the wild panic of the troops who scurried into the town on the 19th, as also of the executions by martial law that took place in consequence.

We enjoyed glorious rides this hot summer's day in the wonderful avenues of the park, which remind me of Sanssouci, and likewise visited both Trianons; these I had last seen in the year 1867, when the Empress Eugénie was at that moment arranging a display there of all such articles as could be got together which Queen Marie Antoinette had personally possessed or used. On that occasion I sat for some considerable time by the Empress's side in the carriage; it was the time she and Napoleon enjoyed the triumph of seeing all European sovereigns appearing at the Court of the Tuileries, and the development of the supremest brilliance of the French Court was taken as the surest guarantee for the maintenance of European peace. Three years later, barely six weeks sufficed to bring to ruin the edifice of pretence and falsehood built up by the Bonapartists. To-day the Empress languishes in exile with her consort and their heir—sharing a like fate with Bourbons and Orleans. A moving sight, with such thoughts in one's mind, to view the gilded coaches here standing idle in which the Duc de Reichstadt, Comte Chambord, the Comte de Paris, with the Prince Imperial, drove to the baptism.

Headquarters: Versailles, 25th September.—To-day, a splendid, hot Sunday, a field service was held in the open, at the foot of the great terrace under thick chestnut avenues. I think Louis XIV would have turned in his grave could he have known how we heretics were using his creations for our devotions. The singing from hundreds of voices of gallant soldiers who had many a time looked death in the face, accompanied by instrumental music, while in the distance the gunfire from the Paris forts could be heard, gave the whole an extraordinarily solemn air. The service was simple and dignified. We sang the same hymn: "In allen meinen Taten," that was chanted before marching off for the front on July 31st at Spires. The thought of all we had done in these two months, and how victory had manifestly been given us from on high, moved me strangely as I listened to the words. French onlookers appear to have expressed amazement that German Protestants should actually hold a divine service and knew something about religion.

Yesterday and the day before some sorties took place, but they were repulsed with considerable losses for the French; as these will be frequently repeated, I lay the greatest stress on this, that the troops should abstain from all unnecessary engagements and the outposts be exposed in no superfluous degree to the enemy's fire.

To-day a half-crazy Prince Max of Württemberg turned up to see me, who for years has been taking part in lion-shooting expeditions in Africa. After a breakfast he did ample justice to, and when he had suitably quenched his thirst, he refused to avail himself of my suggestions and went off to roam about recklessly outside the chain of outposts—result he soon got a glancing shot wound on the head.

A telegraph cable has been discovered in the bed of the Seine; this we immediately tapped, by fixing on a wire, so now we are in a position to control the correspondence of the French authorities (in Paris on the one hand and Rouen and Tours on the other), notwithstanding that much of this is in cipher.

In the afternoon I made a journey to Saint-Germain-en-Laye, and thoroughly enjoyed the noble view from the vast terrace there. Three years ago, in 1807, I had been attracted by the situation of the place and the panorama over the valley of the Seine, with Paris in the background. To-day, as on that occasion, everything looked peaceful, and the conical summit of Mont Valérian, standing directly in face of the beholder, looked down just as it did then on the smiling country-side. Only our bridges of boats over the river and the patrols moving here and there afforded indubitable evidence of the seriousness of actual conditions.

Headquarters : Versailles, 26th September.—I gave myself the pleasure to-day of personally distributing Iron Crosses among officers and men of the 17th Infantry Brigade and other detachments of troops before the assembled garrison under arms. To this end I had had the troops drawn up in the " Cour royale " of the Palace round the statue of Louis XIV, mounted the steps leading to the monument, and from that point of vantage handed out to each individual the noble decoration in question, finishing up with a cheer for the King, after which followed a march past in the Avenue de Saint-Cloud. If the ghosts of the French monarchs who founded and dwelt at Versailles, above all Louis XIV, are angry at this profanation added to the offence of the service held yesterday, I for one cannot blame them. The marauding raids in Alsace and the Revocation of the Edict of Nantes occur to one's memory, but at the same time the phrase that has more than once before in the course of this campaign come involuntarily to my lips : " Alle Schuld rächt sich am Erde ! " (On this earth every guilt finds vengeance).

Jules Favre has had the interview between Count Bismarck and himself printed—according to his biased reading of it—and distributed over the country by balloons. Already two of these air-borne copies have come into my hands; still the tenor seems to me to be fairly accurately reproduced. According to information received, Favre's attitude meets with the highest approval, and France, startled at our demands as communicated to him, would seem resolved to continue the policy of war to the knife. It may be many are averse to the struggle, but it is none the less clearer than ever that at this moment nothing is to be done with the arrogant French nation, who, for all they must feel how things are with them, will *not* give in. Incidentally the just completed municipal elections have again been cancelled, and the votes for the Constituent Assembly already recorded will have to be given again, on the ground that these matters ought not to be carried on under the stress and strain of foreign invasion.

I rode out to-day to the outposts at the Château de Meudon, the former residence of Prince Napoleon, whose father had occupied it before him. The French wanted to construct an entrenchment round the magnificent five-storeyed building, but were disturbed when the work was already far advanced by our arrival on the 19th, and quitted the place, which might have done us a great deal of mischief, so hurriedly that trenching tools of every conceivable sort were left lying about. The fine trees of the park, particularly those standing close to the château, must have enormously facilitated the French works, while the interior of the building, now completely empty, is like a barracks. The view over Paris is famous, affording a peep into the city, beginning with the Bois de Boulogne. On a bright, sunny day like this it is particularly enjoyable. However, we only durst go to the windows with the utmost precaution, for the enemy's outposts, stationed quite close opposite, as well as the guns of the enceinte, fire at sight on every living creature.

Headquarters : Versailles, 27th September.—First thing this morning I rode over to the great basins, the "Grandes Eaux," in the park of the Palace, which one descries from the terrace as an extension of the "bassin de Latone," and occupied a whole hour in the survey. On my rides here in the park I recognize again and again the leading idea that served as pattern for the pleasure-grounds at the "New Palace" at Potsdam, and I cannot but think to myself what a great extent of shrubbery was probably to be seen there before the main avenue was modernized. When, as is the case everywhere without exception at Versailles, all the grounds follow the formal, old-fashioned French fashion, one may very well find pleasure in a mishandling of Nature so systematically carried out. On the other hand, I gather that the Court, which year in, year out, spent its life here, at last reached the most maddening pitch of deadly ennui, or else built Trianons for itself, just to have a change of scene. Louis XIV's apartments I greatly admired; their design is tasteful, royal, magnificent, and I delight in the recollections of the Royal Palace at Berlin that are here awakened. Yet as a building the Palace at Versailles does not produce the imposing impression our " New Palace " evokes, even though the latter lacks the unique beauty of the great terrace and the vast extent of the edifice.

No fresh news from the outposts, except the arrival of an intermediary to discuss terms, who brought with him letters for His Majesty and Count Bismarck; he belonged to the General Staff, and seems to have looked extremely low-spirited. The gist of letters captured coming from the Parisians is indignation at our demands and bellicose vapouring; at the same time a certain depression of spirit is hinted at and anxiety at the prospect of hunger and high prices. Another trouble that worries most French heads is the conviction that a civil war will not be long in coming, and every sort of pillage occur, once our soldiers have quitted the places they now occupy.

Prince Adalbert arrived. I put him up as well as might be in one of the few salons left unoccupied in my house, to get him at all costs out of the odious quarters that had been assigned him in a gloomy neighbouring street.

General von Hindersin and General von Kleist are at present inspecting our positions, so as to have the ground reconnoitred in view of firing from Paris—this in case of our blockading the place. The former wanted to call for volunteers and capture Mont Valérien by a night attack. I think he will change his mind altogether, once he has examined this magnificently situated work a little more carefully and viewed it quietly at close quarters.

The European Cabinets appear to have received hints of a well-organized system of affiliated branches of the Social Democratic party, and one and all to be in a great quandary about it. The otherwise unaccountable arrest of Jakoby at Königsberg [1] might possibly be connected with this.

[1] This occurred on September 20th in consequence of a speech delivered at Königsberg on the 14th by the Deputy Johann Jakoby, in which he inveighed against the annexation of Alsace and Lorraine.

THE EMPEROR FREDERICK III. 137

Otherwise nothing intelligible is to be made out of the existing state of affairs, each piece of news contradicting another. There is great talk of attempts at opening negotiations on the part of all parties in activity in France; but the outstanding difficulty for us still remains, to find an authority at present possessing a recognized, established and secured position with which to negotiate.

We are so many at table we are obliged to use the great reception-rooms of the Préfecture for the daily meals; this for mere outside observers gives it a look as if we were every day indulging in brilliant festivities, an impression enhanced by the glitter of the serried masses of wax candles.

In the afternoon I rode out to the outer posts at Saint-Cloud; I was last here in the year 1867 to see the little Prince Imperial, and later again on a drive with the Empress Eugénie through the pretty park; my wife had stayed at the château in 1855 on her first visit to the Continent, and to-day it lay there within the chain of Prussian outposts, and is the pet target of kind enemy marksmen, who instantly open fire from the houses opposite if so much as a head appears. One can no longer cross the courtyard of the Palace at all, as this is forthwith raked by a cross-fire. Should it come to a bombardment of Paris, the French would themselves end by destroying the building, as it lies directly in their line of fire.

Colonel von Bothmer, whose brigade is at present on outpost duty, was unwilling for this reason to let me go any nearer to the château; but I contrived, by creeping up under shelter of the dense clumps of laurel and taking further advantage of the orange trees in the garden, to get myself and my attendants into the château so completely hidden that nobody had an inkling of our being there. From the noble Gallery decorated by Mignard the painter in the Louis XIV taste, now arranged as a hospital, standing behind the lowered jalousies, we enjoyed the view over Paris, which lay directly at our feet, and afterwards strolled through the rooms, already stripped of their costly embellishments. A patrol of the 38th Infantry Regiment had just entered the building from the garden front as I was examining the great oil painting that hangs on the wall of the staircase and represents the moment of arrival of my mother-in-law, Queen Victoria, at Saint-Cloud in the year 1855. I explained to my people who the chief personages in the picture were; it struck two of them as quite incredible for my wife to be portrayed there; the third, however, was more sagacious, and made out from this circumstance that I was his Commander-in-Chief! By way of a joke I next took the three men with me to show them Napoleon's apartments; this was a piece of fun for them, and gave opportunity for some naïve speeches about the originator of the whole War. On the Council table, at which the decision to declare war was taken, lay nothing but pictures of the Prussian Army. The Library was filled with books, but nowhere were traces to be seen of the living-rooms having been abandoned suddenly and without preparation, except that a small table held a hint in little work-baskets and invitation cards, beginning "Impératrice Régente," which still lay on the writing-desk of the chamberlain on duty. The interior equipment of the private rooms of both their Majesties was no less charming than luxurious, and perfectly new; but articles of value, except for sundry timepieces, there were none remaining but two marble busts of Napoleon I, and another of the Empress Eugénie. Hardly had we left the château before a lively musketry fire began. Inasmuch as we slipped away by the same route we had come by, no marksman could possibly see us, so it must certainly have been some domestic or other had made a treacherous signal.

Headquarters : Versailles, 28th September.—An early morning ride in warm autumn weather through the noble avenues of the park of Versailles is a true pleasure, enhanced to-day by the fact that just at starting came the news that Strasburg had capitulated. These tidings I communicated to everybody in the streets, to the troops drilling or otherwise engaged, and everywhere cheers of jubilation broke out. The capitulation of Strasburg is a specially important success, which my old friend, Lieutenant-General von Werder, has won, thank God! without great losses, so far as we know at present. We are now in possession of the capital of Alsace, and need no longer include its surrender among possible conditions of peace. The troops hitherto employed on the siege operations, together with the siege material, we can bring to Paris, while the rich war booty will eventually contribute directly to the defence of our country against France; even the prisoners—inhuman as it seems—might be utilized for the reversing of the lines of front. With such a "place d'armes" in our hands, another and a stronger language may be used with the French, as I immediately wrote to the King to suggest. I also directed stringent orders to be instantly given that all measures should be taken in hand for the repair of the Minster, the restoration of the ruined churches, the Library and such like edifices.

We must, in fact—so I consider—give immediate proof that we intend to make good again the damage that, alas! is inevitable in war. In such wise are moral conquests made. Our officials, of course, sitting round the green cloth will raise a thousand new points for consideration, and so let precious time slip by, but I will at least do my very best to "put fire under," so that Strasburg may have real help given her. I am overjoyed at the recovery of this German city, which I pray heaven will now for ever remain German, and where, with God's good help, we shall know how to awaken true German sentiments of mind and soul, and the inhabitants come to realize that in the old, ancestral Fatherland better conditions prevail than in an alien land.

In the afternoon I rode to Bougival on the Seine, to see near at hand this charming part of the river valley, now occupied by our outposts, and watched the sunset from the noble terrace of Saint-Germain-en-Laye, the place of all others I best like to visit in this neighbourhood. Only it means some trouble to get quickly to one's journey's end, as everywhere on the main arteries of traffic barriers of felled trees and pitfalls have been constructed, the removal of which can only be effected with the greatest delay.

His Majesty finds Ferrières tedious, and seems to wish to remove the Royal headquarters to this neighbourhood. I would vote for Saint-Germain, as neither in the Palace here nor at the Trianons can room be made for so many men, and least of all for the horses.

Duke Ernst of Saxe-Coburg is no less bored. The Duke's society always affords me peculiar pleasure, especially under present circumstances, when his heart, that beats so warmly for Germany, is jubilant, and it is a lesson to me to discuss with him his ideas on the reorganization of the Fatherland.

Headquarters: Versailles, 29th September.—In the middle of the night came an advice by telegraph from the Bavarian General von Hartmann that an enemy attack was suspected. All needful preparations were made accordingly, the troops held ready to march off, and waiting; but it came to nothing, and after a long pause everybody returned to quarters.

The officers of my Dragoon regiment, the 2nd Silesian Dragoon regiment No. 8, came to breakfast with me, and as I had taken with me in the field no uniform but my undress outfit as a General, I borrowed Major von Ploetz's (my aide-de-camp in 1866) coat, which fitted me capitally. Again we took advantage of the splendid, hot autumn day for a ride in the park.

Fifteen years ago to-day was my betrothal at Balmoral!

From Paris we hear that the Reds are instituting a reign of terror, and are so eager for the continuance of the War for their own selfish ends that even honourable, peace-loving men, as, for instance, Jules Favre, can make no headway against it.

It is pretty certain His Majesty means to leave Ferrières and will likewise remove his headquarters to Versailles; in that case I shall vacate the Préfecture and occupy Les Ombrages instead, a pretty *cottage orné*, one of several houses standing in a large garden, where it is delightfully quiet and my whole executive Staff can be lodged in immediate proximity.

Headquarters: Versailles, 30th September, and Royal Headquarters, Ferrières.—In order to keep my mother's birthday to-day with my father at Ferrières, I left Versailles as early as five in the morning and enjoyed a glorious sunrise. Hardly had I reached Chatenay before we heard in the direction of Villejuif a lively fire of cannon and small-arms, the noise of which sounded so near I determined to go at once to the Bavarian Lieutenant-General von Hartmann, in quarters at this very place, to learn news of the engagement, and in any case to remain near at hand. After some waiting came the information from the observatory at Sceaux that the French had made a vigorous sortie, supported by their heavy guns from the forts, that our VIth Army Corps was engaged and the Bavarian troops likewise warned for action; but soon after it was reported that the French had again fallen back. I then proceeded at once to the VIth Army Corps to convince myself on the spot of the progress of the fight, and on the way noted how the action was by no means at an end, but was still being vigorously contested round the villages of Chevilly, Thiais and L'Hay. These places lie on the open plain before the forts of Montrouge, Bicêtre and Ivry, quite close, therefore, to the newly-built work at Villejuif, which will certainly give us many a battle yet. The musketry fire was very lively, while shells were bursting in numbers in the air. Major-General von Barneckow, 4th Cavalry Brigade, met me in great excitement, and announced he was hurrying to bring up the available regiment of his brigade, as it was reported by the IInd Army Corps that the Württemberg bridge of boats was still secure indeed, but stray bodies of cavalry were coming in sight. From this I gathered that the XIth Army Corps must be heavily engaged, the more

Villa "Les Ombrages," at Versailles, Residence of the Crown Prince.

so as units whom I questioned on the way spoke of engagements that had already lasted from earliest daybreak. When I came in touch with my escort, supplied by my Dragoon regiment, I made them give me a Dragoon charger, mounted and hurried off to General von Tümpling, passing the 12th Division standing by for action; this though the order had just been received from the General that they should go on quietly with drill—which sounded strange enough in view of an engagement surely worth notice. I found the General halted at Villeneuve-le-Roi near Thiais. An attack by the French on Chevilly had just been delivered, which the 24th Infantry Brigade, Major-General von Fabeck, supported by the Ist Silesian Grenadier regiment No. 10, vigorously repulsed, putting the enemy in full retreat; regiments Nos. 22, 23, 62 and 63, together with the Silesian Jägers No. 6, as well as the Corps Artillery, had taken part in the action, the last-named with conspicuous gallantry; the losses, not yet, of course, to be exactly gauged, were supposed to be trifling, whereas the enemy had left many dead behind, while several hundred prisoners had already been reported. I waited some time for the reports from different points of the scene of action, but was obliged to give up the idea of visiting the whole of the battle-field, as I had still a considerable distance to go. Of the VIth Army Corps only two brigades, and those never once with all their battalions, had been engaged; on the French side some ten battalions seem to have been counted. For all the thunderous noise of the firing, that lasted from five to nine o'clock, the engagement was only to be called a comparatively simple one, though it is true it lasted longer than the last sorties. The VIth Army Corps is delighted to have found itself in action at last. Of the XIth Army Corps and of their having been engaged in a fierce encounter nothing was known. Later on I came across Lieutenant-General von Schachtmeyer near his headquarters, and learned that he had indeed ordered the XIth Army Corps to stand by for action, but it had only come to an artillery duel with some detached columns of the enemy on the march from the Charenton neighbourhood, which very soon after had retired on Vincennes or Saint-Maur and back to Paris.

One can see by to-day's doings how necessary it is to deal with reports with all the cool deliberation possible, since these as a rule bear quite a different complexion from that presented by the reality, for the persons bringing the information, especially if they were eye-witnesses, are only too apt in the first excitement to make more of things than they merit. So it was to-day with General von Barneckow, who was only in the second line and a mere onlooker, and yet spoke in his report to me as if a sortie on an enormous scale had been made from Paris in which the XIth Army Corps had already suffered important losses, whereas not a man there had come into action.

There had indeed been a sortie against the Vth Army Corps in the neighbourhood of Meudon and Sèvres, but only by three battalions, and this had been forthwith repulsed. Thus at almost all points my Army has been busy and kept in breathing, as in fact must always be the case in sieges and will be repeated many a time yet before Paris. For the troops this sort of thing is all to the good, as it saves them from going to sleep serving all day long in cantonments.

At Ferrières we dined in full dress and wearing decorations, which means a great deal with His Majesty, who never wears anything but the great-coat. The Crown Prince and Prince Georg of Saxony were there.

With Count Bismarck I had several intimate conversations; favourable news had just come regarding the discussions between the Minister Delbrück and the Munich and Stuttgart Cabinets. I see from these reports that German interests, to Bismarck's surprise even, especially in Bavaria, are making gratifying progress; the general temper there and in the neighbouring States could not for the moment be better; thank God, this time we are not missing the opportunity of taking advantage of existing circumstances.

To-day I talked over the Imperial question with His Majesty, pointing out to him how it was becoming evident that this was now come to a head; but he replied that he did not look upon this possibility as so much as in sight. To this I answered it was now nearer than ever, and he must make up his mind shortly to see steps taken that would make any talk of refusal impossible. The King displayed much indifference towards the matter, though his attitude was not one of unconditional rejection. As his feeling was opposed to the whole scheme, it was some time before little by little he grew more reconciled to the idea; yet later on again he was for evading the issue, referring to the contents, shortly before come to his knowledge, of the inaugural address of the newly-appointed Rector of the Berlin University, Professor du Bois-Reymond, in which the latter maintains that " Imperialism " is over and done with, and in future there can be in Germany only a King of Prussia and " Duke of the Germans." I then sought to prove to him that already the mere existence of the three

THE EMPEROR FREDERICK III. 143

Princes—in Saxony, Bavaria and Württemberg—made into Kings by Napoleon I compelled us to assert our supremacy over them by the assumption of the title of Emperor, yet further that the ancient Imperial or Royal crown of Germany, over a thousand years old, and only in abeyance since the year 1806 by the abdication of the Emperor Francis, had still nothing whatever to do with the purely and entirely modern Imperial crown of Austria or France.

In the end it struck me his opposition had grown weaker, unless perhaps a long-existent and just conception of the situation had been forced to give way before a momentary effervescence of feeling.

His Majesty did not appear in the evening in consequence of a slight indisposition.

Headquarters: Versailles, 1st October.—Yesterday's engagement, to be known as the battle of Chevilly, has still cost us over a hundred men as well as several officers. The losses of the French are so considerable that they have asked for a truce to bury the dead and remove the wounded to the rear. The great number of these drew from the French on the spot expressions of evident surprise, while many of them gave repeated utterance to the depressing thought that ever new actions, to which by this time their troops of the line found no sort of inclination, must inevitably follow. In fact, officers frequently told Dr. Boeger and Dr. Wilms that almost all troops of the line had already been used up, and the defenders therefore saw themselves thrown back upon the men under arms in Paris, who were in no condition to meet any regular soldiers, let alone our Prussian Army; hence they looked upon their position as desperate. The brigade recalled from Rome appears to have fought us with great gallantry; the general retirement, on the contrary, was accomplished in much disorder. I am persuaded yesterday's engagement will give the French food for reflection. There was actually found on the corpse of a General who had fallen the plan of action for the day. Chevilly was to be taken and an advance pushed forward to our pontoon bridges to destroy these or else occupy them. Nothing of all this came about, every advantage, on the contrary, remaining with us. But I verily believe, such arrant liars are the French, they will find a way to picture yesterday as another victory and celebrate it as such.

Headquarters: Versailles, 2nd October.—To-day, Sunday, field service in the open air, the same as a week ago, only the Minister had brought no altar with him and did not wear his robes.

I visited the Hospital in the Palace and in the afternoon rode to an Observatory situated above Bougival. From here again one has a superb view over Paris, La Malmaison lying immediately below one's feet, and enjoyed a noble prospect over the valley of the Seine as far as Saint-Germain-en-Laye. Directly opposite this Observatory lies Mont Valérien, which with its heavy Naval guns can throw a shell as far as here, and thanks to a large telescope unearthed in one of the neighbouring villas can be quite minutely observed; everything that occurs there is faithfully recorded in a book kept for the purpose.

On the way back, which took us through whole woods of chestnuts and past countless delightful villas, we rode by the supports of the same outposts we had just visited. Their bivouac is quite close to a kiosk, the fittings of which were presented by the Sultan Abdul Aziz to the Empress Eugénie, and over which the figure of a pigmy imp keeps guard. Our people here make a regular feast on the countless edible chestnuts, now just fully ripe. The whole place appears to have been only quite recently given to the Empress and to have been destined by her as a sort of model holiday resort.

My mother-in-law,[1] who follows our achievements with touching sympathy, has telegraphed to His Majesty to exhort him, in view of Jules Favre's efforts for peace, to display magnanimity in his negotiations and decisions, but without finding any practical means whatever to recommend. I am of the opinion that we ought certainly to act towards the vanquished in the high-minded spirit that is consonant with our honour; still England should not for her part forget how, on the conclusion of the Crimean War, she imposed conditions on vanquished Russia with the object of checking that country's growing influence in the East—conditions which to this day the latter finds hard to bear and seeks to shake off at every opportunity that offers. If then the neutrals so ardently desire peace, why do they not support our demands so persistently that France must realize that help is nowhere to be found for a defeated foe?

Headquarters: Versailles, 3rd October.—I inspected regiments of the 5th and 6th Cavalry Division (von Rheinbaben and Duke Wilhelm of Mecklenburg-Schwerin) on the parade-

[1] See also Queen Victoria's letter of the 18th December, Appendix, p. 341.

THE EMPEROR FREDERICK III. 145

ground at Satonay and was greatly affected to see these gallant fellows whose lot it was, in true cavalry style, to fight so brilliantly at Mars-la-Tour on the 16th August and sacrifice themselves so ungrudgingly. The regiments, in whose ranks I saw the Hanoverian Uhlans and the Brunswick Hussar regiments practically for the first time, made a very excellent impression.

The American General Burnside and a Colonel Forbes who was with him some days ago, who had, at their own request, been sent forward right up to the line of French outposts—not without difficulties for us—arrived back again to-day at my headquarters. Both express themselves very outspokenly, and will have it that General von Blumenthal as well as myself are under the impression these Americans are speaking not without the authority of the present rulers of Paris. The gist of their communications comes to this, that the desire for a peace not inflicting too shameful conditions on France is universal, yet that cessions of territory are still regarded as unacceptable. Jules Favre, on the contrary, has assured them he saw plainly how France, beaten once for all, must reconcile herself to the loss of Alsace, but that the present Government cannot act of its own free will in the matter, because to agree to our demands would mean as its immediate consequence their own dismissal from office. That hence the convocation of a Constituent Assembly was highly desirable because, the wish for peace having once found expression in it, and that in the name of the people, this might lend support to the Government. Our demand for the abandonment of Mont Valérien as a preliminary to the granting of an armistice they thought was really asking too much, but that the surrender of other forts might possibly be entertained as an alternative. When I made the observation that we had seen well to put no obstacles whatever in the way of the elections carried out on the 2nd October, the Americans seemed surprised. They said further that, once the armistice was ratified, not another shot, speaking generally, would be fired, but peace would very quickly follow in its train. But that, supposing a peace were not soon concluded, the country was face to face with a state of chaos that was equivalent to the ruin of France. Paris, they said, at present looked perfectly peaceful; outwardly at least no traces had come to light in the capital of any overpowering influence of the Reds on the course of events. The news of the fall of Toul and above all of Strasburg was not yet known in Paris, but men's minds were fully prepared for these catastrophes. On the other hand,

Paris papers glorify the Chevilly engagement as a victory, though at any rate they admit the heavy losses suffered. I must confess that the interview with the two Americans, one of whom, General Burnside, looks a sagacious and able man, especially as it was carried forward without formality and during lunch at my quarters, did not give me the impression that the pair had any wish to give themselves the appearance of being special envoys, albeit they offered to undertake further negotiations with a view to peace.

In the afternoon I took a look at Saint-Cyr, which I had first visited in the year 1866. Now Hanoverian Uhlans and wounded are lodged there. It pleased me to see the names of cadets who had attained the ranks of Marshal of France or held the highest posts as Generals commemorated on stone tablets.

To-day we shifted over to Les Ombrages; I appreciate the comfort of the country quiet, especially as my rooms are furnished in the English fashion.

The Empress Eugénie seems to have made a romantic escape from Paris till the moment when she landed in England; I am sorry for her, for all she was chiefly to blame for the War. But how strangely alike are the circumstances attending the expulsion of all the dynasties that have ruled France in the last hundred years!

Headquarters: Versailles, 4th October.—To-day I have had captured "chassepôts" served out to the outposts, so that our men may turn and turn about, and as required, use their own or the French weapon, which carries farther.

An early morning ride and a view of the sunset from the terrace at Saint-Germain in the evening gave me true pleasure.

Major Schulz of the 47th Infantry regiment, convalescent after his wounds, brought me letters from my wife to-day. Alas! I learn from these that Major-General von Grüter, Commander of the 14th Cavalry Brigade, and Major-General von Stülpnagel of the 1st regiment of Foot Guards have succumbed to their wounds. There is no end to the death lists, so that it is only with a trembling hand I take up the newspapers. My little lad Waldemar seems to be sickly nowadays, a thing I have never hitherto been used to with him.

Headquarters: Versailles, 5th October.—To-day His Majesty with the whole, enormous Royal headquarters arrived here. I had meant to go and meet them, but just as I got near Chatenay I heard the fire of guns and musketry; I called a halt, therefore, and, just as on the 30th September, went off to Lieutenant-General von Hartmann and there waited for news. However, it seems to have been nothing of importance, a mere matter of scattered firing rather than a regular engagement; on this occasion gunboats came into action against us on the river for the first time.

I waited to receive His Majesty on the pontoon bridge at Villeneuve, and as I had ordered all the troops lying in cantonments near the thoroughfare to turn out, the King was able to inspect a good part of the XIth, then of the VIth and after that of the IInd Bavarian Army Corps. At General von Tümpling's quarters a snack was eaten, after which I paraded my Dragoon regiment before His Majesty, and then, after some of the fortified positions held by the VIth Army Corps had been visited in blazing heat and choking dust, all went on to Versailles, which we reached at sunset. The whole town was in the streets and stared abashed at the sight, as the King, after an official reception, entered the place amid the cheers of the soldiery, and established his headquarters in the Préfecture. The vehicle carrying the Royal cooking apparatus having broken down on the road, I was able to give a meal to His Majesty and some of his company.

The mass of conveyances the Royal train requires is beyond belief, as Count Bismarck, General von Moltke, War Minister von Roon, as well as the Inspectors of Artillery and of the Pioneers, together with their bureaux, all belong to it, and even Councillor Schneider and Police Commissioner Stieber have their special carriages—not to forget Prince Karl and Prince Adalbert, as also the Grand Duke of Saxe-Weimar and Prince Luitpold of Bavaria! The latter not only brought with him a carriage of his own, but had likewise to be provided with Royal means of locomotion. How hard it is to marshal such a column in order may be gathered from the fact that, so as not to draw the enemy's attention, I had issued orders that no carriage was to use the high-road by way of La-Belle-Épine; yet right before my eyes Prince Karl gave directions to take that very route and actually drove along the forbidden road.

With regard to the hospital establishments on the Rhine and at Frankfort-on-the-Main, to which my wife devotes especial attention, I hear these spoken of with grateful appreciation. It gives me infinite pleasure to hear in all quarters repeated expressions of the high respect my wife's quiet but strong and efficient activity evokes. In Homburg she has created a perfect model hospital, which it is to be hoped will soon find imitations. I communicated to His Majesty much of what I had learned, but without hearing one word of commendation in reply.

6th October, 1870.—I presented the Iron Cross to a musketeer of the 22nd Infantry regiment who had had a limb amputated, whereat he was so touched and so overjoyed I had to pull myself together not to show the man how deeply I was moved.

To-day, for the first time since we have occupied the town and Palace, the " Grandes Eaux de Versailles " played —by His Majesty's express orders, in fact. The King went on foot, and to the extreme amazement of the French public, strolled about among the crowd without taking any harm; the latter consisted of numerous natives as well as Prussian soldiers and slightly wounded men; before that, he had visited the Hospital and a portion of the Gallery of historical pictures.

Yesterday the Greek Embassy and the Russian Military Plenipotentiary, Prince Peter Wittgenstein, left Paris, but they had to wait for hours between the two lines of outposts before permission to cross ours could be granted. To judge by what individual members say, Paris is provisioned for another two months, but sundry remarks dropped in strict confidence indicate that the scarcity of food now beginning to be felt contributed to facilitate the obtaining of their passes, for otherwise not a soul is allowed out. But now, supposing hunger eventually opens the gates of Paris, what are we to do, who of ourselves add many hundred thousand mouths to those million and a half starving creatures?

Thiers raised the question of setting King Leopold of Belgium on the French throne, but Count Bismarck regards the notion as stillborn. The latter told me also how it grieved him to see no more accommodating temper on the part of England; people there seemed wilfully to ignore the fact that in the future German help is bound to be looked for. Austria remains lukewarm, but yet seems willing to keep quiet; General Burnside and Colonel Forbes are to be allowed to return to Paris within the next few days, for Count Bismarck is quite ready to make use of suchlike private go-betweens, who indeed, while rendering services to Germany, at the same time are equally ready to afford help in the American sense to the young French Republic. They are, it seems, actually to be employed as negotiators.

Not without difficulty I have succeeded in obtaining permission from the King himself to instruct Lieutenant-

General von der Tann to leave Longjumeau forthwith and march on Étampes, but after that to push on to the Loire for the purpose of reconnoitring that section. I am giving him, in addition to his Army Corps and his 105 guns, the Cavalry Divisions Prince Albrecht and Count Stolberg, while the 6th Cavalry Division acting on his right rearward flank keeps an eye on Chartres or sweeps the neighbourhood clear.

Headquarters : Versailles, 7th October.—It seems as though these three glorious, hot, sunny weeks are at an end and inclement autumn weather is warning us of its coming.

So for one more hurried early morning ride in the park and then to accompany His Majesty to Saint-Germain, where the view was still to be enjoyed in all its magnificence. At the moment we left the carriages, Mont Valérien suddenly opened an extremely hot fire for almost half an hour in the direction of Bougival–La Malmaison, just as if they were for showing the King how to do things. Shells were bursting and even set fire to a building at La Malmaison. We breakfasted meantime in the Pavilion where Louis XIV was born, and afterwards surveyed the grand old Castle, together with the Museum of Antiquities, which is rich in models of old Roman camps and siege apparatus. Napoleon III took advantage of the compilation of his *Julius Cæsar*[1] to promote the objects of this Museum, and has really equipped it very learnedly.

Unlike himself, General von der Tann hesitates about moving forward, making me send him the peremptory order, "At sight" to march on Orleans!

I received within the last few days a poem Dr. Strauss has written on me and a letter from Ernest Renan from Paris, who, appealing to our acquaintanceship of the year 1867, asks for a safe-conduct through our outposts and an interview with me to discuss the situation of his afflicted country. Reports are current that Gambetta has escaped from Paris in a balloon.[2]

Hopes of peace, though of a very general sort, are in the air, and it would be well for the elections to the Constituent Assembly to be carried out, for such a body can more easily conclude a peace than the present rulers, who have absolutely no legal basis. People in Paris seem to desire this Assembly, while influential individuals there have given utterance to their conviction that without the cession of Alsace no progress

[1] *Histoire de Jules César*, Paris, 1865/66, 2 vols.
[2] This actually occurred on the 7th October.

can be made with us. May these aspirations soon find realization!

Headquarters : Versailles, 8th October.—Yesterday a fierce engagement was fought at Metz; Marshal MacMahon made a strong sortie, but the French were repulsed with considerable losses. Bazaine's sorties begin to strike me as strange, having regard to their uselessness; at the same time I firmly believe that, though long ago convinced of the impossibility of winning a battle, he desires for his part to keep his men employed as a matter of military prestige,—but possibly, again, he purposely incurs these losses in order to diminish the total of the Metz garrison in view of the increasing scarcity of provisions. The latter supposition I think probable in a man of his character, in fact, quite accordant with it, especially as the French, speaking generally, make light of the sacrifice of their men's lives.

We shall certainly have to make up our minds to a bombardment of Paris, possibly leading to a siege. In my view it is wise to make thorough and adequate preparations for both eventualities, but to postpone as long as possible their actual accomplishment, for I count definitely on starving out the city. This course must inevitably deliver Paris into our hands without any fighting, and we might in this way spare the sacrifice of many thousands of lives.

Within the next few days I look for engagements to be fought between here and Orleans.

We have been much entertained by a Belgian *canard*, repeated in many English papers, according to which I and my whole headquarters with many thousands more have been taken prisoners. The wife of the correspondent of the *Daily News*, Mr. Skinner, has written to ask her husband in all seriousness if this is true or not. The French system of lying prevails to such a degree here that even the English people living at Versailles every day tell Colonel Walker about constant defeats of the Prussians, in which they firmly believe.

To-day the first wet day; a brief clearer interval I utilized for a ride in the " Charmilles " and avenues of the Grand Trianon; the trees are still in leaf, the flower-beds are in full beauty, and at the Orangery the scent of orange blossom fills the air far and wide.

Headquarters : Versailles, 9th October.—To-day, Sunday, divine service for the first time for us Evangelicals in the great Chapel of the Palace! Through an error in the notice His Majesty did not appear, so I with my train of Princes, the officers on my Staff, those of the garrison, along with the

Evangelical portion of the latter, were alone present. The soldiers entirely filled the church, which looked very fine, and the singing sounded superb; strangely enough the Catholic clergy had raised no difficulties about giving up God's house to us heretics to use in God's service.

His Majesty dined at my quarters. The persistent wet weather is harassing our outposts; however, we are making use of captured French tents and are building hutments.

Headquarters: Versailles, 10th October.—To-day it was decided by His Majesty and his advisers that the siege of Paris was to begin. To me are entrusted the preliminaries and carrying out of the operations on the south side of the city. Major-General Schulz as Engineer-in-Chief, Lieutenant-General Herkt with Colonel von Rieff as gunnery experts, are to take the necessary works in hand.

So Garibaldi has actually arrived in Tours; at least the Government there announce the fact. I am truly sorry that the old hero, instead of resting content with his earlier successes and enjoying a peaceful old age in Caprera, is guilty of the folly of lending his name to a senseless struggle. He is for backing up the Republic, which in France itself finds little support, and will only be the cause of unnecessary bloodshed; though he has always proved himself a gallant fighter, he was never a man of great political sagacity and will here again find his enterprise end in a pitiful fiasco.

Gambetta seems really to have escaped from Paris in a balloon.

No doubt the capital will be able to hold out for several weeks with the supplies it has, but longer than that a town of a million and a half inhabitants could scarcely endure this state of isolation; at the same time it is true the Parisians are displaying a tough obstinacy such as would never have been deemed possible by the many sagacious observers there, themselves not lacking in that quality. But, as a matter of fact, the deluded leaders now refusing to take any serious thought or listen to any sober counsel, the whole thing defies calculation. The like might be said of Metz, though I believe myself that scarcity has begun there too.

In Paris folks would seem to be counting on the appearance of a deliverer; whether by this they mean Garibaldi or an Orleans Prince I cannot tell. Actual armies really deserving that name are not reasonably to be counted on, while on the franc-tireurs not much dependence can be placed.

Headquarters: Versailles, 11th October.—To-day proved

rich in news of victories. Yesterday General von der Tann fought a very pretty and successful engagement to the south of Étampes at Artenay, directly on the line to Orleans, in which a thousand unwounded and over five hundred wounded prisoners were taken and the Cavalry Division Prince Albrecht played a distinguished part. The 2nd Body Hussars and another Cavalry regiment, as also a body of Bavarian Jägers, captured a gun each; so General von der Tann is setting out on his march on Orleans under very favourable auspices. Among the prisoners are found lads of sixteen and seventeen, who howled as they were being brought in; indeed pressed men of the sort are to be seen in the ranks of the line regiments as well as among the franc-tireurs. It makes one's heart ache!

Duke Friedrich zu Schleswig-Holstein had on the very first day of the march joined General von der Tann to take a part in his enterprises; but as that day it did not come to any fighting, he concluded that no serious hostile resistance at all was to be expected—and simply went back again. Directly on his arrival at Versailles, he learned, to his no slight vexation, the news of the victory of Artenay, and is now balked of all participation in the very probable storming of Orleans. Poor devil, he was born surely under an unlucky star!

The French are now firing shell, and with quite heavy guns, on the Palace of Saint-Cloud, several having already penetrated Napoleon's bed-chamber and set it alight. What a pity if the shooting as it goes on should cause the destruction of really important buildings!

The condition of the wounded in the hospitals here continues favourable; so far only a few men badly hit have died. Unfortunately a young Dutch doctor has succumbed to blood poisoning; he belonged to a Netherlands Society for the Care of the Wounded, already installed here before our coming, under the leadership of a Heer van der Velde. Dr. Wegner is very energetic and is highly spoken of by Dr. Boeger. Luckily great weight is attached to all possible ventilation and the proper spacing of the patients' beds at wide intervals. The purification of the atmosphere unfortunately is difficult from the fact that all rooms in the Palace have openings only on one side. The doctors would not allow me in the Lycée, as typhus is rife there.

Waldemar, who was getting better, has had a relapse.

Count Bismarck dined at my quarters to-day, and told me how Comte Chambord as well as Ollivier had written to the King. The former would fain give effect to the call of

" his people," but will consent to no surrender of territory; the latter admits having advised the War, but warns the King against demanding territorial concessions! Both letters I read this evening; the gist of both is to dissuade His Majesty from demanding the annexation of Alsace. Really an original enterprise in both cases at the present moment! The one has no power and no opportunity to do anything, the other, on the contrary, is responsible for all the mischief; yet both presume to give advice to his victor.

Headquarters : Versailles, 12th October.—Yesterday Lieutenant-General von der Tann fought for nearly seven hours at Orleans; finally, late in the evening, the town was taken and at once occupied! Thus with three Divisions of Infantry and two of Cavalry we have got possession of the passage of the Loire and by the same blow dispersed the Army of the Loire in course of formation. First Lieutenant von Bissing and Major von Hahnke, whom I had despatched to General von der Tann, arrived towards nightfall from Orleans with the momentous news of the victory just as I reached His Majesty's quarters to take tea, so that the two were able there and then, scalding-hot, to announce the latest news before the assembled Royal circle.

Our loss would seem to be comparatively trifling, the enemy's, on the contrary, very considerable; 2,400 prisoners fell into our hands. The 83rd again fought excellently along with the 32nd, and had to encounter an enemy that in the beginning put up a brave defence, and included troops of the line, Turkos and Zouaves; but they could make no stand against the German attack. Our artillery again, as always, behaved splendidly, whilst the Bavarian did very good work. The Bavarian Infantry fought very well, when they were in close touch with ours. How far from ready was the enemy in his preparations for action was shown, for instance, by the fact that Turkos had been incorporated in the ranks of the franc-tireurs to give the latter more stability; moreover, units from quite a score of different regiments had been brought into line. The success gained is of great importance, as Paris was under the belief they could count on this Army still in the making and hoped to be saved by its help from being absolutely starved out. Now this force will not so soon be in a condition to take the field again, and as we already hear talk of the first signs of scarcity, the final catastrophe might easily be precipitated by the moral effect of this fresh defeat.

Herr von Bethmann Hollweg brought me news from home, but no better tidings yet of Waldemar.

Headquarters : Versailles, 13th October.—I rode to the outposts by the Empress's kiosk, where the supports lie behind entrenchments, and one can conveniently keep Mont Valérien under observation at a distance of some 7,000 paces. To reconnoitre the fortress I took my stand close to a non-commissioned officer, a Berlin architect, behind an old chestnut tree, as no one dare show himself without fire being instantly opened on the place. But once in a way for a change not a shot was fired—at any rate as long as I was there.

On the other hand, news came next moment from the flanking outposts that the Palace of Saint-Cloud was in flames; of the truth of this, alas! I convinced myself when I rode to the look-out post above Garches, and from there saw the great pillars of smoke rolling up. What a pity, and what vandalism of the French to set such a building blazing with their fire! Of course our enemies will immediately proclaim that we had purposely caused the conflagration. It is to be hoped that at least the wing with the Gallery and its splendid painted ceilings of the time of Louis XIV may be saved.[1]

The Bavarians fought an action to-day at Châtillon, the details of which I am not clear about; at first they must have lost ground, but later on, though not without a hard fight, drove back the enemy, who shot with nicked (dum-dum) bullets. The prisoners taken on this occasion declared that for several days now they had had horseflesh to eat.

Every day now members of the Diplomatic Legations still left in Paris are asking permission to leave the city. The Spaniards have their pass already; to-day the Papal Nuncio, Monseigneur Chigi, applies for a safe-conduct through the outposts. This certainly seems to show that life in the place is beginning to have its disagreeables. From Lyons we hear how serious discontent is felt there with the Paris Government, and people sincerely desirous of peace are angry that the stubbornness of the men in power continues to saddle the country with the burden of War. Similar expressions in favour of peace greeted our men again and again on the march to Orleans, where the inhabitants very sensibly maintained that the Army of the Loire, just defeated by us, could no longer offer any serious resistance. Right and true as all this is, I am still afraid nothing will ever teach the deluded, pig-headed Parisians, and that they prefer to wait for famine to come. May this spare us the necessity of a regular siege. Among the working classes great excitement seems to prevail; it is true that so far repeated demonstrations have always been satisfactorily pacified, still we may fairly

---

[1] But see below under the 14th October.

conclude from it all that danger is everywhere brewing within the walls of the capital.

To-day we are expecting a French officer from Metz; in a few days two intermediaries should arrive from the South.

The Americans, General Burnside and Colonel Forbes, came back again from Paris on the 10th. They speak with contempt, nay, with disgust, of the members of the Provisional Government, for one thing because these men act without any reasonable policy and listen to no advice that does not suit their own book, and further because, having no systematic plans to justify their wish to continue the War, they persist in doing so simply to keep themselves in power. The Americans are resolved not to return to the capital again, as the Paris Government refuses all offers to open the way for peace negotiations, and as nothing whatever, in fact, can be done with these besotted fools, who, they declared, had no trace at all of real Republicanism about them. All this was to be communicated confidentially to America.

General Bourbaki's mysterious mission to England appears to have had an arrangement with the Empress Eugénie as its object; but as to any result, nothing tangible is divulged. She seems to have received him badly, but some time later, in consequence of the reproaches which Napoleon addressed to her in writing on the subject, to have announced her willingness to resign her plenary powers as Regent in favour of Bazaine, that he, instead of her, should conclude peace on the terms we demand.

Marshal Bazaine, who, like General Bourbaki, seems to be regarded by the Guards and a part of the other troops as the representative of Bonapartism, wishes to send his Chief of Staff here, not at all with a view to capitulation, but for the sake of military-political negotiations. Count Bismarck is willing indeed to hear what the intermediary in question has to say, but still without any inclination to agree to his offers. The Generals on the Royal War Council wish Marshal Bazaine to act only on the basis of the Sedan Convention, that no interference is to be allowed, and therefore no intermediary to be received here provisionally. They were afraid lest such an emissary would, in Napoleon's interest, demand that the garrison be suffered to march out of Metz, to the end Bazaine with their help might restore the Imperial authority in Paris, and then,—as it must evidently be much to our advantage in any case to see the re-establishment of a legal régime,—of course in conjunction with the German troops, be in a position to conclude peace. Generals von Moltke and von Roon on the one side, Count Bismarck on the other, are often at loggerheads,[1] the gist of their mutual reproaches being that the departments are kept separated by too hard and fast a line and not enough reciprocal interchange of information practised.

Prince Friedrich Karl is against receiving the French intermediary, for he is rightly enough afraid that in the end the capitulation will come to be signed at Versailles instead of before Metz, and he, after being detained there for months, will only be a looker-on; however, he is now pacified on this point, having been assured that he is to sign the stipulations whatever they are.

The Imperial question is now given serious prominence by Count Bismarck; in fact he told me himself that in 1866 it was a mistake on his part to have treated the idea with indifference; at the same time he had never dreamt the desire for the Imperial crown would be so strong as it now is among the German people. An election by the German Princes, who would thus take the place of the old-time " Kurfürsten " (Electoral Princes), is regarded, for instance, by the Duke of Saxe-Coburg as the right procedure. The institution of such a definite system of election, or else one on the basis of popular representation, does not seem desirable. Count Bismarck raises the difficulty that supposing the Imperial dignity—which I should like to see made hereditary—transferred to our House, the style of our Court would likewise be changed and the development of greater splendour of circumstance follow as a necessary consequence. However, it greatly relieved his mind when I explained to him how in my opinion that was the very time when the old Brandenburg simplicity must be more thoroughly observed than is the case at the Royal Court of to-day.

Rather strained relations between him and Russell, *The Times* correspondent, have now been amicably settled. The trouble arose in a peculiar way. The interview between our King and Napoleon on the day after Sedan had been, in fact, printed in *The Times*, while Count Bismarck had not first been made acquainted with its contents. His Majesty had simply forgotten to tell him about it. Presently Count Bismarck finds the conversation in the English paper, repeats it from memory to the King, who corrects sundry inaccuracies, whereupon Bismarck has a telegram sent by the Reuter Agency to Count Bernstorff, saying *The Times* was wrongly informed. But Count Bismarck never revised the draft of the telegram, and Reuter for their part, on its being handed in, add Bismarck's name at the end and in that form disseminate

[1] Though, as is well known, Roon and Bismarck were at one on the question of bombarding Paris and as a rule on other subjects.

it far and wide. The chaos was only cleared up when Russell went to Count Bismarck and by his explanations restored perfectly friendly relations, whereupon Count Bismarck for his part settled the point amicably in London.

Headquarters : Versailles, 14th October.—I sent First Lieutenant Count Seckendorff to Saint-Cloud to see to salving the great picture representing the arrival of my mother-in-law at the Palace in 1855, as it is said only the wing containing the Imperial apartments is burnt out. Unfortunately, however, the fire has spread further, for the soldiers who hurried thither to extinguish the blaze and save property were met by so brisk a fire from the French that they were forced to desist. Yesterday evening, the 5th Jägers had already made an attempt to save the picture, and as this proved impracticable, had on their own initiative tried to cut out for me the figure of my wife, but even this had to be given up. Furniture and time-pieces, with a part of the library, but no objects of value, appear to have been rescued; otherwise the whole beautiful building is utterly burnt out and destroyed.

In the course of a ride to the Villa Stern, the property of the Frankfurt family of that name, I learned accidentally through General von Stosch that General Boyen, Chief of Marshal Bazaine's General Staff, is already at Versailles, having arrived yesterday evening. He asks for negotiations to be opened with a view to the Metz Army marching out unhindered, in order that the Marshal may make an attempt for the restoration of Napoleon III and engage Paris in the enterprise. This proposal certainly strikes me as a trifle strange, for if we agreed to it and fancied we could, in conjunction with French troops, march against Paris, I should not the least blame Bazaine if he casually deserted us and used his Army to fight the Germans before Paris. It is really just an attempt to gain time.

I had had the order given to fit up the two Trianons as hospitals, when a memorandum from His Majesty negatived the scheme, as it might become necessary to reserve accommodation there for German Sovereigns whose arrival now appears not altogether impossible.

From the Villa Stern one looks over Paris and the forts from Montretout as far as Villejuif; immediately before the eye lies the "Crown Prince redoubt" held by us; it was so named by the soldiers "because," as the fellows put it, "it lies the furthest to the front of them all."

Headquarters : Versailles, 15th October.—Rode with His Majesty to the observation post at Garches, which they propose to christen " King's Look-out." In a guard-room was written up for the information of the sentries: *Senklu, Mondöde*—meant to indicate the directions of Saint-Cloud, and Montretout respectively, making me nearly split my sides with laughing. The arrangements for defence against possible attacks by the enemy are excellently contrived, advantage being cleverly taken of the exceptionally numerous and high garden walls with which each proprietor of the locality fences in his gardens and grounds.

An English officer, Colonel Lloyd Lindsay, formerly of the 1st Life Guards, who first arrived here a few days ago, bringing over with him a large sum of money from England for equal distribution among Germans and French, and for this purpose had been admitted into Paris, returned from there to-day. He does not bring much news, but speaks of provisions as likely to hold out for many weeks yet, and describes the prevailing feeling in the city as by no means over cheerful, but still not desponding. Very many English, as well as other families, he said, would be glad to leave the place, as only two pounds of meat per diem are allowed each household. I also received by his hands a letter from the Papal Nuncio Chigi, who would wish, it seems, to be out of the place as soon as possible.

It is encouraging to see how much sympathy with us is felt in England, even if in many cases unavowed; thus a quite poor little Scotch parish is at this moment sending through their Minister, the Rev. Norman MacLeod, contributions for our wounded.

Headquarters: Versailles, 16th October.—The 1st Guards regiment of Landwehr, on the march from Strasburg to Saint-Germain, where it will take up position in support of the left wing of my line of outposts, passed through here; I marched them past His Majesty, who stood on the steps of the Préfecture. The manly, bearded faces made a fine show, only spoilt by the ugly shakos. The native population, which looks upon our Landwehr as equivalent to their local National Guard, must have been mightily surprised.

It is unfortunate Lieutenant-General von der Tann fails to understand how to turn his victory to good advantage, for instead of pursuing the enemy next day with cavalry, he stayed quietly in Orleans and has neglected to push on to Bourges, which could in all probability have been taken by a *coup de main*. This would have given a sure opportunity to destroy the important artillery depôts, cannon foundries, etc. in that town; whereas to-day the place is already organized for defence and can now only be captured given a strong preponderance of force on our side. General von der Tann is a gallant warrior, but one who, whatever he has to do, must be fully and exactly instructed in all details. At present nothing remains but for him to stay on at Orleans, hold the place as circumstances direct and industriously sweep clear the whole surrounding country with punitive columns.

At Saint-Germain Lieutenant von Ivernois, of the Courland Dragoon regiment No. 4, aide-de-camp to the General in Command of the Vth Army Corps, has discovered underground passages, which are conjectured to lead under the Seine and so to Paris. Similar secret ways of communication likewise exist beneath the town, as also at Saint-Cloud and Meudon, the purpose and origin of which are not yet explained, but are supposed to date back to earlier centuries and to be connected with the amorous intrigues and adventures of the inhabitants of high rank.

Reports from different sources all agree in saying that a heavy sortie of the Paris garrison is threatened against the position of the IInd Bavarian Army Corps. I have accordingly ordered the battalions of Landwehr Guards which have arrived at Corbeil to move to the neighbourhood of Longjumeau, in order to march, according to requirements, to Massy and Versailles. Other news from Paris is to the effect that the mood for desperate resistance still continues, though the French troops hate exposing themselves to the daily harassments of duty at the outposts. General Trochu is quiet and composed, and if not in the most cheerful temper, at least resolved to carry out his duties once they have been laid upon him.

Headquarters : Versailles, 17th October.—Once more I gave myself the pleasure of personally distributing the Iron Crosses. The ceremony took place first at Beauregard for the 10th Division, afterwards at Versailles for the 21st, in the magnificent Avenue de Viroflay. The day was so fine and bright I proposed to His Majesty to go to the Villa Stern, from which the prospect was again superb.

The Château Beauregard just mentioned used to belong to the notorious lady-love of Napoleon III, Miss Howard, who lent him moneys for the *coup d'état*, had from him first millions and then the title-deeds of this château, and subsequently made it into a little fairy palace of luxury for herself. Her " son " sold it to a much talked of Duchesse de Beauffremont, whose latest activities resulted quite recently in a prosecution for poisoning, now pending, being instituted against her.

In a few days' time the Bavarian and Württemberg Ministers arrive here, so that next Saturday is already fixed for the commencement of negotiations.

If the enemy does not attack us to-night or early to-morrow morning, I shall have to swallow the bitter pill to-morrow and receive whatever country gentry are still here in the town and neighbourhood; besides these, all the Princes wish to be present, the " Grandes Eaux " are to play, and dinner and grand tattoo to follow at His Majesty's quarters. Certain indications lead us to suppose that the Parisians contemplate a sortie for that very day. If they do carry it out, it will be of no advantage to the French and merely involve the loss of many lives; I trust we are mistaken in our conjectures, for I should not like to think of blood flowing on my birthday.

Looking back at the past year of my life, which opened at Corfu in the course of my Eastern travels, my heart is full of thankfulness for all the good God has given me and mine to enjoy. For wife and children are safe at home, the home-land has been preserved from the firebrand of war, magnificent successes, of the happiest augury for the future, have so far marked the course of this campaign; I can only hope that at the end of all the bloodshed, that, alas! still continues, a brilliant but at the same time a whole and complete consummation may be reached that will stablish the German Empire on a solid and unassailable basis and assure for us and it a true and lasting peace. It is hard for me to be parted to-morrow of all days from wife and children, especially as this was also the case last year; yet, on the other hand, there is something rarely elevating in the thought that we are celebrating a day of commemoration of German triumph in the Wars of Liberation[1] on French soil and actually before the gates of Paris, beleaguered by us.

Headquarters : Versailles, 18th October.—Among the memorable events of my life will be counted for all future time the unique fashion in which my birthday was kept this year. I feel that in a very special sense it would seem to focus my attention on the seriousness of the tasks I have to perform in the field of German politics, for I hope I may have no more wars to go through in days to come. Undoubtedly many look with confidence on this task which will one day be entrusted to my hands, and I am conscious of a certain assurance of its due fulfilment, knowing as I do that I shall prove myself worthy of the trust reposed in me. For the immediate future, it is true, I look for a host of difficulties

[1] Anniversary of Battle of Leipzig.

that must arise in connection with the deliberations with the South German Ministers. May I succeed in my endeavours to lend strong support to the German demands already authorized by them for eventual unity! For the moment Count Bismarck, so I believe, is seriously considering the matter, especially as he can now no longer bring it to nothing; incidentally, indeed, he will do all in his power to assure his complete ascendancy in his position as Imperial Chancellor, and to this end will suffer no Federal Minister to take responsibility.

The lovely sunny day opened with a salute of music performed by the band of the 9th Division quartered here. Men of the Royal Grenadier regiment in particular had hung up festoons of flowers, and without a sound decorated the outside of the house and my room with them. Bonbons and tokens of affection from far and near took me by surprise at breakfast. I found, however, a quite special satisfaction in the fact that the two-and-twenty Iron Crosses of the First Class which His Majesty had decided to grant arrived on this particular day for distribution. I immediately took the first of these to General von Blumenthal, and afterwards was able to take advantage of the throng of soldiers and civilians come to offer their congratulations that assembled about noon in front of my house to present this noble token of distinction to such of the Generals and officers concerned as were present—an honour, in fact, adjudged to only one Captain, Von Strantz of the 5th Jäger Battalion.

The King was at my quarters at an early hour, and to-day at last granted my request made many weeks ago, and himself presented me with the First Class of the Iron Cross; he remarked jokingly as he did so, referring to the oak leaf of the Pour le Mérite and its Grand Cross in 1866, that it was I who conferred on him all the higher classes of war decorations. He appeared again at lunch, this time accompanied by all the Princes. The King proposed my health as of the one " who had led us all to victory hitherto."

Twenty years ago, on a holiday tour as a Bonn student, I was at Lyons on this day. How times and circumstances have changed since then. At that time France was a Republic —and now?

The Papal Nuncio Monseigneur Chigi, who wishes to quit Paris, paid me a visit, during which I was interested to hear him speak of the Roman question and its possible solution. He saw no help save in God's good will, who had always hitherto succoured the Papacy in its troubles, but could think of no better scheme than the division of Italy into three parts, as the Neapolitans in particular were urgently desirous of a restoration of their banished dynasty. The Pope, he held, could not possibly reside in Rome at one and the same time as the wielder of temporal power, and Pius IX must therefore quit the Eternal City, both to avoid living there as a prisoner and so as once more to enjoy free intercourse with his flock. There could be no question of compliance now or ever, and, supposing the Pope to fall into financial straits, he can never accept money. But he does so already in the way of Peter's pence!

Headquarters : Versailles, 19th October.—Later yesterday evening we heard a rather heavy cannonade; all Versailles was of the opinion that we should make a forward move because of its being the day of commemoration of Leipzig, while we, on the contrary, thought for the same reason that the French would attack us.

Rumour has it that Trochu has announced by proclamation that he proposes to make no more sorties; that provisions are in hand for four weeks, and that later on horseflesh will probably secure the inhabitants against famine for a further period.

General von der Tann, whose reports breathe a certain uneasiness on account of the enemy forces concentrating to the south of Orleans, I have ordered, despite that massing of troops at Gien, to remain in Orleans with his Corps and the 2nd Cavalry Division and only to leave the town in face of superior forces.

Headquarters : Versailles, 20th October.—In company with His Majesty I visited the Villa Beauregard and afterwards the Villa Seine, famed for its flower gardens, belonging to the daughter of Napoleon's former Minister, Achille Fould.

More books were saved from Saint-Cloud than could have been expected; the furniture, clocks and vases are of no great value.

An odd character, the Marchesa della Torre, Garibaldi's lady-love, who keeps " free and open " house at Saint-Germain for gentlemen visitors, and also does amateur work as a nurse, begins to annoy me, every moment dragging me into her conversation and referring to me as her authority without my having ever exchanged one word with her.

In the neighbourhood of Villeneuve-Saint-Georges is a château of the Minister Rouher (Cerçay by name), where quite unexpectedly a mass of political papers of the year 1866 has been found—an interesting piece of war booty.[1]

[1] In 1919, under an article in the Treaty of Versailles, these papers were given back to France and published in the *Origines diplomatiques de la guerre de 1870*, Vol. XII.

At Metz the decisive blow seems likely to fall very shortly. Paris, on the other hand, will certainly be able to hold out for another four or six weeks, but after that absolute starvation will begin. That moment already fills our Commissariat officials with dismay, for as a matter of course the feeding of the hungry inhabitants will fall upon us; but in less than a week of the signing of the capitulation this will become impossible, all means of communication having been utterly destroyed by the French. The Parisians must then either go on starving or we shall be forced to provide from the store of provisions destined for our own soldiery for the necessities of the inhabitants of the capital.

Bavarian and Württembergers report that on the evening of the 18th shots were fired into the town from the north-eastern forts, as if a rising had occurred there. I do not believe it.

I continue to receive numerous birthday letters and telegrams, and am touched and delighted to see how kindly all think of me at home.

Headquarters: Versailles, 21st October.—Again to-day exhibited a true picture of life in war-time. Early in the morning I rode out in the grandest autumn weather, accompanied by a brief cannonade from the enemy. Then an invitation to dine with His Majesty in honour of the officers of his Grenadier regiment, and after that, while some Potsdam acquaintances from the Landwehr Guards for the moment at a loose end at Saint-Germain are sitting with me at lunch, suddenly a cannonade increasing so rapidly that the garrison is warned and turned out; we have our horses brought round in all haste and swing into the saddle, as a heavy sortie is reported.

I rode first to the Préfecture, partly to be at a more central point, and also to await further reports. The King was just getting into his carriage to see the action, but without any clear idea where he wanted to go. Nor could I myself come to any definite decision, as the reports received did not yet indicate sufficiently what were the decisive points; meantime His Majesty drove off, calling out to me he was bound for Beauregard. This struck me as somewhat rash, as the stable people know nothing, and above all as those about the King's person never deemed it worth their while to get their bearings in the surrounding country; so I galloped after, to be at hand if needful, though I should have preferred to ride to the Empress's kiosk, where I could find an excellent point of view. I caught up the King close to the garden wall of Beauregard, but separated from the scene of action by the wood of La Jonchère, so that we saw nothing of Bougival, and only shells bursting in the air at some distance from us indicated the locality of the battle-field. After some while, acting on Colonel von Gottberg's advice, we left our stand and went to Marly; by this move indeed we got no nearer to the fighting, but were now able instead to overlook the whole of the enemy's dispositions from the top of the old, gigantic aqueduct that stands there.

A long line of batteries stretched across the western slope of Mont Valérien and was firing in the direction of La Celle and Saint-Cloud, while another similar deployment seemed to have taken more the direction of Saint-Cloud itself. At Bougival, just below our look-out station, several houses were on fire; yet already columns of enemy infantry were again advancing from La Malmaison in the direction of Rueil. Reports showed that an infantry engagement had come about with the 10th Division, in which the 1st regiment of Landwehr Guards had intervened very opportunely, a hundred French prisoners having been taken. The enemy never once succeeded in shaking our line of outposts, though he developed an extremely lively fire from mitrailleuses and big guns. The French, apart from considerable reserves, may have brought into action against us one strong Division with some forty guns; their main attack was made on La Malmaison and Saint-Cloud. Our losses are not yet known precisely, but, thank God, they would seem to be slight. The most joyous excitement followed the news that the 5th and 8th companies of the 3rd Lower Silesian Infantry regiment No. 50 had captured two cannon.

It was dark before we reached home. Still, at a late hour in the evening the dinner at His Majesty's for the assembled officers of his regiment took place, after being postponed for some time by the events just described. The officers of the Royal Grenadier regiment, returned from the battle-field, were also present, just as they arrived from the march.

All Versailles, the inhabitants of which, as came out in the evening, had known perfectly well that a sortie was fixed for to-day, was in feverish excitement. Every soul was in the streets, eagerly awaiting the moment when the French soldiers should march in; indeed, many a householder had taken a sympathetic farewell of the men billeted upon him, because, as we learned subsequently, everybody was certain of our defeat. It was therefore with profound astonishment the Versaillese gazed at us when we came back home that evening in the greatest content; the troops betook themselves to their usual quarters, and no doubt remained that the French had been beaten.

The Royal Grenadier regiment came back singing the "Wacht am Rhein"; this tune is heard everywhere among the troops; it has already become a true national air.

Prisoners, as well as letters found upon them, speak of high prices and scarcity of salt as increasing; they mentioned further a sortie on the largest scale that is being planned against Versailles and Saint-Denis, with the object of bringing into Paris a convoy of provisions from Rouen. One can see from this that hunger is making itself sensibly felt. Would it might spare us further bloodshed!

I have been carefully watching at this moment our political attitude towards England;[1] for I have discovered that for a long time secret designs have been entertained hostile to that country; thank God, this insane intention has fallen into abeyance again, and the tension would seem to be over. But whether Bismarck's predilection for Russia and America may yet give an opening to his hatred of England no man can say.

It is intended, when the South German Ministers arrive, to let them speak first and divulge what offers they have to make. Only when this is done shall we express *our* views.

Headquarters : Versailles, 22nd October.—To-day the first works were begun for building the siege batteries. Though I have ordered the preparations for a siege to be carried out with the greatest energy and all possible judgment, I am still in hopes that Paris will be forced simply and solely by hunger to open her gates to us and that many lives will thus be spared to us.

Yesterday cost us, however, four officers killed and three hundred men put out of action; among the latter are some very badly wounded cases. The total of casualties is very easily under-estimated if we trust to casual information, for in practice it generally amounts to half as many again as was originally supposed.

The personnel of the Royal establishment that remained behind at Versailles had such a scare over yesterday's sortie that everything was packed up in all haste; even to-day many were still of the opinion that it would be repeated and our lives would no longer be safe here.

We learned from prisoners that the troops fighting against us yesterday had some time since been condemned, as punishment for grave breaches of discipline, to bivouac on bread and

---

[1] In this German-English "tension" reference is, of course, made to the exchange of Notes between the Ambassador of the Bund in London, Count Bernstorff, and Lord Granville, in which the former protested strongly against the English delivery of arms to France.

water rations in the Bois de Boulogne, the conclusion they drew being that advantage had been deliberately taken of the sortie to get rid of as many of them as possible! The officers complained openly of the unpardonable way they are sent into action without rhyme or reason, for no object or motive whatsoever.

At Metz bread is run out altogether, while the horses are given as provender the hay once used to stuff mattresses with; clearly surrender cannot be far off.

Headquarters : Versailles, 23rd October.—To-day I visited the wounded in the engagement of the 21st. Alas! two officers have since died, another had to have a limb amputated. It seems to me that again the men have rushed into battle too boldly and recklessly, without heed to the orders repeatedly given to observe caution; yet again linesmen and Landwehr have as always fought only *too* gallantly. The French lost many more than we, without gaining any corresponding advantage. They are living now without heed of consequences from day to day, and reckon human life as nothing.

After divine service in the Palace chapel His Majesty with his own hand conferred the Iron Cross on all the men left of the 50th regiment of Infantry, who captured the guns on the 21st, and the two cannon in question were mounted in front of the equestrian statue of Louis XIV.

I had a longish talk with Herr von Bennigsen. His impression of Count Bismarck's intentions is of a favourable sort, and as the latter declares he wishes to hold fast to his principles once established, Bennigsen looks forward hopefully to the commencement of negotiations and the further rapid and definite solution of the German question. " Emperor and Empire " are, according to the impressions he has gained in South Germany, very generally regarded there as highly desirable eventualities; so this vexed question has already taken firm root in those quarters. Letters and other expressions of opinion on the part of the Bavarian troops in the field here, as also of the wounded sent home, seem already to have brought about a quite noteworthy change of feeling, so that for the moment the voices of the hostile Catholic clericals find no echo.

Storm and rain greeted the arrival of the Bavarian Ministers; the Württembergers had made a special point, so General von Suckow himself told me, of being here half a day before the former. The Baden Ministers, as also Dalwigk from Darmstadt, will follow immediately. I trust a Congress of Princes may soon be the sequel of the sittings of their Ministers!

My sister-in-law Alice [1] has given birth to a second son, and my wife, the mother not being equal to the task, has several times already acted as wet nurse.

His Majesty, it seems, speaks disapprovingly of my wife's staying away from Berlin, and finds fault with all the children being with her, on the ground that in such times the Royal family should keep all together. Yet my mother is likewise gone to Homburg, and Princess Karl and Princess Friedrich Karl are at this moment on their travels. The King has so far said nothing to me personally on this subject.

Headquarters : Versailles, 24th October.—News of the capitulation of Schlettstadt arrived to-day, while for once in a way not a shot was heard from Paris. I made a tour through the galleries of the Palace and attended the dinner given by His Majesty in honour of the South German Ministers. On that occasion I learned that Thiers proposes to come here, and that permission will probably be given. A glimmer of hope for peace possibly?

It has now been definitely made clear to Marshal Bazaine at Metz that any offer of negotiation, not having surrender as its object, would be refused. A telegram to the King and a letter to Count Bismarck have come from the Empress Eugénie, in which she adjures them on every possible motive not to drive the garrison of Metz, on which she seems still to count, to extremities; she will now, it appears, acquiesce in the cession of Strasburg with a small area of country round it, and into the bargain be willing to give up to us the colonies in Cochin-China (!), simply to avoid offering any French territory.

Under the walls of Paris starving civilians of the better classes are by now digging for potatoes, enemy infantry being told off to act as cover. While the latter lurk concealed in trenches, the potato diggers come up to our outposts, begging and beseeching them not to forbid their getting this supply of food, as otherwise they could get absolutely nothing to keep them alive. Naturally our fellows find themselves in a painful fix, as it is impossible under such circumstances to fire either on the defenceless wretches or on the marksmen lying in ambush behind them.

For hours this evening there was a brilliant aurora borealis that glowed over nearly one-half of the evening heavens, the bright glitter of which we at first mistook for some great conflagration, and the magnificence of which surpassed anything of the kind I have ever seen.

[1] Princess Alice of England, consort of Prince Ludwig of Hesse.

I regret to observe that the German Press, but in especial the "inspired" papers in Berlin, continues its spiteful attacks on England, using every petty occasion to bring up the reproach that the status of neutrality is being used there to our disadvantage. America, on the contrary, which quite openly delivers weapons of war to France, indicates the ships engaged in their transport and publicly announces their intention to sail in this business, is left entirely uncriticized. It makes me sincerely sorry to see people in Germany behaving in such a blind and small-minded fashion, if only because we can gain no advantage thereby; but I am convinced that Count Bismarck cherishes secret designs against England, and for that reason chooses to treat America indulgently. On no other grounds whatever could I explain this attitude to myself.

I cannot help myself at this crisis from thinking a great deal of the plans my late father-in-law,[1] as also the late King of the Belgians,[2] in conjunction with old Baron von Stockmar, entertained for a united Germany under a monarchical head. God so willed that those men should conceive the notion of a free German Imperial State, that in the true sense of the word should march at the forefront of civilization and be in a position to develop and bring to bear all noble ideals of the modern world, so that through German influence the rest of the world should be humanized, manners ennobled and people diverted from those frivolous French tendencies. In such a State we should gain a bulwark against Socialism, while at the same time the nation would be delivered from the oppression of bureaucracy, despotism and priestly domination. Jesuitry and Catholicism would be knocked on the head, and men's souls delivered from the tutelage of the Church. Once we Germans were recognized as honest champions of such convictions, an alliance might well be attained with England, Belgium, Holland, Denmark and Switzerland against Russia and France, and thereby peace be assured for many a day. Then in course of time the way would be again paved for an understanding with France and thus bring about the utilization of rich resources in the domain of Science, Art and Commerce, to the reciprocal advantage of both nations.

I gather from current rumours that it grows more and more likely the Russian Chancellor, Prince Gortschakoff, may regard the present moment as propitious for achieving a revision of the Paris Compact,[3] and that it is generally

---

[1] The Prince Consort.   [2] Leopold I, *d.* 10th December, 1865.
[3] At the Paris Congress (1856) the Black Sea was declared neutral and Russia was prohibited from maintaining a fleet there.

supposed Count Bismarck will be inclined to gratify Russia's wishes in order to manifest his enmity to England. Whatever one may think of the English Government's behaviour during the present War, it would certainly be a gross mistake to alienate the sympathies of the English people to please Russia; accordingly I still hope the rumour referred to is not true.

Headquarters: Versailles, 25th October.—Another rainy day; the South German Ministers dined at my quarters. Prince Friedrich Karl telegraphs from Corny (near Metz) that great events are preparing. Are we really and truly to look for a capitulation of the city?

A whisper from Vienna indicates that Count Beust is losing his footing and Count Andrassy's prospects of being his successor improving.[1]

Thiers is now expected for to-morrow;[2] he seems to be bringing proposals for an armistice and intends to go on from here to Paris.

Headquarters: Versailles, 26th October.—To-day we celebrated the seventieth birthday of our honoured hero Moltke; betimes in the morning I brought him a wreath of laurel, which I presented in streaming rain. In the evening all the officers on the General Staff now here gave him a dinner, which I attended, and at which the Crown Prince of Saxony, staying here just for the day, appeared.

I had a conversation with Count Bismarck; our demands in view of possible Peace negotiations will extend to Alsace and the German-speaking portion of Lorraine, including Metz. Whether, supposing the wretched French resistance lasts longer, as unfortunately seems more and more probable, our claim will be pushed further, to embrace still more French territory, I cannot yet tell, but something of the sort may be brought up as a threat and scarecrow. Alas! we cannot avoid the imputation of having waged a war of spoliation, but I ask anyone whether any other course is left to us but to win and hold in possession French land when the French after and in spite of every new defeat grow more obstinate in their resistance and more mendacious.

All persons in authority, I at the head of them, are at one in this, that we must use every endeavour to force Paris to surrender by hunger alone; General von Moltke is in full

[1] Count Beust's dismissal from office did not come about till the 1st November, 1871; Count Andrassy was appointed to succeed him on the 8th November.
[2] He had returned from his circuit of the European Courts on the 21st October to Tours, and started from there on the 28th for Versailles.

agreement with me as to this, and approves every measure directed towards postponing the opening of the parallels, because, like myself, he now, more deeply than ever, deplores the doubled loss of human life.

Since yesterday Prince Friedrich Karl has been in negotiation with old General Changarnier for the capitulation of Metz. Can this much-to-be-desired event be really imminent at last? The Empress Eugénie does not relax in her efforts to save the Metz army, announces, in fact, that she would fain put herself at its head and fall with it. As for Marshal Bazaine, he seems actually to be negotiating solely with reference to the troops under his command, but to refuse to include the garrison and fortress of Metz. Thus the task would still be before us to deal afterwards with the fortress properly speaking and its garrison, as the Commandant, General Coffinière, declares he is independent and that Marshal Bazaine's arrangements concern him not at all. Naturally we cannot consent to recognize this, as we are bound to hold the key of France, in order to have the power more easily to keep in respect our always quarrelsome, and from now on, of course, embittered neighbour.

Count Bismarck permits the foreign Embassies to leave Paris in troops. Thiers, Marshal Bazaine and a brother of the latter are hourly expected here.

Headquarters: Versailles, 27th October.—We have known since yesterday morning that the capitulation of Metz, following exactly the pattern of that of Sedan, was to take place yesterday afternoon at five o'clock.[1] To the war prisoners already in our hands are now added 150,000 more, so that by this time we have captured 300,000 men from the enemy. Nevertheless I am convinced that the French will not be a whit more disposed to listen to reason, and that Paris, to begin with, will not believe it at all; then lies and protracting things on and on till at last famine masters the city. How many more unhappy sacrifices will have to be made?

The whole German Army before Metz has immediate orders to march for Paris and Orleans, thus not only substantially strengthening our fighting forces, but also at last releasing our men from the pestiferous atmosphere of the battle-fields round Metz. What else will France be able to oppose to these contingents save the wreckage of the Armies I have beaten and undisciplined hordes of franc-tireurs?

[1] It only actually occurred on the 27th October at the Château Frescaty.

BISMARCK AT VERSAILLES.
Lithograph from a Painting by Camphausen.

When we have crushed these again as we have done hitherto, remain only chaos and despair for this unhappy people, which, worthy of a better fate, has little by little sunk so low that lying has come to be for it the very bread of life.

His Majesty during the military report of to-day was not a little excited, which may well be accounted for by the heavy exertions he has lately undergone. On the other side, present signs make it more than ever manifest that France is everywhere restlessly engaged in making preparations for the relief of Paris. Hitherto little weight was attached to the news, especially as Lieutenant-General von Podbielski demonstrated with the utmost calm and confidence that the French were in no position to make the strenuous efforts that could be of any sort of danger to us. Certainly we have no reason for any special alarm, still we should keep our eyes open, and, just because so far we have won such successes, we must not venture to go to sleep on our laurels. The withdrawal of the troops from Metz comes in very opportunely for us.

Count Bismarck told me that an insolent Note had arrived from Vienna, speaking in ironic terms in favour of an armistice; Bavaria appears to be already taking fire, so we must be prepared for a dear, sweet little intrigue of Count Beust's. If this goes on, we should be eventually forced to send troops back again to the Silesian frontier, from which those hitherto posted there have been withdrawn. However, it is more likely that Count Beust is only trying a little bluster; afterwards, should an event such as the capitulation of Metz intervene, to be able the quicker to creep to the foot of the cross; shortly before Sedan the language of Vienna was likewise unfriendly, but it quieted down momentarily in consequence of the victory. For the rest, it is surprising this Note was only communicated verbally to Herr von Thiele at Berlin, but was not delivered to him textually.

Lord Granville sends a Note to us, in which, without exactly developing any definite views, much less making any definite proposals, he seeks to show that it would be a misfortune to bombard Paris or starve the city out.

The Empress Eugénie, in her efforts to save Metz, has actually gone so far as to wish to resign in favour of Marshal Bazaine [1] as a " Lieutenant de l'Empire." The unhappy woman, who not a year ago in the East saw Emperors, Sultans and Viceroys at her feet!

---

[1] The original of the telegram here referred to, from the Empress to Bismarck, speaking of Bazaine as " Lieutenant-Général de l'Impire " (*sic*) is in the family archives of the Bernstorffs.

Americans leaving Paris confirm what we had already heard from other quarters, that in ten days beef will have run out, after which only horseflesh, already growing dear, will be left; that of grain, flour and vegetables, on the other hand, there were still considerable stores, though salt and fats were becoming scarce.

Headquarters : Versailles, 28*th October.*—My time will now be largely claimed by conferences with the Ministers of the South German States, as well as by the surrender of Metz, which involves all sorts of discussions at His Majesty's quarters, conversations with Count Bismarck, General Moltke, etc., while the reports I have to deal with myself here must not, of course, on these accounts suffer the loss of a moment, and into the bargain I ride out every day to the troops.

We are warned by various indications of a new sortie of the Parisians, this in spite of our knowing that General Trochu has declared all sorties of whatsoever sort to be useless. To our great content we are already reinforced by as good as two fresh Divisions, and shall soon have still more important accessions at our disposal.

Metz actually capitulated yesterday. Marshal Bazaine with his whole Army, besides this the garrison and the fortress itself, in all three Marshals (Bazaine, Canrobert, Le Bœuf), and 175,000 men, amongst them 20,000 wounded and sick, have surrendered as prisoners of war ! This highly important success, which I do not for a moment grudge to our gallant troops and Prince Friedrich Karl, is the final consummation after seventy days of trials to patience of every sort in the most poisonous air and under the most arduous conditions. But will this new and gigantic triumph alter the state of things in France? That is a question that causes much shaking of heads and, alas ! gives occasion for well-founded doubts; but it is a matter now, as so often before in this War, of waiting.

The King is altogether overjoyed, and at once at yesterday's dinner drained a glass in honour of the victory. Now all disposable troops, it seems, are to march at once on Paris and Orleans. My old Pomeranian Army Corps is already on the road; its 4th Division will soon be here, to my great joy. General von Manteuffel is to command the 1st Army and take the direction of Rouen and Lille. Unfortunately we are bound first thing to detach nearly an Army Corps and a half to convoy prisoners.

I visited the Orangery of Versailles, planned on a gigantic

scale and of such a height that the trees might be twice as big as they now are without touching the roof; the fine vaulting is constructed so as to give bomb-proof shelter. Whatever was built in those days is as strong and solid as if meant to last to all eternity; nowadays most construction is superficial and aims only at outward show. The very fine colossal statue of Louis XIV, of marble and representing him as a Roman Emperor, stands amid the green foliage of the orange trees, of which some would seem to go back as far as the fifteenth century. With many others historical legends are connected. Napoleon III did not like orange trees and accordingly, as the Court gardener told me to-day, made over many of them to the Comtesse de Beauregard! I ordered the man to have the trees still standing in the open air at Saint-Cloud brought here.

Headquarters : Versailles, 29th October.—To-day is Prince Adalbert's birthday. Before I went to him, I received a telegram from Prince Friedrich Karl: " Congratulate my worshipful General Field-Marsh."; I thought he wanted to play a joke on me, but an hour and a half later comes a letter in His Majesty's own hand dated yesterday, appointing me Field-Marshal. The touching, beautiful and affecting wording of this appreciative letter, and above all the declaration that my gallant Army should see in this promotion, never before granted to a Prince of the House, a token of recognition of their exploits, helped me to get over the uncomfortable feeling that here was a breach of the really fine old family tradition to confer the rank of Marshal on no scion of the Royal House. Prince Friedrich Karl indeed, having for many a long day earned the dignity of Field-Marshal for himself, will look upon his promotion merely as the fulfilment of a long-justified claim.

The King, when I reported myself, was deeply moved; he conferred to-day on General von Moltke, who before all others should have been made Field-Marshal, the rank of Count and gave the War Minister von Roon the Order Pour le Mérite. Generals von Boyen and von Treskow have received the First Class of the Iron Cross, without anything so far having come to our knowledge of their actual doings in face of the enemy.

I dined with His Majesty, my Uncle Prince Albrecht and the Grand Duke of Mecklenburg-Schwerin, the latter of whom has once more come under my command, being also present.

Headquarters : Versailles, 30th October.—After the service in the Palace chapel the Division of Landwehr Guards marched through here on their way to take up position to reinforce a part of our line between Saint-Cyr and Saint-Germain. Anything more inspiring, or for a soldier's eye finer, cannot be conceived than these tall, bearded, manly figures. The Versaillese simply cannot hide their astonishment at the sight. Prince Karl, albeit he was there only as a spectator, discovered something to find fault with in the way the march in was marshalled, and spoke so roughly about it to General von Blumenthal that the latter there and then gave him back as good as he got, not to be forced into the necessity of officially reporting the King's brother; amongst other things, the Prince said suchlike confusions could only happen in such an Army as the IIIrd was. I too came in for my share, because he had not been informed beforehand that a battery of artillery also belonged to the Division in question. In general, as came out later, a whole crowd of others had to-day enjoyed marks of favour of the same sort.

Just as this really quite unusually fine-looking body of men was marching through Versailles, Thiers entered the town from Tours and met them. For to-day he avoided entering into any political discussion with Count Bismarck, as he wished first to have visited Paris before revealing his intelligence; nobody, therefore, knows precisely what he is bringing us. May it be Peace proposals at last, for we have been long enough now before Paris! At noon Thiers did actually go on to Paris, intending so far as possible to be back again by to-morrow evening; yet he appears to have himself expressed doubts whether his object would be gained so quickly, or indeed if he would be suffered to leave again at all.

Headquarters: Versailles, 31st October.—It looks more and more as if the French are beginning fresh concentrations in order to advance on Orleans, and we should decide to send reinforcements there, to disturb or stop such designs. But the King refuses to have any troops detached from the army of investment.

Yesterday the 2nd Guards Division fought a glorious but bloody battle in the neighbourhood of Saint-Denis, the point in dispute being the village of Le Bourget. As yet I cannot see into the whole thing, but it certainly seems to me the possession of that village was not of such great importance that it had to be retaken with such relatively heavy sacrifices, especially as it lies inside the outposts and was always hitherto occupied only by a half-company. Count Georg Waldersee, Commander of the Queen's Regiment of Grenadiers, just returned ten days ago to his regiment on recovery from his severe wound received on the 18th August, fell in the action. My former personal A.D.C., Major von Zaluskowski, Battalion Commander in the Queen Elizabeth Grenadier Guards regiment, appears to have been very seriously wounded; the regiment has in all lost seven officers dead and seven wounded! But, on the other hand, the Parisians would seem to have left no fewer than 1,200 men and 30 officers unwounded in our hands. Where eventually these masses of prisoners are to be interned is more and more a riddle to me; I have accordingly strongly advised the immediate construction of great barrack-buildings on wide, airy levels, such as the Lüneburg Heath, for instance; so that, above all things, these masses may be rid as far as possible of infectious complaints before they reach our fortresses and large towns.

I regret to hear from Berlin that people there grow more and more bloodthirsty, burning with impatience to see the bombardment of Paris begin at last; nay, that many wish to have some of the forts stormed, deeming it would be more honourable for our arms to capture Paris downright and take the city in due accordance with all the scientific rules of siege warfare than to force it to surrender by mere starvation. It is verily a bad business when the laity, safe at home in well-warmed rooms and sitting round a table, presumes to give judgment on questions which they know nothing about and do not understand. Yet surely it is the very first thing prescribed to aim at winning the greatest possible successes with the smallest possible sacrifices of men, and this is the object I set before myself, for by now we have quite enough bloody victories to show.

In spite of shockingly rainy weather, the building of the batteries progresses, and already 232 siege guns are parked, while the necessary ammunition is already on the road.

An Englishman, Captain Hozier, and an "Inspector of Hospitals," Mr. Innes, have arrived here; just now, in fact, there are many English here.

Thiers really returned back from Paris this evening. He appears to have wept when he noted the traces of war on the localities close to Paris.

Headquarters: Versailles, 1st November.—Thiers had two conversations to-day with Count Bismarck. His offers were of a very vague sort, and, so far as the armistice is concerned, as undisguisedly French as could well be; thus, among other things, he wishes us to feed Paris during the continuance of such a truce and not to require the surrender of any of the forts. Yet as to conditions within the city he seems to have received a highly discouraging impression. Confusion, infatuation, along with an insane determination to resist, rule the day; nobody will listen to reason, all waiting helplessly for salvation to come from imaginary great armies. Thiers has come back sooner than was expected from Paris, where immediately after his arrival a Council of Ministers sat late into the night; its attitude would seem to have been one of depression.

English people who left Paris to-day declare that the crazy mania of resistance knows no bounds, and it may be some weeks yet to the time when suddenly famine will manifest its dread compelling powers. Though a general reign of terror forms the ruling element, no excesses have so far occurred.

I have still no really trustworthy particulars of the battle at Le Bourget; only this much, alas! is certain, that it cost us 30 officers and poor Zaluskowski has already succumbed to his wounds. Count Georg Waldersee seems to have been the victim of French villainy. He saw French soldiers signalling with white flags, whereupon he went towards them to talk to them, when suddenly they opened fire and he instantly collapsed, shot through the lungs. An officer who hurried to his assistance to support him was likewise shot, and the same fate befell yet another who also tried to help. As we are still lacking precise accounts of the action, and in particular of the necessity for keeping Le Bourget in our possession, I am still at liberty to hold to my yesterday's view. General von Schlotheim, Chief of Staff to the Crown Prince of Saxony, has been summoned here to give explanations.

The King declared yesterday evening in an interview with Herr von Roggenbach that he regarded the constitution of the North German Confederation as in need of revision and alteration, and expressed himself generally well-disposed on the " Imperial " question.

Lieutenant-General von Werder has fought a victorious action at Dijon, in which Prince Wilhelm of Baden distinguished himself.

The Empress Eugénie appears actually to have been to Cassel, but has already left there again. What can have induced her to make such a sudden, quite secret and yet brief visit to Wilhelmshöhe?[1]

I rode through Jouy and the pretty valley of the Bièvre

---

[1] The ex-Empress, in obedience to a wish expressed by Napoleon, had started from Chislehurst on the 29th October and reached Wilhelmshöhe on the 31st, quitting it again next day.

to visit such as remained of the Landwehr men of my Berlin Landwehr Guards battalion, left behind to guard the gunpark, who in inimitable, typical Berlin style fired off their jokes and pert sayings.

The inhabitants of Versailles persistently deny the possibility of the surrender of Metz; to-day I saw some of them in front of the official printed notice giving the news laughing out loud as they cried, " Ç n'est pas vrai; ce ne sont que des mensonges ! " (It isn't true; it's all nothing but lies). When it was put to a barber here that we could not possibly publish such impudent lies, and above all that our King invariably telegraphs the leading events to the Queen with his own signature appended, a thing he could not do if it was not true, came the answer : " Of course it'll be lies, for weren't Napoleon's despatches to the Empress always falsehoods ? " and so it will always be, " car on ment des deux côtés naturellement ! " (for both sides tell lies—of course).

Headquarters : Versailles, 2nd November.—To-day, in addition to the daily report to His Majesty, General von Moltke and the War Minister von Roon being present, a discussion took place with Count Bismarck on Thiers' proposals and the deliberations so far held with him. The gist of it all is that in order to elect a Constituent Assembly, in France twenty-eight days are required for taking the suffrages, that during that interval Thiers demands an armistice, that furthermore not only are we to allow a reprovisioning of Paris, but are actually ourselves to contribute substantially to it, and finally that we are to stand still doing nothing exactly at the point where our troops shall be at the commencement of the truce. On Count Bismarck's asking what corresponding advantages it might " perhaps " be contemplated offering *us,* Thiers expressed great surprise and added that the intention to elect a Constituent Assembly was, in fact, the concession to be accorded, for in virtue of that Assembly a lawfully appointed Government would be created. To the observation that at the very least we must demand the occupation of several of the Paris forts so as to preserve the military *status quo,* he replied indignantly, and being told that the revictualling of Paris was refused and the investment of the city must continue—which, however, need not interfere with the elections—he let slip the hasty words : " Mais nous aurions donc alors la capitulation au milieu de l'armistice ! " [1] This exclamation should seem to reveal that

[1] " But then we should have the capitulation coming in the middle of the armistice."

things may be yet worse in Paris than we have hitherto supposed.

Thiers, it appears, talks vivaciously and shrewdly, and for a man of his years, and considering his just completed journeys to London, Petersburg, Vienna and Florence, to be remarkably fresh and vigorous; but his education shows gaps, for in reply to a remark of Count Bismarck's blaming the employment of Khabyles and Turkos against us, he retorted: "Mais vous vous servez donc tout de même des uhlans!"[1] and refused to believe that our Uhlans are just as much civilized Christian folk as we all are. The answer he will receive is that an armistice can only be concluded on condition of the maintenance of the military *status quo*, as well as the continuance of the investment of Paris, but eventually, even in case war goes on, the holding of elections to be permissible.

I cannot myself think that much more can come of further negotiations with Thiers; this though he is provided with plenary powers from Tours as well as from Paris. An armistice which still keeps Paris closely invested, and for the duration of which a line of demarcation should be drawn at the exact point up to which our troops have advanced, we might accept; but it is quite clear we can consent on no other conditions.

The Duke of Coburg and likewise Count Solms had conversations with Thiers, who also gave them the impression of being depressed and deeply discouraged by the situation of his country.

At Tours great confusion appears to prevail, and at Marseilles such a state of excitement that by now a price has been set on Gambetta's head. A proclamation, it seems, accuses Bazaine of treachery in league with "the man of Sedan."

It is reported from various quarters that General Bourbaki too has sent in his resignation, either because he cannot use the troops forthcoming or because he cannot serve under a Government that calls Marshal Bazaine a traitor.

Headquarters : Versailles, 3rd November.—News comes in that enemy masses are gathering to the southward; in fact, according to the *Daily News* these Armies already total 60,000 men, who, under cover of the 16th Corps stationed at Blois, are on the march for Le Mans. I deem it needful, therefore, to send reinforcements to Orleans in order to encourage General von der Tann, who is halted there doing

[1] "But anyway *you* use Uhlans."

nothing, and regards himself as too weak for independent action or even for resistance now becoming necessary, to push forward. Still, it will only be with difficulty His Majesty can be induced to detach troops from here.

In compliance with a request made him, Thiers has reduced to writing the proposals discussed yesterday; now they strike one as even more monstrously arrogant than they sounded verbally, so that really no possibility of agreement exists.

From different sources come reports, confirmed by prisoners and peace emissaries, that in Paris the Reds have attempted a new rising, this time without success, and that "la Commune," with men like Dorien, Félix Pyat, Blanqui as government, is at the helm. Trochu and Jules Favre were arrested by this charming gang, but released again with the help of Gardes Mobiles; Trochu, nevertheless, would appear to have been dismissed from his office. Thiers states that when he left Paris again on the 31st the city was already greatly excited, and he only got away more or less at the risk of his life, especially as he had brought confirmation of the rumours as to the capture of Metz, which no one up to then would believe. Anyway, he only did get out under escort of a strong body of Cuirassiers, and neither Trochu nor Jules Favre were able, as they originally intended, to accompany him as far as the outposts, because neither now felt himself safe. Thiers seemed to have a high opinion of the sagacity and integrity of both of these, of Gambetta, on the contrary, to make no account whatever.

If one reckons up the demands regarding provisioning by the figures Thiers has given, three weeks would not suffice to supply the cattle required to feed the inhabitants; from this we may conclude that stores must soon come to an end—and yet from the point of view of their adversaries they offer no compensating advantages! We all shudder to think of the moment when famine shall declare itself, and yet the infatuation of the Parisians must inevitably bring about such a consummation.

A mutiny, it appears, has broken out in the French fleet and to have been the occasion for the hitherto unexplained return of the ships and their running into Dunkirk.

To-day a year ago I landed at Jaffa and started on my ride to Jerusalem.

Headquarters: Versailles, 4th November.—I now daily attend the reports of the Generals to His Majesty. To-day the pressing necessity of undertaking some offensive measures from Chartres against the Army of the Loire now forming was brought up, but the King declined to consider it.

The prospects of an armistice are not unfavourable, for in the course of the conversations held for hours together between Count Bismarck and Thiers, many reasonable grounds to pave the way for the desired peace will be calmly and quietly debated, and it is to be hoped the authorities in Paris, moved by similar considerations, will likewise show an accommodating spirit. Thiers, who desires to remain here till to-morrow, so perhaps still has something up his sleeve, though this cannot be anything much, yesterday sent one of his companions into Paris to find out for certain what precisely has occurred there. After long waiting came the information from one of the Divisional Generals in command of the forts outside the city, that a rising had taken place, but had been suppressed by a victory of Trochu's; so that the original Government was again in office. Still no unqualified belief was as yet accorded this news, as now reports are coming in of mitrailleuse fire interspersed with musketry volleys being heard inside the city, while yet another source of information has it that Trochu was again overthrown, after having succeeded three days ago in establishing himself in power; we may assume, therefore, that a pretty wild state of things must prevail in the capital.

In the next few days we shall have to despatch heavier mobile columns to the westward in the neighbourhood of Orleans and Chartres, as fresh units are beginning to be formed round the remains of the troops of the line still to be found there, the main constituents of which must be Mobiles and franc-tireurs, but whose more solid organization we shall be bound to break up or frustrate betimes.

The King will not consent to troops now in position before Paris being withdrawn for such purposes, and as his nervous condition now manifests itself in the form of rather irritable tempers, the progress of business is often made more difficult. Otherwise His Majesty looks as hale and hearty as if he were at home, in spite of his never taking exercise even here, never riding and always living in over-heated rooms. His diversion he finds in the daily dinners at four in the afternoon and tea in the evening at nine, at which meals the whole personnel of the Royal headquarters and the Princes who are members of the Royal suite invariably appear. Regularly at eleven o'clock Count von Moltke and War Minister von Roon arrive, together with Lieutenant-General Podbielski, for the reports, which Generals von Boyen and von Treskow attend; I too make one of the party, albeit uninvited.

The Army of Metz is already well on the march here. To help its strength my old Pomeranian Army Corps, moving under my orders, has already reached Palaiseau, and will rendezvous here up to the 12th. Prince Friedrich Karl, it appears, is marching southward to the Loire, while General von Manteuffel goes to northern France. A powerful body of troops, therefore, will be in a position to reinforce us.

Headquarters: Versailles, 5th November.—Thiers went out personally to-day to our outpost, to discuss affairs with Trochu, or rather with his representative Ducrot, and Jules Favre. The circumstance that he has invited the Parisian authorities to an interview there rather than elsewhere leads one to conjecture that he might prefer to decide the fate of the immediate future *outside* Paris, and this makes it possible that our demands may yet find acceptance, especially as Count Bismarck too noted in Thiers certain dispositions towards a peaceful settlement. But I can hardly think myself that present conditions in the capital allow common sense to prevail, while the conjecture is becoming more and more of a probability that the disturbances in Paris will cause Thiers not to go back there at all.

Again to-day His Majesty refused to discuss proposals for an offensive against the Loire, though indications from far and near point to the probability that fighting forces of no insignificant strength are included in the muster that at this moment could still be broken up.

On Austria the capitulation of Metz seems to have had the effect of cooling down her ardour, and at last they realize there that our successes are of such a substantial sort as to have determined them quietly to look on at the development of events in lieu of everlastingly craving to have a finger in every pie. If only wise counsels should at last win the day in Paris, then perhaps the given moment might present itself when a forceful word from the neighbouring States would be welcomed; now any such proceeding would be entirely premature. The proclamation in which Gambetta admits the fall of Metz is a pitiful production full of high-sounding, bombastic phrases à la Victor Hugo.

Headquarters: Versailles, 6th November, Sunday.—At divine service to-day in the chapel of Louis XIV's Palace we kept the Reformation festival, singing " Ein' feste Burg."

Thiers designates his mission as a complete failure. Why so? That is still obscure to me; probably something has occurred in Paris that has brought about a sudden change of views. So once more hopes of peace are gone to water. As the King told me, the Paris authorities refuse to agree to any of our demands. Is there any language adequate to characterize the perversity of these infatuated hot-heads? Surely no clearer proof could they give that all they heed is to enjoy and preserve their momentary power. But it may be they themselves live under the constraint of a moral terrorism. So now no choice is left us but to take Paris; all the same I still hold by my policy of starving the city out, for this procedure, cruel though it seems, will spare more lives than a regular siege and storming of the city would cost us. There will be fighting enough yet, for we shall certainly force them to make a stand at Orleans and Chartres, as also at Rouen, even though no organized forces, in the strict sense of the term, will meet us at those points.

When Prince Friedrich Karl heard of his appointment as Field-Marshal, all he exclaimed was: " At last." This one word says everything. Subsequently he expressed the opinion that the fact that he as senior General of the Army did not receive this rank has prevented others from obtaining it. Proposing a toast at a dinner, he declared he could not tell whether he had already earned the distinction in 1864 or only in 1866, but anyhow the year 1870 had given it him and so he thanked the Ist and IInd Armies for having fetched him the Field-Marshal's bâton out of Metz (!). It is plain, as I said just now, how he looks upon this honour as a right hitherto unwarrantably withheld. For how long will the possession of this rank he has laid claim to satisfy his boundless ambition and overweening vanity? Not a doubt he will soon be dreaming of fresh distinctions and privileges of exceptional sort and will never show himself contented, making a point of it at every opportunity to gratify his own will and pleasure. When to-day I said something like this to Lieutenant-General von Treskow, Head of the Military Council, he made an express protest against the notion that the circumstance of the Prince's having made claims to the rank had influenced his appointment; nevertheless I am still of the same opinion.

A balloon captured yesterday, which carried two men, a number of carrier-pigeons and a hundredweight of letters, supplied valuable data for picturing the state of things in Paris; to judge by the letters, the inhabitants are not yet starving, though the meat ration has already shrunk to three-quarters of a pound. General Trochu means for the present to make no more sorties, in order that the Mobiles may first be properly trained to stand fire, and so be fit for a sortie on a grand scale later on. The Paris *plébiscite*, which declared¹ for the maintenance of the present Administration as against the Commune, was a comedy staged with tricky scenic effects worthy of the Napoleons; all the same it has had the effect of confirming Trochu in power.

Our Press still continues its attacks on England; I mean to speak about this to Count Bismarck in all seriousness, for we must *not* quarrel with that country.

Lieutenant-General von Stosch returns to-day from Metz, and, thank God! makes a more favourable report as to the health of our troops than we have so far been able to presume to be the case.

I have written to Colonel Lloyd Lindsay expressing my grateful thanks for English efforts for the benefit of our wounded; I trust the English will see by its wording that my feelings towards their country remain unchanged.

Thiers has again sent one of his suite into Paris, but intends to set off himself for Tours at six to-morrow morning; I sent Major Lenke of my General Staff with him as escort as far as Orleans. Thiers' Secretary, Monsieur Cochery, stays on here, so it almost looks as if a last and final discussion with the Parisians is still a possibility. For the rest, Thiers is earnestly and actively working for peace, in fact he has actually been quite near concluding an agreement; thus we may even yet hope something might turn up unexpectedly in the way of renewed prospects of peace. But there has surely been enough now of allowing individual Frenchmen to make their way into Paris, for otherwise only too welcome opportunities are afforded our enemies for espionage and the examination of our positions and defences.

The firing from the forts has slackened to a surprising degree during the last few days.

Headquarters: Versailles, 7th November.—General von der Tann reports that he believes he must soon expect an attack. Accordingly I have once again urgently insisted at the conference with His Majesty on the necessity of not leaving General von der Tann without reinforcements, and on Count Bismarck's asking me if I really thought this was necessary, I answered bluntly with the one word: "Absolutely!" This had its effect, and at last the King agreed to the despatch of troops to Orleans. Against my wishes, however, the 17th Division (Mecklenburg), which was under the command of Lieutenant-General Schimmelmann, a man who provokes serious anxiety by reason of his excitable temper, was desig-

¹ By 556,000 votes against 63,000.

nated for this duty; my own preference had been to send thither the 4th Division, Lieutenant-General Hann von Weyhern, which was ready to march and the nearest to Chartres; however, it was decided in preference to take the Mecklenburgers from my extreme right wing, thereby causing at the very least two days' more waste of time. Still the all-important thing is that in any case troops are to be sent there, for we are bound to admit that before the IInd Army can reach the line of Orleans, another full week must elapse, consequently putting us in a critical position. General von Manteuffel needs even longer time before he arrives northward of Paris at Amiens and Rouen respectively. The Grand Duke of Mecklenburg is to take over the supreme command of the troops to be detached from the sphere of my Army, and to make arrangements to be at Chartres on the 12th with his whole Staff.

It looks more and more as if the Marshals [1] taken prisoner at Metz were far from anxious to remain in the neighbourhood of the Emperor Napoleon at Cassel, and it almost seems as though dissensions had broken out there.

Headquarters: Versailles, 8th November.—Verdun has capitulated!

The Grand Duke of Mecklenburg-Schwerin reported himself to-day to obtain his instructions, as he now takes over the supreme command of his 17th Division, the 22nd Division, the von der Tann Corps and the three Cavalry Divisions already at Orleans. His duty will be to act according to circumstances and such news as comes in, to get in touch with the enemy, that is to say, the Army of the Loire, and embarrass him in massing his forces wherever he comes upon him, and compel him to retreat by way of Le Mans. Should the French 15th and 16th Corps, as reported, be really concentrated at Blois and Le Mans, perhaps they could be beaten separately and their union rendered impossible. Over and above all this, there would be another, no doubt less important, object, viz. to break up the enemy's concentration between Tours and Rouen, and to keep an eye on utilizing that fertile stretch of country for the Army. An interesting piece of strategy, calling for calmness, coolness, determination, and admitting of no looking on the dark side of things.

General von der Tann's reports speak of the advance of French columns in the direction from Blois to Orleans. Within the next few days it must surely come to an encounter

---

[1] Viz. Bazaine, Canrobert, Le Bœuf; only the first-named stayed on at Cassel.

THE EMPEROR FREDERICK III. 185

in that region, with which a sortie from Paris will undoubtedly coincide, Trochu having, it appears, told Thiers a pitched battle must first be fought before negotiations can be thought of. Our outposts report almost every evening that nothing is to be heard on the fortifications and in the Paris forts but the disorderly cries of dissolute fellows killing time in lewd orgies and suchlike dissipations; so it seems the seriousness of the crisis fails entirely to bring these frivolous French to a proper sense of their position. On the other hand, there is certainly something heroic about this stubborn resistance of our foes, who, hurrying in crowds to the colours, follow Gambetta's behests, and there in Paris are ready with the most exemplary patience to wait on and on till the longed-for relief arrives. This does not hinder deserters gathering in increased numbers under the walls, all complaining of the scarcity of provisions. Civilians too join them, begging for food. It almost seems as if beef can only be bought at increased prices, and the practised Paris cooks will soon have to direct their skill to the dressing of horseflesh. At the most the troops of the line appear to be allowed ample sustenance. Preparations have already been made, in case of the capitulation of Paris, to help the hungry population at any rate out of the first distress by contributions from the storehouses. The transport of siege munitions proceeds so slowly that weeks must yet elapse before the necessary total of cartridges required for a regular bombardment will have arrived; so I still cherish the unspoken hope that Paris will surrender before we resort to shelling the city.

A Mr. Oliphant, coming from the south of France, gave us amazing accounts of events at Lyons and Marseilles, where the Reds several times gained the upper hand. At the former town the Préfets set up respectively by the two hostile factions used to speak simultaneously from the same balcony. There must be wild doings in those parts, and we can only wish the confusion may grow wilder still.

An American, Mr. O'Sullivan, a former diplomat, was Count Bismarck's neighbour at a dinner at my quarters; expressions used by the stranger roused suspicions of an ill-disguised preference for the French, and the object of his stay being in any case obscure, he is to be requested to leave Versailles at the earliest possible moment.

General von der Tann again reports that an attack is imminent; they seem to be in a state of nervousness there, knowing no Prussian helmets to be any longer in the immediate neighbourhood. It is wonderful how strong is the moral influence our arms exercise over the Bavarians, the very people who once laid such stress on their military independence and distinctive character. General von der Tann has left a Division in the town to secure Orleans and with the others taken up a position to the west of that place in the direction of Coulmiers. He must know how to act independently according to circumstances in localities with which he is now become familiar, but I cannot so far understand this separation of his forces. But seeing General Count Stolberg, as all reports certify us, keeps a sharp eye on the enemy by means of reconnaissances, we shall know exactly what is going to happen in that quarter.

Headquarters: Versailles, 9th November.—A rainy, dull day; we relieved the tedium by a walk in the pretty park of the Trianon in company with Duke Ernst.

To-morrow the elections are held at home in Prussia.[1] I pray our people may fall into no mistakes in consequence of our military successes, and choose only such men as are heart and soul for the free development of our national life, for otherwise we shall be faced with a period of reaction that would only too closely resemble that following on the War of Liberation. It is true the coming elections of members of the Reichstag will be more momentous, as the development of the united German Fatherland will depend on the view of things they take.

The system of requisitions hitherto practised by our Commissariat Department with its oppressive regulations is at last to be given up, deliveries against cash payments to take its place. An immediate proof of the advantages of the new method is the fact that provisions of all kinds are now coming in in greater quantities and with more regularity than before, while the markets are again well stocked.

I have written a note to Count Bismarck regarding the hostile language of our Press against England, to leave no means untried that the two nations, so decidedly meant to be friends, may learn to know and understand one another better. There is one thing that will probably be exploited to our disadvantage, the fact, namely, that numbers of Englishmen leaving Paris are bound to pass our outposts, and these, as both sides are equally ignorant of the other's language, can only manage after endless difficulty to obtain passes; under these circumstances it may well be our fellows' behaviour leaves something to be desired on the score of urbanity. But besides this, it is very annoying how most of the English doctors and ambulance men who come here, in

---

[1] To the Prussian House of Representatives.

the first place, can speak no German, and, moreover, pay no heed to the orders of the Physicians-in-Charge, but insist on acting independently, a thing that will never do. The same applies to the English ambulances; one of these, under a Mr. Shee's direction, is halted at Saint-Germain and will not move on because its members are counting on a heavy sortie; they refuse to follow the urgent recommendations of our Physicians-in-Chief and go to Lunéville, where help is needed.

Headquarters: Versailles, 10th November.—The first snowflakes fell to-day; it was cold out of doors, dull and disagreeable weather, anything but propitious for military operations.

M. Cochery, Thiers' Secretary, to-day left for the south by way of Corbeil under escort of Colonel von Faber.

A telegram has it that yesterday General von der Tann fought a seven-hours' engagement at Coulmiers, then broke off the action on his side and made good his retreat in the direction of Fleury, where he made junction with Lieutenant-General von Wittich, who had been sent out from Chartres. It sounds very much as if he had painted his not over explicit report of a reverse in as favourable colours as possible, as later on he made the strange announcement that yesterday he had lost no guns, but to-day that two reserve cannon, the gun-crews of which lost their way, had fallen into the enemy's hands. The French losses appear to be considerable, the Bavarians' comparatively trifling, but the troops to be greatly exhausted. The IInd Army must now push on by forced marches, so that the IXth Army Corps can reach Fontainebleau on the 14th.

No doubt France from one end to the other will break into a mighty shout of jubilation over this their first success; its importance will be exaggerated and efforts will be made to exploit it as a moral lever to foster a yet more obstinate spirit of resistance. Had General von Wittich been there, we should never have fallen back, but have repulsed the enemy, that is what everybody here feels to-day. It was the first time the Bavarians fought unsupported in this campaign, but the luck seems to have been against them. May this stain soon be wiped out again!

Headquarters: Versailles, 11th November.—We have yet another proof how needful it is in war to receive the first news of incidents that have occurred coolly and calmly and wait for subsequent and more exact information as to details. For to-day it is now plain that General von der

Tann has come off quite well. Posted in a position well adapted for defence, he repulsed energetically and brilliantly three well-supported French assaults, and only when he realized the superiority of the enemy in numbers did he voluntarily evacuate the field as dusk was coming on, without ever being attacked or hard pressed. The enemy appears not to have sent a single man in pursuit; indeed a French report speaks of a check to their troops on their left wing.

With the exception of the severely wounded, von der Tann has saved all that could be transported out of Orleans, by means of such locomotives, just made serviceable again, as were procurable. It is true, many wounded were left behind, who accordingly fell into French hands, the French having reoccupied the town he had abandoned. The two guns previously mentioned were lost because, the day after the engagement, a Bavarian reserve column, taking reserve cannon with them, lost their bearings and were made prisoner by enemy patrols. The fact of possessing German guns will cause vast jubilation among the French, albeit the capture of them was no victory, still less a deed of prowess. The prisoners appear to speak with great disfavour about continuing the War, in which they declare the men were forced to serve, actually saying they were invariably driven forward from behind—a manifest indication they have lost every spark of patriotic ardour.

English people who left Paris two days ago confirm the statement that with to-day the supplies of beef come to an end; the inhabitants can now rely on the 32,000 horses still remaining. It is pitiful to think how the wretched children in particular must suffer under the ever-increasing privations. But what will it be presently, if the worst comes to the worst! Trochu has no feelings of humanity, and Gambetta is simply beside himself with pure lust of battle and defiance, ever since the day Thiers began to find it impossible to do anything effective.

Headquarters: Versailles, 12th November.—I rode out to-day to the Villa Stern to show my brother-in-law of Baden the view of Paris and the forts from there. Since it has become known what an excellent survey of the city and its defences can be had from the said point, all the world comes thither in crowds, and mention has already been made of it in the newspapers. An order that no access to the place be permitted without a pass from my headquarters was the natural consequence. Since then the sentinel at the gate must allow no one inside, and above all not before the main front. So to-day when I found myself at this very spot, the Jäger (5th Battalion) who stood sentry there, quite respectfully, but with an ineffable smirk strode up to me and said he had orders to admit no one whatsoever. I commended the fellow's behaviour, of course, and had the commendation repeated in General Orders to the guard.

From there I rode on to Villeneuve L'Étang, a charming spot, a sort of *dépendance* of the Park of Saint-Cloud and often used by Napoleon and the Empress for teas and the like. A few days before a shell had burst on the sill of a window in the upper story, had knocked to pieces rooms on two different floors and done all sorts of other destruction, but, thank heaven, hurt nobody, although the officer in command of the outposts and his staff were lodged there. Before ever we blockaded Paris, French working men had gutted and pretty well ruined the house, which, of course, is all set down to our account. It is a wretched thing how much destruction of this wanton kind was wrought by the enemies of Napoleon and of order generally immediately after the establishment of the Republic. When in the year 1867 the European Sovereigns made their progress to Versailles, the carriages drove by way of Villeneuve L'Étang; on that occasion I was actually sitting by the Empress's side, as we passed through here that glorious summer's day. How times change!

Next I rode to visit the outposts, where the patrols of the 4th Posen Infantry regiment No. 59 entertained us with the most fantastic reports in broken German. The place had to be put in a condition for defence, and I really cannot blame any journalist if, seeing all the destruction necessitated by this, he upbraids us for our vandalism.

I could not deny myself a peep at the ruins of the Palace of Saint-Cloud, now utterly destroyed and burnt out, a truly miserable spectacle; really and truly one ought not to venture so far out, but I managed to slip unobserved close up to the building, once so fine, through which you can now look just as if it were a sieve.

Various indications point to yet another heavy sortie being imminent, making, as it were, an honourable end to the investment. Deserters confirm the prevailing wish for peace among the troops, conscious as they are that all is over; indeed, some days ago, they say, all the men manning the forts had gleefully pledged one another, when it became known that Thiers was engaged in negotiations.

Surprising stories are current regarding the constitution of Garibaldi's legions; the condition of these bands must be quite lamentable. The old man seems to have bitten off a bigger mouthful than he can chew, fondly imagining he could enlist an efficient body of troops. It would be a downright embarrassment for us if we ever took Garibaldi prisoner. What could one do with him? He would only be one more added to the 350,000 already in our hands.

Headquarters: Versailles, 13th November, Sunday.—After divine service in the Palace chapel we took advantage of the warm sunshine to make an expedition to Saint-Germain to give my brother-in-law of Baden the pleasure of visiting this noble point of view; His Majesty had given orders for a breakfast there. On his arrival the King was greeted with much jubilation by the men of the Landwehr Guards in cantonments at the place.

It was with real gratification I read the leading article of the *Volkszeitung* on the elections to the Prussian House of Representatives; its warnings not to be led astray by our successes in the field, but to stand firm by liberal principles under all circumstances, meet with my heartfelt approval, as indeed generally the language of that paper all through the War has been sober and dignified.

A right pleasant distraction for many gloomy thoughts was afforded me to-day by the arrival of photographs of my youngest little daughter, whom I scarcely know yet.

A balloon coming from Paris and captured in the lines of the IInd Army Corps contains a mass of correspondence, the language of which no less than that of the newspapers indicates beyond all denial that famine is beginning to be felt in the capital. Some speak of coming sorties, others hold this would be sheer folly and would lead to nothing. Caricatures turn the Garde Nationale into ridicule, in which Trochu too has his share.

Headquarters: Versaïlles, 14th November.—I am at present having three entrenchments, each of three guns of heavy calibre, thrown up at Plessis-Piquet to protect our engineer depôt and artillery park. The Bavarians working at No. I greeted me with cheers; as I rode on, Major-General Schulz overheard one of the men say: "If *he* had led us in 1866, we'd have beaten the lousy Prussians."

The Grand Duke of Mecklenburg-Schwerin is sending our 22nd Division back again to Chartres, but himself remains where he was, half-way between Orleans and Chartres. Why, we fail to see; still, he must know what he is about, being there on the spot; so I prefer not to scare him with questions and instructions rather than interfere with his independence.

The King is downright nervous at the daily report; indeed this is only natural, a place like Versailles offering so little distraction from all the daily worries that beset him. Besides which, it is no easy task for him to induce the Foreign Office, the General Staff and the War Ministry, which simply refuse to work in harmony, to pull together.

Mr. Woodhouse, Lord Kimberley's brother, is just coming from Paris, where he has hitherto been in charge of affairs at the Embassy. He passes for a francophil and spoke only with great circumspection; he quite declined to admit that famine was already making itself felt—in positive contradiction, therefore, to the language spoken by the letters seized in the balloon. I explained to him, as well as might be, that our Government was not responsible for the hostile language of the Press against England and enlightened him on the present attitude of German policy. At the same time I gave emphatic expression to my gratitude for the actual sympathy shown by England; I hope he will make good use in that country of what I told him. To my very great satisfaction, however, I learned that Mr. Odo Russell is on his way to Versailles, for under existing circumstances England could send here no one of a more suitable type. What precisely is the object of his mission no one knows, but it might well be connected with some idea of intervention; in any case I am very glad to see a man of his good sense and wide experience here.

The Grand Duke of Baden hopes through acquaintances of his to bring influence to bear on America in such a way that, in the event of Paris capitulating, measures will be taken in that country to find means of helping in the provisioning of the city.

We are daily expecting sorties as well as fighting on the Loire; so we must be prepared for more days of bloodshed. All the same, the power of stubborn resistance shown by this people, already sunk so low and so utterly beaten by us, has something heroic about it, but I can hardly bear the thought of the new sacrifices we shall be bound to make.

An American General, Burnside by name, dined with me.

Headquarters: Versailles, 15th November.—Nowhere has it come to actual fighting to-day. Probably the French are concentrating at Chartres, whereas up to now the likelihood had been they meant to do so at Dreux. Accordingly, the Grand Duke of Mecklenburg is marching on Rambouillet, but leaving one Division (the 22nd) to remain at Chartres. General von Manstein, who is pushing on in the direction of Étampes, has already, thank heaven, with the advance guard of the IXth Army Corps, reached the position Melly–Fontainebleau. As he is moving at the head of the IInd Army Corps, it is a great relief to know of these reinforcements in the south, which take a weight off my mind, as I need feel no more anxiety for my own safety on the road to Orleans. The IInd Army Corps must either take Orleans or else, if a Paris sortie should threaten us seriously, will have to intervene for our assistance. It will be three days before the IIIrd Army Corps can come in line with my position, the Xth will be correspondingly later still in coming up.

Prince Friedrich Karl, since leaving Metz, has left no stone unturned in the way of urgent applications to get such regiments as belonged to the IIIrd Army Corps under peace-time arrangements assigned to him, on the ground that he must have under his immediate command officers and units whose merits he knows by personal experience. To do what he wishes is on the face of it a sheer impossibility, the regiments in question being actively employed all the time at Chartres and so absolutely indispensable. To grant his desire these troops would have to be recalled from the front and sent many days' march across country, and that without the possibility of providing others to take their place.

I rode out to a factory of percussion caps, which lying near the Jägers' entrenchment and the park of Meudon, serves as lodging for the officer in command of the outposts of the 21st Division, at present Colonel Preusz, and at the same time for our best point of observation, affording as it does a most admirable view over Paris. The spot is so close to the city you can see people in the streets and easily read sign-boards in big lettering. To-day the city lay in bright sunlight, that lit up the freshly-gilded dome of the Invalides; further off, I could make out amid the sea of houses the Rue de Rivoli, the obelisk in the Place de la Concorde and the Louvre.

Once the siege is well over, may the Peace that might soon be expected to follow bring with it a new and better life for this city, and through it for France generally! But I am almost tempted to think that the days of splendour are past for ever for city and country; the blows Fate has inflicted on France in this War are hardly likely to lead to any root-and-branch reform, demoralization having already eaten too deep in. Letters from foreigners now in Paris that have fallen into our hands declare openly that the authorities now in power are ruining everything and invariably do things in just the wrong way, though all the time a population is there at their disposal ready and fully efficient for the most

FRIEDRICH KARL
Prince of Prussia.
(The "Red Prince".)

serious undertakings; that in military matters every good measure is choked at birth and even from the sorties that are still sometimes contemplated nothing of consequence is to be expected.

I went on subsequently to the Château de Meudon to pay a surprise visit to the outposts and inspect the building of the batteries on the terrace. Suddenly my horse shied violently, as something whizzed close past my head, while at the same time a whistle made itself heard as when a buzzard gets up. In vain I looked about to see the bird till a soldier on sentry duty near by told me it was the fifth rifle bullet that had buzzed past in the last few minutes. I confess I had not given a thought just then to rifle shots, for riding though I was over heavy, muddy roads, I had been so deeply absorbed in contemplation of the woodland beauty that it was only this warning made me aware we were directly in the line of fire.

Headquarters : Versailles, 16th November.—The letters coming from the captured balloon, the amazing number of which my whole Staff cannot master even just skimming through them, speak with one voice of the growing scarcity of food in Paris; so it seems we may once more believe in the speedy starving out of the city.

The King regards the possibility of a fresh sortie in an excited and very anxious mood, whereas Moltke, Blumenthal and myself do nothing of the sort, seeing we are fully prepared beforehand, reinforced, moreover, to a large extent by the moving up of the IInd Army Corps and well secured on both fronts—Paris and the south. Information received makes it probable that a sortie can only be undertaken in the direction south and south-west. Granted the French should for once really break through the line of investment, they would gain nothing more than to be immediately driven back again with very sensible losses, without having found any means of provisioning the city, while Prince Friedrich Karl covers the neighbourhood of Orleans, the Grand Duke of Mecklenburg-Schwerin that of Chartres.

Headquarters : Versailles, 17th November.—The Grand Duke of Mecklenburg has marched to Épernon and means to attack Dreux to-morrow. It is not quite easy to see what his crisscross movements mean, but I am convinced he is only acting as the result of inquiries made and is going where he conjectures the main force of the enemy to be concentrated.

His Majesty has given over to Adjutant-General von

Treskow the command of the 17th (Mecklenburg) Division, Lieutenant-General von Schimmelmann having fallen ill; as things stand, the former may soon witness some serious fighting.

The Pomeranian Army Corps is now moving up here in full force and will go into cantonments in the position Palaiseau, Longjumeau, Saclay. The entrenchments at Villa Coublay are already armed with heavy guns, so that our engineer depôt and siege artillery park no longer offer the enemy a favourable point of attack.

It is indeed a delightful thing to treat of German affairs with German people (as we are finding out in the negotiations now proceeding with the different States in connection with the constitution of a united Germany). First endless difficulties of every sort and kind, then, when you think you have at last gained your object, a perfectly eel-like nimbleness in slipping out of the conclusions already arrived at. This we witnessed even here in view of events of world-wide importance. Suchlike experiences are well fitted to make His Majesty positively nervous, whose strained attention must be given at one and the same time to the activities of the troops and both foreign and domestic policy. Moreover, he sadly misses the social intercourse that should afford him relaxation, for the guests who daily appear at the dinner at five o'clock and tea at nine grow downright wearisome in the long run.

Everybody here must have strong nerves, but above all are they needful for those who are all day long on outpost and observation duty. Many of our officers come back to quarters positively shaking with excitement when the two brigades in cantonments here are relieved in the regular course of events.

For myself I cannot complain of my health, for apart from a few attacks of giddiness connected with excessive blood pressure in the head, the only time I have really felt ill was at Ligny-Revigny at the end of August. I sleep well, though often enough of nights the expectation of a sortie or the thunder of the guns from the forts, now increasing, now diminishing in loudness, makes me start up. As I wake early, my time for reading is from six in the morning, for in the course of the day the never-ending claims of business made on me prevent my making any regular partition of my time. Still, after the War is over, my nerves will need a thorough rest.

Headquarters : Versailles, 18*th November.*—The Grand Duke of Mecklenburg has, to begin with, again taken the direction of Tours and Le Mans respectively, from which it seems as though the main force of the enemy is in those hills. These up-and-down marches will greatly fatigue the troops; nevertheless I do not mean to interfere, as orders given from a distance may only too easily give rise to annoyance and even injustice.

Prince Friedrich Karl receives orders to march in the direction of Orleans, where the French are throwing up strong entrenchments; so we shall very soon see some bloody work there. At this moment it is Orleans seems likely to be the deciding point for the future course of events in France; consequently a successful engagement fought there might well bring the War to an end.

The Times contains an article in acknowledgment of my letter of thanks to Colonel Lloyd Lindsay for his efforts on behalf of the wounded which has given me true and sincere pleasure. I feel this language to show a right appreciation of my views and sentiments, a thing to which in England of all places I attach the greatest importance. May I only succeed in my unceasing efforts, in accord with the principles of my ever-to-be-remembered father-in-law, to forge an enduring chain between the two countries so unmistakably meant to be friends with one another. A word like this in *The Times* means more in my eyes, particularly at the present moment, than the usual expressions of benevolent appreciation over ordinary everyday incidents, for it will make men say that England reposes confidence in the future of Germany. If only the War were at an end, this peaceful work of bringing England and Germany into closer accord could be carried on with fresh vigour.

Effusions in letters and journals which reach us from Paris refuse to hear a word more of sorties or longer resistance. May these sentiments finally carry the day ! Thoughts of the unhappy children, who above all others must be suffering from bad food and lack of proper nourishment, trouble me day and night, for it is a known fact that the poorer classes are already starving. The well-to-do are not feeling the strain yet and can comfortably indulge in this senseless and aimless parade of resistance to the death. Granting it should come to a capitulation, I can still form no right conception as to the immediate consequences of that event. It would in any case have no direct influence on the conclusion of an armistice or of peace, but the Great Powers surely would then press for the assembling of a Congress to bring about the reconciliation of the contending parties. But who will be in a position to make the French realize that they are really beaten, nay, that little by little their whole country must be ruined if they themselves will not take thought for its future?

Headquarters: Versailles, 19th November.—Many indications point to another sortie being imminent. Let them come, we are ready.

Yesterday the gallant 22nd Division, in a successful action at Châteauneuf-en-Thimerais to the south of Dreux, drove the enemy to the westward to such effect that now no relief can any longer reach Paris. If only the Parisians could learn this soon, perhaps they would become more sensible.

Mr. Odo Russell, my esteemed and amiable old acquaintance, whom I first knew in Rome in the year 1862, has arrived here, coming straight from London. His mission is connected with the Black Sea affair. His first impression of Bismarck, thank the Lord, and generally of what he saw here and learned on the way, is entirely favourable and satisfactory. May his mission prove a harbinger of peace!

Headquarters: Versailles, 20th November, Sunday.—I presented Mr. Odo Russell to-day to the King. He had breakfasted with me first, when I took the opportunity to discuss with him in detail the serious questions of the moment.

Chartres yesterday had a false alarm. The news of this quickly led us to believe that the enemy was actually on the march by that road for Versailles.

An attempted relief and sortie at La Fère was repulsed with brilliant success.

Deserters, who refused to eat the bad food any more, are come here from Paris; they say nothing is heard yet of positive famine in the city, though the poorer classes certainly had by this time to endure much privation; that a sortie was to be made directly, and to this end a provision of food for several days was ready for distribution. This shows the object of the sortie is to effect a union with the Army of the Loire. If the luck we have hitherto enjoyed does not leave us in the lurch, we shall win through one way or the other, but we cannot shut our eyes to the fact that we are up against a very serious crisis.

Headquarters: Versailles, 21st November.—A year ago to-day, my dear wife's birthday, I was on the Nile—a pleasanter reason, that journey of mine to the East, for our separation than the one which this year perforce keeps us apart.

The day was lovely, favoured with warm sunshine, and after a greeting of military music in the morning, I was able, as before on my own birthday, to receive my well-wishers' congratulations in the open air. The King appeared, together with all the princely grandees, at the luncheon, to which all Englishmen at present here received invitations, after which the whole company adjourned to the Palace, where the "Grandes Eaux" played before a numerous contingent of the military and native public. A big dinner at His Majesty's and tattoo concluded the day. I was delighted to feel the conviction that everywhere in the range of my Army the day was kept with genuine good-will; everything indicated a sincere affection for my person, so that I look back on the day with real gratification.

The Prince of Wales speaks with cordial appreciation of our successes, albeit he feels deeply the humiliation of France.

I received a letter to-day from Prince Friedrich Karl, dated Puiseaux, the 19th, in which he tells me he learns from deserters that two enemy Army Corps, one of them under command of General Aurelle-de-Paladines, had marched from Gien and Bourges on Loury; they were, it seemed, troops of the line and 30,000 to 40,000 strong; further, that a third body of 20,000 men was at Auxerre, so that he will find himself faced by an army of something like 100,000 men, without counting the host of franc-tireurs with which the district swarms. He puts the strength of the IIIrd, IXth and Xth Army Corps at only 40,000 to 41,000 men and appears to feel no great inclination, considering this inferiority in numbers, to attack the strongly entrenched enemy.

Headquarters: Versailles, 22nd November.—In all likelihood the whole Army of the Loire, which received further reinforcements brought up in forty trains on the railway from Autun, is on Friedrich Karl's front; for this reason the Grand Duke of Mecklenburg, who was already entering Nogent le Rotrou, which he found unoccupied, is to aim at co-operating with the IInd Army, and to pursue the retreating enemy with cavalry only, but with his contingent at once to turn off to the southward and intervene on the right flank of the IInd Army. It is to be hoped the Grand Duke may reach Beaugency and Blois by the 25th November, for which day Prince Friedrich Karl plans his attack, and by a surprise advance get possession of at any rate one of those strongly defended passages of the Loire. Failing this, the IInd Army Corps must furnish materials for temporary bridges. A simultaneous advance with the object of attacking on the left bank of the river must be jointly organized with the officers in chief command of the IInd Army Corps; I have urgently recommended the Grand Duke to get in touch with Prince Friedrich Karl's headquarters at Pithiviers.

We conjecture that General Keratry's Corps has come to a stand before the Grand Duke of Mecklenburg, but that troops from the Army of the Loire have been sent to his assistance. The latter force (the Army of the Loire), which has entrenched itself at Orleans and will there await our attack, may run to 100,000 men, but will not have many trained soldiers in its ranks, making the efficiency of the whole a very doubtful quantity.

Nothing definite can be gathered from the Paris news. First there is *no* meat, then they would seem to have enough to last four weeks. Swarms of women come out of the town every day in search of potatoes, and push forward, regardless of all the threats of our outposts. Men too have now appeared in front of the Saxon line with the same object in view, but into the bargain have been shooting at our sentries; the latter naturally returned their fire, the unfortunate result being that women were hit. One of these, however, was proved later on to be a man in women's clothes—so stratagems, it seems, are mixed up with this business of potato digging, the whole thing putting us in an embarrassing and painful position.

Garibaldians, led, they say, by Ricciotti, fell upon the baggage train of the Xth Army Corps at Châtillon-sur-Seine and inflicted losses upon us. I am sorry to say Major von Alvensleber of the Garde du Corps regiment lost his life on that occasion. Not a doubt of it, the longer this wretched War lasts, the more of these painful pin-pricks shall we receive, for as a result of Gambetta's appeal, the whole country-side is up in arms, waging a guerilla warfare against us. This again forces us to resort to measures of retaliation that lead to acts of cruelty, however much such things are contrary to our national character. It makes one despair the War should take this form, and in spite of all our victories no end be in sight.

I dined at " Les Réservoirs " with the Junior Staff. Before the meal I took yet another stroll, for it was raining hard, through the Galleries of the Palace and was much interested to note a large number of original portraits of the family of King Louis Philippe, the work of the painter Winterhalter in earlier days. The pictures are kept in store-closets, in fact quite hidden away; a charming one is a view of the arrival of Louis Philippe at Windsor Castle, in which my wife is represented amongst others, and shows a quite remarkable likeness to my little Viktoria.

Headquarters: Versailles, 23rd November.—We are at a crisis of the most exciting and interesting strategical combinations. Day by day Count Moltke expounds the situation of affairs with the utmost clearness, nay, to some extent with over-much sobriety; he has always thought out and calculated everything and invariably hits the nail on the head. War Minister von Roon, who has an asthmatic cough, spits copiously, and is fond of shrugging his shoulders if any piece of news sounds strange; this sort of pantomime, joined to the Olympian calm and confidence that Lieutenant-General von Podbielski shows under all circumstances, often makes more impression on the King's now highly nervous temperament than Count Moltke's admirable clarity. Added to all this, disturbing news has reached us from Holland of my Aunt Luise's critical state of health, so that the poor King is really to be pitied. At reports the special maps of France are, of course, of no small importance, and our General Staff does its very utmost to provide His Majesty and the commanding Generals with these. But for all the King's tables are covered with maps, one can never from one day to the next count on finding those used to-day being there again to-morrow. It is really a funny thing how the maps disappear, and a troublesome one to boot to be compelled every day to institute a thorough, but mostly unsuccessful search in the King's study. Nobody can explain how this happens, as the domestics all swear no unauthorized person ever enters His Majesty's private apartments.

The Parisians celebrate the successful skirmish of Coulmiers–Orleans as an all-important victory, or at any rate pretend to do so to give themselves fresh spirit for putting up an efficient resistance. General Trochu appears to have planned a sortie for the 19th, but then to have put it off again because he had received information that the enemy was aware of his intention. Letters we have captured say that every day the orders issued are changed merely to keep the men's minds occupied, but that all enthusiasm for resistance is over and the longing to see the War ended universal. But even if this is true, it is certainly not what Trochu proposes, and weeks and weeks will go by before the final settlement comes about; this means that the IInd Army will not escape the battles yet to be fought at Orleans.

The Duke of Mecklenburg announces that he cannot carry out the change of direction towards Orleans before to-morrow, because his troops have already marched too far in advance for the order to be by any possibility executed to-day. He will therefore, more is the pity, only be able to intervene two whole days later than was counted on.

A very cheering dinner at General von Kirchbach's finished up the day. His quarters are in the residence, a house furnished with a luxury that passes belief, of a Général Comte de Clérembauld, who commanded the French Division stationed at Versailles in peace time.

Headquarters : Versailles, 24*th November*.—Yesterday evening the Treaty with Bavaria was signed here. So at long last we seem to have taken another step forward in the unification of Germany. Württemberg is proceeding with her negotiations in Berlin and is now réally ready to come into agreement with us. Thank heaven, all Germany is at last united in the Confederation, and the main line of demarcation no longer exists; if only " Emperor and Empire " come soon, how infinitely much will have been accomplished, what a victory won ! At any rate there before the eyes of foreign countries, which fortunately do not understand our internal conditions—and these will not always be as they are now— stands the *fait accompli* of Unity finally consummated.

To-day French deserters were examined here; they declare they would not go on any more eating the scrap of meat, and that of a " highly flavoured " sort, to which and nothing else they had been reduced. Everywhere prognostics of approaching famine, but no actual starvation yet ! For the rest, future relief supplies are already being got together in England and forwarded across the Channel.

The French themselves are by now finding the institution of franc-tireurs a curse to the country, for all sorts of rabble are doing mischief under cloak of the system. Only to-day we received another request from a number of influential landowners begging us to employ our troops in clearing out certain tracts of forest, as these gentry shot without distinction Prussians, game and well-to-do people !

General von der Tann appears to have won a success, strangely enough only now reported, as long ago as the 17th November. Nor has he ever yet sent me information about Coulmiers ! Before Orleans Prince Friedrich Karl is carrying out reconnaissances; " The Prince Field-Marshal " is the only title he now has himself called by !

Headquarters : Versailles, 25*th November*.—In honour of the departing Baden Ministers, His Majesty gave a dinner at which I had a talk with Count Bismarck, who is extremely desirous of seeing the bombardment begin immediately, in order to hasten the capitulation. The same proposition he had already some days ago discussed with General Blumenthal and received the same answer I gave him to-day. As a result of these conversations the General, in agreement with myself, has written a memorandum to General Count Moltke expressing his views as to the senselessness of a bombardment, inasmuch as till all requisite munitions are on the spot the guns ought not to open fire. But even if the bombardment has begun, it will be exclusively the forts and not Paris itself that will be affected by our fire, the actual capture of which can only be accomplished by opening parallels and eventually storming the positions, and this, of course, is bound to involve serious losses. After that, the next step would be to occupy the said forts under the active fire of the enemy, and then from these to proceed to the assault of the strongly fortified enceinte of Paris, and at long last only master the city street by street.

Headquarters : Versailles, 26th November.—To my regret I hear ever-fresh complaints from England of the language held by our Press on the wrongful export of weapons of war. Still, there is nothing more to be done about it, as the bulk will not listen to reason, while on the other hand the English mark on the rifles we are now every day taking from prisoners constantly stirs up the old abusive talk afresh, the fact being that our people find it impossible to distinguish English from American trade-marks.

To my great chagrin, the Berliners have taken not the slightest notice of my wife's birthday, whether of herself personally or of the day; this after she had been urgently exhorted to be in residence on that particular day. On the contrary, it was with a touching sympathy the wounded in her Homburg hospital celebrated her birthday, as indeed in Homburg generally genuine and grateful affection was displayed.

People in England are asking whether, supposing after the capitulation of Paris the neutral Powers wished to see to a speedy provisioning of the city, we should raise military objections to this course. We have nothing to say against preparations of the kind, and in particular against supplies lying warehoused at English harbours till we declare the moment come for making use of them.

The Grand Duke of Mecklenburg is criticized for operating over slowly, so Lieutenant-General von Stosch is to be sent to him, especially as telegrams coming from that quarter are not properly intelligible. He seems to be extremely desirous of making for Le Mans, where heavier concentrations of enemy troops are to be found.

Headquarters: Versailles, 27th November, Sunday.—By accident I learned to-day that Prince Lynar was several days ago sent with invitations in His Majesty's own hand to the Kings of Bavaria, Saxony and Württemberg, and this the King confirmed.

Colonel Count Holnstein, equerry to the King of Bavaria, has arrived here and announces with more or less certainty the coming of his Sovereign, for whom he is seeking lodging and even stabling. He speaks very unfavourably of the Bavarian Ministers, who should have been compelled to do more than has hitherto been the case for the German cause. They are thinking of putting the two Trianons in readiness for the invited Monarch.

Should the Garibaldians succeed in falling on Vitry-le-François or any other point of our railway lines, they would be in a position to cut off for the moment all our communications with the frontier and home. As we are bound to keep united the bulk of the troops lying before Paris no less than those on the Loire, we can despatch only a few troops to secure our lines, especially as further operations will aim solely at the successes it is hoped will be won.

It was expected to-day that General von Manteuffel would be engaged with the so-called French Army of the North. To-morrow the Grand Duke of Mecklenburg ought to have made junction with Prince Friedrich Karl.

In Berlin they seem shocked by the conduct of Adjutant-General von Bonin, appointed Governor-General at Nancy, because he enforces stern reprisals whenever acts of an unbecoming sort are perpetrated upon our soldiers. My mother, whose help has already been invoked, recommends leniency and forbearance.

Headquarters: Versailles, 28th November.—Again our window-panes rattled with the thunder of guns from the Paris forts that goes on at night for hours together; yet this cannonade cost us only four men, making us ask ourselves what all the noise and commotion really comes to. Probably the enemy thinks to destroy our siege works or that he can force the troops lying in advanced positions to evacuate their cantonments.

Apparently it is becoming a perfect mania in Berlin, this eagerness for the bombardment of Paris, and I even hear that Countess Bismarck-Schönhausen points me out to all and sundry as more particularly the guilty cause of its postponement. And she is quite right, for above all things I do not wish fire to be opened till in the opinion of professional gunners and experts the necessary ammunition each single siege gun requires for an effective, uninterrupted bombardment is there on the spot. If that were all, we could have begun firing long ago, but we should very soon have had to stop and have gained nothing by it save a ludicrous failure. Everyone at the moment is loud in giving his views on this question, but above all others the amateur quidnuncs whom Versailles provides in ever-increasing numbers and from all classes of society do this with especial confidence, sagacity and profundity—fellows who in all comfort and security and without any sort of responsibility or special knowledge join in the military life of the place. These are pre-eminently the people who are keenest in their adherence to Bismarck's theory, to wit, that the Parisians would find a few bombs and shells quite enough for them and would very soon capitulate. These critics forget one thing: by the way our guns are laid on Paris, only the wealthier quarters of the city would be hit, whose denizens are at this moment without influence, as the working classes exercise a reign of terror; the specially industrial districts, on the contrary, would be unaffected by the bombardment, and the labouring section of the population, who have the power in their own hands, would be little the worse. I guard myself by begging everyone who talks in this fashion to assume the responsibility involved in my position and for once take it on his own shoulders, adding that, so long as I am in chief command, I meant to be answerable for all measures or none at all—for middle courses were no part of my business. To my great satisfaction I hear from home that General of Infantry von Falkenstein shares my views on this question.

Yesterday La Fère capitulated and General von Manteuffel won a great victory at Amiens. The city was occupied by him to-day. The King's Hussars rode down a naval battalion, while 700 prisoners as well as the colours of a body of Gardes Mobiles fell into our hands; the enemy's losses appear to total several thousand, but ours to be not inconsiderable.

Headquarters: Versailles, 29th November.—In the night I was roused out by a telegram from the Crown Prince of Saxony, followed by another from Saint-Germain, saying that the French at Bezons, therefore opposed to our IVth Army Corps, were actually building bridges, whereupon I immediately sent orders to the Landwehr Guard lying at Saint-Germain and thereabouts to occupy the bridges at Sartrouville. During the night again the roar of heavy firing went on for hours, but this time, as the reports from all sides announce, without doing any harm whatever. What powder they must have shot away and squandered there! Later in the night I likewise learned that yesterday the Xth Army Corps north-eastward of Orleans had fought a hotly contested but victorious action against the superior attacking forces. The 5th Division, supported by the 1st Cavalry Division, had reinforced at midday and helped to take possession of the field of battle. The losses seem to be considerable on both sides. Thus the night wore away in alerts of one sort and another, as I was also momentarily expecting to receive news of a sortie.

In the course of the day Prince Friedrich Karl reported that only to-day could the whole import of the victory be appreciated, the major part of the Army of the Loire having suffered complete defeat and the enemy been driven off in disorder. The thought of the prowess of three Prussian Divisions matched against the French superiority of force is arresting and at the same time encouraging.

Till to-day's telegram from the Prince arrived, General Count Moltke did not feel justified in crediting any permanent success; but the particulars prove in the most unmistakable fashion that the victory is with us. Still, even now our minds are not quite at ease about the Prince's left flank, for it is easy to imagine that a forward movement of the enemy for the relief of Paris is being made by way of Montargis; then, should the sortie, so often announced, succeed, its main attack being along the Seine, a junction of the Paris garrison with a section of the Army of the Loire would not be beyond the bounds of possibility.

Our VIth Army Corps victoriously repulsed to-day at L'Hay a strong reconnaissance of the enemy. No doubt the Parisians think we have been forced to detach troops from our line of investment to send against the Army of the Loire, and accordingly are trying if they cannot break through by way of the VIth Army Corps. However, the sortie, not a strong one in itself, brought them in exchange only several more hundred prisoners taken, who together with five officers fell into our hands. Our loss might well exceed a hundred men. Strangely enough, the French wounded found by our men begged they might under no circumstances be sent back to Paris, as things were altogether too unpleasant for them there; as to food, they said they had nothing to complain of, but it was utterly impossible to get on any more with the Mobiles, as the latter would never go into action, and invariably demanded that the line should show them the way. The temper of the latter, therefore, seems to be such that what would please them best would be to join up with the enemy and fight the folk in question. I cannot but guess that the long-promised sortie has never been really carried out as proposed; possibly that to-day was only a feeler leading up to a more serious enterprise, and that this latter will come off if the Army of the Loire should succeed in winning through to the Seine and somewhere about Creteuil make a junction with the Paris garrison. Happen what may, we are all well prepared.

We are very vexed with the newspapers at home, which just at this present moment talk with a naïve innocence of movements of troops, dispositions and plans of defence, for all the world as if it were a question of peace manœuvres; the smallest bit of information may give the enemy a welcome basis for his calculations or strike him as a useful hint. We have therefore been obliged over and over again to give the severest warnings against printing news of this sort. A chief delinquent indeed is to be found at the Royal headquarters itself in the person of the Court Chamberlain, Louis Schneider, reader and confidential secretary to His Majesty. Notoriously the man has never had any tact, and shows by the news he sends as correspondent to the papers, as well as by outspoken, boastful, pretentious speeches, which are quickly repeated everywhere, that even in the field he cannot rid himself of this failing. He means no harm, but cannot keep to himself what he hears and sees, especially as every day he reads aloud to the King over coffee and receives almost all telegrams that come in addressed to His Majesty, and these in most cases are actually sent in through him to the Federal Chancellor—greatly indeed to the latter's despair. Yet nothing, of course, is to be done with a man holding such a position.

It affords me indescribable pleasure, amid all the daily excitements that military command and political problems bring with them, to hear from home that my two youngest children, Viktoria and Waldemar, think of me and often ask after their papa.

I went again yesterday to Villeneuve l'Etang, and took the opportunity to inspect the enormous defence works constructed in the course of the last few weeks by the 9th Division. By the felling of numbers of trees and the thick undergrowth that has sprung up, the woods have everywhere been transformed into natural, impenetrable abattis. I was convinced that, really without exaggeration, an enemy trying to break through anywhere by way of Saint-Cloud and Sèvres could not possibly now win his way to Versailles. The owners of the ground sites, among whom is a Comte de Fénélon, who laid down a running ground for himself here, will certainly not be edified by the state in which they will find their properties when one day they return.

The 5th Jägers as also the 58th Infantry, whom I encountered in their cantonments and at the outposts, were in the gayest of spirits, having this morning driven in the enemy's reconnaissance with so little trouble. To-day our prospects are once again quite favourable, and if only Prince Friedrich Karl could make up his mind to take Orleans, the Parisians would have to abandon for good their hopes of relief.

Headquarters: Versailles, 30th November.—All night long raged such an unceasing cannonade from all the forts I could scarcely close an eye; the same uproar went on throughout the day up to five o'clock in the evening. At eleven in the forenoon, a sortie was made against the positions between Seine and Marne held by the Württemberg and Saxon contingents. The Württembergers, to begin with, lost Mesly, but subsequently stormed and retook the high ground adjacent to the village. Thereupon two Prussian brigades drove the enemy right back, while, on the other hand, the Saxons have not won back two villages they lost after some hot fighting.

Late in the evening arrived Count Moltke to report the news of the Saxon failure to His Majesty, at whose quarters I had just come in for the usual tea, and brought the further information that the Württembergers and the Saxons too were greatly exhausted. After a short deliberation it was decided to despatch before the night was out General von Fransecky with my old Pomeranian Army Corps to reinforce the Württembergers and the rest, as in all probability the engagement will be continued to-morrow. I approved this step, for all I knew that at that very hour the IInd Army Corps had only just got back to its cantonments at Palaiseau after being all day long on the move; but delay might be dangerous. Lieutenant von Bissing was then sent, late as it was, to General von Fransecky with the order immediately to rouse out three brigades along with the Corps Artillery and set off on the march to the scene of action at Champigny; so that the Pomeranians will to-morrow recapture the villages lost by the Saxons.

Till a late hour this evening no clear information was forthcoming as to how exactly the engagement had developed, especially as the reports speak of the Württemberg outposts having been relieved in the morning by the Saxons, in carrying out which the latter appear not to have reached the spot agreed upon at the appointed hour, the consequence being that the French attack was delivered just at the very most inconvenient moment. But more than this, unity of command was lacking, as while Lieutenant-General von Obernitz fought for his own hand, Prince Georg of Saxony had on his side only just arrived on the spot where he was being attacked, so that there was no common action according to the plan of one leader supervising and conducting the whole operation. Suchlike incidents will be avoided in the future by the fact that General von Fransecky at once takes over command of the troops between Seine and Marne.

I sent Lieutenant von Gustedt to Lieutenant-General von Obernitz; with him rode Prince Wilhelm of Württemberg.

All day long I was on tenterhooks. The persistent gunfire in the distance spoke of hot fighting, and I must not go near it. My duty bade me stop at Versailles, as the central point for the transmission of all orders, for one could not tell whether the Parisians would make sorties to the eastward only. Besides which, the troops engaged did not belong to my Army, the Württembergers having for the present been attached to the Army of the Meuse because of their being so far out of reach from here.

Apart from anxiety about this fighting before Paris, the inactivity of the IInd Army at Orleans also keeps us in suspense. Every day came reports from the " Prince Field-Marshal," as he calls himself, with fresh reasons why the attack cannot be made, so that General Count Moltke is by this time quite beside himself at the dilatoriness displayed there.

I thought that perhaps from the Villa Stern I might see or hear something of the action, but this was not possible. A détour by way of Sèvres in company with an old friend of my young days, Captain Robert von Dobeneck of the Guards Artillery, who arrived a few days ago, afforded me distraction in some degree from my anxieties.

Headquarters : Versailles, 1st December.—The roar of gunfire from the forts has not been so loud or long-continued as during the last few nights, and again this morning we are not expecting it to come to fighting.

The Württembergers yesterday retook the scene of the fighting with great gallantry, but paid for the success with the considerable sacrifice of 40 officers and 800 men ! Sad as these losses are, still it cannot be denied that it was highly important for that Field Division to engage for once in a regular battle, as up to now only one brigade, and that on the day of Wörth, had been under fire. I am extraordinarily glad about my old friend Obernitz, that he has distinguished himself and is everywhere highly spoken of. Why the Saxons with equally heavy losses were less successful is still unexplained, but the news that their troops did not make their stand, fight it out and take their part in the action when they were ordered finds confirmation.

It seems to be more and more likely that yesterday the long-expected sortie did actually take place, and statements made by prisoners amply confirm our conjecture, for they say that in the orders issued for the action the object of the enterprise was indicated as being to break through our line of investment with a view to a junction with the Army of the Loire. Moreover, it appears that 150,000 men had been told off for the undertaking, each man having orders to carry reserve rations for six days, together with complete kit as in full marching order. It was part of the plan to keep us busy meanwhile with sorties and so on from the capital. In conclusion the fellows told us they still got quite enough to eat, but that once a week horse flesh was substituted instead of the daily issue of salt meat. Of news from the city itself they had little to give us, as the garrisons of the forts were forbidden all traffic with Paris, and only exceptionally were single individuals allowed to enter; still they admitted they had heard say that the poorer classes were already suffering great privation. Again the French fought well yesterday, but lost considerably and left many hundreds of prisoners in our hands; to-day they asked a truce of several hours to bury the dead.

Again to-day there was heavy firing all day long, but no engagement on yesterday's scene of action, the reason being that Prince Georg of Saxony had come to an agreement with General von Fransecky not to try to recapture the villages of Champigny and Brie. The possession of these villages, already lying outside our line of outposts, is of no importance; they have never hitherto been occupied except by troops on a reconnaissance, it being impossible to hold them under the enemy's heavy shell fire. I confess I approve of General von Fransecky's decision, which is entirely wise and saves a host of lives. There is really nothing to be gained by the possession of these two villages, and though the circumstance that we failed to take them yesterday is unfortunate, as it will give the French a chance of crying victory, well, we can quite easily put up with that. If only the French could just for once attack us in our entrenched positions at the outpost reserves, to find out what we are really and truly like, when strongly posted, by running their heads against our defences! Always hitherto we have fought on the outpost line, where we can by no means bring our full superiority into play.

The Ist Bavarian Army Corps, General von der Tann, seems once again to have met with a reverse; but, besides this, the news we hear as to discipline sounds so bad that the General himself admits he cannot be answerable for the internal condition of his Corps.

Headquarters : Versailles, 2nd December.—To-day there has been more bloody work at Champigny and Brie, the Crown Prince of Saxony having given the order to retake the villages mentioned. An early morning attack proved successful and at first gave us possession of these; a subsequent advance, however, of the French, added to the never-ceasing hail of shells from the forts and from a height known as Mont Avron, very favourably situated for the French, worked havoc among the Prussians—Pomeranians strictly speaking—Württembergers and Bavarians, with the unfortunate result that Champigny could only be half occupied, while Brie, together with the neighbouring heights, had to be abandoned again altogether.

Who had been right? That only the sequel will show. The losses are not inconsiderable and have led to no satisfactory result. Was it then really necessary to order the attack? I think not! Luckily, for all this, the French have made no further advance since that of two days ago. As we gather from rumours, General Ducrot appears to have been in command of the sortie and on leaving Paris to have vowed solemnly either to break through our investments or to fall on the field. The first he was little likely to accomplish.

All arms seem to have fought well in the eight hours' battle, albeit I cannot clearly make out what happened to the Saxons again to-day, as the reports, like those on the 30th November, lead us to conclude they could have acquitted themselves a great deal better. Prince Georg is at the same time depicted as a man little adapted for high command; anyway he has gone to-day to ask help of General von Fransecky.

The unsatisfactory state of the engagement I only learned in the evening as I was sitting at dinner with the Junior Staff at " Les Réservoirs "—also known as the " Aquarium." I went at once to see His Majesty, then drove on myself to General Count Moltke's, to bring him to the King's quarters, and was present at the discussion of eventualities for the following day. It gives an unpleasant feeling to hear news of this kind without being able to judge how far the dispositions of the Generals actually on the spot should be interfered with from here. However, seeing the supreme command between Seine and Marne is now given over to General von Fransecky, things are in the hands of the right man for the work.

The Grand Duke of Mecklenburg with his contingent, supplemented by other troops, Prussian and Bavarian and a Cavalry Division, has fought a victorious action at Artenay before Orleans, in which there is little doubt Lieutenant-General von Stosch lent a helping hand. So far as we can judge from here, this successful undertaking has no connection with the plans of Prince Friedrich Karl as known up to the present; but in any case the victory is, in view of the inactivity of the IInd Army Corps, an important and welcome event on the Loire, as surely Prince Friedrich Karl will now at least have occasion to push forward on his side too.

In these times our military experiences from day to day are for all the world as they are laid down in the books. Combinations have to be made for three Armies, quite separate and distinct, but still working in co-operation; successes alternate with reverses and surprises—in a word, the higher Strategy and Tactics are the order of the day. General Count Moltke in all this remains always his own calm, clear-headed, matter-of-fact self—a veritable worker of miracles; for me it is a pleasure of the rarest sort to hear him make his daily report. If only the dark side—our inevitable losses—were not inextricably bound up with these impressions and experiences!

Night after night now I can get no restful sleep, for my thoughts are all the time busy with the fighting before Paris and Orleans and the efforts of the enemy to relieve the capital from the Loire. Our Generals who fought at Brie and Champigny believe they had near on 100,000 men, if not really more, against them, and think that the big, long-expected sortie is at this very moment in course of execution. All this is cause enough for anxious thought, while the incessant cannonading again is anything but a lullaby.

The King of Bavaria has really and truly written our King the letter suggested by Count Bismarck, and Count Holnstein is already on the way back to Versailles as its bearer. He may be here with it to-morrow.

Headquarters: Versailles, 3rd December.—Yesterday's bloodshed does not seem to have satisfied the French yet, for at first dawn to-day we could again hear the sound of brisk firing, till the thick snow clouds deadened the sound altogether.

Ludwig II.
King of Bavaria.

THE EMPEROR FREDERICK III. 211

Of the Pomeranian Army Corps the Grenadier regiment Kolberg and the 6th Pomeranian Infantry regiment No. 49, as also the artillery, seem to have suffered severe losses. The 1st Württemberg Infantry Brigade and certain Saxon regiments appear to have been literally decimated by heavy gun-fire. But the French losses too amount to a very considerable total.

My God, what torrents of blood must yet flow, though surely sound common sense should at last tell the French that their continued resistance, heroic as it is, can only lead to their ruin! May these sortie actions have no other meaning but this fine vindication of French honour, after which its debt can in the end be paid to ever-increasing starvation.

Prisoners' statements, supplemented by other sources of information, lead us to suppose a fresh collision likely tomorrow between Seine and Marne, as the three Corps of the line in Paris appear to be concentrated there.

The Grand Duke of Mecklenburg's victories may be called brilliant, for at Artenay 12 guns were captured, and a General, 25 officers and 1,600 men made prisoners. Probably the whole IInd Army is in action to-day before Orleans, so the next few days must prove very bloody. Disturbing as this thought is, still everyone must feel glad that at last the decision to attack has been taken in that region.

Krupp from Essen has sent here a model of a balloon gun, as it is called, and believes that with this, an invention resembling a rocket battery, the balloons ascending from Paris can be hit and destroyed.

To-day, one I have for so many years held in honour and affection as my sister's birthday, has acquired a special importance for our House and country from the fact that the King of Bavaria, in an official communication in his own hand to our King, has begged him to assume the Imperial dignity. Colonel Count Holnstein, the Bavarian King's equerry, arrived to-day at the Royal headquarters with the letter in question, and brought his Sovereign's orders to Prince Luitpold of Bavaria to hand the document personally to His Majesty. The Prince acquitted himself of his mission, one naturally to the last degree obnoxious to him, immediately before the big dinner held at His Majesty's in honour of the birthday, without my having an inkling of what had occurred. It was whispered in my ear by one of the guests that a letter had arrived from Munich. Some profess to have observed that the Prince to-day was noticeably self-absorbed.

After the meal I told His Majesty of my curiosity about the rumour that had come to my ears, and as the result received permission to attend the report just arranged for by Count Bismarck, who thereupon read out the King of Bavaria's letter. The gist was something to this effect, that now the German Confederation had been restored, it seemed to King Ludwig to be only right that it in turn should further develop into the old-time Empire with the Emperor at its head, and that, if His Majesty showed himself disposed to adopt the idea, he was ready to invite the German Princes and Free Cities, whom he had informed of this step, to offer him the Imperial Crown. The contents of this letter put His Majesty quite beside himself with displeasure and took him altogether aback; so he seems to have no inkling that the draft of it went from here to Munich. The King held that the matter came just at the most inopportune time possible, as he looked upon our prospects at the moment as very black and our position highly perilous. Count Bismarck replied that the election of Emperor had nothing to do with the fighting now going on, but was rather a victory in itself and a consequence of the victories won up to the present, and that, even if we were driven back to the Meuse, the question was distinct from military incidents and a matter of simple right. But the King was not going to change his mind to-day and saw in " Emperor and Empire " simply a cross for himself to bear and for the Prussian Kingdom generally (!). After leaving the King's room, Count Bismarck and I wrung each other's hand, without saying much—for we felt that the decision was made and that from to-day " Emperor and Empire " were restored beyond possibility of recall.

A new summons to our House, a task of the highest importance, is involved in this continuation of the thousand years' old Empire of the German nation. I thank God that the sixty-five years' interregnum is over, a time to which the poet's line : " Vorbei ist die schreckliche, die kaiserlose Zeit " (Over the dreadful days, the days without an Emperor), is as fully applicable as to the years that preceded the election of Rudolf of Habsburg. The circumstances under which our King will mount the Imperial throne of Germany are the direct consequence of a campaign in which the Prussian hosts led and gave example to the allied Germans. May our House, in due recognition of the task laid upon it, know how, not only on battle-fields, but also in the paths of peace, duly appreciating the needs of the age we live in, to pave the way for a liberal development of the German Empire ! A costly gift has been bestowed on the German people, and if this must for the moment be in a sense regarded as only an assurance of the ultimate realization of what is still only in the bud, and the result secured still leaves many a fondly cherished wish unfulfilled, yet does the mere fact of the restoration of this proud and ancient title afford a guarantee for the growth and prosperity of the newly-founded Empire. Only for the evening of his days will my father probably enjoy its honours; but on me and mine devolves the task of setting our hands in true German fashion to the completion of the mighty edifice, and that on principles consonant with these modern times and free from prejudice and prepossessions.

Headquarters: Versailles, 4th December, Sunday.—Thank God, all the anxious forebodings which beset us yesterday and all night too have not been justified, for no new engagement occurred on that day at Brie and Champigny; so we can attend divine service untroubled by fresh cares. At the subsequent report at His Majesty's quarters I heard the joyful news of Prince Friedrich Karl's victorious advance and that of the Grand Duke of Mecklenburg on Orleans. Most likely the decisive action will be fought there to-day; then at last we shall be done with this Army of the Loire, on which at present all France keeps its eyes fixed in feverish expectation of victory.

I visited the Trianon to-day, a spot I am always glad to linger at, and came upon some dragoons of my regiment standing lost in admiration at the old gilded coaches kept there. To the fellows' delight and that of the bystanders, but certainly to the no small horror of the attendant in charge, I made them get into Charles X's Coronation coach and seat themselves in it. This carriage has in its time driven the King of Rome, the Comtes de Chambord and de Paris, as well as the Prince Imperial to the font.

As the news we have from Berlin runs persistently to the effect that the Reichstag is unwilling to approve the agreements with the South German Governments, but may accept the Bavarian treaty, Count Bismarck has urgently begged Baron von Roggenbach to go there and, though he is not a Deputy, still to make his influence felt. In this way I shall miss, alas! my interesting and instructive talks with him.

It would be really too dreadful if on the eve of the final consummation of the great work of Unification, spoiled and stunted as it may be, the people's representatives ruined the harvest the War has ripened so rapidly and to which " Emperor and Empire " is actually the assured sequel. Should we now let slip, as has, alas! too often happened, the favourable opportunity, one can guarantee nothing. It is certain

Count Bismarck will as little suffer himself to be shaken in his ways of thinking and acting as in his views, whereby incalculable mischief may be done. Then once again would German philistines have frustrated the realization in practice of a noble ideal.

No doubt in theory the Deputies are right in their objections, but at this moment only facts count, for such an opportunity as now offers to decide for good and all the German question will never occur again. What is unwelcome in it can be put in hand later on for improvement, if only the Empire itself is first established as one united whole. I am positively horrified at the mere possibility of failure, for if nothing comes of it all now, we have made ourselves a hideous laughing-stock and the old régime of Beust and his intrigues will come back again. Were I in Berlin, I could certainly, as I did in 1867 with regard to the settlement of the North German Constitution, say a conciliatory word to the party leaders, perhaps bring them to see things in the right light, and so accomplish a good piece of work. May Roggenbach's influence carry its full weight.

As winter is now upon us, we have sent for furs and warm clothing; Count Bismarck advised this specially on the ground that it would, he hoped, be perfectly well known in France and show our enemies that we are preparing for a long duration of the War.

Headquarters: Versailles, 5th December.—Last night towards midnight I was awakened by the joyful news: "Victory at Orleans that has put us in possession of the railway station and the Saint-Jean suburb," so that I tried to get to sleep again in the exciting expectation that the city would be captured in the course of to-day.

At Villiers-Brie the French are actually abandoning the much-talked-of Hill No. 100, from which they brought to bear the considerable superiority they possessed in their artillery fire; as a result of this we can now push our outposts further forward. The enemy is also breaking up again the bridges of boats they threw over the Marne during the last few days. What this should mean I do not yet gather, but I look upon it as a favourable sign indicating that they do not propose to resume the fight; in other words, that they have had enough of the tussle with us, at any rate for the present.

But what will be the consequence of this victory on the Seine and Loire? Nothing else, we may be sure, but this, that in a few weeks we shall have to fight again just the same, for in this War no single event is any longer decisive, in the same way as we have always hitherto found to be the case. For certain we shall now get much to do with the franc-tireur bands, which are continually growing in numbers and whose organization has already given us so much trouble, inasmuch as the native population is all in its favour. One cannot but think highly of the obstinate power of resistance shown by the French, for from it we clearly see what a united people can do when swayed by a great national ideal. This makes the duration of the War impossible to foresee, though the Paris catastrophe is perhaps nearer than we suppose. I am tempted to think that, when the capital has fallen, it would be opportune to say to the Great Powers that on grounds of humanity we should be rejoiced to see an end to the struggle. Of course we must exhibit no trace of longing for peace, as otherwise they would think we were using considerations of humanity as a pretext because we could not carry on the War longer.

General Count Moltke in conjunction with Count Bismarck has sent by the hands of Captain of Cavalry Count Nostitz, carrying a flag of truce, an official letter to General Trochu, in which he informs him in a few words that Orleans is occupied by us and the Army of the Loire beaten and in full retreat, adding that his reason for writing was the supposition that news of this sort might be of importance to the recipient in view of the distressed condition of Paris; for the rest, that he left it to him to send a French officer to Orleans who could convince himself personally of the truth of the tidings. I imagine we shall receive an ingenious, mock-polite answer to the letter.

We are curious to learn what the Parisians will say to it, but for my own part I think everything will remain just the same and the capital will exclaim, like naughty children: " Now we will *not* give in ! "

Headquarters: Versailles, 6th December.—Again to-day there was much heavy firing from the forts; amid the uproar I had the great satisfaction of decorating Colonel von Gottberg, my tried and trusty Quartermaster-General, with the Iron Cross of the First Class, which the more delighted him as it happened to be his birthday to-day. The outposts reported great movements of men inside the city from east to west.

Prince Friedrich Karl is pursuing the enemy towards Bourges, the Grand Duke of Mecklenburg in the direction of Tours, though the troops are greatly fatigued, and their footgear in a lamentable condition by reason of the never-ending forced marches they have of late had to make. The last few weeks have given 45,000 French as prisoners. The soldiers of the Army of the Loire must be much demoralized, for when our men entered Orleans, French soldiers sitting round camp fires in the market-place did not even get to their feet, and let themselves be disarmed without a blow; the same was the case with others found in the houses we took possession of. It is typical of the French how, so long as the struggle lasts, even when they are in the field against their will, they always fight bravely, but directly it is all over they throw to the winds, so to speak, all that is generally expected of soldiers. May we conclude from this that, though having no great battles to expect any longer, we may well find after a while fresh armed hosts gathering in the south—an achievement of which the heroic temper of the nation, firmly resolved on the most desperate resistance, is fully capable?

General Trochu has answered Count Bismarck to-day; his communication reads politely, couched in almost identical terms with ours, but declining the suggestion to send an officer to Orleans.

In honour of the birthday to-day of the Duchess of Saxe-Coburg-Gotha His Majesty and the Duke dined with me. The King was not a little taken aback by the news received a little while before that yesterday the Minister Delbrück in Berlin had read out in the Reichstag the whole contents of the King of Bavaria's letter. I, on the contrary, am rejoiced to hear of this proceeding, for the young King is now firmly pledged; there can be no going back now on "Emperor and Empire." Moreover, I feel that an occurrence of such high significance will bring over those members who till now meant to vote against the treaties.

Already the majority of the German Princes in the field have telegraphed their acceptance of the Bavarian proposal, and now Saxony and Württemberg could not well do anything else than say yes, even though it be with gnashing of teeth.

In company with my brother-in-law I took a long walk to-day, in the course of which we passed the "grand bassin," on which people are now busily engaged in skating—certainly a rarity under climatic conditions here. But the cold air is healthy and a corresponding decrease of sickness is found among the men.

Rumours have it that Thiers will soon appear again to open negotiations.

Captain von Viebahn of my General Staff returned to-day from Orleans. Judging by his reports, it was from uncertainty as to the enemy's plans that the Grand Duke of Mecklenburg undertook those to-and-fro marches we could not make out, and which exhausted the troops so excessively; into the bargain, the men had to suffer a great deal from the cold for lack of fuel. But the moment Lieutenant-General von Stosch arrived, all became clear and orderly, and we must thank him for the successes already reported.

Once more by way of a change Gambetta has nothing but news of victories printed at Tours, this in spite of the fact that he himself ran the very greatest risk of being taken prisoner when, on his way to join the Army at Orleans, he came quite close upon our cavalry engaged in tearing up the railway. A telegram from the French General Aurelle to him, captured by us, asks what he should do in face of the considerable superiority in numbers of the Germans attacking him; to which the reply, also in our hands, reads: "A French Army of 200,000 men with 500 guns cannot be repulsed!" Delusions again, and nothing but delusions!

General von der Tann's Army appears to have done well, though before the decisive day several positions had to be evacuated; but the losses are remarkably heavy, for in the last four days 133 officers and no fewer than 3,000 men were reported as put out of action.

Headquarters: Versailles, 7th December.—Quite early I was wakened by a telegram from The Hague, in which poor Uncle Friedrich in Holland begs me to notify my father on his behalf of the death yesterday of my dear Aunt Luise. Before eight o'clock I was on my way to see His Majesty, who only too quickly caught the meaning of my appearance at so unusual an hour when I spoke of a telegram from The Hague; he received the news, which, alas! we had only too often before expected, calmly and composedly and only turned a little pale, tears welling in his eyes, as he pronounced the words: "She had a true, faithful heart, full of burning love for Prussia!" Then he spoke of my uncle and decided that Prince Wied should proceed at once to The Hague, and that to-day he wished to be alone with Prince Karl at midday; the report with the Generals, however, he appointed as usual for ten o'clock, and was as calm and composed at it as ever.

Among the officers in high command in the IInd Army great surprise seems to have been felt that the Grand Duke of Mecklenburg had already occupied Orleans on the morning of the 5th December, and instead of a fight, a friendly arrangement had been come to with the French officers in command, surrendering Orleans to us without a struggle.

Headquarters: Versailles, 8th December.—Lieutenant-General von Stosch writes me to-day that he regards the engagement on the 2nd December at Bazoches as a brilliant victory, 25,000 Prussians having beaten the French, 100,000 strong, albeit not without difficulty and anxiety and, alas! not without sensible losses. The actions on the other days prove in his opinion that the French were ready to take to their heels and would do so if involved in the smallest danger.

With endless trouble a gigantic field-piece has been mounted on Mont Valérien, intended to shoot right up to the Préfecture. Already, indeed, it is stated that shots have struck only some thousand paces short of the suburb to the east of Versailles, but this still needs confirmation. Anyway, we are *not* yet driven out of the place by long-range cannon.

Headquarters: Versailles, 0th December.—Yesterday the Grand Duke of Mecklenburg, advancing against Beaugency, was fiercely attacked in the wood of Marchenoir by three enemy Corps of the Army of the Loire in retreat in different directions, but without his being stopped in his victorious progress, so that one after the other the villages of Cravant, Beaumont, Messas and Beaugency were captured. I am extraordinarily glad that Lieutenant-General von Stosch should see his advice and tactics prove right under such favourable circumstances.

In Paris yet another vote—whether war or peace—would seem to have been taken, when the majority declared for going on with the War. So neither the defeat of the Army of the Loire nor the abortive sortie has made an impression, and the Apostles of Civilization will have fresh pools of blood and heaps of corpses! Thank God we are in no way responsible for this wickedness.

To-day the proposal as to "Emperor and Empire" was brought forward in the Federal Council.[1]

The Bavarian Ist Army Corps also played a glorious part in yesterday's action in spite of its weakened state. Apart from its losses in the engagements, it has been weakened by the unusually large number of marauders encountered everywhere; more than that, the doctors there make the mistake of discharging men slightly ill and wounded straight home instead of sending them into the nearest field hospitals.

Public feeling at home was, generally speaking, shocked on hearing of the treaties, especially of that concluded with

---

[1] The motion being to substitute for "President of the Bund" and "Bund," "Emperor—and Empire," in the text of the Constitution of the North German League.

Bavaria. In fact people are asking each other in amazement, if then all the blood spilt, if all the generous sacrifices of the German people are to serve no other end but to patch up a miserable Confederacy on which they clap the caricature of an Imperial Crown. Others, on the contrary, see in the Constitution to be framed a temporary expedient that suits only the individuals for whom and by whom it is adopted. These, therefore, put their hopes in the Reichstag, where the decision will be made, with clear head and cool brain, to bring to a right issue the great work of the nation itself and to set up a Constitution calculated to confer blessings on generations to come.

Headquarters: Versailles, 10th December.—Meantime the Tours Government has been transferred to Bordeaux, which may surely be taken as a significant sign in our favour of France's increasing difficulties; but with Gambetta's utterly perverse character, no sensible calculations can be made. His colleagues would like to see an intervention on the part of the Great Powers, but dare not make any proposal tending in that direction to him.

The Reichstag would seem to have accepted the Treaties to-day[1] at Berlin; thank God, this has come about! We are bound to recognize the self-denial of the Deputies, who have done violence to their convictions, they certainly deserve the credit of having acted rightly; one day they will surely find that the seed they sowed to-day will bear good fruit.

After a long and agreeable conversation with my brother-in-law, I had an intimate and equally pleasant talk with Mr. Odo Russell. He finds that in principle Count Bismarck is favourably inclined to an alliance of Germany with England, though the Chancellor's natural sympathies draw him to Russia. Mr. Russell laments the isolation of England that is ever growing more evident and will soon make dependence on an allied Power a necessity—above all, at the present moment, when the Envoy of the President of the United States of America has taken a hand in European developments, whereby an aggravation of the dangerous Alabama question is brought into closer prospect.

Headquarters: Versailles, 11th December, Sunday.—At the military report from the Generals to-day His Majesty was greatly agitated. Besides events in the field, the com-

[1] The Reichstag accepted the treaties with the South German States on the 9th, the inclusion of the words " Emperor " and " Empire," in the text of the Constitution on the 10th December.

munication of the King of Bavaria's letter to the Reichstag gives him endless worry, above all because Delbrück produced the complete text, whereas the King, so it appears, had only sanctioned a confidential reference to the document in question. Can His Majesty be still unaware of the fact that the draft of this all-important letter was composed by Count Bismarck, despatched from his Chancellerie to Bavaria and just simply copied out by King Ludwig?

The enemy is withdrawing from the Loire to the south and west; for the moment then fresh bloodshed ought at any rate to be spared till the time when fresh French concentrations are carried out, which will then, of course, be followed by fresh battles. Prince Ludwig of Hesse captured at Chambord five guns with their full supply of ammunition, and is now posted before Blois on the left bank of the Loire.

In yesterday's brisk cannonade before Beaugency twenty-four of our cast-steel four-pounders belonging to the 22nd Division were completely shot out, so that the barrels had to be sent back as unusable and new ones substituted in their place. Krupp's artillery critics here are rejoicing over this failure, at the head of them being General von Podbielski. The IInd and VIth Army Corps report the arrival of numerous deserters; the Gardes Mobiles amongst these state that the rations served out to them are now very short and bad, and that it can hardly go on another fortnight before the city surrenders. Believe this or not as you please. I have given up making guesses and just live from day to day in complete resignation; by to-morrow it will be now three months since we began to blockade Paris, the outside limit conceivable of possible defence that even the most sanguine could fix. Nevertheless, I stick to my opinion that a bombardment would be no good, strong as is the tide of opinion at home in the opposite direction. General von Blumenthal, Count Moltke and I will never, so long as we are in office, allow anything to confound us in our conviction, for only on the spot itself, and not in Berlin, can anyone properly judge what is going to happen here. I informed these two what confidence my wife reposed in them, and how she shared their views, to the evident delight of both.

Headquarters: Versailles, 12th December.—Pfalzburg has capitulated, and that unconditionally; we have been blockading this eyrie of a mountain fortress ever since August. Shortly before the victory of Sedan I had signed conditions of capitulation, which the Commandant had accepted, when he changed his mind again; since then the place went on now offering, anon refusing to surrender. The defenders are worthy of the highest honour, for all concerned, from the Commandant, Colonel Denfer, downwards, have done amazingly under the most arduous conditions. On our side I sincerely congratulate First Lieutenant Giese, whose steady perseverance, no less than the courage and devotion of the besieging troops, deserves all praise—the more so as Pfalzburg has never before surrendered to an enemy in any war.

Prince Peter Wittgenstein, who as Russian Military Plenipotentiary has been long in Paris and is deeply versed in the customs and ways of the city, together with his English colleague, General Clermont and the Belgian Legation, has arrived here from Paris. For what reason General Trochu has now withdrawn his absolute prohibition against leaving the capital we cannot understand. Possibly it is that for the moment he has no thoughts of a sortie, and in consequence the new arrivals here could not betray his plans; in any case I do not, as so many other people do, see in this a sign of any intention of a speedy capitulation. General von Podbielski opined to-day : " The rats always leave the ship before she sinks ! " It may be hunger is grown more acute, but the new-comers just referred to have made no mention of it, but rather declared that they themselves could no longer make head or tail of things. They certainly believe that one fine day the capitulation will come about quite suddenly and, in fact, just when the language held by the powers that be indicates the exact contrary—or perhaps yet another utterly senseless sortie will be made, whereby to secure the appearance of having saved the last shred of honour.

Headquarters : Versailles, 13th December.—One cannot but recognize the tenacity of purpose shown by the French, who, despite their woeful moral decadence, still preserve a heroic spirit, of which they themselves were probably unconscious when the War broke out. On the other hand, the more clear-sighted among their responsible guides and leaders should at last realize that, by the continuance of bloodshed and the never-ending sacrifice of life, France is crippled for many a day to come; may the country avail itself of the ample means of recuperation still existing.

On Friday, the 16th December, the deputation from the Reichstag may be expected here. As the King insists on not receiving it until expressions of agreement have reached us from all the Princes, to ease his mind, a telegram has been despatched to the King of Bavaria to say he may at last forward to us the official notifications that have long been in his hands.

I am glad to see these Deputies here, actually on French soil, in the enemy's country; in the midst of war's alarms sounds the swan-song of the last of the North German Reichstags as a pæan of welcome to the future Emperor of Germany!

Headquarters : Versailles, 14*th December*.—My thoughts are busied in a very special way to-day with my beloved, never-to-be-forgotten father-in-law, who this day nine years ago was taken from us. Had he lived, much would have gone differently and turned out differently in the development of the world's history; above all would it have been a subject of congratulation in his case if only he could have witnessed the restoration of the Empire, the complicated questions involved in which so often formed the subject of his talks with me. In particular, I recall perfectly a conversation we had during a stroll in the gardens of Buckingham Palace, in which he more especially stressed the point that we Prussians would have to give up this idea of playing a decisive rôle without assistance from Germany. His notion was not that of gaining by force of arms the ends the attainment of which was hindered by the stupidity of the Princes and the narrow-mindedness of the nation; but indeed no one in the year 1856, when peace at any price was in fashion, could have imagined that a time could ever come for such a magnificent and puissant revival of the manly spirit of Germany as we witness at the present moment. What a great mind like that of the enlightened Prince Consort wished and worked for can only gradually come to maturity; his blessing will not fail to be upon the building up of the new Empire.

My mind still dwelling on the day, I took a walk with Duke Ernst in the lovely peaceful garden of the Trianon, with its wealth of evergreens; the spring-like breeze and the abundance of greenery made me fancy I was in dear old England.

In Berlin it is now the order of the day to vilify my wife as being mainly responsible for the postponement of the bombardment of Paris and to accuse her of acting under the direction of the Queen of England; all this exasperates me beyond measure. Countess Bismarck-Schönhausen and the Countess Amélie Dönhoff, a lady of the Court of the Dowager Queen Elizabeth,[1] have repeated the scandal quite openly. But who in Berlin can judge what is best to do before Paris? Did we by any chance consult these wiseacres about Weissenburg, Wörth and Sedan? And yet our exploits at that time

[1] Widow of King Frederick William IV.

have been deemed quite exemplary. But now in this case, where the bombardment calls for the most thorough preparations, especially so because of grave sins of omission on the part of the War Ministry, and in which we are faced with a siege on an utterly unprecedented scale, for which the necessary material has not been got ready, we should, of course, without more ado just loose off our guns, simply because the laity are of the opinion that Paris must then quite obviously capitulate! Yet, if only one of these clever people would be so good as just take the trouble to get a pair of compasses and measure how far our batteries, armed with the heaviest cannon, can actually reach, and if folks at Berlin would only realize that though shells may fall in the forts, the houses of the city itself are far out of range, so that the inhabitants would not be in the slightest degree incommoded by the firing, then perhaps they would understand that we are not the dolts they take us for at home. If we did proceed to a regular siege, the storming of the fortifications that must inevitably accompany any such operation would cost us a frightful toll of men. I should just like to see the outcry that would then be raised at home! No, we shall not allow ourselves to be moved one hair's-breadth from our conviction just to please these gentlemen sitting at home in comfortable, cosy rooms. I should like these experts to come along here, take matters in their own hands and show whether they understand the job better than we do!

Montmédy has capitulated. It's for all the world as if we took a table-spoonful of fortresses every two days.

Prince Wittgenstein and the English General Clermont dined with me, but I avoided for my part putting leading questions to them regarding conditions in Paris. Their remarks confirm what was said yesterday, and though neither says so expressly, one can see they do not believe Paris can hold out much longer. General Trochu would seem to have no illusions on the point, but rather to be convinced of the hopelessness of his position, only as a matter of military honour he is resolved to protract the defence to the uttermost limit. General Clermont, who knows him well, regrets that a man like Trochu is at the head of affairs, as his one-sided, purely military mind can do little good; on the other hand, he holds him perfectly right in principle in his doctrine of resistance to the very last—a view I find it altogether impossible to share.

Headquarters: Versailles, 15th December.—The spring-like air enticed my brother-in-law and myself to the Petit Trianon, where the birds were twittering as if the warm weather were come. In the garden of my house there is a camellia tree covered with buds standing in the open air.

His Majesty is in great excitement and ill-humour not less over the military situation than over the course of politics.

In the next few days General Count Moltke looks for the capitulation of Longwy and Mezières, this more especially because the Commandant of the first named had declared that rather than surrender he will be buried under the last stone. He says most of the man's colleagues had expressed themselves in the very same way, only immediately afterwards to give up the fortress. Count Moltke's bearing and way of speaking at such moments are quite inimitable.

Headquarters : Versailles, 16*th December.*—It looks more and more as though our military situation is once more to become critical in the north, as it already is in the south; so we must concentrate our forces that we may be able to meet, before it is too late, the masses of enemy troops accumulating against us.

His Majesty's outlook on the immediate future is of the blackest; indeed he is so depressed that at dinner at the Préfecture, at which I was present, it was actually noticeable to others. We believed Prince Friedrich Karl to be fighting to-day at Vendôme and Cloyes and that Châteaudun would be attacked. But telegrams say that the enemy evacuated Vendôme to-day as a result of the attack delivered by the advance guards. Whether General Bourbaki is undertaking something from Bourges cannot yet be substantiated.

The Deputation with the Address from the Reichstag arrived this evening.

The King will not hear a word about receiving the Deputies. Gentlemen of the Court are asking quite openly what exactly these fellows would be after here (!). But, on the other hand, His Majesty is beginning to get a little more accustomed to the Imperial scheme, and is no longer so steadfast as he has hitherto been in his refusal to accept the consequences depending on it. What Count Bismarck may propose being at this time of all others of paramount importance on the question, an attack of gout just now torturing him, combined with the strained state of his nerves that necessitates the utmost quiet and care, is a cause of very serious inconvenience.

Headquarters : Versailles, 17*th December.*—To-day the Council at His Majesty's sat longer than usual; General von Blumenthal also attended, and the question whether Paris should be blockaded or just bombarded was discussed at

General Blumenthal.

length. Thank God, the opinion was expressed that we should rest satisfied with a blockade, only the forts to be bombarded. True, this will not do much to alter the present state of things, but in this way we shall be spared the fearful losses that would be involved in a bombardment of the city and the storming of the fortifications that must necessarily go along with it.

I had just concluded a visit to our wounded officers lying in the Palace when I happened to come upon Prince Karl's Court Chamberlain, and learned from him that a dinner was to take place to-morrow at His Majesty's quarters in honour of the Deputies from the Reichstag, which makes it a fair guess that they would previously be received by the King. To get some more definite assurance at last, I waited for Count Bismarck at the Préfecture till he came out from the report at His Majesty's, and was informed by him that the King had really made up his mind to receive the Deputation to-morrow, as a telegram to-day from the King of Bavaria had announced the actual arrival of the original documents embodying the Princes' declarations of agreement, so ardently desired. No Proclamation is to be issued; but His Majesty's reply will state that he is willing to accept the Imperial dignity. Not before an official notification from Bavaria certifies the arrival of the assenting documents or else these written declarations of the Princes are in our King's hands, will any further step be taken, whilst, further, all the German Parliaments must first have expressed their assent to the assumption of the Imperial title. Count Bismarck deems it very possible that the Bavarian Second Chamber may reject the Treaties, though the Bavarians here on the spot say the contrary. News privately received speaks of the unspoken chagrin of the Kings of Bavaria and Saxony at the good prospects of "Emperor and Empire" becoming an accomplished fact.

I had a long conversation yesterday with Dr. Simson, the President of the Reichstag; I find his point of view entirely correct, and his arguments were no less interesting than logical.

Headquarters: Versailles, 18th December, Sunday.—I was deeply stirred by the reception of the Deputies of the North German Reichstag come to present their Address to His Majesty, for it all went off well and decorously; by it we have made a great step forward in our work for the Unification of Germany and the establishment of the Empire. All German-thinking people felt with me to-day that we were witnessing a momentous event, and that the birth of "Emperor and Empire" was appreciably nearer. The Deputies themselves felt as if they were in a dream. But is it not, in very deed, a wondrous stroke of fate that allots them the duty, on enemy's soil, and at a place that, like Versailles, recalls above all others the bygone ignominy of their country, there to prefer the request to a victorious Prince that he will graciously become Emperor of Germany?

In the sermon preached by the Potsdam Garrison Chaplain, Herr Rogge, who had been specially summoned from the cantonments of the Guards' Corps, the event was tactfully brought into connection with the coming Christmas festivities and the temper befitting them. What I particularly noticed, to begin with, was the greater importance attached to the reception than I had supposed would be the case. Otherwise, the preparations did not so much indicate this, for till that morning, by His Majesty's directions, only those in daily attendance on his person had been invited; then later on I too, and later again the Princes of the House, had been ordered to appear at the ceremony. But subsequently, as we came out from the service, the North German Princes came to me with the request that they likewise might be present at the reception, and the same desire was expressed by all the Generals present. I conveyed their wishes there and then outside the church to the King, who was quite astonished and at most wanted to include the Generals, but in the end after much hesitation I obtained the answer, that if anyone of those named really wished to be there, His Majesty would raise no objection. The natural result was that all the Reigning Princes and Hereditary Princes of the German Confederation now here, together with their suites, as also the Princes attached to my headquarters, put in an appearance, not excepting, of course, the Grand Duke of Baden, though the King expressed himself surprised at this. Similarly all the Generals appeared, while at the last moment the King's A.D.C.'s were also told to attend. The Staff Guard posted guards of honour inside the Préfecture; but to my regret the fine marble staircase was not used. In the main hall of the central building His Majesty took up position in front of the fire-place, the Princes of the Royal House and the others on the right, the Reigning Princes on the left of the King; the rest of those present settled themselves along the walls, standing in a half-circle. The thirty Deputies, Dr. Simson at their head, were introduced, whereupon the President immediately addressed His Majesty in frank and open language. The speech was a complete masterpiece, and so finely delivered that its genuinely patriotic ring actually drew tears from me, who am not generally easily moved in this way. Nay! more, at that moment positively not an eye was dry, and this, particularly in the case of the Generals, means a great deal. After the speech followed the reading of the Address, also by Dr. Simson, whereupon the King read out his reply, as usual on such occasions rather haltingly, for he cannot easily read now without spectacles, but he was also more than once brought to a standstill by his emotion. I have not yet actually seen the contents of the reply, and can only judge by this one hearing of it. It struck me as being over-long, and I thought the part referring to the Princes' consent a trifle hazy. But it gave general satisfaction, and everyone realized that it could only be a question of a brief period of waiting before the momentous words "Emperor and Empire" should be pronounced. His Majesty next had the Deputies presented to him individually, after which all the gentlemen came to me. The President and Vice-President drove in Bismarck's carriage, drawn by a team of four white horses mounted by men of the Transport-train. Throughout the ceremony the guns of Mont Valérien could be heard; the guard, at that moment relieved, played: "Was ist das deutschen Vaterland" as they marched past the Préfecture, and whatever Germans were not on duty at the moment stood in closely packed masses before the King's lodging. In the evening all the Deputies dined at the Royal table.

After the ceremony and again in the evening His Majesty looked happy and pleased and, strongly opposed as he had been at first to the reception and what it implied regarding the Imperial status and the Empire, he seemed henceforth less heavy-hearted, in fact decidedly well satisfied.

We are daily expecting a sortie of the Paris garrison; it would be a curious coincidence if the Deputies were to witness such a thing, as not one of them but would have been glad to see something of war during their short stay in the enemy's country; in any case I shall make an exception in their case and allow them to visit the outposts. The VIth Army Corps reports to-day the results of an accurate survey of the defences lately constructed by the Parisians on their front, the gist being that the ground has been very carefully made the best of and trenches dug everywhere. Our own notion is that General Trochu is counting on fresh attempts at relief, with which he would presently get in touch, or else that he is now for carrying out his last forlorn hope in the way of a sortie so soon as he is convinced that his men cannot hold out any longer within the walls. The state of the enemy's troops retreating before ours in the south and west seems to be deplorable. We read as much in the many private letters captured just now, and above all in the papers of General Chanzy, commanding on the Loire, who reports the wasting of his force to one-half the original number. Gambetta, on the contrary, as usual announces victory upon victory, and lies away gaily about them as he always does. The private servants of the English and Americans who have lately arrived here from Paris appear to tell quite a different tale from what their masters do, making me feel pretty sure that the situation in the city is more distressing than the latter wish us to think.

I received a letter from Paris from Ernest Renan, which was delivered open, as is ordered for all papers coming from there; it is dated the 20th September and its contents are the same as one that reached me in October, and to which I had had a reply sent according to my instructions through Count Seckendorf, albeit written in the third person.

One single exception in the case of sealed correspondence is enjoyed by the American Embassy, which every Tuesday, by special agreement, has packets of despatches handed in at our outposts and receives others back. At the same time deliveries are allowed under our control to enter and leave the city. For the rest, the preference shown the Americans provokes no little surprise.

The question of the form the Empire is to take in the future is at present in everybody's mouth, but no one knows what precisely is proposed in responsible quarters. Personally I am for a monarchy which will independently, in the true sense of the word, face the questions and claims of the day, and by the immediate introduction of a free system of election by districts, as also by granting the laity a share in Church government, will impress the seal of its authority on the People's will.

Furthermore, the re-established Empire must be reformed root and branch and be free from all connection with the principles and traditions of the erstwhile "Holy Roman Empire," the very nature of which was essentially rotten, hollow and utterly effete. Otherwise and barring this difference, I regard the Empire of to-day as identical with that which existed in Germany for over a thousand years and which has only been in abeyance since the abdication of the Emperor Francis II in the year 1806 till the present moment, when, after a sixty-five-years' interregnum, it is re-established, purged of defects and made hereditary.

Headquarters: Versailles, 19th December.—I went out to-day to Villeneuve L'Étang to visit the outposts, and after-

THE EMPEROR FREDERICK III.   229

wards gave a dinner in honour of the Deputies from the Reichstag as well as my limited accommodation permitted; many of them have really been out to the outposts to-day. They all seem to be leaving us well content. It is difficult to describe how much good the change brought about by their appearance in our everyday war-time existence has done us all. After five months of warfare, of which we have already spent three before Paris, it was truly refreshing and exhilarating to see these men with us who bore witness to an achievement there is no going back upon any more, and which, however imperfect the manner of its inception and completion, has yet brought us a gigantic step forward in the history of Germany.

Everybody is eager to be home for Christmas-time. My heart aches to think I must spend this festival so specially dedicated to the joys of family life far from wife and children. But sharing this fate as I do with hundreds of thousands of others for the great cause of Fatherland, I am content to endure the like sacrifices and deprivations in common with my gallant fellow-countrymen.

Headquarters : Versailles, 20th December.—Accompanied by Mr. Odo Russell, I made a long expedition to Louveciennes, near Marly, where the charmingly situated and tastefully appointed villa of the notorious Dubarry is situated. Our presence had been observed from Mont Valérien and it was not long before sundry shells struck pretty close to us.

I dined with Count Bismarck, who is full of all sorts of complaints. Besides myself and my A.D.C.'s, the company included only two other guests along with the subordinate officials, who never spoke one single word at table, but all sat there as dumb as so many statues. The lights instead of being in candlesticks were stuck in the necks of bottles!

Headquarters : Versailles, 21st December.—To-day, the shortest day in the year, the guns of Mont Valérien and the other forts, which we had heard all night long, without intermission, boomed away harder than usual; when dusk came, a sortie was made against the XIIth Army Corps and the Guards' Corps, but it was mainly an artillery duel and caused us little loss.

Here at Versailles a general house-to-house search for arms is all of a sudden being carried out to-day, prepared in dead secrecy and directed by the celebrated Police Agent Stieber (Chief of the Field Police), who accompanies the King everywhere. It seems, in fact, that repeated intimations have been received to the effect that a company of franc-tireurs had little by little smuggled themselves into the town, intending to carry off His Majesty, and more particularly Count Bismarck. True, it is substantially only Stieber himself who hawks about these rumours, still it is always advisable in time of war to take double precautions, and so this entirely unexpected surprise was sprung on the good folks of Versailles to-day. House by house, room by room was searched by our soldiers, house-doors and windows being kept shut and barred meantime and nobody allowed out. The net result was, an individual, well known in the place for a lunatic, was caught with a pocket pistol in his possession!

The Ist Bavarian Army Corps von der Tann is from to-day to join up again with my Army. Opinion in the IInd Army Corps was unfortunately not very favourable to the Bavarians, for it cannot be denied that every time the said Ist Army Corps fought alone for its own hand, it found itself at a disadvantage; on the contrary, directly a mere handful of Prussian troops appeared anywhere near, its courage and capability rose again.

The troops of the IInd Army are already suffering quite sensibly for the want of boots; ill luck too will have it that the French have decidedly smaller feet than the Germans, so that boots taken as booty as well as prisoners' footwear are of no sort of use for our men.

The fashion in which our home Press publishes abroad military news with explanations and prognostics that quite look as if they were inspired, leads people astray; especially must this mischief not be underrated on the question of the bombardment of Paris, for every amateur soldier arriving home from Versailles is always at the utmost pains to proclaim in his shrillest voice the disadvantages involved in the neglect of this pet idea of the Berliners.

It was a more cheerful piece of news for me to learn that my wife's doings as an expert in matters of nursing and tending the sick is rightly appreciated. Thus a detailed report from the Consulting Surgeon to the Hospitals of the XIth Army Corps, Professor Schillbach of Jena, has appeared, which describes the results achieved in the Homburg Hospital, in which my wife never ceased to take an active interest, as the best of all those connected with the Corps.

Headquarters : Versailles, 22nd December.—Already we are busy buying Christmas presents and ransacking the shops, which certainly do not offer much in the way of pretty things.

An icy frost and a north-east wind have come all of a sudden.

Under these circumstances it is lucky that some time ago I ordered hoods to be provided for my Army; these will come in very opportunely to-day. Already we come across the most extraordinary costumes and disguises, the uniform clothing worn up to now being little adapted to keep the men warm. It is to be hoped things will be different in another campaign. Instead of the furs introduced in 1864, the sentries are being given padded cloaks lined with frieze, with which the fellows are well satisfied.

Headquarters : Versailles, 23rd December.—This morning seven degrees of frost (nineteen degrees Fahrenheit, thirteen below freezing point), a temperature unheard of here in France so early in the winter, but fortunately accompanied by bright sunshine and no wind, and also without snow. Our men are used to such cold, but the French cannot stand it at all.
Yesterday Paris rained 350 shells on the Vth Army Corps, but, for all result, hit only one man ! The French Infantry of the line appears in yesterday's sortie to have penetrated much less far than on previous occasions. Two Württemberg batteries the same day forced two enemy brigades threatening the Saxon left wing to turn back again. Prisoners are loud in their abuse of their officers, this even in their presence, and though they know very well they are always given the best of whatever can in any way be got in the way of food, yet they grumble openly at the bad rations.
From one o'clock till five heavy firing could be heard; in fact the Parisians are for again repeating the folly of a sortie against us, for the Landwehr Guards and the Vth Army Corps report that the enemy seems to be planning to break through by way of Chatou to the west and north-west. Such an attempt on the south front could only end in disaster for them, as the 9th Division, by felling whole tracts of woodland, has established three such formidable lines of defence that literally not a soul can force a way through these obstacles. These are generally known by the humorous title of " Sandrart's embellishments of the landscape." It is just as if the French were deliberately choosing this Christmas week for provoking more bloodshed, while their prospects of any possible success to follow grow more and more hopeless.

Headquarters : Versailles, 24th December.—Christmas Eve, the great day when gifts of goodwill are distributed, in an enemy's country and in the midst of war's alarms ! So this time we are not to spend this chiefest festivity of German family life with our dear ones. My heart is heavy indeed, yet for this year it seems that every feeling of kindly sentiment, nay, every instinct of humanity, must be overshadowed by the grimmest horrors of war. Next after my beloved ones at home, my thoughts are above all for the unhappy widows and orphans; for indeed for thousands this Christmas will be a time of mourning. God grant that when a year hence at the home fireside we recall the many sacrifices of this War, its results may at any rate be such that we can say with full conviction, they have been made to secure a lasting and honourable Peace!

I cannot but believe things are coming to a climax, for more and more urgent every day in France are the demands for peace at any price and the summoning of a Constituent Assembly. On the other hand, it sometimes seems to me that the longer the city's resistance lasts, the more are new and hitherto hidden possibilities of holding out discovered. In no other way can this obstinacy be explained. The prisoners taken two days ago declare that the disinclination of the troops of the line for further sorties has risen to such a pitch that they were informed of the proposed fight only on the preceding evening, and that with the intimation that this sortie would be the last. Moreover, battalions of Gardes Mobiles are purposely paraded before those of the line in order to show the latter that these would share in the action —yet nobody observed any Mobiles actually engaged. As to provisioning, only small rations of horseflesh, a great deal of bread, but less wine than before and no vegetables at all are now served out. They said the Mobiles only fought when officers gave the example, but as all serviceable men were already prisoners of war in Germany, there were no efficients left.

Yesterday General von Manteuffel won a victory on the Hallue by Amiens over an enemy of twice his force.

For Christmas Eve I had organized a raffle under the Christmas tree for the eighty members of my Staff. The same was arranged in separate rooms for domestics, Staff guard, stable and escort squadrons; of course punch, pepper cakes, nuts and apples being provided as far as possible for the occasion. Every member of my Staff, as well as other invited guests, was bound each to bring with him two trifles for distribution, so that the caprice of fortune had a free scope; for instance Mr. Odo Russell won an officer's sword-belt. The 160 prizes were soon disposed of amid much laughter and merriment, whilst I, to my surprise and delight, found a number of useful presents, thoughtfully chosen by wife and mother, laid out on a table specially reserved for me. In particular, a miniature pocket-revolver met with much applause among the company; purses, pincushions, riding-satchels and other little toilet requisites were not wanting.

Another raffle like that at my quarters was held for the Princes and the subordinate members of my Staff at the Hôtel des Réservoirs, from which we went on afterwards to His Majesty's, where there was a formal distribution of gifts and a supper. Every guard-house was gay with Christmas trees and their glittering lights, which were to be found even at the most distant outposts. Everything wore quite the look of Christmas-tide at home, and a spirit of gay good-humour enlivened every German heart even at points where the enemy's shells were whistling by. The French could not conceal their astonishment at the doings of these northern barbarians, for even by our purchases in the shops and by meeting us about the streets they saw how friendliness and the wish to give pleasure to others animated every man amongst us.

Headquarters : Versailles, 25th December.—Nine degrees of frost (sixteen degrees Fahrenheit) and an east wind as we went to service in the Palace chapel.

It sounds almost like irony, amidst the miseries of war and in days that speak only of death and destruction to the foe to listen to the Christmas message of salvation : " On earth peace and good-will toward men." Christendom is still far from acting in the spirit of those words. The clergy have a difficult task set them to explain the contradiction involved in the strife of Christians against Christians, where each side invokes God for its own as the only just cause, and at every success holds this to prove that the adversary has been forsaken by Heaven. I leave the solution of the problem to professed theologians, and look simply to Him who has helped us hitherto; and then I turn my thoughts to all those who are no longer with us and to those left behind who to-day can be filled only with feelings of sorrow.

At the report at His Majesty's, General Count Moltke mentioned how, according to General von Manteuffel's latest reports, the latter this morning was still faced by his opponent, so that the victory announced yesterday could have been no decisive or final one. In view of this doubtful situation of the Ist Army he deems an immediate reinforcement desirable, to include six battalions and two batteries of the IVth Army Corps, to be despatched by rail from Gonesse to Amiens. To take their place, a brigade of Landwehr Guards of the

Army of the Meuse was to be made available, while the Vth Army Corps was to step into the gaps caused thereby in the investing lines round Paris. However, towards midday came a telegram from General Manteuffel reporting that, after the repulse of certain offensive movements on the part of the enemy, the latter were now in retreat and he was pursuing in a north-easterly direction, whereupon Count Moltke cancelled in all particulars the order he had just issued. So to-day there was enough and to spare of writing and telegraphing, the more so as indications reached us to the effect that an attempt to break through and attack the Army of the Meuse was preparing and supports might have to be sent out to its assistance. In fact, ever since the engagement at Champigny, contingents in ever-increasing strength are gathered before the east face of the city and may at any moment carry out a movement against the XIIth (Saxon) Army Corps; but besides this, the Parisians have now opened a regular system of parallels against Le Bourget, in order to gain possession of this village that has so often already been a bone of contention. All day long we expected the sortie, but it hung fire; then, late in the evening, it became known that in Paris, in spite of drizzling snow and a cutting north-easter with ten to twelve degrees of frost (fourteen to ten degrees Fahrenheit), a great parade had been held to-day, so that the marchings of troops in the streets necessary for this purpose had been taken to indicate movements with a view to a sortie.

Skating is in active progress; for myself, I am not taking part in the amusement.

Headquarters : Versailles, 26th December.—The reports at His Majesty's now often last a long time, for it is no trifle for us, in view of the powerful efforts of the French to relieve Paris from three different sides, to keep good watch on these and estimate the disposition and application of our forces necessitated thereby, especially as in an enemy's country the difficulties of transmitting and receiving news and those of transport are infinitely intensified. In particular, we find it troublesome to discover what exactly is preparing to the south of the Loire, where Bourbaki is now busy organizing a fresh Army; as to the route it will take and its plans, nothing whatever is to be learned. Rumours are rife that General Bourbaki is to relieve Belfort, liberate Alsace and then invade Baden, whereas others point to Montargis or Orleans as his objective. In any case the IInd Army fails to reconnoitre adequately to the southward, to Count Moltke's great vexation. To-day we have reasons to conjecture that General Bourbaki is marching on Châlons-sur-Saône, indicating that at last he is really making for Belfort. But it might also be possible that a junction and co-operation with General Chanzy is intended, so that eventually the latter, advancing from the south-west from Lille, Bourbaki from the north, both are planning to cut our lines of communication with Germany.

To-morrow our batteries will at last be so far completed against Mont Avron that its bombardment can begin.

Headquarters : Versailles, 27th December.—At seven in the morning, in bitter frost, fog and driving snow, our siege artillery opened fire on Mont Avron, where, so they say, subsequently to the engagements of the 30th November and the 2nd December, entrenchments, equipped with heavy cannon, were constructed by order of Colonel Stoffel as commanding officer. We had been firing for six hours without a break, when about midday the roar of the guns little by little fell silent. Was our heavy cannonade at last making its effect felt? We are eagerly awaiting news of the results, of which Paris really knows as good as nothing, for in the first place the forts are at a great distance from the city, while, besides that, fog and snow entirely shut off any distant view.

Belfort appears, as a matter of fact, to be threatened by General Bourbaki, for we hear that auxiliary forces of all arms are actually being hurried up in fast trains from Lyons and the south; Generals von Werder and von Zastrow will consequently have a heavy task before them. Bourbaki's enterprise is an insane one; still, if it should result in two or three successes, it may for the moment inspire the Parisians and the French generally with an overweening confidence and fresh spirit, one consequence of which will undoubtedly be an immediate and effective *levée en masse* that will cause us serious difficulties. However, Lieutenant-General von Blumenthal is really overjoyed at the folly of the French in undertaking such an enterprise and is convinced that General Bourbaki will make a conspicuous fiasco.

To-day the Ist Bavarian Army Corps von der Tann returned to its quarters at Arpajon; the General received the Order *Pour le Mérite.*

I got a letter to-day from my little daughter Viktoria, the first she has composed herself, though her hand was guided in the writing.

It is said the Duc de Chartres and the Duc d'Aumale are serving and fighting in the French Army.

Ernest Renan has written a wonderfully fine letter to my wife, in which his noble and elevated sentiments for humanity, no less than the pure sincerity of his character, are mirrored. If only we could find more Frenchmen who like him possessed insight and impartiality combined with human kindness, and courage to boot, then Gambetta's bloody handiwork would soon be at an end.

Headquarters : Versailles, 28th *December*.—General von Werder is to march on Vezoul, while General von Zastrow with the available troops of his VIIth Army Corps will be withdrawn from Auxerre to act eventually as a covering force for General von Werder. At Le Mans new French forces are concentrated, and while in the north, it is true, the enemy is all the time retreating before General von Manteuffel's pursuit, yet it begins to look more and more as if fresh auxiliary forces are expected at Lille and the neighbourhood. We must therefore be prepared before long to see vigorous and desperate attempts carried out simultaneously from north, west and south for the final relief of Paris; while at one and the same moment we are on the defensive on three fronts, a sortie on an imposing scale will likewise be made from the capital. Generals von Manteuffel and von Werder have now the stiffest task to tackle; but battles and bloodshed will go their course—nor must we forget that the French will have no lack of war material, as they always have ample consignments of arms and ammunition from America to congratulate themselves upon.

It has been snowing for two days; five degrees of frost (twenty-three degrees Fahrenheit) is the lowest reading of the thermometer at noon. Fog and snowflakes make it difficult to see far, notwithstanding which we keep up a continuous fire on Mont Valérien, which for once in a way is silent to-day. Thank God, our yesterday's loss was only four killed and nineteen wounded; but indeed we too can have inflicted but little damage on the enemy under such unfavourable conditions of weather.

Headquarters : Versailles, 29th *December*.—We have enjoyed a fine success we never expected; the enemy after a forty-eight hours' cannonade was forced to abandon his strong position on Mont Avron, after the railway station of Noisy-le-Bec had been well knocked about and the French artillery in cantonments at Bondy reduced to silence. Arms, ammunition and dead men were left behind in the fort. The Berliner will be triumphant. His Majesty too as early as yesterday received a telegram of approval from the Köpernicker Strasse because the bombardment had begun at last (!). What drove out the French, particularly in this weather, is still an unsolved riddle; but anyhow, under these favourable conditions, we can now bombard at our pleasure the forts of Rosny and Nogent.

Deserters say that the rations in Paris get smaller and smaller and that the cavalry horses were already disappearing.

We received to-day the glorious news how First Lieutenant von Boltenstern of the 3rd Hanoverian Infantry regiment No. 79, with six companies, a squadron of horse and two guns, had at Montoire-La Chartre, after a courageous defence against a superior force, which had actually surrounded him, triumphantly fought his way through and with a loss on his side of some hundred men had brought in 10 officers and 230 men as prisoners. A noble example for the Army, over which General Count Moltke, altogether against his wont, came very near breaking down.

On January 1st the Imperial Constitution, embodying the principle of "Emperor and Empire," is to come into existence. But no one has an inkling whether this great event will be smuggled into Germany, so to speak, without a word or will be announced by an official proclamation, or whether possibly people generally will just stand by waiting to see the results of the change. All the more, therefore, I shall find myself obliged to seek information at the Office of the Federal Chancellor by a series of very pointed questions. At all events I have, in collaboration with my brother-in-law, drafted a Proclamation for His Majesty, which, while sparing as far as possible the King's peculiar susceptibilities, still possesses patriotic spirit; it is indeed more than doubtful if it will meet with approval in the highest quarter of all. I resolved on this composition, although on principle I do not as a rule lend my name to creations of Bismarck's, to try whether, in view of the unedifying quarrels at the Royal headquarters, my hand might perhaps be helpful in the way of reconciliation and explanation, for at all points and with all the strength I can bring to bear, I am fain to do what I may to avert greater evils.

The dominant idea underlying the Proclamation is to represent our King as successor to the German Emperors, albeit the future Empire, as compared with that borne to the grave in the year 1806, is in its essence a new and entirely different thing. The continuity, therefore, between the two is only to be recognized in purely external matters, which, however, must be modelled neither in any sort of way on the old Holy Roman Empire, nor yet on any foreign example whatsoever. If only on the ground that many a German Prince would rather see the old Empire of shreds and patches restored than the Hohenzollern established, any rigid adherence to what is over and done with is to be avoided. I hold that, just as in 1848 the old Prussian Kingdom died and was buried, straightway, thank God, to rise again fundamentally changed as a constitutional monarchy, while keeping its title and external forms unaltered, so in like wise should be the case to-day with the newly-founded Empire. At the same time, of course, with the so-called " new " Emperor of Germany the modern Imperialism as displayed in the creations of Austria and France ought not to be introduced; what I desire is that the present Empire should preserve only in its outward manifestations any close and clear connection with the old Empire of a thousand years and more, whereas its inward constitution, framed on entirely new lines, must be something essentially different and adapted to meet the claims of the present day. For the rest I can only hope I have in my draft hit the taste of the King and Bismarck. Could I express freely and from the heart my own inmost convictions, I should indeed speak in quite a different tone.

A year ago to-day I paid a visit in Paris to the Emperor Napoleon and the Empress Eugénie on my return from the East, and was told by the former that Ollivier had become First Minister of the Crown on that day. How everything has changed since then!

Headquarters: Versailles, 30th December.—Heavy firing kept us long in suspense; probably it is the commencement of the bombardment of Nogent and Rosny from Mont Avron.

My Secretary Pilch, who ever since the 9th December has been on his way from Berlin with letters for us and presents for the regiment from my wife, arrived to-day after a thousand perils on the road.

Headquarters: Versailles, 31st December.—We had to-day a rather lengthy sitting at His Majesty's, at which General von Kameke and General Prince Kraft zu Hohenlohe were present; at this all arguments for and against bombardment and investment were again discussed at length, and finally the order was given by the King for the bombardment of the city, to begin at the earliest possible moment. At a consultation held immediately afterwards with the Generals named I fixed the 4th January as the day for the opening of this wretched bombardment. May we not have to repent our folly!

Indications lead us to believe that the temper of the Parisians is beginning to weaken, but we have heard this so often already that I have altogether ceased to credit it. In the evening, newspapers from Paris were read out at His Majesty's containing official reports of what happened on Mont Avron, from which we gather that as early as the 27th December we were inflicting heavy losses on the enemy.

. . . .

How glorious it would be if, as we greet the New Year, we could at the same time hail the dawn of peace! But the future is still veiled behind dark, heavy clouds, whose shadows fall on anxious hearts and make it hard to keep a bright courage and cheerful hope. The spectacle now displayed before our eyes is in very deed one to fill all Germans with serious, if not troubled thoughts. Everything has fallen out differently from what we seemed justified in expecting, and we cannot therefore shut out the fear that it might even go from bad to worse with us. Both the two contending nations in this bitter struggle have come to regard it as a point of honour not to give in or to remit anything of the demands formulated. The basis for an understanding will accordingly from day to day grow harder to find. It may be the Governments of both countries are equally open to the reproach that they have called up spirits they cannot now lay, and heedlessly given currency to watchwords that public opinion has now appropriated for its own.

It is at this time of day a simple impossibility for us to cancel our possession of Alsace and Lorraine, even if we have to tell ourselves that the gain is precarious and hardly worth the streams of blood that have been shed for it. Even Bismarck, whose genius is pre-eminently displayed in discovering ways out of inconvenient obligations, would find himself in the greatest embarrassment if he were forced to search for excuses to cover the surrender of the two Provinces. Every man in Germany, be it rightly or wrongly, desires their retention, and even from the military point of view this is deemed a necessity. If we look back to the beginning of the War, Germany was manifestly the aggrieved and attacked party. All Europe was angry and indignant at the way we were assailed and startled from our peaceful quietude. The world sympathized with the noble burst of enthusiasm that swept through all Germany and brought about a swift unity; it admired the heroic spirit that fired the sons of the Fatherland to the holy War. In all humility and earnestness we were one and all ready to fight and die, and to the same degree as men applauded us, they execrated the insolent and overweening enemy, and cordially rejoiced at the punishment that quickly overtook him for his pitiful lies and boasting. We were well prepared to suffer reverses at the start; all the more, therefore, did our wonderful successes fill us and all the world with breathless amazement, and never did victories effect mightier and more glorious results than those of Weissenburg, Wörth and Sedan. The collapse of the Napoleonic régime, with its Army, its Officialdom, its whole organization based on falsehood and deceit, frivolity and corruption, delighted the thinking portion of mankind, which had suffered long enough under the deadly influence of this jugglery. The assumption seemed justified that France after the battle of Sedan was utterly crushed, that the nation was broken in morale and incapable of further resistance, that Paris itself, the capital city of pleasure, would instantly capitulate " if it were only a single day without strawberries." But in all points the exact contrary was manifested. The French people day by day rose higher from its degradation; it seemed as though the downfall of its former Government had given it back strength, courage and honour, as though Generals and Statesmen it had hitherto so sorely lacked had sprung up again to win back what was lost. Men like Gambetta and Trochu were not wanting at any rate in boldness and capacity. And on all sides we see new Armies, made up of volunteers, arise out of nothing; never, it is true, have these become a force of trained soldiers, but they are often much superior to us in numbers, and day by day gain in efficiency and fighting capability, to vanquish which will cost us heavy sacrifices. But it is the capital holds us at bay before her gates and puts our endurance to the severest proof.

The longer this struggle lasts, the better for the enemy and the worse for us. The public opinion of Europe has not remained unaffected by the spectacle. We are no longer looked upon as the innocent sufferers of wrong, but rather as the arrogant victors, no longer content with the conquest of the foe, but fain to bring about his utter ruin. No more do the French appear in the eyes of neutrals as a mendacious, contemptible nation, but as the heroic-hearted people that against overwhelming odds is defending its dearest possessions in honourable fight. Nay, in their sympathy with France men go so far as to hate Germany. In this nation of thinkers and philosophers, poets and artists, idealists and enthusiasts, the world will recognize nothing but a people of conquerors and destroyers, to which no pledged word, no treaty concluded, is sacred, which speaks with rude insolence of others that had done it no hurt and scornfully makes mock even of the gifts offered it as tokens of sympathy and good-will. Utterly false as these views are, we cannot, unfortunately, deny their existence and are bound to own that they are indeed well fitted to tarnish the brightness of the good name we have hitherto enjoyed. True, we are indisputably the foremost people of the world in civilization, yet at the moment it must seem as though we are neither loved nor respected, but only feared. We are deemed capable of every wickedness and the distrust felt for us grows ever more and more pronounced. Nor is this the consequence of this War only—so far has the theory, initiated by Bismarck and for years holding the stage, of " Blood and Iron " brought us ! What good to us is all power, all martial glory and renown, if hatred and mistrust meet us at every turn, if every step we advance in our development is a subject for suspicion and grudging? Bismarck has made us great and powerful, but he has robbed us of our friends, the sympathies of the world, and—our conscience. I still hold fast to-day to the conviction that Germany, without blood and iron, simply by the justice of her cause, could make " moral conquests " and, united, become free and powerful. A preponderance of quite another kind than that gained by mere force of arms was within our reach, for German culture, German science and German genius must have won us respect, love and—honour. The insolent, brutal " Junker " willed it otherwise. In 1864 his schemes and intrigues spoilt the victory of a good cause; in 1866 he broke up Austria without making Germany one, and now by the publication of Benedetti's offer has made it seem as though under certain circumstances we had not been disinclined to enter into Napoleon's perfidious designs.

The future holds for us the noble, but infinitely difficult task of freeing the beloved German Fatherland from the baseless suspicion with which the world to-day regards her. We must prove that the power acquired is not to beget dangers, but to bring with it a blessing, the blessing of peace and civilization. But how hard it will be to combat the worship of brute force and mere outward success, to enlighten men's minds, to direct ambition and emulation once more to worthy and healthy objects ! God grant it may soon be possible to find the means to bring about an honourable peace and put an end to useless bloodshed, before it has cost us too excessive sacrifices ! Even now the Bavarians,

Saxons and Württembergers have suffered terribly, and the ranks of our officers are sadly dwindled, without any prospect of speedily filling the gaps. But at home the lofty spirit of holy, patriotic enthusiasm such as was shown in those unforgettable days of July, has materially declined and given place to a feeling of discouragement. Yet our gallant Army bears all privations and sufferings with unparalleled courage; to our soldiers and Fatherland we owe it to be steadfast in patience and confidence and to face the future with a strong heart and undaunted eyes. As the beginning of the mighty War was fortunate beyond all hope and expectation, so must we in thankfulness and confidence trust that, in spite of all changes and chances that may still befall, the end will correspond with the beginning.

Headquarters: Versailles, 1st January (1871).—Seldom indeed has a New Year's Day been kept under such remarkable circumstances and conditions as the present. Every man is asking himself and his neighbours what the New Year will bring us, and, first and foremost, will it at last bring peace? To both questions there is but one and the same answer: Who can tell?

After I had, at an early hour this morning, distributed Iron Crosses of the First Class to officers, regimental sergeants and non-commissioned officers of the Vth Army Corps, I proceeded, in very unpropitious weather, before the hour of divine service to visit the King, whom I found less downhearted than I expected, but rather in the holiday mood customary with him when he has to address a number of people. In serious and kindly tones of emotion, he greeted me with the wish that it might be granted me to live to see in times of peace the fruits of the work now being done here, adding that he could not indeed suppose for his part that a permanent unity of Germany would really be achieved, as so very few of the Princes were acting in such a way and in such a spirit as was to be wished and as the Grand Duke of Baden had shown the example. I found nothing to answer, seeing I regard the disruption again of our at last united Fatherland as an impossibility, so long as Prussia and my House do not desire it.

Then after a very hearty greeting to the Grand Duke of Weimar, the King received the congratulations of the surprisingly numerous—a good thirty in all—Princes and Hereditary Princes who had appeared in the hall of the Préfecture; then came divine service in the Palace chapel, and directly after that congratulations from all the assembled officers and officials off duty at the time in the celebrated and beautiful *Salle des Glaces,* the whole length of which down one side was completely filled by the numerous company present standing at the wall three deep. His Majesty entered briskly, made a short speech of greeting and thanks to the company generally, walked rapidly once up and down the front of those marshalled in line, addressing a few friendly words to individuals, and in barely ten minutes the whole thing was over.

The military report at His Majesty's was to-day a highly important one. In the first place, acting in agreement with Prince Kraft Hohenlohe and Lieutenant-General von Kameke, on the ground of the conclusions we had lately arrived at together, and since their reconnaissances were now concluded, I urged His Majesty to order the bombardment to begin on the 4th January, which thereupon the King agreed to. Furthermore, at General Count Moltke's urgency, I was ordered to have the IInd Army Corps march at once for Montargis, there to await General Bourbaki's further movements. This Army Corps consequently is withdrawn from the line of investment round Paris and, separated from the IIIrd Army Corps, comes under the direct orders of the General Staff and will be relieved by the Ist Bavarian Army Corps von der Tann. At the same time it was ordered that the IInd Army should take the offensive to the westward, that is to say, advance in the direction of Le Mans; meantime Orleans remains occupied and the enemy forces conjectured to be about Bourges and Nevers on both banks of the river are to be kept under observation. Prince Friedrich Karl accordingly will oppose the forward movements of the French General Chanzy in the west, while the Pomeranian Army Corps has to keep in uninterrupted touch with him, as well as with the VIIth Army Corps under General von Zastrow, now ordered forward in a south-westerly direction from Montbard by Châtillon-sur-Seine. In this formation we wait upon General Bourbaki's movements, in case he pushes on to the north. All the same we conjecture it to be more and more likely he is actually marching against Belfort and General Werder's position, so that we shall soon have to send reinforcements there.

So it seems the bombardment is really ordered, and thereby Count Bismarck's and the Berliners' wishes are fulfilled. But I still hold to the same opinion, to wit, that with the scanty material so far on the spot, and considering the insecurity of transport for keeping up the indispensable supplies of ammunition, we ought never to have taken in hand the bombardment of a city and fortress like Paris; the planting of heavy guns in positions specially well adapted for defence would have been the right course. As it is, the Parisians will just laugh at us, and if famine does not eventually force them to surrender—which indeed in the long run it cannot fail to do, and to which end the blockade was in fact directed—I fully expect that at the sound of the first shot the spirit of resistance will flare up again more hotly than ever. But into the bargain we may yet find ourselves under the agreeable necessity, one fine day when the firing ceases, of being precious sorry for the mistake we have committed.

I had invited to second breakfast all the men of my old Pomeranian Army Corps who have been nominated as Knights of the Iron Cross First Class, in order personally to bestow on them that splendid badge of honour. It gave me particular pleasure to be able to pin this high distinction on the breast of a common soldier, a lance-corporal of the 6th Pomeranian Infantry regiment No. 48. He is doing his second year's service and is a day labourer from the neighbourhood of Stolpmünde. After that I brought the whole delighted company to report to His Majesty. The day ended with a big dinner at the King's quarters, at which His Majesty spoke a few words. The Grand Duke of Baden, however, referred to the " Empire " that was ratified to-day by the official publication of the Constitution, but which the King refused to recognize before all princely lines had given in their consent, and, using the King of Bavaria's words, had his health drunk as " King William the Victorious." The effect of this toast, as noble in thought as in expression, on all present was unmistakable, for my brother-in-law had ventured to express in words what all felt. Prince Luitpold of Bavaria was the only one who appeared not to like the phrase. Thus at any rate this evening of New Year's Day some mention has been made of the poor Empire, whose re-birth would else have passed entirely unnoticed.

Mr. Odo Russell found the spectacle very imposing of all the many German Princes gathered to-day about the King, but noted on his part too how evidently hopes had been entertained in all quarters of a Proclamation of the Empire to be made to-day. One cannot maintain that in principle a mistake has been committed in postponing it, as the fact is established of the Empire's being again in existence; at the same time it is a sad pity that our talent for belittling really great things by a clumsy way of doing them, and thereby as good as diminishing their value, has again been manifested on this occasion.

From King Victor Emmanuel I received a New Year's

telegram very cordially expressed, and—a noteworthy fact—dated from Rome.

Mr. Odo Russell has meantime also heard of the American longing for a disagreement between Germany and England; nevertheless, and in spite of Prince Bismarck's antipathy to England, he hopes the latter country's common sense will preserve her from senseless alliances, as for instance with America.

Headquarters : Versailles, 2nd January.—Mezières capitulated yesterday—another triumph for Lieutenant-General von Kameke, who received the oak-wreath to his Cross *Pour le Mérite* for it.

I went to visit the batteries, now ready for the guns, on the terrace of the Château de Meudon, as well as the orangery underneath it destined to serve as bomb-proof shelters for the covering units; I took advantage of the field telegraphs that have just been fitted up here to inform Lieutenant-General von Blumenthal, who was particularly anxious to prevent my going to this certainly rather exposed spot, that I was on forbidden ground. The enemy below at Bas-Meudon, whose outposts are quite near, appear to have discovered nothing yet of our preliminary works, but will surely before long be again pitching a ruinous hail of shot this way, after he has for months now been doing such fatal damage to the old château as makes it nothing more than a pitiful, nay by this time a sickening sight.

Headquarters : Versailles, 3rd January.—I visited to-day, under guidance of Major Salbach of the War Ministry, batteries Nos. 5 and 6 at Clamart, which are planted almost directly opposite Fort Issy, and whose equipment had just been completed and the guns hauled in. The prevailing frost—the noon reading to-day was six degrees below zero (twenty-one degrees Fahrenheit)—facilitates the latter operation, for otherwise it would be enormously difficult in this heavy soil to shift the cannon. All conceivable measures are adopted to provide bomb-proof shelters for our artillerymen and the troops acting as cover and reserve. As it can hardly now come to a regular infantry engagement, we shall, please God, suffer no great losses. The open throats of the heavy 24-pounders are going to give the Parisians a surprise to-morrow.

A little before I reached the batteries in question, a shell struck close by them not far from us and exploded. The fragments were picked up at once and brought to me; it was a greeting from Issy, the garrison of which must have contrived to get wind of our preparations. The men were very pleased and excited, eagerly at work to finish the last of the earthworks, no light job with the ground frozen hard; everybody is delighted at the bombardment, long desired both by officers and men, all hoping this would bring about the conclusion of the War. Many a look of astonishment was cast at me, for the fellows could not at first believe their eyes when they beheld the Commander-in-Chief coming to visit them there. Certainly my proper place is not in the batteries, but I wanted the gunners to have seen me for once before their heavy work begins.

On the way home I met the long train of the rest of the siege guns leaving the gun-park of Villacoublay, and now again ordered for removal; the gun-crews marching with them carried every man his woollen blanket with him, which gave the column a very odd look. Many cheery greetings were exchanged; but I was more particularly diverted when I came upon the men of the Pomeranian Garrison Artillery, a number of whom, recognizing me as an acquaintance of earlier days, gave expression to their delight with their own inimitable national phlegm. Fortunately our troops do not suffer from the cold, for to every man going on sentry duty is served out, besides his service cloak, a second one lined with thick, woolly material, to which is fastened the hood that proved so serviceable in 1864. Ever since that winter campaign I had longed to have this for the Army, of course without seeing it introduced—now the cold does what I never could, and they had to be put in hand in headlong haste.

At the Army of the Meuse a French officer of the line with several files reported himself with the announcement that, if they received him well, he gave his word of honour to fetch over his whole company. He was allowed to go—and duly brings in the whole body. His men declared they could not put up any more either with the bad, scanty rations or the insults superiors heap upon them as if they were dirt. May this really vile behaviour prove at any rate an indication pointing to a speedy capitulation.

My brother-in-law and the Prince of Schaumburg-Lippe dined with me. The latter has a perfect passion for taking dangerous rides outside the outpost line, which will one day cost him dear. Once you have got used to his queer personality and let him say his say, he can talk quite in an interesting way and develop shrewd opinions. Little as he has been a *persona grata* to us since 1866,[1] he is now decidedly on our side on the German question.

[1] In the year 1866 he had sided with Austria, had withdrawn from the German Confederation and had subsequently been excluded from the Treaty of Alliance with Prussia.

I live in expectation of the bombardment which is to begin at daybreak to-morrow; it is kept a profound secret, the same as on the eve of a battle; whatever else it does, I pray it may bring peace a step nearer! All orders are issued and carried out, and all batteries under my command are connected by wire with my headquarters; if we are favoured with the same good luck as heretofore, the bombardment may perhaps lead to important results. May we then soon see an end of the resistance of this reputed metropolis of civilization, and finally break the chain that surrounds this so-called " holy city "—" the modern Babylon " were the better designation— and inflict on her the chastisement she deserves. At the same time it would grieve me if the buildings that are part of History or dedicated to art, or if the collections should be damaged, for all that is in question is to punish that section of the population whose wickedness was the guilty cause of the War. But, unfortunately, in a bombardment we can, of course, make ourselves responsible for nothing. The only definite aim for the moment is to bombard and silence the forts; we can only await further developments.

Headquarters : Versailles, 4th January.—The eager antici- pation with which from daybreak on we watched for the first shot was frustrated by an impenetrable fog, that refused to clear for even one instant, so that there was no real daylight whatever. At the same time an icy wind was blowing that covered the whole landscape with hoar- frost.

I went to-day to the Bavarian entrenchment, so well known from the 19th September onwards, to visit the batteries there, in which Bavarians and Prussians serve the guns. Off and on a French shell flew by not far from us, but this was only the usual afternoon cannonade from the enemy's batteries, so that we could only conclude they were not yet aware that we were standing by fully prepared to open. The wind and thick atmosphere have so far been our good allies, but now it must be clear to let us aim properly—and already the glass is rising and promises good weather. In the com- munication trenches, as in the batteries themselves, it was comfortably warm because of the shelter the walls of earth afforded against the icy wind.

It is really worthy of the highest praise, the unwearied perseverance with which the construction of the batteries was pushed on, for, not to mention the cold, the ground is frozen several feet deep, and into the bargain larded all through with stones. Besides this, the keen frost prevailing freezes the earth just dug out so quickly that our fellows have to deal far more with clods of earth than with ordinary soil.

It gave me no little pleasure to be able to speak a word or two of recognition to officers and men for their diligence in this heavy work, and for all I feel convinced that strictly speaking I ought not to be there, on the other hand I am very sure that all ranks like to see their commander exposing himself in places of danger, especially where, as in this case, a trying duty is further aggravated by out-of-the-way conditions. During the bombardment I certainly ought not to come here again out of the regard I owe to my position, but should a big sortie occur, I know where my place will be.

Rumour has it that in consequence of events at Mont Avron disturbances had broken out in Paris, necessitating the calling out of the National Guard; the dearness of everything seems to be really increasing seriously; for according to the official lists of prices issued daily, two or three eggs cost ten francs and a few herrings the same. Supposing this true, our bombardment might really seem to have been of some effect.

It is so cold in Berlin my wife has had the sentries come indoors and has sent out hot ale to the guard-rooms.

Headquarters : Versailles, 5th January.—Yesterday's fog was succeeded to-day by bright sunshine, so at a quarter after eight this morning the first shell, from Battery No. 8, fell on Paris. The Bavarian Field Artillery opened fire from Sceaux on the hollow way at Bièvre and silenced the terraced batteries there. The remaining batteries only fired as the clearness of the air and the possibility of taking aim permitted; so, for instance, Batteries Nos. 11 and 12, after being briskly but ineffectually shelled from Montrouge, only began to take action at midday. Now will the wiseacres of Berlin be triumphant indeed and expect the capitulation to come about at latest this evening. Only what will they say, if in a fortnight's time everything still remains *in statu quo ?*

The first day's bombardment gives the impression that the French are obviously aware of the superiority of our fire over theirs, for up to nightfall only a few isolated points of our lines were under fire; more than that, the very much exposed batteries at Meudon suffered no losses at all—indeed a report ran to the effect that the guns in Fort Issy had apparently been removed from the embrasures. Yet it transpired that Plessis-Piquet, the very spot where Dr. Boeger and Dr. Wilms had established their dressing-station, was so heavily shelled that several times they had to shift it, and that in the middle of operations. Possibly the enemy will only open fire on us when night comes; but should he by any chance decline the artillery duel altogether, he will by such conduct shake the morale and confidence of his troops, for to be continuously under fire without having the least chance of returning the punishment is one of the most searching demands to which a man is exposed in war. Our losses to-day amounted to four men killed, four officers and eleven men wounded, but, alas! several of the latter very severely.

I drove with my brother-in-law to Villa Stern, from which, however, in spite of the sunshine, the heavy mist that hung about the sky prevented our seeing much. His Majesty, General Count Moltke, Duke Ernst and others were likewise there. A horrible, biting wind got up suddenly as we stood there, quickly veiling the sun with clouds and quite benumbing us; but with evening came a change of weather, so that after eight degrees of frost (eighteen degrees Fahrenheit) in the morning, it was almost a thaw at night with a temperature of one degree above zero. What a piece of luck that the ground remained frozen just till the arming of the batteries was completed.

Great excitement was caused by the sudden hoisting of a flag of truce, whereupon, of course, sundry hot-heads jumped to the conclusion that the bombardment had already done its work. But it was merely a question of an old, infirm American General who desired permission to leave the city.

Prince Friedrich Karl may have the opportunity within the next few days at Le Mans of completely defeating the Western Army, still in course of formation at that place and already once beaten, so as afterwards to march the quicker on Orleans and look for General Bourbaki, as we do not even yet know the strength of that force, and conjecture that at least one Corps of it will march on that place with the object of disturbing us before Paris by an onslaught from the south.

Headquarters: Versailles, 6th January.—When yesterday a French shell exploded in the battery of Clamart, a panic seized the gunners, but next instant Colonel von Rieff, who was there at the moment, sprang on to the parapet and from there fired on the men in so vigorous a fashion that the first consternation was quickly overcome, and thereafter all did their duty without demur.

Paris shows hardly a trace of the bombardment, for this is directed solely at the forts and the enceinte of the city, and only here and there does a shell go astray into the sea of houses. To-day and yesterday we received news by roundabout ways from spies to the effect that, owing to the increasing scarcity, a very despondent temper prevails in the city, and that the shortage of horses is making itself felt. However cautiously suchlike news is to be accepted, still it cannot be denied that this time they sound more probable than heretofore, but without our being able on that account to form any notion as to how long resistance will still last. With regard to Gambetta, a notable change seems to be coming over French sentiment..

My brother-in-law and I, favoured by the very mild weather accompanying the thaw and the bright sunshine, went out to the "Tinder-box," as the men call this particular outpost, and enjoyed, amid the thunder of the siege guns, the magnificent view of Paris from this point. We could accurately observe the firing from the French batteries as well as from the enceinte; that from Montrouge was particularly noticeable and effective, as so far we have built no batteries that could deal specially with that fort.

At dinner with His Majesty every single telegram that arrived from the batteries was read out to the assembled company, so that in the course of the same evening the most insignificant occurrences there will certainly be keenly discussed.

We are still without any certainty as to whether General Bourbaki with his Corps is still at Bourges, or whether he has marched thence, whether on Montargis or Belfort. True, we have received fairly trustworthy information from spies that confirms the oft-times repeated statement of the Press that Bourbaki is on the march to relieve Belfort and invade Alsace and Baden; but our own cavalrymen of the IInd Army, so fully occupied on other duties, afford us no enlightenment, so that at present a painful state of uncertainty prevails.

On Tuesday, the 10th January, so we hear, the vote is at last to be taken at Munich after all these everlasting delays, and we may look upon it here as a good omen that to-day a War credit has already been approved there. By yesterday it seems a majority was secured within two votes; so at last there is an actual prospect of the Treaties being ratified, saving us thereby this scandal of offering the world the spectacle of fresh disunion. Furthermore, as all the documents, so I heard to-day, sent in by the German Princes in attestation of their assent to the King of Bavaria have now been delivered at the hands of the latter's Envoy to the Federal Chancellor, the ceremonial Proclamation may very well take place without further difficulties on the 18th January.

FRIEDRICH I.
Grand Duke of Baden.

Headquarters: Versailles, 7th January.—The experts are very well content with the result of yesterday and to-day. We are building more and more batteries, pushing up gun emplacements nearer Paris; have so far not been interfered with in any way in carrying out these works and, in proportion to the difficulties involved and in view of the enemy's artillery fire, have, thank God, suffered but slight losses. Already shots have fallen in the city that are bound to have set buildings on fire, while before long we shall be able to do yet more havoc in the town itself; all the same I think myself the Parisians are in such a mood of sullen defiance that even such horrors will make little impression on them. There is news come from Bordeaux that provisions in Paris would be exhausted about the end of January, and at best could only last till early in February. I trust this may be true.

Yesterday the IInd Army Corps pushed forward victoriously, but with terrible losses, from Vendôme in the direction of Le Mans, after a hot fight hurled back over the Azay brook two enemy Army Corps taking part in the advance, and gained possession of that sector as well as of Montoise. The IIIrd Army Corps seems in the same action to have again lost many officers. To-day and to-morrow the struggle will no doubt be continued, while General von Werder on his side will in all probability finally take the offensive against the advancing enemy. In addition, General von Manteuffel, in supreme command of a Southern Army to be made up of the IInd, VIIth, and XIVth Army Corps, is to march at once to the southward to cover Belfort and Alsace and attack Bourbaki's flank. It is true at least a fortnight must elapse before this Southern Army can get fully to work, but for certain the mere knowledge of its approach will have a bad effect morally on Bourbaki's projects, and meantime this is always something to the good.

Thus we are once again politically and strategically in an extremely critical situation, calling for attention to every quarter of the heavens at one and the same time, inasmuch as the efforts to relieve Paris are being directed from all sides and with great masses of men. The King's mind is naturally greatly exercised by all this, and for the last few days his outlook on the immediate future has been of the blackest; we have accordingly had to do what we could to encourage him and raise his spirits, whereas General Count Moltke never loses his quiet composure.

It is positively amazing how quickly, after an Army has been beaten and put to flight, ever fresh masses of men are again got together and armed, which in their turn fight well.

We, on the contrary, must always bring the same troops into the field, troops whose ranks cannot, of course, be so rapidly filled up, even if we do train the new additions a trifle less pedantically; and consequently we should regard it as a godsend if Paris finally capitulated and we had troops available to send to the reinforcement of the other Armies. How under such circumstances peace could ever be arrived at, seeing the calling up of new levies, enforced by violent threats on the part of the local authorities, goes on at an ever-increasing rate, is a riddle.

Information brought in by spies indicates that before another ten days are out many an anxious hour will strike, and that more sorties from Paris are projected; nay, more, that the Parisians are aiming at seizing the person of Count Bismarck, because, directly he ceases to have a hand in the game, it is obvious the War will at once come to an end; lastly, that Saint Germain should be more strongly held than hitherto, and that a search for arms and a round-up of vagabonds should be carried out there, the same as was lately done here.

Headquarters: Versailles, 8th January, Sunday.—After divine service I proceeded, in alternate snowstorm and sunshine, but no fog, to visit the outposts in company with my brother-in-law, hoping to get a look to-day at the effects of our bombardment from the newly-built Observation Post No. 0. This stands only four thousand paces distant from Fort Issy and consists of a bomb-proof roofed-in blockhouse, in which several very good telescopes afford an accurate survey of the effects of our gun-fire. The enemy's shells whistle over it constantly and strike not far off, as the terrace of the Château de Meudon, on which are four of our batteries, borders on the Observation Post in question. But as since the beginning of the bombardment battery fires on battery, and consequently a quite definite mark is aimed at by the enemy, one can without recklessly exposing oneself linger well within range of the guns. All the time we were in the blockhouse we could every moment hear the screeching hiss of a French shell, immediately after which came the explosion close beside us. Forts Issy and Vanves were so close in front of us, you could easily see how their parapets have suffered, and even verify the traces of our hits on the earthwork itself. At Montrouge the barracks on the western face could be seen burning fiercely, while pillars of smoke rising in different parts of Paris told of fires having broken out in the city. Our men are overjoyed at the bombardment, and since the enemy's fire is confined to the batteries, the fellows on outpost duty and with the outpost reserves are in much less danger than hitherto, so that music and song are everywhere to be heard intermingled with the noise of the shells.

I must confess that with every shot that fell in the city I felt a lump rise in my throat, as I thought of the innocent folks who have to suffer from this curse of war; but above all I cannot get over the thought of the children who may possibly be hit, especially as I have only lately learned that at Strasburg, as a result of the siege, a hospital for children who have lost limbs has had to be established. Considering my personal aversion to war, it is a veritable cross for me to be forced under present conditions to carry out this painful obligation. But in this war of giants there is no duty I can shirk. May its results at any rate be such that the true blessings of peace in all directions, progress and full development of all that can only thrive in times of quiet and good order, may grow out of it. Then, I think, would the dreadful doings of to-day be expiated at least in part. For the rest, my aversion to this bloodshed is well known in France, as I have already had repeated opportunities of learning; indeed they say of me, as I heard to my silent delight, that in all cases where it was in any way compatible with the stern demands of duty I let kindliness and forbearance govern my actions.

At Danjoutin before Belfort our troops have had a fine success, taking prisoner 300 unwounded men; the siege there proceeds unhindered, though we know that General Bourbaki is on his way to relieve the fortress. News has reached us according to which reinforcements for General Faidherbe's Army were embarked at Cherbourg, and as these will land at Boulogne, it cannot be much longer before he attacks us once again. The Ist Army also believes for its part that the enemy will soon take the offensive again and actually push forward at Bapaume.

I had to-day at my quarters a lengthy discussion with General Count Moltke, in which I talked over the present situation with him in detail, and convinced myself that he is deeply offended at Count Bismarck's arbitrary and despotic attitude. He has the feeling that, in military matters no less than in political, the Federal Chancellor is resolved to decide everything himself, without paying the smallest heed to what the responsible experts have to say; besides which, he is offended because Count Bismarck addresses inquiries and writes communications to the General Staff relating to circumstances so exclusively concerned with recent strategical questions that he (Count Moltke) has already more than once been compelled summarily to abandon matters of the sort.

His Majesty, having called upon Count Bismarck to give an opinion on Emperor, Empire, title, insignia and appellations, received a memorandum in reply, and ordered me too to give my present views in writing on these questions.

Headquarters: Versailles, 9th January.—General Bourbaki appears to be taking the road for Nancy and Belfort; so to-day he should very likely come into collision at Villersexel with the troops under General Werder, who is on the way to meet him. Still we are not yet sufficiently informed in what force Bourbaki is advancing, or whether he has not sent an Army Corps towards Montargis.

Last night 500 incendiary shells were pitched into the city, but without causing any conflagrations. I cannot myself look for any great results from these shells, for apart from the few occupants of houses in the immediate neighbourhood of which they strike, those who are undisturbed will know nothing of the matter, while damage done on the defensive works and fires inside them can produce no impression in the city itself. Weeks ago Count Bismarck promised himself the most prodigious results, once three shells had exploded in the place, yet on this the fifth day of the bombardment these still remain unrealized!

The Minister of War, General von Roon, celebrated to-day the fiftieth anniversary of his military service, but received only the King and myself, as his terrible asthma, which for the last fortnight has been complicated by catarrh and prevents his attending the reports at His Majesty's, is so indescribably severe that every day he gets choking fits. The physicians want to send him as soon as possible to Berlin; his condition strikes me as highly critical, so that I with many others expect he will sooner or later have to give up his duties. Who will then be his successor, whether General Podbielski or another, is the question everybody here is asking himself.

Count Bismarck is only just recovering from nervous rheumatic pains in the feet that set up a state of nervous irritation in every part of his body—a doubly unwelcome state of things in such all-important days as these.

Headquarters: Versailles, 10th January.—The bombardment follows its prearranged course. The losses amount daily to some ten to fifteen men. The forts are suffering damage, while on our side only a few limbers and one gun have been dismounted. Otherwise everything is in the same state. The Paris papers have now discovered the reason of the bombardment—the Crown Prince of Saxony's defeat is to be kept hid, while at the same time the rattle of the mitrailleuse fire of Chanzy's troops, already come to Étampes in their advance, has to be drowned by the roar of our guns. Lying is a trade like another; still I should like just for once to find out whether there really are people in existence who credit such news. Whether loss of men's lives is to be mourned, of this no newspaper ever says a word.

General von Manteuffel is on his march to the Southern Army, with which, if he carries out successfully the duty assigned him, he may well add yet greater laurels to those he has already won and make a glorious name for himself. He, like myself, is distressed at my and Prince Friedrich Karl's appointment as Field-Marshals and laments the prodigal distribution of Iron Crosses, which already all members of the suites of those amateur warriors the Princes have received.

An interview of some length with Count Bismarck, who still suffers pains in his feet, afforded me the agreeable assurance that he is well disposed to discuss in my presence with General Count Moltke the measures to be taken in case Paris capitulates and the preliminaries of Peace that will follow on that event. He gave me to understand further that the hostility that exists between his Department and the High General Staff, and is growing more and more acute, would not be allowed to go on any longer.

Headquarters: Versailles, 11th January.—The war and thunder of the bombardment go on unceasingly, but, without any visible effect, and already the interest felt in the event, having lost the charm of novelty, begins to cool down; indeed sundry hot-heads, who before were never tired of preaching up this bombardment as an indispensable necessity, are now asking themselves whether under the given conditions it has really been decided to go on with it. Naturally enough this gives me a good deal of malicious pleasure. It gets more and more to seem as if—indeed I feared as much from the beginning—in consequence of the poor results of the bombardment, we shall be downright sorry for our mistake. The reports of the first few days, to the effect that we had silenced some of the batteries, are proved by what we actually see from day to day to be unfounded, for after stopping for hours together the fire is resumed only the more vigorously.

General von Werder reports that, since the action of the 9th January had given him the certainty that General Bourbaki with three Army Corps was opposed to him, and a fourth, the 21st, was likewise being brought up, he had abandoned Villersexel and withdrawn to the position, already put in a state of defence with heavy artillery, on the passes of the Vosges between Lure and Delle, where he preferred to await the enemy's attack. He lost on the 9th 13 officers and 200 men. On the 12th, General Manteuffel reaches Châtillon, and on the 13th can begin his march on Vesoul, so as to take simultaneous action on Bourbaki's flank and against Garibaldi. Thus the next few days with be a sufficiently bloody and anxious time.

Fresh difficulties about Bavaria's acceptance of the Treaty greatly disturb His Majesty, while, on the other hand, Count Bismarck's irritability gives him many a bad half-hour.

The probability increases that the Proclamation of the King as Emperor will take place on the 18th January.

Headquarters: Versailles, 12th January.—New important but sanguinary victories of the IInd Army in conjunction with the XIIIth Army Corps round Le Mans and Saint-Corneille lead us to hope that General Chanzy, with whom Gambetta is for the moment, is completely defeated and rendered harmless for the time being.

Prince Friedrich Karl is very jealous of the Grand Duke of Mecklenburg, whose successes are brilliant, but less bloody than is the case of the IInd Army's; so he never mentions him in his despatches, nay, people go so far as to declare openly that the Prince would be delighted if only the Grand Duke were defeated, so that he might come to his rescue and win fresh laurels for himself.

General von Werder has shifted his defensive position before Belfort to the passes of the Vosges, without the enemy pursuing him.

In company with my brother-in-law I paid a visit in bitter cold, eight below zero (eighteen degrees Fahrenheit) to the "Tinder-box." Though the fog prevailing generally to-day shut off all distant view, I was able nevertheless to convince myself that the forts are every day suffering more and more severely from our fire, but the damages so caused are really nothing more than the natural consequences of the long-continued bombardment, which would be of importance only in case breaches were established or an attempt to storm the works was made.

Papers, which again came to hand secretly from Paris, speak of shells that fell among a crowd of people just come out of church, and of course did not spare women and children.

Such a piece of news wrings my heart. But otherwise my impression is that the bombardment does nothing to damp the Parisians' spirits, albeit telegrams from other countries say that shells were flying as far as Saint-Sulpice, the Sorbonne and the Val de Grâce, while the Ceinture railway, the imposing viaduct of which one can plainly see to the northward of Fort Issy, had been destroyed. I still think to myself that we are doing the Parisians a favour they have long been hoping for, seeing they can now under present circumstances persuade themselves they were vanquished by their opponent's gun-fire and not simply driven by hunger to submit. On the other hand, I believe that, as the general population can see but little of the effects of our fire, they will soon recover from their terror of the horrors of a bombardment and defy us now in good earnest.

Count Bismarck is to meet General Count Moltke to-morrow at my house and enter into a preliminary discussion towards an understanding as to the treatment of Paris after a possible capitulation, the question of Armistice or Peace, and lastly how to deal with Alsace and Lorraine.

Headquarters: Versailles, 13th January.—The victories of Prince Friedrich Karl during these last days brought us 18,000 prisoners, 12 guns, 2 to 4 flags, 6 locomotives and 200 railway cars! What are we to come to with these ever-increasing masses of men!

Our yesterday's victory at Le Mans must have been a pronounced defeat for General Chanzy's forces, as for the first time the French reports admit such a thing as a reverse. It is made even more important by the fact that Gambetta was a witness of the battle, and the rout that ensued will exercise a lasting and prejudicial effect on the defeated Army.

All eyes are now directed with the utmost anxiety on General von Werder, who will be hard put to it to defend the passes of the Vosges until such time as General von Manteuffel's advance on Bourbaki's position, to begin to-morrow, makes itself felt. But for certain the latter, long before he is attacked by the Southern Army, will realize that his line of retreat is threatened, and will be at once crippled thereby in his undertakings.

The fog to-day prevented much firing on either side; the French, however, are bringing up numbers of guns every day, and never cease to give our batteries trouble, but, thank God, without causing us great losses.

General Count Moltke and Count Bismarck had an hour and a half's conversation at my quarters and stayed to dinner;

still, it will need a good many other discussions before they reach an agreement. Both talked quite plainly to the other, and Moltke, generally so sparing of words, speaking in tones of reproach and quite eloquently, upbraided the Federal Chancellor, bringing forward all the grievances he had already confided to me on the 8th; the other protested in return, and I had repeatedly to interfere to bring back the conversation into smoother water. The two were least of all in accord as to the consequences of an Armistice, inasmuch as Count Bismarck desires peace, but General Count Moltke a war of extermination. Then Count Bismarck attacked the General on his tenderest point, developing the theory that after the battle of Sedan we should have stayed on in Champagne to await further developments and ought never to have gone to Paris. Under such circumstances agreement was clearly out of the question, and I could not even gain this much, that at any rate at coming reports at His Majesty's, mention might be avoided of the differences of opinion actually existing. It will rather come to this, that each separately for himself will lay his views before the King, and His Majesty must decide between them.

I received full authorization from His Majesty to telegraph to the Minister of the Household, Baron von Schleinitz, to inform him that the King ordered him to come here at once, for if we are to hear his views at all, this is the very last opportunity, as he must be consulted before the date fixed for the Imperial Proclamation, viz. the 18th of this month, and the journey here is so full of difficulties. He answered he could start to-morrow.

Headquarters: Versailles, 14th January.—General von Werder reports that his outposts were attacked and fell back, but at the same time he could hold his ground, that four massed French Corps and a fifth still in course of formation were opposed to him, whose attack he expected to-morrow. We trust to heaven that, in his extraordinarily strong defensive position, he will succeed in holding back General Bourbaki until General von Manteuffel's forward movement, to begin to-day, produces its immediate moral effect on the enemy's rear. For, directly Bourbaki has news of the advance of the Southern Army, he must make front in two directions and betimes look to his way of retreat, which can only take the line Besançon–Lyons, if he is not to find himself forced on to the Swiss frontier. So it is there for the moment that the all-important decision is to be reached, for, if Werder's flank were to be surrounded, the siege of Belfort must be abandoned and a position further to the rear be sought for the defence of Alsace; but no doubt in that case General von Manteuffel would have greater difficulties in marching to the Vosges than he has now to face.

The frost is a right trusty and welcome ally to us, for it works great mischief on the Parisians no less than the rest of the French in contradistinction to our men. I myself visit the outposts almost every day and thus am for hours together in the open air, and when I do stay in Versailles I contrive to take regular exercise out of doors, so that I feel perfectly well.

I went out to the Observation Post No. 0, but the prevailing fog that has come on with the increasing frost prevents my making out anything clearly. I took Duke Friedrich of Holstein and the Hereditary Grand Dukes of Weimar and Strelitz with me, as otherwise it is strictly forbidden for anyone to visit the spot. How necessary such strictness is, is proved by the case of the Prince zur Lippe and his brother-in-law, Duke Eugen of Württemberg, who, when riding about at Meudon without a guide, so completely lost their way that eventually they found themselves in front of our batteries and exposed to the cross-fire of the shells, so that there was nothing left them but to dismount and have themselves dragged up by the gunners over the parapet into the battery.

It was a sad sight, the numerous charming villas, no doubt nothing but the pet summer resorts of wealthy Parisians, that have for many weeks now been occupied by the troops on outpost duty and of course look badly used. As these buildings possess only thin walls and not much provision for heating, the necessity for securing warmth in the cold weather has a substantial share in the damage done to these premises.

Headquarters: Versailles, 15th January, Sunday.—After church, where it was very cold, as out of doors a raw, cutting wind was blowing, with nine degrees of frost (sixteen degrees Fahrenheit), the usual report was held at His Majesty's, at which the King was extremely excited and unstrung. General von Werder telegraphs that he deems his left wing to be threatened, inasmuch as strong enemy columns are marching on Lure, and accordingly asks, likewise by telegraph, whether he would not do better to abandon Belfort, as he believes he could then defend Alsace. One must have seen General Count Moltke's face and known him too as well as I do to form a conception of the look with which he communicated this telegram to me in the King's antechamber, then read it out at the report, and with what an air of imperturbable, icy calm he added: " Your Majesty will, I trust, approve of this answer to General von Werder, that he has simply to stand firm and beat the enemy wherever he finds him." I cannot say how admirable beyond all praise I thought General Moltke at this moment; any other man would have launched out with reflections and exclamations—*he* in one second relieved the whole strain of the situation and, thank heaven, restored General von Werder's steadiness.

Thus we may daily expect to hear of a great united attack below the passes of the Vosges; I feel confident that General von Werder, who after all has important forces at his disposal, and has also taken with him the heavy guns for the fortresses defending the mountain passes, can hold out over the decisive days. The siege of Belfort will go on unchanged.

General Count Moltke to-day received a formal, official protest from General Trochu regarding shells that had fallen on hospitals, inasmuch as this infringed no less the laws of humanity than the Geneva Convention; now as these shells struck repeatedly and with marked regularity precisely in that quarter of the city where the muncipal hospitals, as the Val de Grâce, the Salpêtrière and others stood, he could only assume that we were aiming purposely in that direction. General Count Moltke's answer runs, that so soon as we should have pushed forward our lines of investment so near Paris that we could distinguish different buildings or make out the white flags flying on those to be spared, we should certainly as little think of firing at them on purpose as we did now. That our principle was to take account of the dictates of humanity so far as was at all possible, and we still held fast to this principle even after the Provisional Government had on the 4th September introduced a new fashion of carrying on war against us.

Unfortunately I cannot but fear these facts alleged by General Trochu are true, seeing it is not impossible that the buildings named stand precisely in that sector which lies within range of our guns directed against the city. The thought of this is, if possible, yet more terrible to me than that of the innocent women and children. At the same time the Parisians for three months past have been firing on all the places where military hospitals have been established by us, so that in the end the Maire of Sèvres has sent a protest to General Trochu.

In company with my brother-in-law I was to-day at the " Tinder-box," from which, in spite of fog and hoar-frost, we enjoyed a remarkably clear view over Paris. The bombardment goes on unchanged, in the same manner as hitherto; after the forts have been silent for a while, they presently open a heavier fire still, which again drops, as soon as ours grows brisker. Surely by this time the French must observe that we are now shooting only for shooting's sake, and the sight of those hit is bound to stimulate their courage and spirit of resistance all the more violently.

The King is at last agreed that the Proclamation of his assumption of the dignity of German Emperor shall take place on the 18th January in the *Salle des Glaces;* yet he is quite unhappy things should already have reached such a point. On the one hand out of conviction, on the other from anxieties of his own invention concerning reproaches from the party of hard-bitten " Old Prussians," he opposes from the latter's point of view what is now a strictly National question, which in 1848/49 was repudiated simply as a democratic usurpation. I think that otherwise it must have been nothing but a satisfaction to his mind to mount the ancient Imperial throne as a result of the German victories. Indeed there is so much here to remind one of the election of the leaders of German hosts by their warriors or of the elevation on the shield of those chosen as Chieftains in the earliest centuries of our history. However, the King will have nothing to do with preparations of any sort or kind, but insists on leaving it to others to make the needful arrangements. Meantime nothing is settled as to title, escutcheon, armorial bearings, etc., so that Minister of the Household von Schleinitz and Count Stillfried will have to help out to reach a decision even now at the eleventh hour. Mohr and Speier, the Superintendents of Military Stores, now here from Berlin, so far as field conditions allow, will see to the cutting out of velvet, after Count Harrach's design, an Imperial Eagle, and sewing it on a piece of gold brocade, so as to have the new escutcheon decked out for the occasion more or less as it ought to be.

It gave me a great shock when it was brought home to me that by the King's election as Emperor my own personal relation to the Crown and the Empire would call for a special designation—" Imperial Highness " or the like—for I had never thought of the thing, and that style is not in the smallest degree to my taste. Unless we have to meet a sortie just on that day, I shall provide all troops of my Army then off duty, regiment by regiment, as well as the Knights of the Iron Cross, with a flag or standard, so that a good seventy such colours will be massed in the historic " Salle des Glaces." His Majesty approves this; would he might see the others, the Army of the Meuse that is, take part in the ceremony, but I am sorry to say he will not give the order.

As a matter of judicious discretion I am having letters written to the two Bavarian Army Corps, merely by way of information, and not as an order, as I did in the case of the Prussian troops, so as to leave it entirely to the judgment of the Generals how they choose to behave in view of this purely political and non-military event; for one cannot tell what attitude the Bavarian House of Representatives, which is again and again putting off its vote, will yet take up towards us. Next Tuesday the decisive sitting is to be held; but one has almost ceased to expect a favourable outcome for the questions at issue.

From my mother-in-law arrived a grey necktie crocheted with her own hands, which I immediately handselled.

Headquarters; Versailles, 16th January.—Yesterday General von Werder victoriously repulsed in a nine-hours' battle an attack undertaken by four enemy Army Corps along the whole line Montbéliard–Chagey; the artillery action was particularly fierce, yet our losses came to only 400 men. So the day was certainly ours; may the others be equally favourable to us. Now the enemy has for once had an opportunity of learning thoroughly what we Germans are like on the defensive. General von Manteuffel with the VIIth Army Corps has put to flight a force of Mobiles on the plateau of Langres, which will undoubtedly set General Bourbaki thinking, for he must by this time know that his rear is no longer safe and that he stands between two fires.

In the Army of the Meuse preparations are so far advanced that with to-morrow the bombardment of Saint-Denis begins, which cannot but make an impression in Paris, as many of the inhabitants are in flight and will be compelled to seek safety in the city. By this time the hotel-keepers there should be doing splendid business with the people frightened away from their own houses, who, shirking the danger, seek protection and refuge at the inns. Still I hold to my opinion that the Parisians must be well aware of the fact that with our bombardment we aim at nothing more than just to intimidate them, and that for that very reason they will not give in.

The last engagement before Le Mans cost us 140 to 150 officers and 3,000 men, of which total the IIIrd Army Corps alone loses 100 officers. It is really dreadful. The number of prisoners there is already risen to 20,000 men.

Lately Jules Favre has asked for a permit for London to allow of his journey to attend the Black Sea Conference there. I had been instructed to give it him as far as my Army is concerned; but Favre never appeared. To-day I was ordered, supposing he still reports himself at the outposts, to ask instructions first from the King. At the same time it was stated that Favre had also requested a safe-conduct for his family, but had acquiesced in a refusal. Whether this is true or no I cannot say; anyway, we may regard it as noteworthy if he has actually sought a suitable opportunity to secure the safety of his belongings.

Other significant facts are the difficulty the French Government finds in raising its loans, and the attempts that are being made to pay for deliveries of grain by Treasury notes, which, however, no contractor will take up.

To my chagrin I hear once more that at home, especially in Berlin, a temper of unbounded and embittered hostility to everything French prevails, everybody longing to be able to bring the whole nation absolutely to their knees; this seems to me to be as petty and narrow-minded as can possibly be, but is regarded as patriotism, and everyone thinking otherwise is loaded with abuse. Instead of bragging and boasting and giving themselves airs, it would really and truly be better for our countrymen if they rejoiced at our great successes in a quiet, dignified way, at the same time recognizing the fine persistency of the French in their devotion to the cause of their country. Besides, experience teaches us that those who are insolent in their triumph are always the first at the moment of a reverse of fortune to fall into the opposite extreme. Only too natural, I allow, is the feeling of bitter indignation in view of the ever-increasing sacrifices which the long continuance of this War demands of us; nay, I can understand the longing for revenge that overmasters many a sorrowing heart, but excessive indulgence in this sentiment is both injurious to our own character and lowers us in the eyes of contemporaries.

I am sorry to say the news of Prince Woldemar of Holstein sounds very bad; we shall certainly lose this gifted, experienced and trusty friend, who might yet have done us such good service.

The King is excited, disturbed and anxious beyond all belief; he says himself that his inclination to look on the dark side of things has in these truly critical days notably increased; so much so that at the report I spoke to him in all seriousness, urging him to drive away his black thoughts and keep a good heart. The inevitable excitements such events involve are bound to interfere with the cheerful carrying out of a great State ceremony such as that appointed for two days hence.

The inhabitants of Versailles, who are frequently quite well informed as to news current in France and preparations being made there, without our being able to discover the sources from which they draw their information, would seem all of a sudden to be very confident; but in particular the many old retired Army officers living here appear all at once to entertain high expectations, whereas up to a short while ago they were greatly depressed and declared the cause of France to be as good as lost.

Von Schleinitz, Minister of the Household, has arrived; nevertheless, again to-day nothing whatever has been settled, and I cannot yet get any inkling of what exactly is going to be done on the 18th January. Nothing can be quietly and deliberately thought out and arranged here, for either decisions are indefinitely postponed or else they are slurred over. We had given orders for a daïs with a throne for His Majesty and seats for the German Princes, behind which the flags were to be ranged; yet the King, in spite of what he announced yesterday, that he would listen to nothing about preparations but leave it all to me, directly he heard to-day of the proposed arrangements, ordered a host of new alterations, of which again I was told nothing; this makes it difficult, if not impossible, to settle anything for certain. The King will have no throne and no raised platform, because "if we were now in summer-time, the ceremony would go forward in the open air" (!)

I had the order to inform the Crown Prince of Saxony, but without directly inviting him, that the ceremony was fixed for the 18th. Whether the Württembergers are receiving a like notice is not to be learned.

The voting at Munich is, by way of a change, once more postponed to next Friday!

Headquarters: Versailles, 17th January.—Yesterday General von Werder again successfully repulsed a heavy attack by Bourbaki's Army; his right wing, however, under command of the Baden General von Degenfeld, could not hold its ground against superior numbers at Chenebier-sur-Oignon and fell back, so that General von Werder immediately despatches reinforcements there, to win back the position. So it is in no little suspense we look for the arrival of the next news, for, although the occurrence mentioned is in itself no real disadvantage, yet we have grounds for supposing that it is just at this point the enemy's main force will concentrate; thus even so small a success will no doubt duly set aflame the French spirit of enterprise. General von Moltke takes this information quietly, in fact all he said to it was: " The good God will not allow us to suffer reverses," but otherwise went on unshaken in his usual calm composure. The King's mood is already so depressed that he cannot be talked out of the conviction that at the very moment of his installation as Emperor we shall receive the very worst news from the Vosges.

General Faidherbe is moving on Saint-Quentin with a view to march from there on Reims, cutting our communications and joining hands with General Bourbaki. As to the latter idea, General von Blumenthal, who always looked upon the attack on Belfort as the maddest scheme the French can possibly attempt to their own destruction, is perfectly delighted at it, as the impracticability of carrying it out is obvious at a glance. For the like reasons General von Goeben has for several days past been hoping for General Faidherbe's advance southwards, as he can then make sure of being able to come to grips with him and drive him back; I trust he will gain his purpose.

Our flags and standards are already arriving, and will all be taken to my quarters, from which a colour party of men from the King's Grenadier regiment will fetch them tomorrow. I am glad to know that both Bavarian Army Corps are likewise sending theirs.

The Military Council, without informing me of the fact, has had direct orders sent to the Guards' Corps with regard to sending in their colours. What precise directions were given is not yet made known, but in any case one of those muddles so frequent in Berlin played a part in the matter, for the colour party was already half-way to Versailles when it received the order to turn back again and to bring along the colours of the 1st battalion of the 1st Guards regiment, riddled with shot at Petit-Iblon and Le Bourget.

In the afternoon a sitting was held at the King's quarters, which Count Bismarck, Minister of the Household von Schleinitz and I attended. When Count Bismarck met von Schleinitz in the ante-room, he told him pretty sharply he really did not understand what the Federal Chancellor in conjunction with the Minister of the Household should have to discuss with the King. In an over-heated room the discussion dragged on for three hours over the title the Emperor was to bear, the appellation of the heir to the throne, the relation of the Royal family, the Court and Army to the Emperor, etc.

With regard to the Imperial title, Count Bismarck admitted that already in the discussions as to conditions the Bavarian Deputies and Plenipotentiaries had refused to agree to the designation " Emperor of Germany," and that finally, to please them, but all the same *without consulting His Majesty beforehand*, he had substituted that of " German Emperor." This designation, with which no really special idea is connected, was as little to the King's liking as it was to mine, and we did all we possibly could to secure the " of Germany " in lieu of it; however, Count Bismarck stuck to his point, that, as this title would be adopted simply to secure a combination with the Bavarians, any other would be totally inadmissible, in fact at the present moment an arbitrary alteration would be bound to have the worst possible effect on the Bavarian House of Representatives. Moreover, he endeavoured to prove that the expression " Emperor of Germany " implied a territorial dominion, which we did not in any way hold over the realm, whereas, on the contrary, " German Emperor " followed in natural sequence on the old-time *Imperator Romanus.* So we had to make up our minds to it, though for my part I shall never like it. The official style will therefore run : " We, William, by the grace of God German Emperor, King of Prussia," a corresponding formula to which is to be adopted for the Empress. Nevertheless, in colloquial speech the " of Germany " is pretty sure to come into use. The form of address is to be " Your Imperial and Royal Majesty." As to the appellation of the heir to the throne and his consort, all conceivable, possible and impossible titles were canvassed, ending at last with that of " Crown Prince of the German Empire, Crown Prince of Prussia," though without any definitive decision being reached on the point.

Seeing that by virtue of these designations we expressly signify that we possess no territorial dominion over the Empire, the wearer of the German Imperial Crown, together with his heirs, is within limits chosen exclusively from the Royal family of Prussia, and as such set at the head of the Empire, without the rest of the House being affected by this proceeding; but in this way again my view becomes untenable, that our whole family should receive Imperial rank, and consequently the title " Imperial Highness " will be given only to the heir to the throne and his consort.

In this connection arose a very painful debate on the relation of Emperor to King, because His Majesty, in contradistinction to the old Prussian traditions, holds an Emperor to be higher than a King. Both Ministers, and I with them, controverted this view most emphatically, appealing to historical documents in our archives. But the King was by no means convinced by the instances we quoted, got angry rather, and declared that, as King Frederick William III, on the occasion of meetings with the Emperor Alexander I, had laid it down that precedence belonged of right to the latter, at this present time the will of his Royal father was authoritative and decisive for him. It was finally decided that on this point and on that of the future status of the rest of the Royal family, nothing should be definitely settled for the present, the decision to be postponed till the conclusion of peace or till a possible Coronation.

For the Court, no change was to be made for the immediate present with regard to the Minister of the Household, nor was there any question of an Imperial Ministry; only Count Bismarck's title was to be that of Imperial Chancellor, albeit this designation putting him on the same footing with Count Beust, was so little to his taste that he exclaimed this was really bringing him into too bad company.

No objection was made to the escutcheon proposed by Count Bismarck and myself, but again it was not expressly adopted.

The more clearly, however, did the consequences following on " Emperor and Empire " show themselves, the more irritated grew the King. Finally, he broke out with the words that the Imperial dignity he would be assuming was just a matter of form, nothing more than another name for " President "; he could only compare himself to a Major on whom " brevet rank as Lieutenant-Colonel " was bestowed. Still, as it had gone so far, he must indeed bear this cross, but he chose to be the only one to do so, and he therefore forbade their expecting him to put the German Army on the same footing as himself; accordingly he would listen to no word about an " Imperial " force, as he would fain guard our Army from anything of the sort and could not endure to see the troops obliged to put up with simply " German " names and designations. The Navy, he granted, may be entitled " the Imperial." In the greatest agitation he went on to say he could not describe to us the despairing mood he was in, as to-morrow he must bid farewell to the old Prussia, to which alone he clung and would always cling. At this point sobs and tears interrupted his words. Thereupon I spoke to him in all kindness and seriousness, referring to the history of our House and briefly describing how it had gone on from the status of Burggraf to that of Elector and from that to the Crown, so that the Princes at each step had been compelled to add to the dignity that had hitherto pleased them well enough yet another new one, without this prejudicing Country or Family. True, King Frederick I in his time had created in Prussia a kingship that was "only a matter of form," but yet Prussian history proves clearly enough what had come eventually of this originally shadowy Royalty; so powerful, in fact, had it grown that at this day the old German Imperial dignity naturally devolved on us. The King simply refused to hear these historical facts, undeniable as they are, and exclaimed in boiling excitement: " My son is heart and soul with the new order of things, while I refuse to go one hair's-breadth out of my way for it and hold by Prussia only." I pointed out to him further that he and his successor after him were called upon to make of the Empire, now nominally re-established, a true and actual reality—but in vain ! Finally, in furious anger, the King sprang up, broke off the discussions and declared he would not hear another word of the ceremony appointed for to-morrow.

With nothing effected and asking one another what would happen now, we left the Préfecture, where one of those scenes had just taken place that are only too familiar to me, having become so used to witness them at the Ministerial Council board with His Majesty, on occasions when a definite decision on important matters was to be taken. Indeed it was long since the King had been so hot as to-day, and it was astonishing how he had managed further to exaggerate the difficulties and inconveniencies that must in any case exist and which are already causing quite enough annoyance, invariably gainsaying every logical argument advanced against his own opinion. I was so ill after these scenes I had to take physic; subsequently I heard that the King had not appeared at all at tea that evening.

Such were the impressions under which we were preparing for the imposing German ceremony appointed for to-morrow ! My brother-in-law came again in the evening with the Minister von Schleinitz, who, like me, had been made quite ill by the discussions; with one accord we expressed our sympathy with the King, who by his pessimism makes everything so enormously more difficult for himself, and loves to exalt the most insignificant details above the essence of the whole.

Headquarters: Versailles, 18th January.—So Emperor and Empire would seem at last an acknowledged fact, to be proclaimed on the very birthday of our Prussian Monarchy. God grant this league between German Princes and Houses may never be broken, and more and more Princes arise who seem

WILLIAM I.
German Emperor, King of Prussia.

worthy to devote themselves to such a task! My own opinion is that from now on my duties and my wife's will have become twice as heavy, important and responsible, but I welcome the increased burden, because I shrink from no difficulty, because I feel sure I have no lack of fresh courage to set about the work fearlessly and steadfastly, and lastly because I am convinced it was not for nothing it came about that between the ages of thirty and forty I have been again and again called upon to make the most weighty decisions, and, looking the dangers connected with them fairly in the face, to carry them to completion.

The long-cherished hopes of our ancestors, the dreams of German poets, are fulfilled, and, freed from the accumulated dross of the Holy Roman curse, rises an Empire, reformed in head and limbs, yet under the old name and the thousand-year-old symbols, from its sixty years' eclipse. Great are the duties thus undertaken by my House, great the expectations and legitimate claims on us, but by a right understanding of the demands of our age, and with an honest determination to move forward, the great work will reach fruition.

As a good omen, first thing in the morning came the news from General von Werder that, after Chenebier had been already retaken last night, the enemy losing 400 prisoners and his baggage, he had further to report that in a second engagement he had now found Bourbaki's troops less tough customers to deal with than the day before, and that on the French side the action had been fought more as a rearguard skirmish, and General Bourbaki was really drawing off. Belfort and Alsace are therefore no longer threatened; this we owe to the German troops under General von Werder's command, who won a brilliant and highly important success under difficult circumstances. Thank God for it! May General von Goeben be equally successful in beating General Faidherbe.

The news had a visibly cheering effect on His Majesty, or at any rate lightened the weight oppressing him; indeed an important announcement could not have come more opportunely. Just as General Count Moltke had read out the report, the band of the Guard of Honour struck up, as, with all the flags and standards that had arrived for the ceremony, it marched past directly under the King's window on its way to the Palace. The sight evidently served to enliven him; indeed, calculating on this very effect, I had ordered the colour company, which looked really splendid, to make a détour so as to pass before the Préfecture just at the usual hour of report. A sunbeam at the same moment broke through the clouds veiling the grey sky on this otherwise cold, damp day.

The ceremony may in the strictest sense of the word be called unique, and I am truly rejoiced to have lived to see it. Only in the course of time shall we realize its full importance, what it means to have witnessed in the stately " Salle des Glaces " of Louis XIV's Palace at Versailles the re-establishment of the German Empire achieved on the French battlefields and the proclamation of the chosen, hereditary Emperor.

There were present at Versailles to-day, besides the King and myself, and with us Prince Karl and Prince Adalbert: the Grand Dukes of Baden, Saxe-Weimar and Oldenburg, the Dukes of Saxe-Coburg, Saxe-Meiningen and Saxe-Altenburg, the Princes of Schaumburg-Lippe and Schwartzburg-Rudolstadt, the Crown Prince and Prince Georg of Saxony, the Princes Otto, Luitpold and Leopold of Bavaria, the Princes Wilhelm and August, and the Dukes Eugen, father and son, of Württemberg, the Landgrave Friedrich zu Hesse, the Hereditary Grand Dukes of Saxe-Weimar, Mecklenburg-Schwerin, Mecklenburg-Strelitz and Oldenburg, the Hereditary Princes of Hohenzollern, Anhalt, Saxe-Meiningen and the Duke Friedrich zu Schleswig-Holstein. Absent were: Prince Friedrich Karl, as also the Princes Albrecht, father and son, who are still in the field against the enemy, and besides these the Prince zu Hohenzollern, whose invalid state prevents his taking part in the War and in this great day, which sees the fulfilment of his ardent desires also. All the above-named assembled in the " appartements de la Reine," which the company reached by the stairway famous under the name of the " escalier de marbre," occupied by doubled guards posted at successive stages, to wait the King's arrival in the " Salle du sacre de Napoleon I." Fires burned everywhere in the open grates, but diffused only a moderate degree of warmth. While we were waiting for His Majesty, Prince Karl communicated to me a note sent him by the King, in which the latter notified that, as he was to-day assuming with the designation of " Emperor " only the outward form of that dignity, as a Major sometimes takes brevet rank as Lieutenant-Colonel, this title had no wide signification, and therefore would make no alteration whatever either in the designation of the Royal family or in my own! Typical of the difference between the formal recognition and the real significance of to-day's ceremony is the wording of the official notification from the Court Chamberlain, which ran: " The ceremony of installation will be held in the Hall of Mirrors at the Palace of Versailles at midday twelve o'clock, a short prayer and after that the proclamation," etc. The whole of our domestic Household had earnestly begged to be allowed to attend the ceremony, a request I gladly granted. The mounted Military Gendarmes asked expressly to be allowed to ride before my carriage, a privilege I also accorded to my Dragoon escort; so it was with a highly imposing cavalcade I made a formal entry into the " Cour Royale." I had given leave to all men of the garrison not on duty to promenade as they chose between the Préfecture and the Palace, so as to be able to see the King; thus we arrived at the latter between a regular lane of soldiers. Cannon salvoes, however, I could not sanction because of the numbers of wounded men lying here. The dress ordered for the occasion was tunic, helmet, sash and decorations; but I had not laid aside my high boots even for to-day, but retained this service equipment, nevertheless wearing the English Garter at the knee in honour of my wife and as an omen of an intimate union of the Empire with England. The guard of honour in the " Cour Royale " and to escort the colours was supplied by the gallant Royal Grenadier regiment. The King appeared in the uniform of the 1st Guards regiment, with the ribbon of the Order of the Black Eagle, which, considering its special connection with the War, implies a good deal; besides this, he wore to-day many German Orders, Stars and Crosses, but along with these the insignia of the Russian Order of St. George. To begin with, he addressed the German Princes in some words of thanks for their share in adding importance to the ceremony in hand; after which we followed him to the " Salle des Glaces."

In the salons and the " Chambre à coucher de la Reine " was stationed the guard of the King's Staff as Guard of Honour. In the " Salle des Glaces," to the left if one came in from the " Salon de la Paix," and with backs to the window, stood the Prussian and Bavarian non-commissioned officers and men appearing as deputations, and over against them the officers—all decorated with the Iron Cross. As, over and above these, all officers and officials who were not on duty and could be got at in cantonments had permission to be here to-day, the gigantic hall was so full that the " Salon de la Paix " had also to be used. The platform was at the opposite end in front of the " Salon de la Guerre." In the central window stood a field altar, before which the King took his stand, surrounded in a half-circle by all the Princes, and where Chaplain Rogge from Potsdam was to read the abridged liturgy and offer a simple prayer. As the order to the men, " Off helmets for prayer," had been forgotten, I was obliged myself to give it out loud, on which the choir of singers, made up of musicians from the different regiments here, accompanied by the band of military music, struck up the hymn "Sei Lob und Ehr" with fine effect in these great rooms. But the "simple prayer" consisted of a criticism of Louis XIV, with a rather tactless and tedious historical-religious dissertation on the significance of the 18th January for Prussia; the conclusion, which dwelt upon the German question and its solution as affected by to-day's event, struck another note by its fervent and effective language. During this part of the ceremony I let my eyes wander over the assembly and turn to the ceiling where Louis XIV's self-glorifications, expressed in allegories and explanatory boastful inscriptions, have for special contrast the disruption of Germany, and asked myself more than once if it was really true that we were at Versailles to witness there the re establishment of the German Empire so like a dream did the whole thing seem to me.

Then, after the Te Deum had been sung, the King proceeded, followed by us all, to the platform erected before the "Salon de la Guerre," on which the non-commissioned officers with the flags and standards were already posted, and summoned the ensign with the shot-riddled colours of the 1st battalion of the Foot Guards regiment, as well as the three of his Grenadier regiment, one of whom carried another no less torn, to come right up to him, so that they stood close behind His Majesty and elbow to elbow with me. To right and left of these specially conspicuous central groups the German Reigning Princes and Hereditary Princes took their place, behind whom again the flags and standards were lined up.

After His Majesty had read aloud in the familiar fashion a short address to the German sovereigns, Count Bismarck came forward, looking in the grimmest of humours, and read out in an expressionless, business-like way and without any trace of warmth or feeling for the occasion, the address "to the German People." At the words "Enlarger of the Empire," I noticed a quiver stir the whole assemblage, which otherwise stood there without a word.

Then the Grand Duke of Baden came forward with the unaffected, quiet dignity that is so peculiarly his, and, with uplifted right hand, cried in a loud voice: "Long live His Imperial Majesty the Emperor William!" A thundering hurrah, at the least six times repeated, shook the room, while the flags and standards waved above the head of the new Emperor of Germany and "Heil dir im Siegerkranz" rang out. The moment was extraordinarily affecting, indeed overwhelming, and was in every way wonderfully fine. I bent a knee before the Emperor and kissed his hand, whereupon he raised me and embraced me with deep emotion. My feelings I cannot describe, all quite understood them; even among the flag-bearers I remarked unmistakable signs of emotion.

Then the Princes, one after the other, offered their congratulations, which the King accepted with a friendly handshake, a sort of defile past being formed, though never really marshalled properly because of the unavoidable crush. Next the King went along the line of flags and their bearers; then he stepped down from the platform and, making his way down the hall, spoke a few words in passing to the officers and men standing on either side. I had sent orders to the band, directly the Emperor was on the point of leaving the hall, to play the Hohenfriedberg march, so that His Majesty parted from the assemblage to the strains of that noble air, and finally left the Palace amid the cheers of the Staff Guard of Honour.

A dinner at the Préfecture, at which His Majesty said to me that from now I ought to be addressed as "Imperial Highness," though indeed my precise title was still unknown to him, concluded this noteworthy day, the evening of which the Princes in a body spent at my quarters.

The Versaillese understand the matter in the sense that our King is being proclaimed as French Emperor, but they cannot comprehend why we did not first consult the French. Some imagined we were capitulating to the victorious Parisians, and that was why we were removing the flags (!).

I have witnessed Coronations, Oaths of Allegiance and many unusual ceremonies, but I have known none either so august or so well contrived and so incomparable in external significance. For one thing, the vast importance of the moment was directly connected with our victories, and further, all witnesses just now gathered in these rooms were not any customary guests, but men who for months past had devoted their lives to the common cause of the Fatherland, which now, before their eyes, was receiving its consecration. Germany had her Emperor again!

The temper of the Court personnel was again to-day one of discontent; indeed we heard people saying how nothing further had come of it in particular, seeing that for the future everything remained Prussian and no external changes were to be made. But the groups of officers and men thought and felt otherwise, for when His Majesty was reviewing the flag-bearers in the "Salle des Glaces," and I at the same moment was talking with the non-commissioned officers of the Royal Grenadier regiment, at the first word in reply the file on the flank at once addressed me as " Imperial Highness." For the rest, so little was I prepared for this address that I was visibly startled, thereby giving the man a corresponding fright on his side—an incident several times over repeated as I was conversing with the Knights of the Iron Cross who were there as deputations from the rank and file of the soldiery.

Headquarters : Versailles, 19th January.—Yesterday's intrinsically warlike ceremony in celebration of the re-establishment of Emperor and Empire was immediately followed by a bloody baptism of fire to-day. That is to say, the Parisians made a sortie, which was directed in the early hours of the forenoon from Mont Valérien first against the IVth Army Corps and the position of the 10th Division by La Malmaison and Bougival, then subsequently took the direction of Saint-Cloud, but was everywhere repulsed. Immediately on receiving the first reports I had the Landwehr Guards from Saclay and a Bavarian brigade from Châtenay concentrate here, and only when I was sure of a reserve thus constituted, did I start out with Lieutenant-General von Blumenthal. In the first instance I struck into the road to Marly, whither His Majesty had gone and Princes as well as officers of both Headquarters were streaming in crowds. The inhabitants of Versailles were just as excited as on the 21st October, wished us all conceivable disasters, and would seem to have been aware for several days past of the sortie planned for to-day. However, before I reached Marly, I received—at Rocquencourt—from General von Dresow the information that the engagement with the 10th Division was over and that nothing more of note could now be observed from the Marly aqueduct, but, on the other hand, enemy columns now seemed to threaten an attack on Saint-Cloud. Of course I at once abandoned the idea of going to Marly and drove hard, accompanied on horseback by Major von Hahnke, whom I met on the road, for Vaucresson—which the soldiers call Vokersdorf !—where I knew of a hill not far from the Hospice affording an excellent point of view. Arrived there, I found in the gun emplacement called the " Hospice battery," Battery No. 3 in action and firing on the height of La Bergerie near Garches as well as in the direction of the Montretout entrenchment. Major-General von Sandrart, who was likewise in the battery there, told me that entrenchment had been taken by the French early that morning, and he could not learn with any certainty whether it had yet been retaken or not. This earthwork, left unfinished by the French and now lying within the outermost line of our outposts, we have always held with a patrol of non-commissioned officers, whose duty it would, of course, be to offer no sort of serious resistance; consequently the men occupying it early this morning, after holding out a good while, had been forced to yield to superior numbers and evacuate the position. From the Brigade Bothmer engaged in the fight a message asking for reinforcements had reached Major-General von Bothmer, who at this moment was sending forward the Fusilier battalion of the Royal Grenadier regiment to Garches and Montretout to their help, so that I had the opportunity of having the gallant Silesians, who were just moving off in the gayest of spirits, march past before me. When, after being some while in the field, one has become known to the different units, it affords those in command a feeling of pleasure that is well-nigh indescribable to note how delighted the fellows are at meeting one again. Such was the case to-day, while the shells fired from Mont-Valérien whistled over our heads and crashed into the Park of Villeneuve l'Étang lying directly below us. It did not last long, as a brisk infantry engagement, now more, now less intense, developed on the heights of La Bergerie, where the French had managed to take up a strong position behind the garden walls. I had an excellent view of this infantry engagement from the "Hospice battery," for so close were we to it that the chassepôt bullets came flying right into the battery. I must own that it was not quite the thing to take up my stand actually in a battery, as the action was fought only by single battalions and I had no direct concern with it, and I shall certainly not do it again should opportunity occur. But I confess it was particularly welcome to me just on this day, as after yesterday's event, which in a certain sense brought me promotion, I received as it were a new baptism of fire.

Then appeared Lieutenant-General von Boyen, whom His Majesty had sent to get him information as to what the firing meant, as it was supposed at Marly that the engagement was at an end, and so General von Kirchbach had already given the order for the reserves to march away. There could, of course, be no question here of anything of the sort, though it was getting dark, as preparations had to be made for storming Montretout. Presently, late in the evening, the entrenchment was actually taken, this happening directly we had regained possession of the heights of Garches.

His Majesty is not satisfied with the reports submitted to him, and again, late in the evening, wrote me a letter with many inquiries, unmistakably revealing great anxiety for the security of Versailles—an anxiety, however, I cannot share in the smallest degree.

So Bourbaki is really retreating, pursued by General von Werder; what a piece of luck and what a triumph for the latter, my subordinate of old days! He deserves the Black Eagle! The precise direction of the French retirement is not known, but we hope General von Manteuffel will yet succeed in barring General Bourbaki's way at Gray or Besançon, or at any rate rendering his retreat extremely difficult.

I had myself vaccinated this morning because of the small-pox that is raging here; I feel tired out with the events of the last two days and am expecting to have more fighting to-morrow.

Headquarters : Versailles, 20th January.—When this morning I arrived at the Préfecture for the usual report with His Majesty, the fourgons were standing there ready loaded, and all preparations had been made for a hasty departure! In fact, the Court marshals and civilian members of the Imperial Headquarters were in great anxiety in view of an impending attack on Versailles, an anxiety His Majesty also shared, while as for me and my Staff nothing was further from our thoughts than such a possibility.

Heavy fog veils the whole neighbourhood.

Quite against our expectations, no enemy attack ensued. Prisoners, who had only to-day been brought in, declare that the Paris authorities were so distressed by the incredible total of their yesterday's losses that all idea of continuing the fight was given up.

I rode out to the outposts, and on the way met a number of ambulances conveying wounded, many of whom had been shot with nicked lead; the " Salle des Glaces," two days ago the scene of a great historic event, was to-day already serving for the accommodation of these unfortunate fellows. The Hospice at Vaucresson offered an excellent refuge for the night, where severely wounded cases found a friendly reception; I could only express my thanks to those in charge.

On my way to visit the outposts on the high ground of the " Porte Jaune " I met General von Kirchbach, who told me an intermediary bearing a flag of truce was reported as coming to me from General Trochu; still, I attached no importance to the news, which sounded too improbable to be true.

General von Goeben yesterday attacked and took Faidherbe's position, and after a seven-hours' engagement threw him back upon Saint-Quentin. Tours is occupied by the IInd Army. Speaking generally then our prospects can hardly be more brilliant than they are at present. Chanzy, utterly beaten, describes in a despatch we have captured his condition as one of "utter defeat"; Faidherbe after two lost actions is in full retreat; Bourbaki declares officially he is forced to abandon the carrying out of his plan and is engaged in a highly perilous retirement; lastly, in Paris so great were the losses in the sortie that they will never make another, even when faced by famine! But how long will it go on, ever new masses of armed men coming on the scene to force us, even if Paris falls, to battle after battle?

To my deep regret I learned to-day that our sincerely respected friend Prince Woldemar Holstein is dead. We are the poorer for the loss of a sagacious brain and a proven, widely experienced officer, an intimate friend such as there are but few left us now.

As we sat with His Majesty at a cheerful family dinner at Prince Karl's lodging, Major von Hahnke had me called outside and gave me the information that Comte d'Hérisson had arrived at Versailles on a mission from General Trochu to me to ask for an armistice, or if not that, at least a forty-eight hours' truce for removing the wounded and burying the dead. Directly I reported this to the Emperor, he looked hard at me for an instant, for we both felt instinctively that such a step must be the forerunner of great things. However, as I scented in this request a covert political move, I at once got Major von Hahnke to apprise Count Bismarck of the matter, and on his reply confirming my supposition, took His Majesty with me to the Imperial Chancellor's, where the answer to be sent was discussed. The latter simply amounted to this, that the outposts in the usual way would have to come to an understanding about looking after the wounded and disposing of the dead, but all other details could only be arranged in writing. I drove on now to General Count Moltke's to lay before him the answer agreed upon with Count Bismarck. The former attached less importance to the circumstance than I did, and saw in the French proposal only an ordinary proceeding common enough after engagements involving heavy losses, with which political *arrières pensées* had nothing whatever to do. For my own part, my first impression remained unaltered, and

I cannot deny that I went to bed in a state of suspense and excitement.

Headquarters: Versailles, 21st January.—Fog again, which has been a great hindrance to the bombardment of Saint-Denis by the Meuse Army, the commencement of which after repeated postponement was finally fixed for to-day; I look for it to make just as little impression on the Parisians as that hitherto undertaken against the southern face. No unprejudiced person denies that the enemy is every day mounting more guns, building new emplacements on the enceinte and is doing us far more harm from there than from the forts. None of the latter has yet been silenced; only too often did we let ourselves be deceived, thinking, if once in a way a longer pause than usual occurred in the French firing, that the enemy's guns had been reduced to silence, but had very soon to realize that, after a brief interval, a brisker cannonade than ever had started afresh. We have reached a stage that was only to be expected under the given circumstances, when we must rest satisfied with keeping the enemy's fire more or less in check, and may congratulate ourselves if it merely remains as it is at present. But should the Parisians in their defensive measures preserve the same obstinate energy as hitherto, I do *not* know what our artillerymen will choose to do. Of course such a view of things is not to be expressed out loud. Hunger will be the determining factor, not arms, for supposing we did decide to storm the forts, to do which we should have to make unheard-of sacrifices of men in order to become masters of these works, even their possession would bring us but little more advantage than our own batteries afford us, as we should then have to hold our ground under the cross-fire of the neighbouring forts as also of the batteries on the enceinte fortifications. Our losses in the batteries are considerable. It had been supposed that with the bombardment the daily, unavoidable losses at the outposts would cease. Instead of that, they are trebled.

God be praised! on the division at last being taken in the Munich Chamber, the Agreement was passed—it is true by a majority of only two votes;[1] so that at last the Unity of the Empire has become a reality unmarred by any exception, and we have all been spared a great scandal.

General von Goeben has now stormed Saint-Quentin itself, and is already in possession of 9,000 unwounded prisoners.

[1] An error. The conditions of alliance were accepted by the Bavarian Second Chamber on 21st January by 102 as against 48 votes.

Headquarters: Versailles, 22nd January, Sunday.—At the service to-day in the Palace chapel His Majesty was for the first time in the public prayers entitled Emperor and King. I was agreeably surprised to gather from the circumstance that people are beginning to take the externals of the Imperial question in earnest.

The Emperor has told his entourage that for them he still remains as before their King, and they are therefore not to call him anything else. Meantime I have the conviction that custom will soon substitute " Emperor " for " King," indeed I hope so all the more as we surely owe the German people at any rate the intention of designating the monarch it has chosen to be its Emperor by a name corresponding to his new dignity. As for myself, I know nothing yet regarding my style. The Princess Karl, Prince Friedrich Karl and Prince Albrecht (senior) appear to have been regularly bombarding Versailles with telegrams, asking for promotion in rank! The Queen Dowager [1] regards the Imperial dignity with anything but favourable eyes and finds a sympathizer in the mother of the Grand Duke of Mecklenburg-Schwerin,[2] just now staying with her on a visit. The latter—a fine joke —first received the news of the Proclamation on 18th January from a casual remark dropped by the Queen Dowager's black footman. My mother seems, through an oversight of the Post Office, only to have learned the fact of the establishment of the Empire several days after the ceremony by a private letter from the Emperor.[3]

On receiving the news Berlin remained indifferent and unsympathetic; I account for this by the circumstance that a great many people do not understand why the Imperial dignity was first proclaimed so long after the 1st January, and that on our part it is endeavoured even to disavow the facts with the idea of our having to take heed of unknown potentialities, which again cannot be carried through with any stringency.

---

[1] Elizabeth, Consort of Frederick William IV.
[2] Alexandrine, sister of the Emperor William I.
[3] Of the 18th January. The characteristic opening of this reads: " I am just back from the ' Emperor ' act! I cannot tell you what nervous (!) emotion I have been in during these last few days, partly because of the high responsibility I have now to undertake, partly and above all to see the Prussian title supplanted! In a conference yesterday with Fritz, Bismarck and Schleinitz I was so nervous (!) at the last I had there and then to retire and hand over everything to Fritz! Only after I had turned to God in fervent prayer did I win composure and strength! May He grant that so many hopes and expectations may through me be brought to fulfilment, as desired! There should be no lack of honest purpose on my part."

To-day I mounted the tower of the Villa Bussières, from which the clear weather for once allowed a view of Paris free from mist and fog; yet, except for sundry conflagrations I could not observe any traces of destruction in the town itself. A new fact there is no denying—for some days the optimists among the newspaper correspondents and private letter writers, who hitherto were always talking of the supply of provisions and the defensive strength of Paris, are playing quite another tune. Whether this language betokens merely a momentary discouragement or else an actual sense of defeat, only time will show. I remain as heretofore mistrustful and resigned.

The despatch of the intermediary by General Trochu seems to have been meant less for me personally than generally for the holders of high command. But in any case the forty-eight hours' truce remains a striking fact.

The Grand Duke of Oldenburg gave a family dinner at his lodging, which thanks to the amazing sallies of Prince Karl, went off with uncommon cheerfulness.

Headquarters: Versailles, 23rd January.—Von Schleinitz, Minister of the Household, who returns home to-morrow, was with me a long while discussing questions of form arising out of "Emperor and Empire." But he knows as little about these as about the designations to be given Court officials, the theatre, etc. Only my own appellation was made known to me late in the evening by a Cabinet order addressed in His Majesty's own hand, by which the designation " Crown Prince of the German Empire, Crown Prince of Prussia," with the style of " Imperial and Royal Highness " is granted me. This new title pleases me and sounds well, but is a side-issue after all in view of its inward significance. May I fitly respond to the great demands this dignity makes on me, its wearer; with it I feel myself for the first time a true "German." Henceforth I know no distinction between Bavarians or Badeners or Hessians and whatever else the inhabitants of the three-and-thirty Fatherlands used to call themselves, and from now on regard every German as being no less nearly related to me than I have hitherto considered my own Prussian fellow-countrymen to be; but by no means do I therefore propose to concern myself in the internal affairs of the several countries, or to wish in any way to deprive them of their individual privileges and peculiarities. But, on their part, may Germans of every Province look upon me and my wife as belonging to themselves and not as North German intruders. My family we must not expect to feel the same; as they will still retain their old name, they will remain separatist till it may be time wears down the sharp edges.

After I had been startled at midday by the news that Jules Favre, who had asked for an interview with Count Bismarck, was to be passed through the outposts, it was presently reported that he had already come; next, the officer of the Field Guard at Sèvres announced that he had passed through there, and a little after I received the definite confirmation of his arrival. He has alighted at Count Bismarck's. All eyes are, of course, now fixed on the discussions between these two; still I fear a great disappointment, for I believe Favre will be much readier to talk about his journey to London for the Black Sea Conference than to discuss the state of Paris and France. On the other hand, it would not surprise me if the Parisians showed an inclination to open negotiations, as the sortie of the 19th January was forced on against Trochu's wishes by the populace, and gained them nothing save several thousand dead. Of this we could make absolutely sure by the number of days required for the burial of their fallen. All are shaking their heads and asking themselves what is the exact object of such enterprises, which never once reached the limit of our first line of defence. The circumstance that in consequence some thousands less hungry people had to be fed one can hardly describe as a military advantage.

Headquarters : Versailles, 24th January.—All Versailles is in the greatest excitement over the sudden and quite unexpected arrival of Jules Favre, which gives us some serious prospect of peace on this the very anniversary of the birth of Frederick the Great.

At a conference at His Majesty's, which Count Bismarck, General Count Moltke, von Roon the Minister of War and myself attended, the Imperial Chancellor in fact presented Jules Favre's offer to conclude an Armistice, Paris agreeing to surrender the forts and lay down arms!! Further, we learned that he did not deny the famine in the city; moreover, that, as Favre himself expressed it, " une sédition a éclaté à Paris " (a sedition has broken out in Paris), resulting in Trochu's dismissal from his post as Governor, which was handed over to General Vinoy, so that now he only remains in office as President of the Government of Defence. Favre could not hide a feeling of something like horror at the thought of a return to Paris, and appears to have developed a perfectly wolfish hunger at the supper provided by Count Bismarck.

Do we actually see a prospect opening before us of becoming

masters of the city without further bloodshed, while at the same time some hopes of peace begin to dawn on the horizon? Yet it sounds incredible; so the French proposals will be kept secret until Favre, who left at midday to-day, has returned. As it happened, he encountered Count Bismarck on the road, who at once stopped and exchanged a cordial handshake with him; so our answer does not seem to have affected his good humour.

News from home, I am sorry to say, makes me more and more convinced that an implacable hatred of the French dominates our countrymen there, instead of the sympathy and gentle, forgiving spirit, especially among the educated classes, that should find expression in view of the calamities of our opponents.

The intention of keeping Jules Favre's aims strictly private is more or less carried out; still the proposals he makes are practically known to everybody, as Count Bismarck actually yesterday evening, when he came out from the Emperor's study, turning to the A.D.C. on duty, Count Lehndorff, whistled the huntsman's call, the " halali "; this, of course, was quite enough to let everybody into the secret of what was toward.

Headquarters: Versailles, 25th January.—To-day, the anniversary of my marriage, the joyful events of the last few days were further supplemented by the news that Longwy had capitulated. When General von Moltke the day before yesterday laid before His Majesty the proclamation issued by the Commandant of that fortress, in which he declares his resolve to hold out to the last man, the General remarked laconically with an indescribable look on his face: " That means he will capitulate day after to-morrow!" No prophecy could have had more exact fulfilment!

Jules Favre is already back to-day in company with his son-in-law, who acts as his Secretary; this could hardly have happened unless his colleagues were willing to agree to our conditions. Again he dined with a monstrous good appetite, as Count Bismarck himself assures us Favre ate up a dinner intended for three all by himself! Indeed yesterday there were people would have it they had noticed he took larded geese and other victuals back with him to Paris. The garrison of Paris is really to lay down arms, the forts will be surrendered to us, and only the National Guard and certain troops of the line will not be disarmed, with the object of maintaining order in the city. The " sedition "

JULES FAVRE.

in Paris spoken of by Jules Favre appears to have been repeated, so that General Vinoy had to order some of the rioters to be shot; the disturbance would seem to be still going on.

Generals Werder and Fransecky are pushing on nearer and nearer to Bourbaki, who seems to be waiting for reinforcements from Lyons; such of his troops as can reach the railway by way of Lons-le-Saunier are making in that direction, though our men will very soon have barred all roads against them. The Grand Duke of Mecklenburg has already advanced almost up to Rouen.

Fairer omens and better news I could not wish for for my marriage-day; my wife, besides some articles of warm clothing, has sent me two charming studs set with emeralds, whose colour forms an excellent match to our hopeful mood. In honour of the day we had a cheery family dinner with the Duke of Coburg at " Les Réservoirs."

Headquarters: Versailles, 26th January.—A conference was held to-day from ten to half-past one for settling the conditions of the Armistice; these will include the following points more or less: truce by land and sea up to the 19th February; a line of demarcation separates the contending parties from one another at a distance of ten kilometres, beginning from whatever day this agreement becomes operative among the troops; only in the Departments of the Côte d'Or, Doubs and Jura the War, as also the siege of Belfort, goes on, pending the receipt of precise information as to the military situation in those parts; Givet and Langres, together with certain northern Departments, remain closed against us; each Army acts independently for the maintenance of discipline; a Constituent Assembly, to be immediately proclaimed and elected by free suffrage, will assemble at Bordeaux and decide as to continuance of the War or the conditions of peace—three weeks, they say, would be required to hold the elections; the Paris forts, with the exception of that of Vincennes, which is indispensable as a State prison for disaffected persons, will be surrendered to us, with war material of every kind; before expiration of the Armistice the Germans do not enter the city, a neutral zone being marked out which no one may cross. This last paragraph roused His Majesty's ire, and it took a long while before he let himself be persuaded to agree to it; still, no other course is possible, for nobody will be responsible for the safety of foreigners, so embittered are the Parisians, and no adequate force is available for the maintenance of order. Further:

the enceinte is to be disarmed and the gun mountings removed at once, though the guns remain, as they cannot be transported. Linesmen, Gardes Mobiles and marines lay down their arms, only a Division 12,000 strong remains under arms to secure the safety of the population; no one to be allowed to leave Paris. So soon as the Armistice expires without peace having been concluded, all become prisoners of war, but the officers retain their swords; only the National Guard and a certain number of Gendarmes keep their weapons for police service in the city; on the other hand all franc-tireurs are at once disbanded; the procuring of food-stuffs may go on wherever no German troops are stationed; anyone wishing to leave the city must have a French military pass, which our outposts check; Paris pays 200,000,000 francs war contribution within the next fortnight and admits no war materials of any sort whatever; the exchange of prisoners begins immediately, among these being included the crews of merchant vessels; we will release the corresponding number of French soldiers of the several military ranks, in return for ours, but not more; letters may be sent by post, if left open and unsealed.

Jules Favre appeared without military retinue, apologizing for this on the ground that he could call upon none of the commanding Generals to accompany him; General Trochu, having vowed he would not capitulate, could not well enter into negotiations, General Vinoy did not feel disposed, directly after he had taken over command, to start off with a capitulation, while we would certainly have refused to receive General Ducrot.

We must hope the Deputies to be elected will decide in a sensible, peaceful spirit, and that without long negotiations, before the completion of which indeed we cannot leave France. There is a possibility now that we may be returning home before Easter. God grant that in a few more days the bloodshed may come to an end, and peace be secured after the meeting of the Constituent Assembly! From midnight fire from the siege batteries is to cease by tacit agreement.

The Pomeranian Army Corps has now barred all the railways to the west against Bourbaki's troops, while General Werder from the north-east is pushing on to Besançon. French rumours speak of the capture of the colours of the Prussian 61st Infantry regiment by Garibaldians at Dijon. There must have been some obstinately contested actions there between the 8th Infantry Brigade (Major-General von Kettler) and the free companies in question; however, we have no news of this, as the activity of the franc-tireurs in the whole district round Dijon and Besançon has suddenly taken such an impetus that our communications are interrupted, reliefs and commissariat convoys broken up, and the Generals in command there unable to correspond with one another. This movement is no doubt connected with Bourbaki's expedition to recover Alsace, and gives us an idea of what, should Bourbaki succeed in his purpose, we should have to expect in France generally in the way of renewed warlike energy.

News coming from England has it that the numerous French people now in that country awaiting the issue of the War are the object of sympathy from many quarters, and that simultaneously the Republican element has of late manifested its activity in a fashion never before known. Mr. Odo Russell does not contest these facts.

Headquarters: Versailles, the 27th January.—To-day is Wilhelm's thirteenth birthday. May he grow up a good, upright, true and trusty man, one who delights in all that is good and beautiful, a thorough German who will one day learn to advance further in the paths laid down by his grandfather and father for the good governance of our noble Fatherland, working without fear or favour for the true good of his country. Thank God there is between him and us, his parents, a simple, natural, cordial relation, to preserve which is our constant endeavour, that he may always look upon us as his true, his best friends. It is truly a disquieting thought to realize how many hopes are even now set on this boy's head and how great a responsibility to the Fatherland we have to bear in the conduct of his education, while outside considerations of family and rank, Court life in Berlin and many other things make his upbringing so much harder. God grant we may guard him suitably against whatever is base, petty, trivial and by good guidance train him for the difficult office he is to fill!

To-day has brought us a step further in the negotiations for the Armistice and the capitulation, for Jules Favre is here again, and with him a military negotiator, Colonel Beaufort d'Hautpoul. But this high-sounding name was ill matched by the behaviour of its bearer, who was already " elevated " when he reached the outposts, had there taken more than was good for him at a breakfast they offered him, and finally at Count Bismarck's had likewise done such ample justice to the refreshments that the difficulty of carrying on negotiations with him seems to have been as great as was Favre's embarrassment at having such a companion. The Commander of the Field Guard, Lieutenant von Uslar, of the 2nd Hessian Hussar regiment No. 14, rode in the same carriage with him from Sèvres here, and related some highly diverting particulars of his experiences on the road.

When the French outposts at the bridge of Sèvres heard with what object Favre was driving under escort to Versailles, instantly officers and men began dancing the cancan together on the bridge, as a token expressing in a fashion very typical of their nature their delight at the dawning of hopes of peace; in fact it was only with the utmost difficulty the men of the VIth Army Corps could drive back the Frenchmen who came in swarms, determined to fraternize with our fellows. Not a doubt of it the French troops of the line are overjoyed to see the end of the struggle, and there is no doubt it was only the Paris elements that wished the War to go on. Jules Favre is decidedly anxious about the disturbances in the city, which make it impossible for him to specify how far the authorities will be in a position to get the pending agreements generally accepted. For our part we must be on our guard, because no one can foresee whether or no the hot-heads may not end by making sorties on their own account. Senseless as such enterprises would be, they might involve the line of defence in more and more fighting.

Since midnight the batteries are fallen silent; we all seem really to miss something, now that not a shot is to be heard, while for five months we have been accustomed night and day to listen to the roar of cannon. The inhabitants of Versailles gathered at once from the unwonted quiet that something out of the common was afoot.

His Majesty dined with me; at table was gathered my whole Staff together with the Princes of all grades and Presidents von Forckenbeck and von Köller, who had arrived as a deputation from our House of Representatives; on the occasion friendly references were made to my son.

Headquarters: Versailles, 28th January.—Jules Favre— I do not envy him his task—appeared again at Count Bismarck's, this time accompanied by a *sober* officer, whose name I did not hear. He is fully in earnest as to all conditions so far accepted, for he gave an assurance that he now had the power to secure the compliance of Gambetta and the Generals, whereas we had been suspecting him of proposing conditions as a mere matter of form, knowing well the authorities at Bordeaux would never ratify them. We must hope it is as he declares. Only towards evening was a meeting possible; so it was somewhere about seven o'clock the compact of capitulation was actually signed by Count Bismarck and Jules Favre. I did not receive information of its conclusion and orders for carrying it into effect till half-past ten at night, then I had first to wait for the arrival of all A.D.C.'s of the different Staffs established in the town; thus many hours were cut to waste and not before three in the morning were we ready for the issue of the necessary orders. I have directed that by not later than ten o'clock my Army shall have occupied the forts from Mont Valérien as far as Charenton.

The stipulation to the effect that we are not to enter Paris before the next three weeks have elapsed is all to the good, for considering the embittered temper prevailing there it might easily, in case of our forcing our way in, have come to collisions that would have compelled us to bring these wild hordes to order. Should the French themselves be unable to maintain discipline we shall, of course, have a word of weight to say from the forts. I think it would not surprise me if the French did all they knew to hinder our setting foot in the " holy " city.

As General von Kettler reports, in an action fought in woods near Dijon on the 23rd of the month, and in which he took prisoner 5 French officers and 150 men, the ensign of the 2nd Battalion of the 8th Pomeranian Infantry regiment No. 61 was shot in the action, which lasted on into the night, and the colours have been missing since. Further particulars are lacking. This disaster will ever be an open wound for the unfortunate regiment, the more painful as Garibaldian levies were their opponents. The French are less liable to suffer such losses, as they usually hide their colours in the baggage wagons.

When we come to Peace negotiations, it will be a chief part of our endeavour to be moderate in our demands. The parts of Lorraine that were once German we can rightly claim, but we should guard against the desire to annex any district really French, because this would afford grounds, always operative, for new French attempts to recover the lost territory. The best guarantee of peace would be alliance with England and Austria; after that, resistance to ultramontane activities, and lastly unceasing efforts to further the work of German unity, the external structure of which is finished, but whose internal completion will have endless disunion, separation, mistrust, jealousy and confusion to contend against. The new Constitution unfortunately favours the development of all these evils, which are nothing more nor less than elements of future weakness.

France's present defeat may easily lead to a regeneration of that State, especially as it is already a unity, not merely aiming at becoming such.

Headquarters: Versailles, 29th January, Sunday.—The occupation of all the forts, together with the pushing forward of the outposts to the line of demarcation, was carried out to-day from ten o'clock on without resistance from the French. In the case of some of the French Commandants, the order for evacuation came so late that many of our units had to wait quietly till the French had packed their baggage before possession could be taken; but again just the opposite happened sometimes, for instance on Mont Valérien and in the fort of Montrouge, so that friend and foe met each other in the fortress without harm done. The general behaviour of the French officers and men is commended—with the exception of that of the Naval troops, who were rough and rude.

I did not go to church, but spent the forenoon at home, to be always on the spot to receive reports, for I was all the while expecting to hear that at one point or another a collision with the troops or with bands of desperadoes from the city would come about. Thus the time passed in great suspense; but later, encouraging reports having arrived from all quarters, I went out in the afternoon to the batteries, to bring Iron Crosses to the gallant gunners.

So far, so good then! The moral effect must be a powerful one on all sides. Now we are anxiously waiting to learn from Bordeaux how Gambetta and the Generals there are taking the news.

They say General Bourbaki has shot himself![1] Can it be that he regards his position as so desperate and hopeless? True, all the outflanking marches of our several Divisions appear to be successful, so that in the end nothing else will really be left him but to cross the Swiss frontier.

Headquarters: Versailles, 30th January.—Accompanied by my regimental Dragoon escort, I to-day visited Mont Valérien in company with my brother-in-law. I cannot deny that I felt greatly elated, to feel myself master of this stronghold, after our having been for four months exposed to its heavy gun-fire. "Forteresse du Mont Valérien" is inscribed over the gate—and rightly so, for Mont Valérien *is* a fortress in itself, which, standing in a dominant situation as it does on top of a conical hill, possesses formidable forti-

---

[1] The General had, as a matter of fact, made an attempt at suicide on the 26th.

fications of masonry, which have evidently been further strengthened during the blockade by cleverly planned earthworks. A storming attack on it would have been a heavy, bloody piece of work, which, thank God, we have been spared. The 46th Infantry regiment and the 1st West Prussian Grenadier regiment No. 6 formed the first garrison; I greeted these gallant regiments, at that moment engaged in calling the muster-roll, with peculiar pleasure at this spot of all others. Our people had the agreeable duty of taking up quarters in the barracks and casemates, teeming with dirt as they were, and wading through the mud to be found on all the roads up there. A huge black, white and red flag waves there instead of the French colours, for I have expressly ordered only the *German* colours to be hoisted and not those of any separate German country. There was no question of a view, thick fog shrouding the whole neighbourhood. On the other hand, we noted the mines now being dug up at different points on the road leading up the hill, the hidden locality of which had been very honourably revealed by the French, and further on the monster cannon Valérie,[1] often mentioned, a very misshapen-looking weapon, which had been left standing there without breech-piece.

On the way to Mont Valérien we touched La Malmaison and then Rueil, where we visited the burial monuments of the Empress Josephine and Queen Hortense in the village church, and then continued our way homewards along the Seine through the burning town of Saint-Cloud and past the ruins of the beautiful Palace. The places lying within the line of outposts on either side have suffered terribly. All the rooms of the fine Palace of Saint-Cloud are burnt out; more than that, the excessive heat of the flames has had such an effect on the solid walls that ashlar and marble were literally reduced to powder. The houses of Saint-Cloud standing nearest the river are terribly knocked about by the French fire and are still burning day and night.

I hear it repeated on all sides that Jules Favre's language and that of his companions is becoming and sensible, and that it is generally felt that they have truly and earnestly striven to deal honourably and act in the interests of law and order.

Gambetta, on the contrary, is said to have certainly misappropriated millions for his personal use during his time in power, and as this report would seem to emanate from the Oppenheim banking circles, there should be some truth in it.

---

[1] Used to stand near the Arsenal in the "Unter den Linden" at Berlin, and since 1918 has been given back to France.

If so, much would surely be lost of the powerful impression that must have been produced by the stubborn tenacity he has exhibited out of sheer love for his native land.

Headquarters: Versailles, 31st January.—Jules Favre is here again and displays the same loyal honesty of purpose as before. For the rest, thank God, it seems more and more as if the Armistice were finding general approval in France. Nay! even Gambetta's language at Bordeaux gives us the impression he is no longer obstinately resolved on war to the knife; all the same his attitude remains the least bit doubtful, and I should not be surprised if next thing he came out as Dictator of the South, for he is just the man and just the character to indulge in the most desperate and ambitious projects.

The Emperor, who was nervous again to-day and in a vacillating mood as to many of the decisions to be arrived at, will stay here to wait for the final conclusion; so too, of course, must I remain on the spot till complete assurance is gained that no further outbreak of hostilities is to be feared. Whether it will then come to a stringent occupation of France for the levying of contributions or whether we shall occupy only German Lorraine and Alsace, this we cannot at present foresee. But in any case, things must then assume a quite *other* character than in war-time, and it will not be consistent with my position to continue longer in France. In the meanwhile I should greatly like to make a tour of Touraine.

I visited to-day, in company with my brother-in-law, the forts of Issy, Vanves and Montrouge; buildings and barracks in all of them have suffered enormous damage from our cannonade.

From to-morrow on, all guns in the forts will be turned against the city and all preparations carried out for a possible bombardment of Paris, to which end in fact a certain amount of French material can be utilized. The rest goes to Germany, so we shall soon be very rich in bronze. The iron siege guns are of no use to us and should therefore be blown up and left behind. Of small arms as well as biscuit and vegetables the French have left no inconsiderable stores behind in the forts.

Headquarters: Versailles, 1st February.—Again in company with my brother-in-law, I to-day visited the forts situated in the range of the VIth Army Corps, those, to wit, of Haute-Bruyères by Villejuif, Bicêtre, Ivry, as well as Charenton, held by the Bavarian Army Corps, where General von Tümpling and the other Generals concerned were taking over command.

From Ivry and Bicêtre we had so excellent a view over Paris we might have been actually in the streets of the city, where regular crowds of inquisitive loiterers lined the ropes that mark out the thoroughfares in the neutral zone and gaped at us; French soldiers who formed part of the throng looked at us as inoffensively as the rest, in fact the fellows seemed more disposed to wave us a greeting than for any hostile demonstrations.

The forts are not, as was hitherto believed, constructed at once against the external *and* against the internal enemy; they are all comparatively weak in the rear, so we shall have to use the three weeks of truce in building reverse batteries to mount guns for a possible bombardment of the city.

Headquarters: Versailles, 2nd February.—Favoured by glorious, hot sunshine I rode to-day with Generals von Kirchbach, von Sandrart and von Schmidt over the battle-field of the 19th January, beginning by Vaucresson and ending at La Malmaison. At the Montretout entrenchment we drank in with delight the noble panorama of Paris, which to-day lay below us with a clearness we had seldom seen before, and we could form a good idea of the heavy task the 5th Jägers had had to perform in the entrenchment here as also at La Bergerie-Garches. Similarly it was only now clear to me here on the actual spot how uncommonly obstinate must have been the fighting in the wood, at the park wall and on the very broken ground which I had looked on from the Hospice battery on the 19th January. The French cannot but have lost a fearful number of men just here, and the reserves in particular suffered heavily from our artillery; even to-day the hideous traces of its annihilating fire were visible. The charming villas at Garches and Saint-Cloud are a pitiable sight; some few, amongst them the composer Gounod's, were spared at the time the place was put in a state of defence, as a result of special favour in high quarters, but the only consequence of this was that in the action of 19th January parties of the enemy established themselves in them and opened a murderous fire on our men from first-rate cover. Our fellows complained bitterly of the favouritism shown, and accordingly, directly the enemy had been repulsed, set fire to the last of the villas left standing. La Malmaison has been badly damaged by French shells. On all sides Parisians and inhabitants of the neighbourhood are streaming past to satisfy themselves as to the condition of their property. I heartily sympathise with those who now find everything in ruins, especially in cases where every movable article had to serve as firewood or be utilized for the defence.

As for the franc-tireurs, we shall have to put an end to the system altogether, even before it is formally forbidden by law, as it has degenerated into mere brigandage and a terror to their own countrymen.

Herr von Keudell of the Foreign Office told me to-day that at the Imperial Chancellerie they definitely count on the conclusion of peace. May it be such as our gigantic successes deserve and prove a lasting one. In the mouths of educated and sensible French people we hear only one wish expressed: Peace at any price. Whether the Republic will follow next, till a new Monarchy is hatched out from it, is what nobody can say for certain. The Legitimists are all for a fusion of the two Bourbon lines,[1] which, however, seems to me so unthinkable as to be the merest waste of labour. On the other hand, we again hear the King of the Belgians mentioned as a candidate for the throne; under him France would certainly not fare badly, but as a friend, I myself hope heaven may guard him from such a consummation.

Count Bismarck has won for himself the reputation of being the instigator of all the cruel reprisals we have, alas! been forced to carry out; they even say of him that he means to establish a reign of terror in Paris of quite another sort from what Gambetta's was; occasion is certainly given for such suppositions by the monstrous maxims and savage expressions one hears openly given utterance to here, and which his wife repeats in Berlin.

More than one of the French Ministers came from Paris to-day to see Count Bismarck, who declares it strikes him he must surely be in the service of France these days, as every Frenchman now comes to him for advice.

I received very pretty letters to-day from Wilhelm and my little Viktoria.

Headquarters: Versailles, 3rd February.—The question has been raised at the report at His Majesty's whether we are justified during the Armistice in blowing up such fortresses as we do not want to hold and use any more for the duration of the War. I maintain that to do so in this interval would be a breach of the Law of Nations.

[1] The senior branch, represented by the Comte Chambord (Henri V), grandson of Charles X, and the Orleanist collateral branch represented by Louis Philippe, Comte de Paris, grandson of the bourgeois King.

Further complaints have been heard in the last few days about looting; as to this I would not mind wagering that on close inquiry it will be found, as so often before, that one-half of the alleged mischief is not true. It constantly happens that appearances are against us, for when the men on outpost duty in the several brigades come to be relieved, the officers are compelled to supply themselves from abandoned houses, so as to have the most necessary and indispensable articles of furniture in the buildings lying inside the line of outposts. Then if a stranger coming upon such a load of furniture in transport regards the whole thing as simple robbery, why, I cannot blame him.

The provisioning of Paris must be seen to far ahead, so that our men may suffer no want of food; day and night the French are at work to restore the railways so that supplies may be brought in sooner and quicker. But should the scarcity become too excessive, we have already, conditionally on the scrupulous observance of the agreement and surrender of arms, informed the French of our willingness to deliver victuals from our own stocks.

Headquarters: Versailles, 4th February.—General von Manteuffel has at last reported officially that the French, to avoid the danger of being completely surrounded at Pontarlier, have crossed the Swiss frontier; further, that 15,000 prisoners fell into our hands and Dijon has been re-occupied by Lieutenant-General Hann von Weyhern. Our men's fine spirit in bearing the hardships of an eight days' march in bitter cold and ankle-deep in snow or on sheer ice the General cannot sufficiently commend. How fortunate we have not this time to guard fresh hordes of prisoners! Switzerland will hardly welcome these guests, who are in the most pitiable condition and utterly disorganized; but no doubt of it many will slip back again into France, for indeed to keep a guard on them is simply not to be thought of.

The stories about the scarcity of food in Paris are pitiful to hear; numerous cases of fatal stomach complaints and a condition of general debility resulting in a total loss of appetite account for a host of victims every day. Moreover, the bad food aggravates all this sickness, as, in fact, the bread itself is no longer baked of flour, but of the most unheard-of and unmentionable ingredients, and the regulation weight made up by adding nails, scrap-iron, even dead cats to the already meagre quantity of dough.

Only now are the Parisians' eyes opened to the system of lies under which they lived, and bitter the disappointments that meet them at every turn. These circumstances, in conjunction with the tragic conditions on the Swiss frontier, cannot fail to be an eloquent warning against the continuance of human butchery and must add yet more weight to the reasons for concluding a speedy Peace.

The streets and roads of Versailles, till now trodden only by German soldiery and almost no civilian folk, now present an unwonted aspect by reason of the crowds of people coming from Paris in daily increasing numbers. Speaking generally, the native population has grown more polite towards us strangers since the Armistice. A host of people come out to Versailles to buy themselves the most urgently needed provisions, but as most of the horses have been eaten, one may now see fine gentlemen and elegantly dressed ladies, who in other days never left their houses except in a carriage, trailing about on foot in the thickest of mud, laden with bread and other comestibles. These visits of Parisians to Versailles are now become so frequent that prices in markets and shops are doubled, and supplies of fuel are running out. Our officers and men are sensibly affected by the scarcity that has thus arisen, and speedy steps are needful to help them out.

The state of uncertainty in regard to the Imperial and Royal nomenclature grows more and more embarrassing, and already serious misapprehensions and positive confusion have arisen in consequence. Strictly speaking, strange as it sounds, nothing has yet been fixed on as the designation of the heir to the throne. A definite decision is sorely needed in these external, as in other more weighty questions with which we are now faced. Otherwise we should undoubtedly be by this time *the* State of all Europe in whose hand lies the final arbitrament of all international business in future times. But so impossible is it to count on Count Bismarck and so fitful his policy that nobody can form a clear conception of his views, still less feel any confidence in his secret plans.

Headquarters: Versailles, 5th February, Sunday.—At divine service to-day, which, however, His Majesty's lumbago prevented him from attending, my wife and I were for the first time designated in public prayers by our new title.

Princes Ludwig and Wilhelm of Hesse have arrived, in whose honour a dinner was held at His Majesty's quarters.

In reply to Count Bismarck's protest against Gambetta's election ordinances the latter has in his turn protested, telling the Imperial Chancellor more or less clearly that the internal affairs of France, and above all the elections, in no way concern him. However, the Paris Government seems disinclined to put up with the Gambetta tactics, and Jules Favre assures us nothing will occur by which our good faith in his loyal purpose might be shaken; more than one commissioner has already been despatched to Bordeaux in order, if the worst comes to the worst, to remove Gambetta from office, should he take any steps to make himself Dictator. All this is very fine and delightful, but as at this moment no one in France exercises a more powerful influence than just Gambetta, one can *not* tell whether he on his side may not equally well declare the " Gouvernement de la défense " to be deposed, and, winning over to himself the south of the country, not yet so harassed by the calamities and miseries of the War, prolong and increase the existing chaos. In that case this unhappy France sees only disruption before her and becomes the sport of parties, delusion and lying. But, to my thinking, any fresh outbreak of hostilities is no longer a possibility, for, though many a hot-head prates of the demand to continue the struggle, it is now clear to every single individual to what this further bloodshed must inevitably lead.

The Parisians' fury against Germans knows no bounds. Shopkeepers who have lived there for decades can only enter the place at the risk of their lives, and are instantly driven out again under threat of long terms of imprisonment. Every day it grows more difficult for us to stop the Parisians from trespassing beyond the neutral zone, hunger no less than curiosity urging them to cross the boundary. Yesterday evening, in fact, a bayonet charge had to be made against the thronging crowds, merely to restore order. My house is every day besieged from morning to night with numberless French, but in particular by Parisians coming from outside asking for permits to enter the capital. These we are ready and willing to give them. General von Gottberg superintends the very worrying work of despatching these people, but manages it all with unruffled good-humour. The " Gouvernement de la défense nationale," however, will allow no one into Paris, so that very often the poor creatures have to come back, after meeting bitter disappointment in sight of the very gates of the city, and can find no way of getting news of those belonging to them.

Headquarters: Versailles, 6th February.—To-day began, as by agreement, the surrender of arms from Paris; the work of taking over these is entrusted to the Artillery officers at Bicêtre and Ivry. Contrary to expectation, the inhabitants in the city raised no difficulties, and already eighty guns and five thousand muskets have been given up, while otherwise petty but murderous rows occur every day in the capital, as to which General Trochu has sent an autograph letter to Prince Radziwill.

Things are taking a highly critical turn. The " Gouvernement de la défense " declares Gambetta's decrees invalid, and is again sending officials to Bordeaux who are pledged to take the strongest measures to see that the orders received from Paris are implicitly obeyed and that General Chanzy's Army help to give effect to the steps taken by the Government. Gambetta, however, on his side points out that the members of the Government were just sitting there shut up in Paris, and so by this time, owing to the long duration of the investment, were quite unable to learn how matters really looked in the country; that accordingly no effect would be given to instructions from Paris, and the Delegates of the Government would not be allowed to enter Bordeaux in an official capacity. It must now come to a definite decision who really and truly holds authority in France and what will be the guiding principles for the elections. Jules Favres goes his way unheeding all these difficulties loyally to act in a manner that certainly redounds to his credit. We must be prepared, should hostilities begin again on the expiration of the Armistice, to show the French that we are then determined to act at once in serious earnest; at the earliest possible moment, therefore, must Army Corps from the Army hitherto investing Paris be sent to reinforce the troops on the frontiers. To this end I shall order the Vth Army Corps to march to the Loire, as to me is assigned the duty of moving southwards; but it is with great unwillingness I part from these gallant veterans, who will certainly now join up with the IInd Army. Still I cannot myself believe tnat the same butchery could ever be resumed by the French, who, it is true, can arm hundreds of thousands of men and send them out to battle, but have ever worse and worse material to work with and can provide for use no efficient artillery, especially if we consider that Paris alone is surrendering to us 600 fieldguns, besides 150,000 muskets.

On account of his lumbago, which is very painful, the King was unable to be present at a dinner arranged by the Grand Duke of Weimar at the Pavilion of Louis XIV at Saint-Germain. At it Prince Karl's humour was again of the most astonishingly lively sort.

Every day more and more house-owners appear from the environs of Paris looking after their property; to our no small

THE EMPEROR FREDERICK III.

satisfaction many express their surprise that the damage is not greater and that Versailles itself remains so absolutely and entirely untouched. It is true, of course, that in certain places self-defence has demanded cruel acts of destruction, but the mischief mainly affects the wealthy classes and speculators; a man who builds himself a summer residence can easily repair any dilapidations and be glad enough to do it. This does not indeed hold good for the unpropertied dwellers in small places. Very lamentable is the felling of so many noble old trees, the loss of which cannot be made good for generations to come. But the greater part of the ornamental trees had already been cut down by the French for barricades and abattis.

All Germany is jubilant over the capitulation of Paris; only Berlin remains without outward manifestations of joy, but is rather inclined to be critical and deems that by no means enough has been gained.

Headquarters: Versailles, 7th February.—Gambetta has resigned his offices!—and hopes of peace have risen considerably in consequence. We learn at the same time that serious demonstrations have taken place at Bordeaux, and further, that Favre and Trochu have invited the Generals of the more important Armies to come to Paris for discussion of the situation. This summons General Chanzy has already obeyed, having passed through here only this evening on his way to the capital. Whether General Faidherbe will be equally compliant it is impossible to say yet; but if he does come, we may gather that the authority of the " Gouvernement de la défense " is generally recognized.

Of the exact course of our policy, no less than of the state of the Peace negotiations with the different dignitaries who appear daily from Paris, I hear just as little as at other times in Berlin; unless I beg for enlightenment, everything remains hid from me. Count Bismarck would seem to show great cleverness in the conduct of the deliberations no less than in his handling of the negotiators, so that he has the members of the " Gouvernement de la défense " well in hand and at the same time keeps on good terms with them. Four to six milliards war contribution is to be proposed, at least so I heard from Count Guido Henckel, who for some days past has been giving a helpful hand at the Imperial Chancellor's bureau. Further, the cession of certain French Colonies and battleships has been mentioned incidentally, albeit Minister Delbrück will not hear of the first of these suggestions, and as to the French vessels of war, it is very questionable if by acquiring these we should be doing a good piece of business for the German Navy. Besides, in this connection another question comes to be considered, whether our age at all admits of great navies of the old type, whether we should afford the gigantic expenses required for this purpose, or whether Germany would not perhaps do better to come to an agreement with England of such a sort that in international affairs her old and experienced fleet would provide for the Empire's safety at sea in the same way as our Army could do for England's well-being on land. As for Alsace, we are faced with serious difficulties, but for the moment I do not yet know whether we are curtailing our demands or mean to claim Metz unconditionally.

I went to see Prince Friedrich Karl, who was in a fairly good humour, and took a rather long ride in company with Lieutenant-General von Stock. My brother-in-law Prince Ludwig of Hesse spent the evening with me, and later on Prince Friedrich also came in.

Headquarters : Versailles, 8th February.—The Emperor had had a bad night because of his lumbago, and at a conference, attended also by Count Bismarck, was in a downright nervous condition. After standing out a considerable time, His Majesty at last yielded to the pressing representations of the Generals and issued marching orders to the Vth and also the IVth Army Corps, so that, on the expiration of the Armistice, they might be ready to reopen hostilities at Orleans, Blois and Le Mans respectively.

The elections were held to-day throughout France, Alsace included. It is thought that among the 700 Deputies to be chosen only about 150 actual Reds will be found, so we may hope for corresponding decisions.

Jules Favre I saw drive by in a closed carriage; he has told Count Bismarck that Gambetta at Bordeaux had made an abortive attempt to get himself acclaimed Dictator at the Theatre there. That to this end a sort of throne had been set up on the stage; but so few sympathizers had put in an appearance that the whole thing had been a fiasco and Gambetta had resigned his office. Count Bismarck finds Jules Favre, in comparison with his attitude at Ferrières in September of last year, notably more moderate, not to say down-hearted; he displays such a surprising lack of business-like qualities and such dilatoriness that the most urgent questions are often left unanswered for days, and, for instance, provision trains cannot be admitted into Paris simply because Favre, who insists on seeing to everything himself, forgets

Léon Gambetta.

under the strain of overwork half the duties he has undertaken.

Whether we shall make a formal entry into Paris has not yet been closely discussed; it would be well to grant such a satisfaction to the troops, but *I* care very little indeed about it, and I should deem it more suitable, in fact, if the Emperor and myself did not take part in it, in order that the very semblance of insolent triumph might be avoided in the eyes of France, already suffering so heavy a penance. Only there is one thing on which we must not fail to put the impress of our power, and that is the French arrogance that goes hand in hand with the most impudent lies, and out of defeats suffered makes out victories won. In this spirit Frenchmen still go about boasting openly " que jamais le pied d'un soldat allemand ne souillera le sol de Paris ! " (that no German foot shall ever pollute the soil of Paris). To these braggarts an entry into the city would be a healthy lesson in humility, and rob them of the last excuse for indulging their vanity.

Some details regarding the loss of the colours of the 61st Infantry regiment are now beginning to throw a clearer light on the occurrence, and it is now established that officers and men defended the flag with really touching gallantry, that it was passed from hand to hand, till, in the end, a great heap of corpses covered it over, under which it was only found later.

Headquarters : Versailles, 9th February.—To-day I gave the regiments of the Vth Army Corps way-leave from the town; I was very loath to see these veterans, to whom I have become so attached, march away, as I am afraid this Army Corps might eventually be taken from my command and join up with the IInd Army. The Versaillese are surprised at the departure of the Corps, which has been in cantonment here for five months, and think we are withdrawing because General Chanzy is advancing for the relief of Paris. A citizen asked a Jäger what the reason was, but all he got from the latter was the laconic reply, " Bordeaux."

The Times gives all sorts of exaggerated reports about the proposed terms of peace, occasioning no small sensation here; still, this misleading information has one advantage, that, when once our real demands become known, people abroad will judge us more justly, as after all it is more than right that Germany should claim the payment of her war expenses, reckoned at four and a half milliards, by her adversary.

I visited in company with the Grand Duke of Weimar the

old and new porcelain works at Sèvres, from which luckily the most valuable articles of manufacture were brought to Paris as long ago as in September last, though, on the other hand, numerous models of burnt clay were left behind and unfortunately have not altogether escaped injury. Still it is really wonderful how out of a hundred shells that fell in the immediate neighbourhood of the buildings, only twenty struck the house and did scarcely any damage. Just when the temper of our soldiers no less than of the French was primed for destruction, I was fortunately informed of it and was able instantly to have strict rules laid down for the gunners. The Sous-Directeur was still overflowing with gratitude for this, as by this means really the chief treasures, to wit, moulds and material, were still available for the continuance of the artistic work. For the rest, so far as good taste is concerned, I must confess I discovered this only in the models of the period of Louis XIV and Louis XV; all the rest could hardly be called really artistic.

Headquarters: Versailles, 11th February.—Only to-day came the official announcement from General von Manteuffel that as long ago as the 26th January an abortive attack took place on La Pêche, causing us losses, particularly in prisoners.

To-day for the first time can the results of the elections in Paris, as also in part of Northern France, be approximately estimated. The capital, against all expectation, voted Radical, due to the excellent organization and discipline that prevails in that party. In the north many Orleanists have been elected, at Boves the Duc d'Aumale. The parties seem once more to be in full ferment in this unhappy country, so that one hears the watch-words : Chambord, Orleans, Bonaparte, Republic shouted indiscriminately. Sensible Frenchmen are utterly discouraged and mournful, feeling as if they had a home no longer, nay, as if France were utterly falling to pieces. No one can tell beforehand what the Constituent Assembly will decide upon, seeing terrorism is of such overwhelming power that it is quite conceivable the misguided creatures might resolve on " guerre à outrance," in spite of what every man knows, that no adequate arms, no money, and above all no trained soldiers are in existence to carry on the struggle. Look where you will, infatuation and obstinacy, evils that are openly admitted by the clear-sighted, without its being possible to remedy them, above all because there is no head knows how to set a limit to the chaos, and because France less than ever now is in a condition to govern herself.

For the moment Jules Favre holds the power, because he is still in the main master of the situation; but inasmuch as he is at the same time suspected on all hands, many regard his position as already undermined. Once, however, he is overthrown, then no man can indicate a Dictator who could take the reins. Thus it might easily come about that, in spite of all the well-deserved reproaches cast at him, Napoleon will even yet be called to be the last saviour of France in her extremity. Possibly again, the Duc d'Aumale might succeed in restoring order, with the object, after he has levelled the ways, of setting his nephew, the Comte de Paris, at the helm of State. In any case, such is the state of things that whosoever to-day craves a continuance of the War, wantonly incurs the guilt of the country's ruin by forcing the sword into our hands afresh; on the other hand, should peace be concluded under the condition that our troops should one and all leave French soil, beyond a doubt civil war must break out.

I drove out with the Hereditary Grand Duke of Weimar to the Bridge of Neuilly, in order to watch for once in the immediate neighbourhood of the line of demarcation the traffic of Parisians passing in and out of the city. At this point all are pressing to get to the surrounding localities to buy provisions, but as no one is allowed to pass our outposts without a certified passport or special permit there is a never-ceasing tumult of tongues, in different languages, leading to diverting scenes, for neither side possesses any great knowledge of the other's speech. Already the " dames du demi-monde " are utilizing the opportunity to make a sensation with their startling costumes.

I went to-day as far as the cantonments of the 1st regiment of Foot Guards, on which occasion I had the pleasure of seeing many an old acquaintance again and was also greeted by the men with decidedly friendly faces. We strolled along the beautiful road leading by the river side to Saint-Cloud in sunshine and a slight frost, and found it so thronged with acquaintances I thought myself transported back to the dear home-land.

Headquarters : Versailles, 12th February, Sunday.—After service the gallant Infantry regiments Nos. 83 and 94, together with the 14th Hussar Regiment, three Batteries and the Pioneer Companies of the 22nd Infantry Division, arrived here under command of Major-General von Roehl. I felt proud and glad to see this Division return to join my Army after being for over three months continuously in the field, acting more or less as the pivot for the activities of the

XIVth Army Corps, and fighting in two-and-twenty battles and minor engagements. The men made a fine show; unfortunately the regiments had had better clothes sent out for them to the last halting-place on the march, so that we no longer had the opportunity of seeing them in their torn tunics and partly dressed in French uniforms. The gallant Commander of the Division, Lieutenant-General von Wittich, to the general regret, was unable to ride at the head of his men, as he still lies seriously ill with the small-pox.

Encouraging results are to hand in the elections in this Department, and Count Bismarck expressed to me to-day his expectation that things were tending towards peace.

Generals Chanzy and Faidherbe appear to have spoken of the impossibility of going on with the War and have found an ally in this opinion in Louis Blanc.

Menotti Garibaldi (son of Giuseppe) has described in a letter, the contents of which we have become acquainted with, how after the fight at Dijon, in which the colours of the 2nd Battalion of the 61st Infantry regiment disappeared, the flag was found under a heap of corpses and drenched with blood.

Could our officers and soldiers have done their duty more nobly or more gallantly guarded the honour of the flag? I find the deed so moving that I feel like weeping every time I think of it.

Headquarters : Versailles, 13*th February.*—It is probable that the Armistice will be prolonged for a short period, as the time is found too short for checking the votes and too few days are left the Deputies for special deliberations. However, we shall not, therefore, infringe the condition originally agreed to, not to enter Paris, but at the same time reserve the right to send troops into the city if it seems good to us. Still, the claiming of this right by no means implies that we are thinking of availing ourselves of it at an early date, particularly as it is a real piece of good fortune for us not to have to share duties with the military police for Paris. Of a formal entry into the city nothing more is being said, but on the occasion of the departure of our troops for home, the men might well march through the capital, to let them for once see the inside of the Paris before which they have lain so long.

Headquarters : Versailles, 14*th February.*—News is to hand from the Army of Investment before Belfort to the effect that all signs point to the surrender of that fortress. We are not disinclined, supposing Jules Favre exhibits a compliant temper in the delimitation of frontiers in the south, to agree to a capitulation under which the garrison should march out free men and with all the honours of war. This event, putting the key of Alsace, as the French call the place, in our hands, would give us complete possession of that German Province of France—a thing that would be of the greatest weight as bearing on our position during the Peace negotiations.

I read to-day the text of my mother-in-law's speech from the throne at the opening of Parliament, and do not think, as many people do, that greater sympathy is therein expressed for France than for Germany. On the other hand, in the House of Lords bitter irony finds utterance against Germany.

Headquarters : Versailles, 15th February.—Jules Favre, who has been to Bordeaux, is back and seems to have gained a favourable impression of the Constituent Assembly; so within the next few days we may look for the election of a regular instrument of Government and may reasonably assume that the movement in favour of peace will gain the upper hand. Most likely Thiers, Favre and Chaudordy will be sent here to negotiate it. Fresh hopes for peace are awakened by Garibaldi's disbandment and the applause with which Favre's speech was received at the preliminary sitting of the Constituent Assembly.

To-day the first ambulance train left Versailles, carrying a great crowd of wounded. The internal fittings of the carriages struck me as not bad; they give the impression of a ship's cabin, especially as the beds are placed one above the other; certainly there was not much ventilation, in fact the narrow compartments were so stifling from the overheated iron stoves that many a patient was streaming with perspiration. But anyway the invention, first suggested in Württemberg, afterwards completed by Professor Virchow in Berlin, marks a very gratifying advance in this department of work for the sick and suffering. It is fortunate that very shortly the Palace of Versailles will be completely cleared of at least thirty severely wounded cases; it was high time, for it was nowhere practicable to establish thorough ventilation.

Headquarters : Versailles, 16th February.—Belfort has capitulated ! Given the condition that the garrison should march out freely with the honours of war and retaining their arms, a prospect was opened to us of gaining possession of the fortress without further bloodshed, and we undoubtedly did right in agreeing to this.

The Armistice has been extended up to the 24th of the month, but without fresh conditions, which came as a surprise to His Majesty. Yet it has been expressly stipulated in regard to this extension that if within this period the conditions laid down by us have not been accepted, we shall be compelled to start hostilities afresh.

I drove out with Mr. Odo Russell to Mont Valérien and La Malmaison in the most glorious, brilliant sunshine, so that we were able to gaze at the noble panorama of Paris in all its splendour. In the course of conversation with this amiable and clever man, he mentioned how he too was surprised at the strictly neutral tone of the speech at the opening of Parliament, but added that one could not well find fault with this, as it was the natural consequence of the course once for all adopted by English policy. In his opinion England might have prevented the outbreak of the War by a decided protest and a declaration in favour of taking the side of Germany. He said Paris seemed to be quickly recovering her wonted aspect, so that only the shortage of carriages and horses was still noticeable and sensibly felt. By this time the Parisians are prepared for a German entry, in fact there is actually talk of windows being let at high prices.

Jules Favre, who was going back to Bordeaux at once, announces very favourable election results, to wit, only fifty Reds and a hundred Moderate Republicans of his own party; all the rest are Monarchists, among whom the Orleanists preponderate, while the number of the Bonapartists seems small to the vanishing point.

17th February.—In company with Count Eulenburg, Majors Mischke, von Winterfeld and von Hahnke I drove by way of Longjumeau to Juvisy, where a special train on the railway was waiting for me and carried me by way of the battle-fields of Artenay to Orleans and Blois.

The Cathedral of Orleans, built in the late Gothic style, recalls that of Halberstadt; the town has no distinctive character and possesses several tasteless monuments in honour of Jeanne d'Arc. The streets swarmed with men of the Vth Army Corps, who let me see they were delighted to meet me again, as well as with French wounded. But most noticeable were a number of Prussian sailors, the crews manning the little Loire gunboats captured from the French.

At Blois I viewed with delight the noble Renaissance

Château and its beautifully appointed rooms. The parts of this magnificent château dating from the times of François I and Henri III are of quite unique beauty, and I could not look enough at the details of the ornamentation. Never have I seen such a wealth of wood carvings, delicate stonework and cunning use of monograms and heraldic devices no less than of artfully interlaced knots and ribbons as here displayed. All these reminders of the re-awakening to a sense of the beauty of the antique date back to the very darkest and most sanguinary period of French history; in the bedchamber of Henri III, here the Duc de Guise was murdered, while the King's confessors in the next room had to pray for the success of a great enterprise of their Sovereign, the nature of which was a secret to them till that moment. Lighted by the red glow of the setting sun we made our way through the town, the streets of which by their narrowness and manifold stairs reminded me of Wetzlar and are highly characteristic; above all is the view of Blois from the Loire bridge particularly fascinating.

The garrison consisted of troops of the Grand Duke of Hesse; also I met here General von Manteuffel and his Staff. I spent the night at Bishop Duparc's, an amiable old man, who lives in a large, richly appointed palace. I had a conversation of some length with him, in which he spoke turn and turn about of the honour he felt it to be to entertain me and his grief at the plight of France; he appealed to my good heart, which everywhere in France is now become the target at which all petitioners for remission of indemnities aim.

18th February.—To-day has been unusually enjoyable, for in the course of it I have come to know Chambord, Chaumont, Amboise and Chenonceaux.

The sun had not yet risen when I started, escorted by Hessian troops, for my next visit—to the Château de Chambord, the gigantic feudal castle, situated in mid forest, and displaying in its ornamentation the finest and most tasteful Renaissance details. Every gable, nay, every chimney is so charmingly decorated that seen by itself and set up where you will, it would immediately excite admiration, but here, owing to the endless variety that prevails, the eye feasts on the tasteful whole. The interior is completely bare and empty, and even in the ornamentation of the walls only what is of stone remains. The famous, ingeniously contrived winding staircase, on which two people can go up side by side without coming in contact with each other, is very original and well worth seeing. Chaumont lies like a Rhineland castle on the high river-bank of the Loire, and looks down on this lovely valley and the hills opposite, which form a landscape that may be fairly styled a miniature of the Rhine valley. As the château is fully inhabited and used, it does not in the least give the impression of a mere cabinet curiosity, but looks natural and attractive.

Taking post-horses, we drove on in warm sunshine through the Loire valley to the castle and town of Amboise, where the two huge suspension bridges have been blown up with quite needless zeal to bar our progress. On the gigantic castle time and revolution have spent their destructive fury, yet without effecting the overthrow of the really colossal pillars and walling.

We went on next to visit the Château de Chenonceaux, built by Catherine de Medici on a bridge over the river Cher. The castle has a bright, coquettish look, possesses an extraordinary wealth of ornamental devices and initials, and handsome fire-places, but has suffered considerably in the course of the centuries. The murmur of the river under the dwelling-rooms and below the balconies has a particular charm of its own, as indeed has the whole situation, so that I can well understand why of all others this beautiful castle is chosen for the scene of the second act of the opera *The Huguenots*.

It was only as night was falling that we reached Tours, where I dined with Prince Friedrich Karl, who " received me as a Field-Marshal," so he expressed it, " as I was travelling incognito." This was indicated by one of his A.D.C.'s coming forward to welcome me to " the third step from the bottom " and halting there—to which my cousin expressly drew my attention, as I myself, of course, never noticed the thing at all. The Prince's riding-whip never leaves his hand even in the house.

Tours, 19th February.—Favoured by sunshine and a cloudless blue sky I took a walk through the pretty streets and across the fine bridge, then spent the rest of the forenoon in the purchase of sundry old curiosities.

Tours is a delightful, prosperous-looking town, rich in pretty shops, quays and boulevards, and especially as seen from the imposing bridge spanning the Loire assumes quite the air of a big town. Round about the Cathedral, dating from the late Gothic period and spoilt by later additions, extend the old picturesque quarters of the town, with ancient buildings, quite narrow streets and ornamentation that is weather-worn certainly, but still beautiful—the whole giving one an idea of what the place was like in the Middle Ages. On one of these strolls I discovered an unusually fine suite of furniture of ebony inlaid with ivory-work in the taste of the Italian Renaissance, which I there and then bought as a birthday present for my wife.

After second breakfast at Prince Friedrich Karl's, who played the amiable, complaisant host, but always riding-whip in hand as token of his dignity, he drove me to the beautiful Azay-le-Rideau, and then to the Château de Vallandray. The day was of a warmth we only know at home towards the end of April.

Touraine, as landscape, I do not find so beautiful as we generally hear it described, but in the highest degree pleasing. Azay-le-Rideau, standing by the water-side, is pretty and picturesque. The Château de Vallandray has not yet been repaired and put in order as some others have, and so, in spite of its splendid situation, fails to produce the same impression as those I have so far visited.

Thiers appears resolved to carry on the Peace negotiations, and is already leaving for Paris to-morrow.

Headquarters: Versailles, 20th February.—Leaving the pretty town of Tours at an early hour, we were able to enjoy another hour's drive along the beautiful bank of the Loire, till once more we reached the stretch of railway available for traffic on the line to Blois, where I met my brother-in-law, Prince Ludwig of Hesse. The return journey was by way of Blois, where I broke the journey to visit the fine castle again and to purchase majolica ware, then by way of Orleans to Versailles, which I reached in the evening.

Thiers, with several companions in attendance, had travelled over the same stretch of line a few hours before me. Newspapers we bought on the way enlarged on his tactful and moderate attitude at the opening of the Peace Conference no less than in view of the proposed demonstrations in favour of Alsace. The end is that Thiers has been chosen by an enormous majority as "Chef du pouvoir exécutif"; may this justify us in concluding that the inclination for peace is in the ascendant. Immediately on Thiers' election England and Austria recognized the now existing, legalized Government. To-morrow Thiers is expected here.

Thus we stand on the eve of the Peace negotiations! May we with all needful firmness and vigour, while preserving moderation, give proper weight to political considerations and a wise appreciation of advantages gained, wherever military questions are not the immediately deciding factor! What offers Thiers will make is as yet unknown, so we cannot tell offhand whether he proffers peace at any price or services in return for concessions; still, the question of the cession of Metz to us should, for certain, be a cornerstone of the controversy. As the situation is not so far clear to me, I cannot judge definitely of these questions, only it seems to me to be incontestably requisite that we should have either Metz or Luxemburg; if the latter could be purchased from Holland, we could perhaps give up Metz.

The selection of Thiers as negotiator, his language, combined with the attitude of the Constituent Assembly on the Alsace question, are looked upon by authoritative circles here no less than by myself as important guarantees of peace, so far as we can hazard any general calculations in view of a France torn to pieces as she is. The friends of order are already wishing that foreign troops might occupy Paris, so that the new Government should have a sure support to rely on—so at least it is asserted.

Headquarters: Versailles, 21st February.—The Armistice is prolonged to Sunday, the 26th February, at midnight, yet another token, therefore, that a favourable issue of negotiations is expected. Thiers has had much talk with Count Bismarck and seems to realize that we as victors have a right to make important demands, but is not willing to give up Metz. Count Bismarck told me during the dinner at His Majesty's that he clearly saw how Metz might be the crucial point of the whole negotiations, indeed the price of peace; to which I replied, that if it were really so, Metz might perhaps be sacrificed rather than see fresh thousands fall on new battle-fields, after we have had to mourn so many. It is a great sacrifice from the military standpoint, yet at such a momentous crisis we must give more weight to a judicious political moderation than to merely strategical claims, however strong. Should we go on with the War, not only is it impossible to foresee its end, but we must be prepared for armed interventions and coalitions. True as it is that our people in arms might be well able to make head against these, yet, on the other hand, the nation has a right to demand that endless blood shall not be spilt merely to carry through strictly military principles.

The date of the Emperor's return to Berlin is not yet fixed, indeed, but might well coincide with the opening of the Reichstag. That event I should like to see accompanied this time by much pomp and ceremony, albeit otherwise I am for avoiding all noisy festivities this year, and for that reason highly approve of my wife's proposal that a day of national mourning should be appointed with memorial services to the fallen in the churches. Whether the three German Kings will condescend to come to Berlin for the opening of the Reichstag is indeed very doubtful.

Of an Imperial coronation there is as good as no talk, as in war-time people cannot think of such things, least of all after a ceremony such as that of the 18th January. For a coronation of the Emperor, who was then raised to the Imperial status, could and would be only an empty and needless anti-climax to that momentous event. If, after peace is concluded, people in Germany should, contrary to my expectations, desire a coronation ceremony, this could always be performed later on, though, it is true, we do not possess the coronation jewels, as these against all right and reason are kept in the treasure-house at Vienna instead of at Nürnberg or Aix-la-Chapelle. Nor do I quite see how at the coronation of an evangelical Emperor the Catholic ceremonial always hitherto observed could be adhered to.

When presently the return home of the troops occurs, at all places, and above all in Berlin, triumphal entries will take place, and the statue of King Frederick William III, long ago finished, will at last be unveiled.

Headquarters : Versailles, 22nd February.—Count Bismarck having asked me yesterday to receive Monsieur Thiers in audience, the present Head of the French Government appeared to-day at my quarters, immediately after the Emperor had seen him.

I opened the interview by expressing my regret at having to make his acquaintance in such gloomy circumstances for his native land, whereupon Thiers, entering into the situation of France, emphasized the point that he had come to-day in hopes of bringing about a peace, a thing he had failed to do on his first appearance months ago. At present, he said, France had many calamities to lament and longed for a peace that could surely be nothing else but welcome to Germany also. He must point out, however, that should it come to pass, the Parisians laid great stress on the inviolability of the capital. Should German troops, however, march into the city, one could not guarantee there would be no excesses. In the last few days, he added, bombs and explosives of all sorts and kinds had been found concealed in different places, of which it was impossible to say whether they had been kept ready merely for the defence of the besieged capital or not rather in case of the entry of foreign troops. If we had not exactly to fear attempts at assassination, such as that on the Tsar Alexander of Russia in 1867, still demonstrations of a very unpleasant sort might occur, the nature of which would induce the troops to take measures of reprisal that must give rise to regrettable incidents. Thiers next turned to the cession of territory demanded, and declared that the cession of the district from the Rhine to the Vosges was a bitter blow, and that no Frenchman would ever consent to the cession of Lorraine; he must therefore earnestly dissuade us from insisting on such a surrender. The demand for six milliards that is talked about he regards as impossible of fulfilment, because nowhere, not even in England, could so much money, or even approximately as much, be found in hand; France was exhausted, he said, and consequently such a prodigious sum cannot possibly be raised. The immediate responsibility of the War he puts on the Emperor Napoleon III; he had told our Emperor, then King, a lie at Sedan, when he stated how he had only been forced into war against his will and in deference to public opinion. Then, when later on an unbalanced idealist like Gambetta had started a *levée en masse*, a great misfortune had befallen France, for which, however, the people had been less to blame than that individual. For nothing could be a clearer proof of the genuine feeling of the French people than the result of the elections held in these last days, especially as France had for long not been really in a position to choose with complete freedom, for even in the provinces occupied by the enemy, this election had gone forward entirely without interference. Yet the attitude of the Constituent Assembly, even though very noisy debates had taken place, had proved by the conclusions arrived at how earnest was the effort for restoration of order and quiet. It could not be foreseen what form would be adopted for the new Government and who would be invested with the supreme power in France, albeit the preponderating section of the Deputies were Monarchists; but anyway great confidence had been manifested in him (Thiers) by the fact of his election. As long as possible, he declared, he had striven against the assumption of that office; but finally had come to believe that under existing circumstances he was bound to fulfil a patriotic duty, and then had straightway had the good fortune, at the very same sitting, to repress a hostile demonstration. He was now here, he went on, to appeal to the noble heart of the Emperor and to me personally (and with that he launched out into flattering speeches regarding the high reputation I had won in France) in the hope that a fair hearing would be accorded to his proposals. It was universally recognized how considerate the Emperor's conduct had been here at Versailles, especially in giving up the great Palace for the wounded, and contenting himself with the modest Préfecture, so that it might confidently be expected he would be guided by similar principles in the present case.

When he came to an end of his wordy exposition, I of course replied as far as possible in general terms, beginning by saying I supposed he had already discussed things with Count Bismarck, and made it clear to him that I myself was obviously not in a position to-day to go more closely into any of the questions raised. No doubt I should feel very much gratified if an understanding could be come to; but he could not fail to realize that in view of the enormous sacrifices made by us and the great achievements of our troops, we were bound to pay regard to the wishes of our soldiers. I said I fully shared his views as to the importance he attributed to the attitude of the Constituent Assembly, seeing it had conferred so highly important an office on him, the man who before the outbreak of the War had declared in the most emphatic terms for peace. In conclusion, I observed that after we had learned his views steps would immediately be taken to consider them, and that I looked forward with confidence to a satisfactory result.

Thiers spoke with little modulation of voice, generally with downcast eyes, preserving all the time a resigned, thoroughly tactful bearing; his language was fluent, yet without in the least degenerating into the style of the phrasemonger. When I spoke, he looked at me with bright, sagacious eyes through big, sharply focussed spectacles, looking searchingly straight in my face. His exterior is more that of an oldish countryman living on his means than of a statesman; his short, thick-set figure, for all his white, but strong, short hair, gives no indication of his seventy-four years.

What further consequences Thiers' presence will have I cannot yet say, because the Emperor has not yet talked with Count Bismarck since the audience. But unpleasant discussions between the Generals and other high officials cannot fail to occur; personally I am with the Imperial Chancellor as against the hot-heads. As to Paris itself, a means will soon be found that will afford our troops the satisfaction of visiting the city without wounding the feelings of the inhabitants by ostentatious entries and demonstrations. It seems to me that even General Count Moltke, in spite of his conviction of the impossibility of giving back Metz, admits that political considerations have under present circumstances a decisive word to say on this question. Whether Monsieur Thiers is engaged in negotiations to-day I cannot discover.

Headquarters: Versailles, 23rd February.—Count Guido Henckel, as also the banker Bleichröder from Berlin, have to-day arrived in Paris to discuss the question of payments on account of the indemnity. Contrary to expectation, no deliberations have been held to-day on Thiers' proposals, while in other respects nothing definite is to be learned, as everything is in a state of mere uncertainty. Count Bismarck seems to be to the last degree peevish and to have caught a fresh cold.

Naturally a renewed feeling of suspense has taken possession of men's minds; my own is exercised by the thought that, even if we do achieve the longed-for peace, we cannot therefore be sure that Count Bismarck, in pursuit of new designs, may not once again, after his own usual fashion, take up such a line of policy that fresh wars will be stirred up. Thank God, in view of the struggle just concluded with France, there is now no pretext for us Germans to go to war, and if our neighbours choose to begin fighting among themselves, we can fairly say we are resting and recruiting our strength now our bloody work is done.

Our next duty in peace-time at home is the solution of the social question; on this lofty aim must all treasures of German erudition and German intellect be concentrated. France is disqualified by the lack of mental balance, England by the too wide severance to be found there between rich and poor; but Germany, where no similar colossal fortunes exist, offers a productive field for a thorough solution of this question. The principles prevailing at the present moment with us will certainly afford no help towards attaining this end, for the prejudice innate in the ruling classes produces only a blindness of the senses or a false conception of the means requisite to reach a solution; we trust the failure of the product of Republicanism in France may prove a salutary warning to our countrymen. For myself, after my return home, a thorough examination of this question is to be an interesting and instructive occupation.

The Parisians appear to be fully prepared for our entry and properly curious. We should do best, little by little, to take up quarters in the district, lying near the Arc de Triomphe, and so unobtrusively push on and on as far as the Tuileries, till one fine day that part of Paris is completely occupied by us; then, on a day not to be made known beforehand, the Emperor to ride into Paris between a double line to be formed by these contingents, hold the march past in front of the Palais de l'Industrie, and, leaving the city again at once, set out on the journey home to Berlin.

I am sorry to say the *Daily News* contains a downright spiteful contribution from its correspondent, Mr. Labouchere, which we all greatly resent; no doubt sharp replies on the part of our Press will not fail to be forthcoming.

Headquarters: Versailles, 24th February.—Feeling grows more discontented from day to day, for no trustworthy information is to be had regarding the state of affairs. On the whole it is said the negotiations are at a standstill, because Thiers, who for the rest is to be here again to-day with Jules Favre, is proving very obstinate and continually appealing to our magnanimity. Count Henckel's impressions of Paris are by no means edifying, in fact he actually seems to believe in a fresh outbreak of hostilities on Monday. Count Solms too has heard nothing very different.

Late in the evening a rumour spread that agreement had been reached to-day on the Preliminaries—the whole of Alsace to become German; on the contrary, that we had given up our claim to Metz, France in return to have to buy Luxemburg and cede it to us, so that we may build up a place of arms there; finally, that four milliards had been fixed as war indemnity. Other people, however, talked of an ultimatum, inasmuch as under no circumstances was an extension of the Armistice to be allowed.

I must confess that I go to bed in the greatest suspense and excitement, for a renewal of war I cannot but regard as something worse than a blunder.

Headquarters: Versailles, 25th February.—When I entered the room to-day for the usual report at His Majesty's, the Emperor at once asked me what then I had to say to the incredible result of yesterday's negotiations, which had lasted well into the night, and when I looked at him in bewilderment, for as usual nobody had thought fit to tell me anything, he would not believe me when I said I had not heard a syllable about the matter. The Emperor thereupon related how the French are ready to cede to us the whole of Alsace, including Metz with the part of Lorraine adjacent to it, and pay five milliards war indemnity, in return for which we consent to the giving back of Belfort.

Furthermore, we have the right from Monday, the 27th February, to occupy Paris from the Parc Monceau across the Champs Élysées up to the Seine; not more than 30,000 men, however, will be quartered there at any one time, and accordingly the troops of occupation are to be changed every four days or so, so that as many soldiers as possible may look about them in the city. A formal entry into Paris is not to take place, but the Emperor will pay one visit to the city unannounced. Lastly, some further small modifications of the neutral zone at Le Mans are to be made and a twelve days' interval to be allowed for arrangements with the Constituent Assembly. I was, of course, quite unprepared for all this, as yesterday's reports had led me to expect just the opposite. Things seem to have gone hot and strong yesterday before agreement was reached; Thiers refused to consent when Count Bismarck desired him to give his help for the acquisition of Luxemburg, whereupon the alternative of Metz or Belfort was proposed, on which Count Bismarck gave the casting vote for Metz. The military advantage we gain is a highly important one; the more surprising is Thiers' compliance, so that many are of the opinion that, recognizing from the first the hopelessness of his efforts, he had merely chosen to begin by offering the strongest opposition before he submitted of sheer necessity to our demands. It is to be hoped the Preliminaries will be ratified by to-morrow, for, as the truce expires at midnight, the gentlemen in Paris have no time to lose. No one doubts the acceptance of the conditions laid down by Count Bismarck, as indeed the main questions are completely settled. I hardly know why the enforcement of such hard demands fails really to please me; it almost seems to me as though we have gained too much to be able to keep what we have won without some bitter hours of regret. At the same time I must admit that our strategical position by the acquisition of Metz and the Vosges has become an extremely favourable one. Mr. Odo Russell too, with whom I had a long conversation to-day, calls our successes " enormous," and shares my opinion that our demands deserve to be called harsh. I can readily suppose that the whole non-German world will characterize the conditions enforced by us as too hard. Thiers in the first instance went to see Count Bismarck and then General Count Moltke, and when the negotiations began, continually went off in long speeches that were copious in vocabulary, but singularly empty of meaning, the end being that Count Bismarck, who after all was in pain, lost all patience and became violent, even positively

ADOLPHE THIERS.

insulting. He actually addressed Thiers in German, as if to show him that he as a German was not in a position to make an adequate reply to such a torrent of words and flux of rhetoric in a language in which he was not fluent. Thiers was not a little taken aback, and now complained of the cruelty with which he was treated, while Count Bismarck, in return, made a grievance of the sending of a greybeard as negotiator, as it was painful to him to have to be impolite to a man of his years. The witnesses of the proceedings, among whom were Count Bray from Bavaria, the Ministers Jolly from Baden and von Mittnacht from Württemberg, cannot speak highly enough of Count Bismarck's superiority as a man of affairs, his quickness of apprehension and mastery of the matter in hand, as compared with the conduct of the French, and declare the conviction was forced upon them that not only on the battle-field but in the political domain also we knew how to carry the day. The violence exhibited would indeed seem to have passed all bounds; at the same time Thiers' lack of business qualities, combined with his habit of continually indulging in oratorical tirades, contributed essentially to the result that the French found themselves always in the wrong.

Headquarters: Versailles, 26th February, Sunday.—The tears are in my eyes as late in the evening I write down my experiences of to-day, for the Peace Preliminaries are actually signed. At last the dreadful, bloody War is over, and in such wise that Germany, after regaining her Unity through it, has earned a noble reward for the countless sacrifices her people has made and won back again her Alsace. And now may peaceful triumphs no less great in the domain of domestic, liberal reforms follow on those of the battlefields, and may we be preserved from reaction and retrogression such as afflicted us after the Wars of Liberation. But where are the men to be found who with due understanding can establish the principles that shall, to the true good of the people, bring free institutions to full development and ripeness, now that such sublime struggles have revealed its wholesome, vital strength to the amazement of the world?

The negotiations were vigorously continued throughout the whole day; again was heard many a rough word, and many a passionate appeal, till at last at five o'clock in the evening the signing of the Preliminaries took place. As we were assembling at His Majesty's quarters for a state dinner in honour of the King of Württemberg, the Emperor joined our circle with this joyful news, unknown as yet to everybody; then, after embracing me as well as General Count Moltke and the War Minister, von Roon, he communicated the fact to each guest as he arrived, his face beaming with delight. Mutual congratulations were exchanged by all, for each felt a ton's weight had been lifted from his shoulders and bloodshed had at last come to an end.

Metz brings us great military advantages, but no less certainly political difficulties, to which blunders in our administration of Alsace that are only to be expected will be added, to our further embarrassment. Still one must hope for the best from the future, and above all welcome with joy the fact now once for all accomplished. In the negotiations Thiers appears to have been quite resolved on the giving back of one of the three fortresses, Thionville, Metz or Belfort, but to have left the choice between them to us, the result being that Belfort was given up, because in that frontier district the key of Alsace can more easily be restored than if Metz remained in French hands.

As to indemnity, six milliards were demanded; of these one was remitted on the condition that five milliards, on which interest will be paid, shall be paid off in three years, while the first milliard has to be paid on the expiration of the current year. Till the last farthing of debt is liquidated, a German Army of Occupation remains in France, which is to be gradually reduced on the receipt of the several instalments. So far as I have gathered, Bavaria and Switzerland are to receive each a small cession of territory, but of what this is to consist I do not yet precisely know. On the 1st March Paris will be occupied by our troops.

I pointed out to Count Bismarck how I was bound to have been surprised yesterday to hear of the French concessions as accomplished facts first through the Emperor, and that even then it was only after manifold questions that I gleaned the more intimate details of the result achieved by us. This surprise, I added, he would the more readily understand as I had previously offered him my assistance should this be needed. By way of excuse he alleged the fact that the negotiations had lasted to a late hour at night and had ended with the complete exhaustion of his officials, making it quite impossible for them to send out reports. In course of the conversation he frankly admitted to me it was his great fear of what our military men would say that had mainly determined him to his obstinate insistence on Metz. But that, into the bargain, His Majesty had used expressions as though, to win the possession of that fortress of all others, he was disposed to go on with the War, whereas Belfort was not of such importance to us as to oblige us to make fresh sacrifices. I only pray Metz may not some day be the occasion of the Peace we have won to-day proving a mere truce after all! I build my hopes on a lasting Peace, and that Germans and French, instead of challenging one another in mutual animosity, will grow neighbourly and enter into peaceful rivalry in commerce, business, industry and art.

It is said the troops are really going to enter Paris; the "how" is still undecided.

One doubts whether the members of the Constituent Assembly at Bordeaux will see their way to decide upon peace without first speechifying for days together.

In contrast to yesterday evening, to-day I go to bed with a feeling of restfulness, peace and genuine satisfaction I have not known for eight months past. My unspeakable bliss and gratitude to know that in a short while now I shall see my wife and my children again are only troubled by one thing, that so many, many families have lost for ever the joy of welcoming their loved ones back, that so many a fond hope is destroyed, so many lives ruined and such woeful gaps made in the home life.

Headquarters: Versailles, 27th February.—On the 1st March, to the number of 30,000 men, as specified by the terms of the compact, contingents from the VIth and XIth Army Corps as well as from the IInd Bavarian Army Corps march into Paris, after a previous grand parade before the Emperor, who does not himself enter the city, on the racecourse of Longchamps. But then, in accordance with agreement, we must confine ourselves to that part of the city comprised within the space from the Seine to the Tuileries, the Rue Saint-Honoré and the Parc Monceau, and our men may enter the Louvre and the Hôtel des Invalides only under command of officers. The troops then entering remain in Paris over the 2nd March and are then relieved on the 3rd by contingents of the Guards' Corps and the Landwehr Guards, followed on the 5th by the Royal Saxon and Württemberg troops. When the Constituent Assembly at Bordeaux learns this, it will at last be moved to ratify with all speed, to the end that as few foreign troops as possible may tread the soil of the capital; yet presumably the orators will first want to be heard before a decision is come to. It is believed the first sitting is to be held to-day at Bordeaux. I have never myself been very specially enamoured of this marching into Paris, little as I begrudge our gallant troops this well-earned satisfaction. In fact, I cannot avoid a certain dread of unpleasant occurrences out of which serious conflicts might only too easily arise; but over and above this, a stay of twenty-four hours in such a city is amply sufficient to cause much permanent damage of various sorts.

The Emperor still declines to make any arrangements for the journey home. Why, nobody understands; in my opinion he ought to be leaving French soil now, as it is fitting for him to remain in the enemy's country only so long as actual war continues. Should the Peace Preliminaries break down, a thing luckily no man expects, the Emperor has still time enough surely to return back again to the Army. It seems that before his return as many more Army Corps as possible are to be inspected, while a little trip to Touraine is contemplated. Unfortunately everything will once again be postponed to the last moment, with the consequence that either the needful preparations cannot then be made, or else, to remedy such an inconvenience, a host of arrangements are hurried through all on the quiet and at haphazard. Most likely we shall not reach Berlin before the middle of March, the date fixed for the opening of the first German Reichstag.

What is to become of the Emperor Napoleon, now his imprisonment is at an end, I have not yet been able to learn from any authoritative source; it is believed, however, that he will retire to his private property of Arenenberg on the Lake of Constance.

Mr. Odo Russell has just been telling me that a tremendous state of excitement prevails in Paris on account of the coming entry into the city; that noisy bands of men were promenading the streets, hunting after "mouchards prussiens" (Prussian spies), and it seems harmless civilians have been drowned as sympathizers with the enemy's design.

Headquarters: Versailles, 28th February.—Nothing has come from Bordeaux; only to-day is the decisive sitting to take place, as Thiers and his colleagues have left Paris later than was expected.

There it has actually come to serious disturbances this time, as the lower classes, enraged at the Peace, have suddenly started nosing out German spies everywhere, and in particular mark down the *sergents de la paix* as secret friends of the enemy. Thus in the open street and in sight of thousands of idle spectators an official of the sort was murdered, the unhappy man being pitched into the Seine bound hand and foot, while every attempt at rescue was prevented by a hail of stones, till the victim perished miserably! Insubordination and evil-doing have certainly largely increased among the masses during the siege, and I only hope that we shall not in the end be called upon to play the part of military police in the city.

Lieutenant-General von Kameke, Chief of the Corps of Engineers, is appointed Commandant of Paris, and accordingly held consultation to-day with the Maires of the different Arrondissements, to get his bearings, before he rides into the capital to-morrow at eight in the morning with the Quartermasters.

I shall be in command of to-morrow's parade of the 30,000 troops on the race-course at Longchamps, on the very same spot where in the year 1867 the review in honour of our Emperor and the Russian Tsar was held, immediately after which the attempted assassination of the latter occurred.[1] Directly after the march past, the regiments march into Paris by different gates.

When and if the Emperor will enter the city is still as uncertain as his return to Germany. *I* only go to Paris if he does, or if it should be deemed necessary; otherwise, a single visit might best be paid quite on the quiet. In any case, there is nothing at present draws me to the place. The Princes have all been forbidden to enter Paris with the troops to-morrow.

The Silesian regiments told off to enter Paris arrived at midday at Meudon, Sèvres, etc., while our Pioneers threw a bridge of boats over the Seine at the Île de Billancourt with very commendable smartness, to facilitate our men's march to Longchamps to-morrow, as everywhere the bridges have been destroyed. I watched the men at work and then rode on to meet the Silesians. The delight is universal at the idea of going into Paris, but very few bethink them that neither officers nor men are going to find entertainment there, but rather that guard duty and restrictions of all sorts will be necessary.

Headquarters: Versailles, 1st March.—A perfect spring day favoured us to-day when after a damp morning fog the sun broke through the clouds and shone on the race-course of Longchamps, where 30,000 men, details from the VIth and XIth Prussian and the IInd Bavarian Army Corps stood drawn up under my command ready to parade before His Majesty before marching off for Paris. I must confess I had a feeling of no little satisfaction as I drew my sword

[1] By the Polish refugee, Anton Berezosky, on the 6th June.

at the same spot where with Napoleon III in 1867 I had attended the races and the great review, at a time when all the Princes of Europe were hurrying to him in order, as all the world then imagined, to confirm the hopes of universal peace. But above all at that moment I was moved by the proud thought how German soldiers were for the third time in this century to enter Paris as conquerors.

His Majesty was as deeply moved as I; that I could feel, without his needing to say very much to me. He appeared to-day, as always on service, in greatcoat, sash and helmet, I too in my usual field kit—tunic and high boots, the star of the Order of the Black Eagle on my breast, as I had worn it in every battle. The faces of officers and men alike beamed with joy to greet the Emperor. It was a true pleasure to mark the bearing and look of our troops.

Not a single French spectator was to be seen, which pleased me; I regard in the same light the wearing of mourning by women announced, as also the stopping of theatrical performances and that no newspapers are to appear. May the signs of mourning betoken the beginning of their moral regeneration; then it would be the better for them, as for many others throughout the world; yet the solution of this problem is indeed immeasurably difficult.

For some while I watched from Napoleon's pavilion the troops in their long-drawn columns march off for the Bois de Boulogne. All woodwork is burnt, and only the iron framework holds the walls precariously together. Obscene insults in word and picture scrawled on the bare walls revile the banished ruler.

Immediately after the march past, at which by my order every regimental band played the march tunes of the entry into Paris in 1814 and 1815, and I myself rode at the head of my Dragoon regiment, the troops moved off to the different gates on their way into the city to take up quarters in the Champs Élysées, in the Trocadero and in neighbouring districts. I had no sort of wish to revisit the Paris of to-day, the city I had enjoyed in its splendours for three whole weeks in 1867, and for myself I desired to avoid the look of a conqueror riding in in triumph. His Majesty wishes within the next few days to hold another parade, perhaps in the Champs Élysées itself; on that occasion I shall come in too, indeed we have not many days left us till all the troops have been in the place.

In fact the rumour actually went about during the inspection to the effect that news had arrived from Bordeaux saying a considerable majority of the Constituent Assembly had declared for an immediate acceptance of the Preliminaries and ratification at the earliest possible moment; still Count Bismarck only looks upon such a step as binding when he has the original document relating to these decisions in his hands and the same is ratified by His Majesty. Meantime the news appears to me very probably true, for under prevailing circumstances it would not be inconceivable that out of love for their capital the Deputies, for once setting limits to their predilection for talk, will reach agreement and peace be an accomplished fact in the next day or two. If the Assembly really decides for peace, I am sorry for the troops, who were to be in Paris on the days immediately following, for, to the Emperor's annoyance and chagrin, it is stipulated in an agreement made between Lieutenant-General Podbielsky and a French delegate from General Vinoy, General Waldau, that the German troops should evacuate the city immediately on ratification being completed. The Emperor too will in that case be obliged to leave Versailles with all speed, inasmuch as the left bank of the Seine must likewise be evacuated by us.

Several of my A.D.C.'s, whom I sent into Paris with the troops, reported to me in the evening that not the smallest offence or disturbance had occurred during the march in, in spite of the fact that Count Bismarck and the majority of the Princes had joined in, though the latter had yesterday been expressly forbidden to do so. Of course a modification may have been made in the order, but anyway nothing of the kind has come to my knowledge.

In Paris all shops were shut, while at every street corner were placards calling upon the inhabitants not to show themselves in the streets. But none the less thousands stood everywhere, who, making bad jokes the while, like so many street Arabs, took good care there should be no traffic whatever between French and Germans. A crowd of such onlookers fell upon an individual who accepted a cigar from one of our officers, elsewhere the proprietor of a café was threatened for giving a drink to one of our men, and more instances of the same sort. In the Champs Élysées, once so animated, there is no traffic to be seen; the plantations about the lake in the Bois are cut down, and the pretty Avenue de l'Impératrice must look quite waste and desolate, whereas the trees in the main Avenues are still left standing. The fury against Gambetta seems to be increasing, because at last his unparalleled system of lies, as well as the fashion in which he has squandered the State funds, has come to light. How quick the transition here from hero to traitor and back again! Woe to him who attaches weight to such-like popular favour or indeed pays any court to it whatever.

The Empress Eugénie telegraphed to-day in the name of all mothers and children beseeching our Emperor to stop the entry of the troops in order to save the inevitable bloodshed.

Headquarters: Versailles, 2nd March.—The ratification has really and truly been signed at Bordeaux, and that so quickly that the document may actually arrive here this evening. The gentry at Bordeaux have thus contrived to free the soil of Paris at the earliest moment possible of the "Northern Vandals," as they could not get their urgent wish to hinder us making any entry at all. By the terms of agreement Paris must now be rid of us again by eleven in the forenoon of the 3rd March.

Jules Favre had already telegraphed from Paris quite early in the morning to Count Bismarck saying the news had reached him through Thiers of the acceptance of the Treaty by a large majority in the Constituent Assembly, and that he had then instantly set off; so it was still quite early when he reached Versailles. But as Count Bismarck was still in bed, Favre was not admitted, consequently he could only repeat his information in writing. Later, however, when he was informed of the wish to see the original document, he had to go back again where he came from.

His Majesty was greatly annoyed at this swift settlement of things at Bordeaux, as we are bound to carry out at once the strict terms of the agreement by which we are bound; he declared we were as good as being chased out of Paris. It was now debated how the Guards at any rate might be allowed into Paris, to give them, if no one else, the pleasure of having paid one visit to the city, but there was nothing more to be done; in particular, General Count Moltke and the War Minister von Roon insisted on the literal observance of the agreement once it had been entered into. Fortunately to-day all the men not on duty are strolling into the city, so that at any rate a great many of our fellows will enjoy the satisfaction of having been in the capital just once. I am most sorry for the Bavarians of the Ist Army Corps and the Saxons and Württembergers, who lose altogether the pleasure of setting foot in the enemy's capital.

By an early hour to-morrow then Paris will be completely evacuated; thus there will be only a single parade of the troops originally told off for entry, that before His Majesty at Longchamps. The Emperor told me I could go to Paris as often as I wanted, whereas this was yesterday forbidden to all the Princes. They will have it they have received no order to this effect, and accordingly the Princes Karl, Albrecht and Adalbert, and with them Count Bismarck and many more, rode in; this, had it come to disturbances in the city, might have proved very awkward, especially as it would certainly have been said I too had been in Paris.

I took a drive with my brother-in-law of Baden in the devastated Bois de Boulogne; it has fortunately not suffered so severely as the papers led us to believe. True, the ground in front of the fortifications is swept clean, and the underwood in many other places cut down; besides this, one can see how single tall trees have been felled to make way for gun emplacements, but otherwise everything is much as it used to be. On the way we had to make repeated détours, because most of the iron gates of the avenues were shut, and presently we found ourselves, before we knew where we were, on a crossroad directly at the foot of the Arc de Triomphe de l'Étoile where there were swarms of Prussian soldiers harmlessly strolling about. When we noted the peaceable surging throng of friend and foe together, we quickly made up our minds to continue our drive further into the city, as we shall for a certainty never have another opportunity of seeing German fighting men enjoying a walk in the streets of Paris. So then we drove on down the Champs Élysées as far as the Place de la Concorde; the whole place was packed thick with German soldiers, each man wearing a leaf or sprig of greenery in his cap, who now in bigger, now in smaller groups, generally singing, were promenading peaceably up and down among the Paris citizens, who had turned out in crowds; it was for all the world as if one was at an annual market holiday at home. No doubt the Parisians were satisfying their curiosity at the expense of the "Northern Barbarians" just as our fellows were feasting their eyes on the sights of the French capital, and already one could see many a soldier talking quite unconcernedly with the inhabitants, among whom the fair sex, though almost universally clad in deep mourning, yet gazed their fill with eager curiosity at the German warriors. Other tokens of mourning were the black crape streamers attached to heads and arms of the statues in the Place de la Concorde representing the divinities of the towns of France, not to speak of the shuttered shops; but otherwise the streets looked just as animated as in the depths of peace, only that the elegant equipages that once thronged them were missing. In their stead to-day the most extraordinary collection of military vehicles improvised for the occasion had been brought out, for every officer who could secure a conveyance for himself had harnessed transport horses to it, handed the reins to the transport driver and crammed in as many friends as ever was possible, so that hay-wagons or two-wheeled light carts appeared side by side with broughams and post-chaises, but equipped in thoroughly military style. At many points the press forced us to ride at a foot's pace, so that we were right in the middle of the general crowd, but without hearing one single disagreeable exclamation. Things would seem to have been otherwise yesterday. On such occasions I could see plainly that a great many faces looked pale and sad. We drove along the Quai de la Seine to the Trocadero, now occupied by several batteries, from which elevation the noble prospect of Paris glittering in the spring sunshine delighted us; immediately below us lay the Champ de Mars, now a French encampment of huts and tents, in 1867 the scene of the assembling of all nations in the peaceful building of the Palace of Glass for the International Exhibition of Industry. We continued along the Seine and came out by the Point du Jour, where the destruction wrought by our fire was in some places even greater than I had expected, and we convinced ourselves how, here as everywhere, the defences and covering works had been planned with circumspection, great precision and neatness.

His Majesty also drove into the city, but seems not to have penetrated so far as we did, but rather to have stopped in the near neighbourhood of the enceinte. Whether the Parisians recognized him I cannot say.

So long as the Emperor remains in France, I am to continue in command, but directly he sets off for home, to resign it and accompany him to Berlin, which, however, he does not propose to reach earlier than immediately before the opening of the Reichstag, as he may perhaps first go to Blois and even Rouen for the inspection of troops. To my way of thinking, he should not, once Peace is concluded, remain another day in France, for there is then nothing more for him to do—little as, in and for itself, I grudge the Emperor the chance of greeting as many more as possible of his gallant troops on the enemy's soil. The troops will only arrive home in April, as those of the IInd Army will not have been able to secure the right bank of the Seine to be occupied by us before the end of March; but more than that, after the release of the Landwehr and men of the reserves, the main part of the Army will still have to remain concentrated along the line of the Seine until the Peace is definitely concluded.

Who will be my successor as Commander-in-Chief is unknown to me; in any case I have spoken decidedly against Princes of the Blood staying on in France on active service.

Headquarters: Versailles, 3rd March.—To-day in really hot sunshine the second great parade took place before His Majesty on the Longchamps race-course, and exactly on the pattern of that of the 1st March, but under command of the Crown Prince of Saxony. One must really confess frankly that the regiments, one and all, showed never a sign of having taken part in a seven months' campaign such as that just completed; one might rather have supposed oneself at manœuvres on the Bornstedt ground at Potsdam or the romantic Kreuzberg. Particularly imposing was the look of the 1st regiment of Foot Guards and the Landwehr troops. Terribly sad, on the contrary, it was for me to discern the manifold gaps death had torn in the ranks of our gallant soldiers, for especially in the Guards' Corps, the number of my acquaintances was a large one.

On Monday, Saxons, Württembergers and the Bavarian Army Corps are to be inspected at Saint-Denis or Villiers, after which the Peace disbandment begins at once.

All went off so well in Paris that everyone has a feeling it would only have needed a few days more for the German soldiery and the Paris population to make friends. But for aught I know, it may be called lucky that no opportunity whatever can now be offered for possible collisions.

The banker Bleichröder enlarged at great length to me on his experiences on the occasion of the financial negotiations of the last few days. The unbusiness-like ways of the French in comparison with what we are accustomed to must be really remarkable. In his opinion the manner in which on our side the requisitions were settled makes it seem doubtful whether we have obtained adequate security that we shall under all circumstances really get payment of our five milliards sooner or later. Count Bismarck would seem to have conducted himself during the negotiations with monstrous brusquerie and intentional rudeness, and by such behaviour to have in particular deeply shocked the Parisian Rothschild, who in the first instance addressed him in French. The scheme to invite all the great money markets of Europe to guarantee the milliards seems to have fallen through.

Headquarters: Versailles, 4th March.—What we shall be doing in the next few days is as uncertain as ever. His Majesty was for going to Blois yesterday to inspect troops, but the idea was found difficult to realize, as by this time all units are already on the march back. General Staff and Household are in silent bewilderment, as no orders are forthcoming. My own headquarters I shall probably shift to Meaux, as my troops are soon setting off for the Seine. The Emperor ought not to stay on here much longer, as the release of the Gardes Mobiles from duty, as also the occupation of the southern forts by the French in accordance with treaty would render residence at Versailles unendurable. Ferrières would again be a suitable place for the Imperial headquarters, seeing His Majesty positively will not make for home.

I contrived a free afternoon for myself to-day and, favoured by real spring warmth and sunshine, went to Chartres, to make acquaintance with the noble Cathedral and the beautiful Château de Maintenon that lies on the way there. The Gothic I might describe as just born into the world, for it still bears traces of the Romanesque style, especially in the treatment of human figures, the characteristic stiffness of which adapts itself to the architectural forms. These figures wear the costume of the twelfth century, and the softness of the sandstone has allowed such an elaboration of workmanship that the most exact details of the embroideries and even of the ornamental braiding of the hair are treated with true artistry. The wall surrounding the lofty choir is decorated with the richest and most perfect Gothic lace-work, till little by little it makes way for the Renaissance. Quite exceptionally beautiful are the old, marvellously well preserved painted windows of gigantic dimensions, which by their skilful blending of colours are in the highest degree instructive. A Romanesque crypt, lately restored, no doubt originally built more by way of foundation than for any ecclesiastical purpose, is very cleverly embellished with paintings and decorations and exceedingly interesting. The situation of the town and Cathedral reminds me of Wetzlar. Maintenon, which gave its name to the famous Macquire and contains many memorials of her and her residence there with Louis XIV, has been cleverly restored by the Ducs de Noailles and in the interior recalls the Castle of Baden, while the outside dates from the time of Louis XIII.

In Paris a ferment appears to be working in the workmen's quarters of the city, the nature of which disquiets the Government to such a degree that already French troops have been summoned in all haste to reinforce the garrison; to these we have readily enough given free passage through the cantonments occupied by us. We must be prepared to see a fight in Paris between the Moderates and the Reds. So bloodshed again already, possibly on the very first day after our evacuation of the place, and when scarce a week has elapsed since this bloody War ended. How sad is the fate of this unhappy people !

The Sovereigns and Princes are hastening to quit Versailles. Among all who resided here at Versailles in the War time, my brother-in-law of Baden stands out pre-eminent; there is but one voice of gratitude and praise for him, for indeed his natural dignity, combined with tact and amiability, has won him all hearts. Of his endless merits in connection with the internal fashioning of the Empire what need to speak?

Headquarters: Versailles, 5th March, Sunday.—So at last it is decided that we quit Versailles on the 7th of the month, and Imperial headquarters will be immediately transferred to Ferrières, where I am to remain until my own headquarters are established at Meaux; however, I propose in any case to visit Rouen, and it is not impossible His Majesty may do the like.

With Mr. Odo Russell, who leaves us the day after tomorrow, I made a round, favoured by the finest weather, by way of Mont Valérien, Saint-Cloud and Villeneuve l'Étang in which agreeable company I then took leave of all these districts and localities that have grown so familiar. The Paris public was strolling about Saint-Cloud and by the Seine; they stared at us with looks divided between surprise and rage, and behind our backs appear to have spoken their thoughts out loud, as my A.D.C.'s stated, who overheard many a downright, coarse expression used of me. However, I cannot blame men so sorely tried by war if they look askance at us, even when we are merely taking a harmless jaunt.

At dinner with His Majesty, Mr. Odo Russell took his leave; he had tears in his eyes at the kind way His Majesty dismissed him. His stay at the Imperial headquarters has been a true blessing, and will, we may hope, be the same in its consequences for Germany.

Headquarters: Versailles, 6th March.—The last day at Versailles. How long have we been yearning to be able to say that word ! It is the first step on the return home, but many days must yet pass before we tread German soil at last, as we are still to stay on in France, without being really able to discover the reason why. Meantime I propose to use the interval in making acquaintance with all interesting parts of this country within reach, for, once out of France, it will certainly never be possible for any of my generation to set foot again within its borders.

I made an attempt to induce Count Bismarck to appoint the Cabinet Minister Baron von Roggenbach as Governor of Alsace, or at the least to prevent the bureaucrats of the Council table making essay to adminsiter that Province; but I entirely failed, as he is determined to put in office there neither the Baron nor a General, but only persons of a sort to carry out his orders directly and implicitly. I gathered the impression to-day more than ever that he means to play the " All-Powerful," the " Richelieu," in these countries.

Paris flings about libels and calumnies of every sort against our soldiers; their lying and the usual French *blague* are here again true to type, for indeed these characteristics have become a second nature with the Parisians. Not the smallest thing was ever reported to me throughout the siege of the capital to the disadvantage of our men.

A last walk to the Trianon, and the last cask of Munich beer, in the enjoyment of which my whole headquarters partook, concluded the day.

Count Bismarck departs to-day, but is not thinking, so they say, of paying his respects to His Majesty at Ferrières before leaving for home; another version has it he is going straight back to Berlin without a stop. There is a quarrel, not yet appeased, between the military authorities and the French Plenipotentiary about the obligations laid on the French to feed our Armies.

Imperial Headquarters: Château Ferrières, 7th March.—So here we are out of Versailles, and at last on the road home.

The parting from this place to which for six months I have been accustomed, and where I have witnessed the most critical decisions taken in such a war as this, and seen and helped to bring about the whole developments of " Emperor and Empire," was far from leaving me indifferent, the whole meaning and importance of this period of time that parted me from home and wife and children passing before my eyes with particular impressiveness. We have seen a piece of world history unrolled, as a consequence of which immeasurable benefits may accrue for Fatherland and society at large if we are well determined to seize the opportunity and if we know how to use it rightly.

But, however many sins of omission are committed, however many serious mistakes check the rapid progress of reconstruction, still I hold this one thing as sure, that not even the greatest folly can any longer succeed in rendering abortive the gains we have now reached. A noble task lies before our Government, if it is firmly resolved to strive earnestly for the internal development of the Empire on liberal lines in accord with the spirit of the age, and by so doing give the world a guarantee for lasting peace.

The envy of all Europe is nowadays, of course, directed against Germany in the same degree as in former days the Coalition united Napoleon's opponents, but with this difference, that, thank God, our neighbours lack any real and palpable handle for disputing our successes with any show of reason. Wherefore I confidently hope that, if only, as time goes on, our love of peace becomes better and better known, this envy itself may turn into a judicious desire for our friendship.

I am sorry to hear from home that there are some there who deem France should have been subjected to yet harder conditions. This is incomprehensible to me, for it was only the circumstance that France was responsible for the wanton instigation of this War, so murderous in its consequences, which compelled us, the victors, to impose harder conditions on the enemy than, especially in view of the distress in France, our age might otherwise have expected between civilized peoples. But suchlike expressions of opinion at home clearly show how arrogant our countrymen have grown as the result of our successes and the sort of vulgar chatter we shall therefore have to combat on our return. For my own part, I bring back with me from the struggle just concluded no feelings of hatred and lasting animosity against the French; on the contrary, I shall use every endeavour to restore as soon as ever possible conditions of reconciliation, good understanding and mutual comprehension.

I left the villa of " Les Ombrages " very early in the morning and proceeded through the cantonments of the VIth Prussian and the IInd Bavarian Army Corps by way of Charenton to Villers-le-Sec, in order, before the parade, to ride over the scene of the engagements of the 30th November to the 3rd December at Brie and Champigny. Everywhere are the traces of the struggle clearly discernible, and the great grave mounds indicate the points at which the fight raged most fiercely. The hilly nature of the whole neighbourhood makes it surprising that the French did not inflict greater losses on us here and did not at all costs push home the offensive with more vigour. Then on the very ground where the Saxon troops fought at Villiers a great parade was held of the Ist Bavarian Army Corps, at which the Crown Prince of Saxony again took command.

Yesterday His Majesty in his room had a heavy fall on his back as he was trying to take the posture of a horseman on the back of a chair. But to-day he was in the saddle again for three good hours without one's noticing the slightest thing amiss with his way of riding, though his old lumbago is not even yet quite gone.

Each Army Corps is forthwith to give up one regiment to form the new Alsatian Corps.

Imperial Headquarters: Château Ferrières, 8th March.—To-day we enjoyed a truly refreshing day of rest, which I took advantage of for a stroll with Lieutenant-General von Stosch. We all feel as though an ebb were come after the exciting days of the Peace negotiations.

From to-day's Berlin newspapers I see that the Preliminaries agreed upon at Bordeaux have been duly ratified by the Emperor, a fact that was never communicated to me, whether officially or in any other way. At Versailles a confirmation of the kind was in many quarters described as entirely unnecessary, while others again maintained that until His Majesty had signed the document from Bordeaux, the troops ought not to quit Paris.

I was glad to note the language held by *The Times*, praising the behaviour of our troops on the occasion of the march into Paris, and tactfully referring to the policy observed by us at the time, as being free from all tokens of a triumphal entry. This is doubly gratifying in view of the bad feeling still existing against us in England.

Imperial Headquarters: Château Ferrières, 9th March.—A bitterly cold wind was blowing when I drove out with His Majesty to the forts of Nogent, Rosny, Romainville and Mont Avron as far as Pantin, near which place the Emperor Napoleon witnessed the battle of Paris on the 30th March, 1814. In spite of the manifold alterations that have since been made, the place was still quite recognizable. The faces of the Saxon and Württemberg troops we came upon in cantonments regularly lighted up when they got a sight of the Emperor. I read an inscription embellished with festoons of flowers, " God bless *our* Emperor," which for South Germans is significant enough.

Report has it we shall enter Berlin on the 16th of this month. To-morrow I am to accompany His Majesty to Rouen, where the Ist Army Corps and the Mecklenburgers will be inspected.

Imperial Headquarters: Château Ferrières, 10th March.—At the moment of starting His Majesty postponed this for another twenty-four hours because of a chill he had caught yesterday;

MOLTKE BEFORE PARIS.
Lithograph from a Painting by Camphausen.

nor will he really be in a condition to travel to-morrow, so I must take his place for the inspections at Rouen and Amiens, and only join him again at Nancy. His Majesty complains of hearing so little of the plans for the entry of the troops into Berlin, and so on. On the other hand, he is full of the idea of having those German Princes who volunteer to come to the opening of the Reichstag attend officially, sitting on stools beside his throne. Only, out of discretion, and not to invite refusals, no formal invitations will be issued.

Count Bismarck is to be created Prince and General Count Moltke Field-Marshal.

Rouen, 11th March.—As a measure of precaution Dr. Lauer forbade the Emperor's journey to Rouen, as the internal pains have not yet quite disappeared. His Majesty finally gave way with tears in his eyes, making one feel really sorry to see his bitter disappointment, as he was so looking forward to greeting these gallant troops and had long ago made his preparations for this journey of inspection. I was charged to represent him and was given Lieutenant-General von Treskow to attend me; Prince Adalbert also joined me.

At an early hour I left the Imperial headquarters by carriage and on the journey made acquaintance with the lovely Valley of the Marne and its scattered villas, breakfasted with Prince August of Württemberg at Margency, his headquarters, and travelled on from there by railway all day up to six o'clock in the evening. At almost all the stations, which were occupied by our posts, a reception was held, so that I had to get out often enough. At Amiens the gallant General von Goeben joined us, after I had, by His Majesty's commission, handed the oak-leaves of the Order *Pour le Mérite* to my cousin Prince Albrecht, to which decoration he had been recommended by the General for the actions at Saint-Quentin. A like decoration is to be bestowed, I am pleased to say, on my brother-in-law, Prince Ludwig of Hesse. The men of my East Prussian Grenadier regiment in full-dress uniform were drawn up in the street from the station and greeted me with evident pleasure, making a monstrously fine show. The quays, along which the road led, recalled those at Königsberg and Dantzig, and the town seems, like them, to have preserved its mediæval aspect, and smelt like a seaport town of tar. At a great many houses mourning flags were displayed or black draperies hung out, while all statues in the place, for instance those of Corneille and Boïeldieu, were draped in black. I find suchlike demonstrations very natural and do not attach the smallest importance to them; the only thing I have to find fault with is that our higher officers and officials are just bursting with rage about it and would fain take measures of reprisal. The less attention we pay to such things, the less do the folk who wanted to give offence succeed in their object.

Rouen, 12th March, Sunday.—I had the pleasure to-day of inspecting the gallant Ist Army Corps, together with the well-proven Mecklenburg Division. The troops looked so splendid it was hard to believe they had really been on war service for seven long months, for bearing and discipline remain unaltered, or if these *have* ever become at all relaxed, have very quickly been re-established. Training strikes too deep in our soldiers for a war to obliterate its effects, it is become a second nature to them. It was a great delight to see my old regiment again, before whose ranks the colours presented by my wife in 1869 had floated in the breeze in seven battles and general actions. After the review, which was favoured by magnificent weather and which the citizens of the town, by the help of telescopes, watched at long range from the high banks of the river, I had a field service held, the day being Sunday. After which I visited the Cathedral and town.

Rouen is one of the most attractive French towns I know. Its wealth of perfectly beautiful churches, its mediæval houses and lanes still surviving in numbers in the old quarters of the town, with ornamentation in wood and ancient timber-work, the same as at Quedlinburg and Hildesheim, are quite well worth seeing. The Gothic here has borrowed largely from the English, as is particularly noticeable in the beautiful Palais de Justice. In the churches, of which Saint-Ouen pleases me best, the old painted windows are everywhere in good preservation and bear witness to the finest style of workmanship, while the decorative embellishments, thanks to the easily worked sandstone of the locality, are carried out with rare completeness. Rouen's speciality is a majolica ware known by the name of the place, examples of which of different periods are brought together in a pretty museum. The public paid no attention whatever to an order issued to stay indoors as long as I was in the town; on the contrary, they filled the streets to overflowing, especially those through which the "Northern Barbarians" marched.

In the afternoon I made a trip to a country house standing high above the river below the town, from which a panorama is unfolded of the city in all its magnificence; on the horizon one catches a glimpse of the Castle where Robert the Devil, Duke of Normandy, was born.

Amiens, 13th March.—From Rouen I travelled by railway, the same as yesterday, to Amiens, where I inspected the gallant VIIIth Army Corps as well as different cavalry regiments of the Guard, formerly attached to Prince Albrecht's Division, on the scene of the engagement near the banks of the Hallue. Several sharp hailstorms accompanied the review, without the admirable bearing of our troops suffering in the least. It moved me especially to see the 33rd regiment, with which my poor friend Jasmund was fighting when he fell at Gravelotte, for I had the opportunity of speaking to his sergeant-major, in whose arms he died.

The Cathedral of Amiens is, next to that of Reims, the finest I have seen in France.

I inspected the Hospital established in the *Musée*, saw Major-General von Memerty, not yet sufficiently recovered from his wounds to be removed, as well as some other wounded soldiers, and afterwards gave a dinner at the Préfecture, where Count Lehndorff-Steinort transacts the business connected with his duties.

Nancy, 14th March.—The journey from Amiens by way of Laon, Ham, Reims, Épernay, Châlons, Révigny to here was one uninterrupted series of receptions by the posts on duty at the various stations. We breakfasted at Reims. Late in the evening I reached His Majesty's quarters at Nancy, where to my surprise and pleasure Generals von Werder and Hann von Weyern were.

Frankfurt-on-the-Main, 15th March.—The first footsteps on German soil!

In rainy weather we left Nancy and then made an hour's halt at the railway station at Metz, where the garrison was drawn up, but the inhabitants kept away. President von Kühlwetter delivered an enthusiastic speech to the Emperor, emphasizing how this ancient Imperial province was once more become German, and will henceforth remain so. I am well convinced of this, but do not expect to live to see the inhabitants feel themselves Germans again after having been French to the backbone for two hundred years. Of Metz and the battle-fields I saw nothing.

About midday we crossed the old frontier of the home-land. I cannot express the feelings I experienced. A great reception here awaited the Emperor, ceremonial in character, but moving in its heartfelt geniality; the Rhenish towns presented him with a laurel wreath of gold.

At Bingen I saw the Rhine again, which I had not seen since I was at Spires in the August of 1870. The " Watch on the Rhine " we had indeed kept well and true.

The Grand Duke of Hesse received us at the frontier of his dominions and accompanied us to Frankfurt, where my sister and her husband awaited us at his Palace, surrounded by all members of the Darmstadt Ducal family, the Princess Elizabeth and my sister-in-law, Princess Alice, at their head.

All Frankfurt was in the streets and had donned their best holiday attire for the occasion. The most important step towards reconciliation with us seems to have been taken as the result of the triumphs of this War.

Weimar, 16th March.—From Frankfurt onwards an uninterrupted series of ceremonial receptions welcomed us at every stopping-place, the same as yesterday when once we had crossed the frontier, to be followed at Weimar by a formal entry into the town, where we spent the night.

Berlin, 17th March.—Joy and jubilation everywhere on today's journey. At the Wildpark station at Potsdam I folded my wife and my eldest boy in my arms after nearly nine months' separation. Both, and my mother with them, had come out from Berlin to meet us.

There the streets were pretty full of people, and along the Unter den Linden, by which we drove, stood more crowds who raised hearty shouts of greeting.

At my house I was welcomed by my troop of children, the youngest member of which, Sophie, was six weeks old when I went away. Soon a throng of the general public collected before my house, and, attracted by the younger children standing at the window, grew ever denser and clamoured to see me, a wish I willingly gratified by appearing on the balcony.

. . . .

On the 12th June the troops of the Potsdam garrison reached the outskirts of the city. The Staff and a part of the first regiment of Foot Guards encamped at Werder, where towards evening I went with my wife to greet our acquaintances. The 1st battalion, on the contrary, was quartered near the New Palace and also on our property of Bornstedt. As they were on the march thither, I welcomed them in the neighbourhood of Kuhfort and escorted the companies up to the Palace, where my wife and her children were waiting for them and watched the battalion march past. Joyful was the greeting the troops gave us wherever they met us, and joyful our feelings to see them again, though this home-coming in just the same old familiar places awakened all the more vividly memories of the fallen, as we noted with pain and sorrow the gaps death had torn in the ranks of our gallant fellow-countrymen.

The 13*th June.*—Next day the whole garrison in Potsdam marched in by the Brandenburg gate. After a rainy morning the sky cleared altogether. My wife in her Hussar uniform, Wilhelm in that of the Foot Guards regiment, rode out with me on the Brandenburg highway as far as the Wildpark to meet the troops. His Majesty the Emperor welcomed the troops drawn up on the different high-roads, and afterwards saw them march past in the Lustgarten. Prince Albrecht (junior) was in command of the whole; I put myself at the head of the 1st regiment of Guards, and with drawn sword led the way through the streets, which were very tastefully, and, considering the poor circumstances of the population, very beautifully decorated, everywhere greeted with really heartfelt cordiality and loaded with garlands and flowers. When after some while Prince Karl failed to see me with the Emperor's suite, he and Prince Albrecht (senior) with him, likewise took up position at the head of the regiment. At noon the city entertained the body of officers and men deputed by the regiments at a great banquet in the Schützenhaus, which His Majesty and all of us Princes attended. At this the only guests to behave in a really offensive way were some Russian officers, who had come to share in the festivities and had soon got into a very " merry " mood. In the evening the town was illuminated, even the smallest houses participating, a fact of which my wife and myself were able to convince ourselves as we made a round of the streets. The day will always remain a fond memory with me.

The 14*th June.*—The birthday of our little daughter Sophie, now twelve months old, found Potsdam still in festive mood, to which an entertainment we got up in the New Palace for the Bornstedt school-children was a very appropriate contribution.

My mother together with the Baden and Hessian brothers and sisters arrived, but four hours after we expected them. The return of the troops from the front and the crowds of visitors coming for the festivities attending the entry into Berlin quite overtax all the resources of the railways.

The weather shows a decided change and promises to be very fine.

The 15th June.—The preparations for the entry into Berlin are on the most magnificent scale I have ever yet seen. For the first time the whole artistic community has taken its share in them, so that the decoration of the Unter den Linden with allegorical subjects shown on great curtains hung across the central roadway, no less than that of the Academy displaying life-size portraits of all the Commanding Generals in the window niches, are really hard to match. Again, in front of the Rossebändiger Portico stands a figure of " Germania " by the sculptor Siemering, the pedestal of which is adorned with figures that excite universal admiration by their beautiful execution. As an accompaniment of to-morrow's celebrations is to take place the unveiling of the equestrian statue of King Frederick William III in the Lustgarten, though the pedestal will only be fully completed after the lapse of some years.

The 16th June.—To-day in positively broiling heat the entry into Berlin took place. The enthusiasm was added to by the circumstance that the Emperor, in spite of representations to the contrary, insisted in riding out to meet the troops on following the same route throughout as they were to use —to my thinking a derogation. His Majesty explained that, as it was not he but the troops were making their entry, it was not for him to receive the honours and tokens of sympathy, and to show this he must ride out in view of the whole waiting multitude, and afterwards escort them in. Nobody really understood this, seeing that in course of the entry the Emperor was addressed by a deputation of young girls dressed in white and by the Burgomaster, and made replies to them. Thus the public had to break out into jubilation twice over; however, on the entry properly so called they had the opportunity of recognizing at least some individuals among the throng of riders following His Majesty, as we took up our places according to a programme made known beforehand, which was not the case when we rode out in the first instance.

The Emperor presented me with a Field-Marshal's baton studded with crowns and eagles and covered with sky-blue satin, to be carried for the first time to-day when, after we had ridden along the front of the troops before they marched off, the actual entry began. So my A.D.C. was obliged to carry it in a great case as well as he could half on the pummel of his saddle, half under his arm, till the prescribed moment was come. Prince Friedrich Karl and Field-Marshal Count Moltke had received similar gifts. Prince Karl and Prince

Albrecht (Senior) were given their badge as Field-Marshals to wear, but no batons.

The heat of the day was as burning as in the East, so that every moment people could be seen falling in a faint, and many on horseback pitching from the saddle. Prince Albrecht fell into such a heavy swoon—if indeed it was not a fit—that he did not come to again till evening. Prince Karl and the Crown Prince of Saxony suffered in the same way, but the former was soon all right again, while the latter slept for the whole time the march past lasted—more than two and a half hours—at the Prinzessinpalais. My son Wilhelm, on the other hand, sat his horse remarkably well all through.

The march past was followed by the unveiling of the statue of Frederick William III in the Lustgarten, at which His Majesty in person gave the order, sword in hand, for the present and dropping of the curtain. The captured French flags and eagles were laid on the steps of the monument.

. . . .

On the 30th June the garrison was to enter Hanover. His Majesty had made up his mind to be present, but a sudden chill on that day compelled him to give up the journey, and he directed me to represent him. I took the salute of the troops in the Herrenhausen Allee and led them, my cousin Prince Albrecht, appointed Divisional Commander, riding beside me, through the gaily decorated streets of the town, which were crowded with people, to the Waterlooplatz, where the march past was held. To my complete and very joyful surprise, all sections of the population gave me a warm, not to say enthusiastic reception, and I found the same feeling prevailing every time I showed myself in the streets during my two days' stay. Our triumphs in the War and the restoration of the Empire are perhaps by way of building a golden bridge for many of the inhabitants of this newly-acquired part of the country, who would otherwise have never become reconciled to Prussia as the conqueror.

. . . .

On the 16th July at Munich the entry of the garrison belonging to that place, together with parties deputed from the two Bavarian Army Corps, took place.

The King of Bavaria, after hearing of my departure, fixed for the 4th July, for a visit to my mother-in-law in England, had invited me to attend this function appointed for the 16th

July. I could do nothing else but accept, though this would force me to leave London again as early as the 13th.

On the 15th, in the forenoon, I was welcomed at Aschaffenburg by gallant old General of Infantry von Hartmann as General in Command and General Count Rechberg, who had been deputed to meet me. At every station from there to Munich unmistakable tokens of unfeigned friendliness were given, vouched for by shouts and hurrahs. At Dachau the King met me—the same spot where he had received me in the July of last year. At the Munich railway station a ceremonial reception was held, the Royal Princes, the Generals, etc., all being present—all except Prince Otto, who has a way now of arriving too late everywhere. Then all drove to the Grand Stairs, where the Queen-Mother with the " grand cortège " stood awaiting me, and welcomed me with a touching joy and cordiality, the more so as I was the first of my House she had seen again since the campaign ended.

Munich, 16th July.—The town was brilliantly and lavishly decorated for the festivity; the whole population was astir, and the country-folk were streaming in in crowds, even from the Austrian border. Of this I was able to convince myself betimes, as eight o'clock in the morning saw me having a bathe in the river—to the no small surprise of the Court domestics.

Then I rode out with the King to the shooting-range near Nymphenberg, and joined him in his inspection of the troops. When this was over and he had ridden off the field, I remained behind with the troops, and amid a quite spontaneous burst of cheering, both long and loud, I distributed Iron Crosses in the Emperor's name, and put myself at the head of the men. We had a long stretch to cover by field roads before reaching the highway leading to the Siegestor. The country-people had gathered in crowds and greeted me with surprising heartiness. The nearer we came to the Gate, the warmer grew the greetings, till finally in the Ludwigsstrasse the enthusiasm reached a height that baffles description. In front of the University the High Burgomaster addressed me in very dignified language; he was accompanied by two young girls, who presented me with a laurel wreath and a bouquet. In my reply I dwelt no less on my grateful recognition of Bavarian gallantry than on my satisfaction at the restoration of Emperor and Empire, interrupted again and again by enthusiastic cries of assent. I was overwhelmed with wreaths and flowers, nay, some of the crowd actually ran up to me to give their gifts into my own hand, or even to pick up such as had fallen to the ground, even under my very horse's hoofs. The only unoccupied windows in the Ludwigsstrasse were those of the Roman Catholic Seminary.

Beside the statue of Ludwig I, tastefully decorated, stands were erected for the Queen-Mother, the Royal Family, the officials and the wounded, while the King stood in front. As I came up, all rose to their feet with cheers and acclamations; the Queen, before whom I stood at the salute, and all the ladies waved their handkerchiefs, making a quite extraordinarily fine and festive show. Next I greeted the wounded and then wheeled my horse about and rode up to the King, whereupon the march past began. An animated and enthusiastic reception was accorded Generals von Hartmann and von der Tann, as also Prince Leopold.

At the military dinner that took place later, the King brought out quite sharply and suddenly the toast: "To my brave Army and its victorious Commander-in-Chief." I replied impromptu to the effect that his people and army had special reason to keep the day, seeing that, this glorious campaign well ended, the returning warriors no less than the restored Empire, for the establishment of which we had to thank the movement first initiated by the King of Bavaria, were being celebrated. Afterwards the King never spoke to a single officer, which made the Queen-Mother and myself do so all the more. At night in the theatre both their Majesties and I were warmly greeted.

Munich, the 17th July.—I had already, while still in London, received an invitation to the festivity given by the city of Munich in honour of the troops and fixed for this evening. This was highly displeasing to the King and his Royal uncles, who never appear at the citizens' entertainments, and after the Princes Luitpold and Adalbert had warned their nephew he could not possibly join this "rabble," the King set every lever in motion to hinder my attending this evening gathering. But I stood firm, and rather sought, though in vain, to persuade him to go there himself. Then he invited me in writing to dine at the Roseninsel in the Starnberg Lake, to see the sun set from there. I accepted the dinner, but explained that I wished to go back to Munich again in the evening to attend the city celebration—and that was what happened. By virtue of my appearing there all the Bavarian Princes were obliged to be present too; their feelings, particularly those of Prince Luitpold, may be imagined. Prince Otto arrived three-quarters of an hour after the banquet had begun, and had to go away again. The festivity had a worthy setting in the imposing rooms of the Palace of Industry and went off in the most successful style. Only the King's staying away disturbed the serenity of the citizens, who had counted on his appearance up to the last moment.

．　．　．　．　．　．　．

After my fine stay in England, where the public everywhere manifested indubitable tokens of lively good-will towards us, we spent the rest of the summer at the New Palace at Potsdam, from which an enjoyable journey was made with my wife to Rheinsberg, a place we had not seen before. Then we went to the Palace of Wilhelmshöhe near Cassel, where we occupied the apartments Napoleon III had lived in a short while before as a prisoner of war.

THE END

APPENDIX

(Compare p. 144.)

Queen Victoria of England to King William I

Windsor Castle, the 18*th December,* 1870.

Dear Brother,
Though I have telegraphed to express to you my profound sympathy in the heavy loss you have suffered, I would wish to repeat the same in writing and to tell you how fully I understand your great sorrow at the death of your beloved sister.[1] Even though I have not written to you again, still you will have learned from Fritz how lively an interest I have taken in your great victories, how much I have admired the gallantry of the German hosts and how deeply I have deplored, and do deplore, the heavy losses incurred. But I would fain now appeal to your magnanimity and Christian charity. The blood of Germans flows almost as copiously as that of the unhappy French; would it not then be possible to call a halt now and make peace? The unhappy, deluded French will fight on, and what is it to lead to? That so dreadful a War can last so long in our days is indeed grievous; and it would surely be so Christian and magnanimous a thing if at this holy Christmas season we could say with truth: " Glory to God and Peace on earth."
It is with sincere regret I have noted the hostile, suspicious feeling in Prussia and the Armies against England. This is, I am bound to say, highly unjust; sympathies were entirely with Germany, and are so still among all well-informed persons. But the exasperation against us, together with the long continuance of the War, will soon, I am afraid, alienate many sympathies to the French side—a thing that would greatly distress me, for I deem it a necessity for the happiness and peace of Europe that between united Germany and England the best understanding should prevail. But now I will occupy no more of your time, which no doubt has many claims upon it, and with the most sincere wishes for your continued happiness and prosperity, I remain,

dear Brother,
Your true
Sister and Friend,
V. R.

[1] The Princess Luise of the Netherlands; died the 16th December.

INDEX

ABDUL AZIZ, Sultan, 144
Adalbert, Prince of Prussia, 136, 147, 173
——, Prince of Bavaria, 323, 331, 339
Adare, Viscount, afterwards Earl of Dunraven, correspondent of *Daily Telegraph*, 55, 69
Adolf, Prince zu Schaumburg-Lippe, 246, 270
——, Friedrich, Hereditary Grand Duke of Mecklenburg-Strelitz, 92, 259, 270
Albert, Prince Consort of England, 168, 195, 222
——, Crown Prince of Saxony, 68, 71, 73, 74, 75, 78, 80, 81, 83, 85, 88, 89, 98, 104, 109, 112, 116, 142, 169, 209, 264, 270, 325, 329, 337
——, Prince of Saxe-Altenburg, Prussian Lieut.-General, 68
Albrecht (elder), Prince of Prussia, 68, 78, 270, 279, 323, 331, 335, 337
—— (younger), Prince of Prussia, 210, 270, 335
Alexander II, Tsar of Russia, 121, 128, 310, 319
Alexandra, Princess of Wales, 18
Alexandrine, Grand Duchess of Mecklenburg-Schwerin, 279
Alice, Princess of Hesse (*née* Princess of Great Britain), 167, 334
Alsace, Alsatians, 47, 51, 65, 102, 104, 113, 117, 124, 239
Altenburg, town of, 11
Altenstadt, near Weissenburg, 23, 24, 27, 28
Alvensleber, Major von, 198
Amboise, Castle of, 305, 306
America, Americans, 145, 146, 148, 155, 191, 219, 225, 236, 245
Amiens, 331, 333
——, battle of, 203, 232
——, Cathedral, 333
Andrassy, Julius Count, Austro-Hungarian Minister, 13, 169
Anhalt, Friedrich, Hereditary Prince of, 270

Appia, Dr., 21, 45, 46
Arago, Emanuel, French Minister, 108
Armistice negotiations and conditions, 276, 277, 281, 282, 283, 284, 286, 287, 302, 304, 308
Arms, export of, English and American, to France, 165, 236
Artenay, engagement at, 152, 210, 211
Attigny, headquarters, 105
Auerswald, Col. von, Commanding 1st regiment Dragoon Guards, 61
August, Hereditary Grand Duke of Oldenburg, 270
——, Prince of Würtemberg, 270, 331
Augusta, Queen of Prussia, 9, 10, 15, 334, 335
Augustin, Lieut., 40
Aumale, Henri Duc d', son of King Louis Philippe, 72, 235, 300, 301
Aurelle-de-Paladines, Louis de, French General, 197, 217
Austro-Hungary, diplomatic relations with, 13, 15, 51, 53, 71, 131, 148

Bacourt, Madame de (de Gonneville), 60
—— Monsieur de, 54, 60
Baden, Friedrich I, Grand Duke of, 30, 32, 188, 190, 191, 223, 226, 246, 249, 250, 252, 256, 257, 260, 268, 270, 272, 288, 290, 323, 327
——, Grand Duchess Sophie, 17
—— Princes :
   Karl, 30
   Ludwig Wilhelm, 16, 176
—— Princesses :
   Marie, 16
   Viktoria, 17, 71
Balan, near Sedan, 85
Balmoral, 140
Bamberg, 11
Bapaume, engagement at, 253
Barneckow, Baron von, commander of 4th Cavalry Brigade, 140, 142

INDEX

Baron, Lieut., 39
Bartek, Wenzel, groom in Crown Prince's service, 101
Baudricourt, Castle of, 66, 67
Baumbach, von, Würtemberg General, 14
Bavarian troops, 17, 19, 21, 23, 25, 28, 31, 34, 104, 109, 127, 153, 185, 187
——, Ludwig II, King of, 10, 12, 13, 46, 72, 110, 202, 210, 211, 244, 337, 338, 339
——, Marie, Queen of, 12, 46
——, Princes:
  Adalbert, 339
  Leopold, 270, 339
  Luitpold, 14, 92, 112, 147, 211, 244, 270, 339
  Otto, 270, 338, 339
Bazaine, François Achille, Marshal, 54, 69, 71, 101, 110, 150, 155, 157, 167, 170, 171, 172, 178, 184
Bazeilles, near Sedan, 83, 85, 89
Bazoches, engagement at, 218
Beaufort d'Hautpoul, Marquis de, French General, 285
Beaugency, 197, 218, 220
Beauharnais, Joséphine, Empress of the French, 30, 289
——, Hortense, Queen of Holland, 30, 289
Beaumont, battle of, 78, 218
Beauregard, Château, 159, 162, 163
——, Comtesse de (Miss Howard), 159, 173
Belfort, 235, 243, 250, 251, 253, 254, 256, 259, 260, 269, 302, 303, 313, 314
Belgium, Belgians, 100, 111, 119
——, neutrality, 53, 100
——, policy, 20, 81
——, Leopold I, king of, 168
——, Leopold II, king of, 111, 148, 292
Bellevue, Château de, near Sedan, 96, 97, 100
Benedetti, Count Vincent, French Ambassador in Berlin, 4, 5, 20, 74, 241
Bergzabern, 21, 23
Berlin, Berliners, 7, 51, 116, 175, 202, 222, 236, 243, 248, 279, 297, 334, 336
Bernhard, Hereditary Grand Duke of Saxe-Meiningen, 18, 39, 68, 270
Bernstorff, Albrecht, Count von, Ambassador in London, 165
Bethmann-Hollweg, Felix von, 153
Beust, Friedrich Count von, Austro-Hungarian Minister, 13, 51, 169, 171, 214, 267

Bienwald, near Weissenburg, 21, 22
Bismarck, Count Herbert, 65
——, Princess Johanna von, 202, 222, 292
——, Prince Otto von, v, vi, 3, 4, 5, 6, 8, 9, 52, 63, 65, 91, 92, 93, 96, 97, 101, 112, 117, 121, 130, 131, 135, 142, 147, 152, 155, 156, 157, 161, 169, 175, 177, 180, 196, 200, 210, 212, 214, 215, 224, 229, 239, 241, 245, 253, 255, 256, 257, 258, 267, 272, 277, 281, 282, 287, 292, 294, 297, 298, 308, 309, 312, 314, 315, 316, 323, 325, 328, 331
Bissing, Baron Moritz, 206
Bitsch, fortress of, 39
Blâmont, headquarters, 54
Blanc, Louis, 302
Blanqui, Louis Auguste, French Communist, 179
Bleihtreu, Georg, painter, 90
Bleichröder, Gerson von, banker, 312, 325
Blois, 197, 304, 305
——, Castle of, 304, 305
"Blood and Iron," 241
Blumenthal, Leonhard Count von, General (Field Marshal), 8, 9, 37, 39, 64, 65, 71, 74, 82, 83, 85, 88, 94, 103, 109, 120, 145, 161, 174, 193, 200, 220, 224, 235, 245, 265, 274
——, von, nephew of preceding, commander of Crown Prince's Staff Guard, 39
Boeger, Dr., 86, 115, 143, 152, 248
Boltenstern von, First Lieutenant, 237
Bonaparte, Emperor Napoleon III, 5, 14, 16, 19, 35, 43, 48, 51, 53, 54, 56, 61, 67, 69, 72, 73, 77, 85, 88, 89, 90, 91, 92, 93, 94, 95, 96, 97, 98, 99, 100, 104, 106, 117, 121, 128, 133, 149, 155, 173, 184, 238, 310, 318, 320, 340
——, Prince Imperial, 53, 73, 94, 99, 109, 114, 117, 128, 133, 213
——, Prince Napoleon ("Plon-Plon"), 54, 106
Bonin, Adolf von, Governor-General Lorraine, 202
Bonnemains, Vicomte de, 31
Bordeaux, 219, 286, 288, 295, 296, 297, 298, 303, 316, 318, 322
Bose, Julius Count von, Lieut.-General, 7, 18, 22, 31, 33, 35, 38, 43, 90, 109
——, Werner von, son of preceding, Captain of Cavalry, 38
Bothmer, Friedrich Count von, Bavarian Lieut.-General, 23, 24, 32, 34, 38, 84, 88, 137, 275

INDEX

Bougival, 139, 144, 149, 274
——, engagement at, 164, 165
——, look-out station at, 144
Boullenois, A. de, Maire, 77
Bourbaki, Charles Denis Sauter, French General, 155, 178, 224, 234, 235, 243, 249, 250, 251, 253, 254, 256, 257, 258, 262, 264, 265, 269, 276, 277, 283, 284, 288
Bourges, 158, 197, 215, 224, 243, 250
Boursault, Château, headquarters, 112, 114, 115
Boyen, Hermann von, General, 100, 121, 157, 180, 275
Brandenburg, 5
Brandenstein, Col. von, 111
Bray-Steinburg, Count Otto von, Bavarian Minister, 12, 13, 315
Brie, engagements at, 208, 209, 329
Bronsart von Schellendorf, Paul, Lieut.-Col., later War Minister, 91
Brühl, Castle of, 97, 104
Burnside, American General, 145, 146, 148, 155, 191
Bussières, Villa, 280
Butz, Bavarian General, Governor of Germersheim, 18

Canrobert, François de, French Marshal, 31, 78, 172, 184
Cartwright, English Member of Parliament, 20
Castelnau, C., French General, 98
Châlons, camp of, 50, 53, 56, 57, 59, 61, 65, 71, 235
Chambord, Henri (V) Comte de, 53, 152, 213, 292
——, Château de, 305
Champagne, 67, 71
Champigny, engagements at, 206, 207, 208, 209, 329
Changarnier, Nic. Anne Théodule, French General, 170
Chanzy, Antoine E. Alfred, French General, 228, 235, 243, 255, 256, 257, 277, 296, 297, 299, 302
Charlotte, Princess of Prussia, wife of Duke of Saxe-Meiningen, 10, 39, 70
Charlottenburg, Mausoleum, 8
Chartres, 149, 180, 184, 191, 193, 196, 326
—— Cathedral, 326
Châtillon, engagement at, 154, 198, 243, 256
Châteauneuf-en-Thimeray, engagement at, 196
Chaume, headquarters, 123
Chaumont, Château de, 305, 306
Chémery, headquarters, 80, 82, 94, 95

Chenebier, near Belfort, 264, 269
Chenonceaux, Château de, 305, 306
Chevigné, Louis Marie Joseph, Comte de, 114
Chevilly, engagement at, 140, 141, 143, 146
Chigi, Monseigneur, Papal Nuncio, 154, 158, 161
Christian IX, king of Denmark, 18
Clérembault, Comte de, 200
Clermont, English General, 221, 223
Clicquot, Veuve, 114, 115
Coblenz, 9
Cochery, Thiers' Secretary, 183, 187
Coffinière de Nordeck, Commandant of Citadel of Metz, 170
Colombey-Nouilly, engagement at, 56
Colson, MacMahon's Chief of Staff, 41
Conseil-Dumesnil, French Infantry Division, 31
Corbeil, headquarters, 124
Coublay, Villa, 194, 246
Coulmiers, engagement at, 187, 199, 200
Coulommiers, headquarters, 119, 120, 122
Crémieux, Isaac Adolphe, French Minister of Justice, 108
Crimean War, 144

Daily News, 21, 48, 69, 150, 178, 313
Danjoutin, near Belfort, action at, 253
Davillers, M., equerry of French Emperor, 98
Degenfeld, Alfred Friedrich von, Baden Major-General, 264
Delbrück, Rudolf von, President of Chancellerie of North German (afterwards Imperial) Confederation, 142, 216, 220, 297
Delongraye, G., of French Embassy at Stuttgart, 14
Del Rio, Martinez, son-in-law of Jules Favre, 282
Denfer, Col., Commandant of Pfalzburg, 221
Denmark, 15, 53
"Deutsche Rundschau," vi
Diel, von, Bavarian Colonel, 127
Dijon, engagements at, 176, 284, 287, 293, 302
Dobeneck, Robert von, Captain, 207
Dohna, Adolf Count zu Dohna-Schlodien, Lieut., 4
Dönhoff, Countess Amélie von, Lady-in-Waiting at Prussian Court, 222
Dönhoff, Count Gerard von, Court Chamberlain, 225
Domrémy, 66, 67

INDEX

Donchery, near Sedan, 81, 82, 83, 84, 94, 95, 96, 97, 100, 101, 104
Dorien, Pierre Frédéric, French Communist, 179
Douay, Abel, French General of Division, 28
Dresky, Capt. von, attached to Crown Prince's household, 115
Dresow, Major, A.D.C. to Crown Prince, 23, 34, 85, 89, 274
Du Bois-Reymond, Professor Émile, 142
Ducrot, French General and military historian, 49, 50, 103, 181, 209, 284
Du Plat, Col., 70

Eberbach, 30, 34, 36
Edward, Prince of Wales, 18, 119, 197
Elections, French, 145, 298, 300, 304
——, Prussian, 186, 190
Elizabeth, Queen (Dowager) of Prussia, 222, 279
Elsasshausen, 33, 34, 35, 36, 38, 39
"Emperor and Empire," 102, 129, 142, 166, 200, 212, 213, 216, 218, 219, 222, 225, 227, 237, 254, 267, 268, 274, 280, 328
Ems, 5
England, diplomatic relations, 9, 74
——, public opinion in, 53, 63, 73, 121, 131, 148, 158, 165, 195, 201, 285, 303, 330, 340
——, Queen Victoria, v, 137, 144, 157, 262, 303, 341
——, Albert, Prince Consort, 168, 195, 222
——, Edward, Prince of Wales, 18, 119, 197
——, Alexandra, Princess of Wales, 18
Entry into Berlin, 336, 337
—— Hanover, 337
—— Munich, 337, 338, 339
—— of German troops into Paris, 297, 299, 304, 309, 312, 314, 317, 319, 320, 321, 323, 324
Ernst, Duke of Saxe-Altenburg, 270
——, Duke of Saxe-Coburg, 9, 19, 39, 63, 76, 92, 112, 139, 156, 178, 186, 222, 249, 270, 283
Esch, Col. von der, Chief of General Staff, 38
Eugen, Duke of Würtemburg (elder), 270
——, —— (younger), 259, 270
Eugénie, Empress of the French, 43, 69, 95, 99, 100, 104, 109, 114, 121, 128, 132, 144, 146, 155, 167, 170, 171, 176, 238, 329

Fabeck, Hermann von, Major-General, 141
Faber du Faur, von, Württemberg Lieutenant-Colonel, 87, 187
Faidherbe, French General, 253, 265, 269, 277, 297, 302
Failly, Pierre Louis Charles Achille, French General, 31, 59, 60, 103
Favre, Jules, French Minister, 129, 130, 131, 135, 140, 144, 145, 179, 181, 263, 281, 282, 283, 284, 285, 286, 287, 289, 290, 295, 296, 297, 298, 303, 304, 313, 322
Ferrières, Château, 122, 130, 131, 139, 140, 142, 327, 328, 330
Finkenstein, Reinbold Count Finck von, Dragoon Guards, 61
Fleigneux, near Sedan, 85, 86
Floing, engagement at, 84, 85, 86, 87, 89, 100
Forbes, American Colonel, 145, 148, 155
Forckenbeck, Max von, President of Prussian House of Representatives, 200
Förster, Sergeant, 27
France, army doctors, 28, 46
——, Republic, 73, 108, 109, 117, 121, 122, 123, 131, 148, 161
——, Napoleon III, Emperor, 5, 14, 16, 19, 35, 43, 48, 51, 53, 54, 56, 61, 67, 69, 72, 73, 77, 85, 88, 89, 90, 91, 92, 93, 94, 95, 96, 97, 98, 99, 100, 104, 106, 117, 121, 128, 133, 149, 155, 173, 184, 238, 310, 318, 320, 340
——, Eugénie, Empress, 48, 69, 95, 99, 100, 104, 109, 114, 121, 128, 132, 144, 146, 155, 167, 170, 171, 176, 238, 322
——, Napoleon Louis, Prince Imperial, 53, 73, 94, 99, 109, 114, 117, 128, 133, 213
——, Napoleon, Prince ("Plon-Plon"), 54, 106
——, Joséphine, Empress, 30, 289
Franchet d' Espéray, commanding National Guard at Versailles, 128
Franctireurs, 70, 113, 115, 119, 151, 152, 197, 200, 215, 229, 284, 291
Frankfurt-am-Main, 147, 333, 334
Fransecky, Edward F. von, General, 206, 207, 208, 209, 120, 283
Frederick William III, King of Prussia, 69, 267, 309, 335, 337
Freyberg-Eisenberg, Karl Baron von, Bavarian Military Plenipotentiary in Berlin, 33, 36, 84
Freytag, Gustav, man of letters, 19, 50, 90, 110
Friedrich I, King of Prussia, 129
——, Duke of Schleswig-Holstein-Augustenburg, 12, 52, 67, 70, 92, 111, 152, 270

INDEX

Friedrich, Hereditary Prince, afterwards Duke of Anhalt, 270
——— (I), Grand Duke of Baden, 30, 32, 188, 190, 191, 223, 226, 246, 249, 250, 252, 256, 257, 260, 268, 270, 272, 288, 290, 323, 327
———, Landgrave of Hesse, Prussian Lieut.-General, 270
———, Prince of Netherlands, 217
Friedrich Franz (II), Grand Duke of Mecklenburg-Schwerin, 46, 92, 115, 123, 132, 144, 184, 190, 191, 193, 194, 197, 198, 199, 201, 210, 211, 213, 215, 217, 218, 256, 283
——— ———, Hereditary Grand Duke of Mecklenburg-Schwerin, 92, 270
Friedrich Karl, Prince of Prussia (the "Red Prince"), 7, 20, 21, 22, 29, 48, 57, 59, 69, 98, 124, 156, 172, 181, 182, 192, 193, 195, 197, 198, 200, 207, 210, 213, 215, 249, 256, 257, 270, 279, 298, 306, 307, 336
Fröschweiler, near Wörth, 33, 34, 35, 36, 38, 40, 41
Fulda, 130

Galliffet, Gaston Alexandre Auguste, Marquis de, French General, 73
Gambetta, Léon, French statesman, 108, 149, 151, 178, 179, 181, 185, 188, 198, 217, 219, 228, 236, 240, 250, 256, 257, 286, 288, 289, 290, 292, 294, 296, 297, 298, 310, 321
Garches, 154, 291
———, engagement at, 274, 275
Garibaldi, Giuseppe, 151, 162, 189, 190, 202, 256, 284
———, Menotti, son of preceding, 302
———, Ricciotto, brother of preceding, 198
Geffcken, Prof. Heinrich, vi
Geissberg, near Weissenburg, 24, 25, 26, 27
Georg, Duke of Saxe-Meiningen, 18, 39, 68, 132, 270
———, Prince of Saxony, 142, 207, 208, 209, 270
———, Prince of Schwarzburg-Rudolstadt, 270
Germersheim, fortress of, 10, 11, 18
Gersdorff, Konstantin von, 90, 109
Giese, von, Lieut.-Colonel, 221
Givonne, near Sedan, 81, 87, 88, 89, 90
Goeben, August von, General, 42, 43, 265, 269, 277, 278, 331
Görlitz, 49
Görsdorf, near Wörth, 34
Gortschakoff, Alexander Prince, Russian Imperial Chancellor, 4, 5, 15, 121

Gottberg, Walter von, Quartermaster General IIIrd Army, 8, 37, 71, 109, 164, 215, 295
Gounod, Charles, composer, 291
Gower, Lord Ronald Leveson-, 48, 69
Gramont, Antoine Alfred Agénor de, Duc de Guiche, French Minister, 69
Grand-Pré, 74, 78
Granville, George Leveson-Gower, Earl, English Secretary of State, Foreign Affairs, 19, 63, 73, 165, 171
Gravelotte, battle of, 64, 104
Gronfeld, Major von, 24
Grossbeeren, near Berlin, 11
Grüter, Otto Baron von, Major-General, 146
Gunstedt, 33, 34, 45, 46
Gustedt, Lieut., von, 24, 25, 34, 68, 71, 93, 103

Haan, Pastor of Obermodern, 47
Hahnke, Wilhelm von, General, Chief of Military Cabinet, 23, 37, 62, 68, 71, 86, 153, 274, 277, 304
Hallue river, affluent of Somme, 232
Hann von Weyhern, Beuno, Lieut.-General, 184, 293, 333
Hanover, Province of, 9
Hanstein, Jäger, 62
Harmel Brothers, proprietors of cotton factory, 106
Harrach, Ferdinand Count von, Orderly Officer to Crown Prince, painter, 33, 261
Hartmann, Jakob Baron von, Bavarian General, 21, 25, 32, 33, 34, 43, 58, 68, 89, 109, 127, 139, 140, 337, 339
———, Lieut.-Colonel, 68
Hatzfeldt, Paul Count von, diplomatist, 93, 112
Hausknecht, Jäger, 27
Heidelberg, 16
Heine, Villa, at Versailles, 162
Heinrich, Prince of Prussia, 54
——— VII, Prince of Reuss, Ambassador at St. Petersburg, 4
——— XVII, Prince of Reuss, Captain of Horse, 61
Henckel, Guido Count, 297, 312, 313
Henning auf Schönhoff, Otto von, Colonel, 34, 86
Hérisson, Maurice Comte de, 277
Herkt, Wilhelm, Lieut.-General, in command of artillery before Paris, 151
Hesse-Darmstadt, Prince Ludwig of, 63, 115, 167, 220, 294, 298, 307, 331, 334
——— ———, Wilhelm, 294

INDEX

Hesse-Darmstadt, Princess Alice of, 167, 334
——, Friedrich Landgrave of, Prussian Lieut.-General, 270
Hicksch, Major, 45
Hindersin, Edward von, General of Infantry, 136
Hohenlohe-Ingelfinger, Kraft Prince zu, 80, 243
Hohenlohe-Langenburg, Hermann Prince zu, 16
Hohenlohe-Schillingsfürst, Chlodwig Prince zu, 13
Hohenthal, Karl Gustav Adolf, Count von, Lieut., 80
Hohenzollern, Prince Karl Anton, 270
——, Hereditary Prince: Leopold, 3, 4, 5, 17, 51, 55, 270
Holnstein, Max Count von, 202, 210, 211
Hoppe, Lieutenant of Police, 61
Horteuse de Beauharnais, wife of Louis Bonaparte, mother of Napoleon III, 30, 289
Hospice battery, 274, 275
Hospital train, German, 303
Howard, Miss (Comtesse Beauregard), mistress of Napoleon III, 159, 173
Hozier, English captain, correspondent of *Times*, 175
Hungary, 13
Hüningen, near Bâle, 71

Illy, near Sedan, 86, 87, 88, 103
Imperial coronation, 309
—— proclamation, 225, 237, 244, 256, 261, 268–274
—— question, 102, 142, 156, 176, 211, 219, 228, 238
—— title, 265, 266, 267, 279
Ingolstadt, 12, 272, 273
Innes, Mr., Inspector-General of Hospitals, 175
Iron Cross, 65, 71, 81, 96, 112, 115, 134, 148, 159, 161, 166, 173, 215, 242, 244, 255, 261, 271, 274, 288, 338
Issy, fort of, 245, 248, 252, 290
Italy, 15, 20, 51, 53, 117, 121, 130, 161
Ivernois, Lieut. von, 53, 159

Jakoby, Dr., Deputy, 136
Jasmund, Captain von, 65, 69, 111, 333
Jeanne d'Arc, 66, 67, 304
Johann, king of Saxony, 46, 202
Jolly, Julius, Baden statesman, 315
Josephine, Empress, 30, 289

Kaisenberg, Major von, 26, 27
Kaiserslautern, 20

Kameke, Georg von, General, 238, 243, 245, 319
Karl, King of Württemberg, 10, 14, 15, 202
——, Prince of Baden, 30
——, Prince of Prussia, 92, 112, 122, 147, 174, 243, 270, 279, 280, 296, 323, 335, 336, 337
—— Alexander, Grand Duke of Saxe-Weimar, 92, 93, 112, 147, 242, 270, 296, 301
—— August, Hereditary Grand Duke of Saxe-Weimar, 92, 259, 270
—— Karl Anton, Prince of Hohenzollern, 270
Karlsruhe, 10, 11, 16
Kératry, Émile Comte de, French politician and military leader, 198
Kessell, Bernard von, Major-General, 64
Kettler, Karl von, Major-General, 284, 287
Keudell, Robert von, statesman, 292
Kirchbach, Hugo von, Lieut.-General, 11, 29, 31, 32, 33, 34, 36, 37, 58, 90, 109, 200, 275, 276
Kleist, General von, in command of engineer and pioneer corps, IIIrd Army, 38, 136
——, von, Major, 61
Klingbach, affluent of Rhine above Germersheim, 10, 11, 18, 291
Knesebeck-Tylsen, Baron von der, 35
Königgrätz, battle of, 20, 42, 64, 94
Krupp, Alfred (of Essen), 211, 220
Kühlwetter, Friedrich Herbert von, 333

La Bergerie, hill of, 274, 275, 291
Labouchere, correspondent of *Daily News*, 313
La Malmaison, engagement at, 164
Lancken-Wakeing, Gustav August Emil Baron von der, Captain of Horse, 32, 62, 68, 71, 91
Landau, 10, 18, 21
Landauer Gate, Weissenburg, 35
Landels, draughtsman to *Times*, 48
Langensulzbach, 32, 33, 34
Laon, 72, 76, 77, 118, 132
Lauter, river, 21, 22, 23
Lauterburg, 18
Lautertal, 16
Lazareff, Frau von, 102
Le Bœuf, Edmond, French Marshal, 172, 184
Le Bourget, engagement at, 174, 176, 234
Lehndorff, Heinrich August Count von, Adjutant-General, 282

INDEX

Leipzig, 11, 160, 162
Le Mans, 178, 184, 195, 298
——, battle of, 236, 243, 249, 250, 256, 257, 262
Lembach, 43
Lenke, Captain, on Crown Prince's General Staff, 23, 58, 60, 63, 71, 89, 90, 183
Leopold I, king of the Belgians, 168
—— II, king of the Belgians, 111, 148, 292
——, Hereditary Prince of Hohenzollern, son of Prince Karl Anton of Hohenzollern, 3, 4, 5, 17, 51, 55, 270
——, Prince of Bavaria, 270, 339
——, Prince zur Lippe, 259
Les Ombrages, Villa, Crown Prince's headquarters at Versailles, 140, 146, 329
Le Sourd, Secretary French Embassy at Berlin, 4, 6
Leszczynski, Stanislaus, King of Poland, 56, 70
Leuchtenberg, Maximilian Duke of, 16
Leusse, Comte de, Maire, 43
L'Hay, engagement at, 140, 204
Ligny, headquarters, 69, 70, 71, 72
Lindsay, Colonel Lloyd, 158, 183, 195
Lippe, Leopold Prince zur, 259
Loftus, Lord Augustus, English Ambassador at Berlin, 9
Loire, French Army of the, 13, 153, 180, 184, 196, 197, 198, 204, 205, 208, 216, 218
Longchamps, racecourse, 317, 319, 325
Longjumeau, 149, 194, 304
Longwy, 224, 282
Louis XIV, king of France, 129, 133, 134, 149, 166, 173, 272
—— XV, 56, 70
—— XVI, 75
Louis Philippe, 111, 121, 198
Lüdtke, lackey of Crown Prince, v
Ludwig II, king of Bavaria, 10, 12, 13, 46, 72, 110, 202, 210, 211, 244, 337, 338, 339
——, Prince of Hesse, 63, 115, 167, 220, 294, 298, 307, 331, 334
—— Wilhelm, Prince of Baden, 16, 176
Lüzelstein, fortress of, 15
Luise, Princess of the Netherlands, 199, 217, 341
——, Queen of Prussia, 8
Luitpold, Prince of Bavaria, 14, 92, 112, 147, 211, 244, 270, 339
Lunéville, 53
——, headquarters, 55, 56, 57

Lussheim, in Baden, 17
Luxemburg, 117
Lynar, Alexander Prince von, 100, 202
Lyons, 60, 118, 132, 161, 185

MacLeod, Rev. Norman, 158
MacMahon, Maurice Comte de, Duke of Magenta, French Marshal, 30, 31, 33, 34, 35, 37, 43, 44, 49, 50, 61, 70, 71, 72, 73, 74, 75, 76, 77, 78, 82, 88, 89, 101, 102, 103, 113
Magnin, French Minister, 108
Maintenon, Château de, 326
Mainz (Mayence), 5, 6, 19
Malet, Sir Edward, English Ambassador in Paris, later in Berlin, 121
Manchester, William D., Duke of, 90
Manstein, Gustav von, General in command of IXth Army Corps, 191
Manteuffel, Edwin Baron von, General in command of Ist Army Corps, 172, 181, 184, 202, 203, 232, 233, 234, 236, 251, 255, 256, 257, 258, 259, 262, 276, 293, 300, 305
Maria, Princess (Karl) of Prussia, 167, 279
—— Anna, Princess (Friedrich Karl) of Prussia, 167
Marie, Princess of Baden, daughter of Prince Wilhelm, 16
——, Queen of Bavaria, 12, 46
Marie Antoinette, Queen of France, 75, 133
Marsal, fortress of, 55
Marseilles, 132, 185
Mars-la-Tour, 58, 100, 145
Max, Prince of Württemberg, 134
Maxau, 11
Meaux, 120, 121, 132, 326
Mecklenburg-Schwerin, Grand Duke Friedrich Franz, 46, 92, 115, 123, 132, 144, 184, 190, 191, 193, 194, 197, 198, 199, 201, 210, 211, 213, 215, 217, 218, 256, 283
——, Grand Duchess Alexandrine, 279
——, Hereditary Grand Duke Friedrich Franz, 22, 270
——, Duke Wilhelm, 87, 144
Mecklenburg-Strelitz, Hereditary Grand Duke Adolf Friedrich, 92, 259, 270
Meisner, Dr. H. O., vi
Memerty, Albert von, Major-General, 333
Merxweiler, headquarters, 45
Metz, 30, 53, 120, 124, 151, 163, 166, 167, 170, 316
——, battles before, 56, 57, 58, 60, 62, 67, 68, 105, 150

INDEX

Metz, capitulation of, 171, 172
——, citadel, 170
Meudon, 142, 159, 248, 259
——, Château de, 135, 193, 245, 252
Meuse, Army of the, 207, 234, 246, 261, 262, 278
Meyer, Sergeant-Major, 27
Mezières, 72, 79, 82, 87, 103, 224, 245
Mischke, Albert von, Major, later General, A.D.C. to Crown Prince, 35, 97, 304
Mittnacht, Baron Hermann von, Württemberg statesman, 315
Mohr and Speier, contractors for army supplies, 261
Moltke, Helmuth Count von, General, Field-Marshal, 3, 5, 6, 9, 18, 57, 65, 70, 72, 73, 74, 76, 88, 90, 92, 93, 94, 95, 96, 97, 131, 149, 155, 169, 173, 177, 193, 199, 201, 204, 207, 209, 210, 215, 220, 224, 233, 234, 237, 243, 249, 251, 253, 255, 257, 258, 259, 260, 265, 277, 281, 282, 311, 314, 316, 322, 331, 336
Mont Avron, 235, 236, 238, 239, 330
Montmirail, headquarters, 115, 116, 120
Montretout, 157, 275
——, entrenchment at, 274, 291
Montrouge, fort of, 140, 248, 252, 288, 290
Moosbrunn, near Wörth, 45
Morier, Sir Robert, English Ambassador at Darmstadt, 19
Mosel, river, 48, 57, 58, 64
Münch-Bellinghausen, Joachim Baron von, of Austro-Hungarian Embassy at Berlin, 4
Munich, 10, 11, 12, 142, 211, 250, 264, 278, 337, 338, 339
Murat, Prince Achille, grandson of King of Naples, 98
Muther, Dr., v
Mutius, von, Captain of Horse, A.D.C. to Crown Prince, 36, 77, 88

Nancy, headquarters, 58, 59, 60
——, town, 202, 254, 333
Napoleon III, Emperor of the French, 5, 14, 16, 19, 35, 43, 48, 51, 53, 54, 56, 61, 67, 69, 72, 73, 77, 88, 89, 90, 91, 92, 94, 95, 96, 97, 98, 99, 100, 104, 106, 117, 121, 128, 133, 149, 155, 173, 184, 238, 310, 318, 320
——, Eugène Louis Jean Joseph, Prince Imperial, 53, 73, 94, 99, 109, 114, 133, 213
——, Joseph Charles Paul ("Prince Plon-Plon"), son of Jérome Napoleon, king of Westphalia, 54, 106

Netherlands, Prince Friedrich, 217
——, Princess Luise, 199, 217, 341
Neweiler, near Wörth, 32
Nicholas I, Tsar of Russia, 14, 16
Niederbronn, in Alsace, 103
North German Confederation, 4, 15, 219
Nostitz, Wilhelm Count von, Captain of Horse, 215
Nüremberg, 12

Obermodern, headquarters, 47
Obernitz, Hugo von, Württemberg General, 31, 109, 207, 208
O'Danne, Captain, tutor to Prince Wilhelm, 62
Oldenburg, Grand Duke Peter, 270, 280
——, Hereditary Grand Duke August, 270
Olga, Queen of Württemberg, 14
Oliphant, Mr., 185
Ollivier, Émile, President French Ministry, 4, 6, 43, 51, 69, 122, 152, 238
Oos, in Baden, 11
Orleanists, 53, 59, 114, 300, 304
Orleans, 150, 152, 174, 178, 180, 186, 193, 195, 207, 217, 243, 298, 304
——, battles round, 153, 158, 159, 162, 211, 213, 214, 215
——, Cathedral, 304
O'Sullivan, American diplomat, 185
Otto, Prince of Bavaria, 270, 338, 339

Palaiseau, 187, 195
——, headquarters, 126
Palatinate, 12, 17, 18, 19, 22
Palikao, Charles Guillaume Marie Cousin Montauban, Comte de, 51, 103
Paris, Parisians, 5, 6, 48, 60, 61, 71, 104, 108, 112, 124, 125, 127, 128, 129, 130, 131, 132, 136, 145, 148, 151, 154, 163, 175, 181, 182, 193, 195, 239, 251, 291, 295, 301, 318, 326, 328
——, bombardment, 137, 150, 201, 222, 223, 230, 238, 243, 246, 247, 248, 254, 255, 257, 262, 290
——, capitulation, 185, 276, 277, 297
——, entry into, 299, 304, 309, 312, 314, 317, 319, 320, 321, 323
——, siege, 151, 165, 167, 188, 220, 228, 293
——, Treaty of (1856), 168
——, Universal Exhibition of 1867, 128, 324
Peace, negotiations and conditions, 287, 297, 307, 313, 314, 315, 321, 325

INDEX 851

Peter, Grand Duke of Oldenburg, 270, 280
Petersbach, headquarters, 49
Petit-Bicêtre, engagement at, 127
Pfalzburg, 54, 55, 115, 220, 221
Pfeufer, von, President, Spires, 17, 21
Pilch, Secretary of Crown Prince, 238
Pius IX, Pope, 122, 162
Plébiscite, French, 57
Ploetz, von, Major, at one time A.D.C. of Crown Prince, 139
Podbielski, Eugen A. Theophil von, Quartermaster-General, 171, 199, 220, 221, 321
Pont-à-Mousson, 57, 58, 64, 65, 100
Pranckh, Siegmund, Baron von, Bavarian Lieut.-General and War Minister, 12
Preuss, Col., commander of outposts before Paris, 192
Princes, German, 21, 59, 81, 97, 112, 131, 161, 226, 242, 255, 272, 273
Prittwitz, Moritz von, Lieut.-General, Governor of Ulm, 13
Proclamation of Empire at Versailles, 225, 237, 244, 256, 261, 268–274
Prussia, King Frederick I, 129
——, King Frederick William III, 69, 267, 309, 336, 337
——, King William I, 5, 6, 7, 8, 9, 10, 17, 18, 19, 37, 49, 57, 58, 62, 63, 64, 65, 71, 72, 73, 85, 88, 90, 92, 94, 95, 97, 98, 99, 100, 101, 112, 139, 140, 142, 146, 147, 148, 162, 163, 171, 176, 180, 190, 191, 193, 194, 212, 219, 221, 224, 242, 249, 251, 256, 259, 263, 265, 266, 267, 268, 269, 270, 272, 276, 277, 279, 290, 296, 298, 308, 313, 318, 320, 322, 324, 329, 331, 335, 336
——, Queen Augusta, 9, 10, 15, 334, 335
——, —— Elizabeth (Dowager), 222, 279
——, —— Luise, 8
——, Prince Adalbert, 136, 147, 173, 323, 331
——, ——, Albrecht (elder), 68, 78, 270, 279, 323, 335, 337
——, ——, —— (younger), 210, 270 335
——, ——, Friedrich Karl, 7, 20, 21, 22, 29, 48, 57, 59, 69, 98, 124, 156, 172, 181, 182, 192, 193, 195, 197, 198, 200, 207, 210, 213, 215, 249, 256, 257, 270, 279, 298, 306, 307, 336
——, ——, Heinrich, 54
——, ——, Karl, 92, 112, 122, 147, 174, 243, 270, 279, 280, 296, 323, 335, 336, 337

Prussia, Prince Sigismund, 10, 119
——, ——, Waldemar, 146, 152, 153, 205
——, ——, Wilhelm (elder), 270
——, ——, Wilhelm (II), subsequently Emperor (the "ex-Kaiser"), v, vi, 285, 292, 334, 337
——, Crown Princess Victoria, v, 10, 62, 70, 115, 147, 196, 198, 201, 220, 222, 230, 236, 238, 248, 271, 307, 332, 334, 335, 340
——, Princess Charlotte (Duchess of Saxe-Meiningen), 10, 39, 70
——, ——, Maria (Karl), 167, 279
——, ——, Maria Anna Friedrich Karl, 167
——, ——, Sophie, 4, 10, 190, 334, 335
——, ——, Viktoria, 11, 198, 205, 292, 335
Pyat, Félix, French Socialist and play-writer, 179

Raoult, French General of Division, 41
Rascou, Don J. de, Spanish Ambassador in Berlin, 3
Rechberg, Ludwig Count von, Bavarian Lieut.-General and Adjutant-General, 110, 337
Reichshofen, 34, 36, 38, 43, 77
Reichstag, North German, 7, 8, 213, 216 219, 220, 222
——, Deputies from, received at Versailles, 221, 224, 225, 226, 227
Reille, André Chr. Victor Comte, French General, 91, 92, 93, 94, 100
Reims, 72, 105, 107, 112, 264
——, Cathedral, 107, 108
——, headquarters, 106, 109, 111
Reinhard, Major von, 111
Renan, Ernest, 228, 236
Responsibility for war of 1870–71, 98, 310
Reuss, Prince Heinrich VII, 4
——, —— —— XVII, 61
Revigny aux Vaches, headquarters, 72, 73, 74
Rheinbaben, Albert Baron von, Lieut.-General, 144
Rieff, Theodor von, Colonel, 151, 249
Right, flanking movement to, of German armies, 70
Rochefort, Victor Henry, Marquis de, French publicist, 108
Roehl, Major-General von, 301
Rogge, Bernhart, Court Chaplain, 226, 236
Roggenbach, Franz, Baron von, Baden Minister, 19, 30, 42, 119, 176, 213, 214, 328

Roman question, 20, 117, 122, 130, 161, 162
Roon, Albrecht von, War Minister, 5, 6, 64, 65, 91, 92, 94, 97, 112, 131, 147, 155, 173, 177, 180, 199, 281, 316, 322
———, Bernhard von, Captain, son of preceding, 95
Rothkirch, Leopold Count, Lieutenant, 30
Rothschild, Mayer Baron, Paris banker, 325
Rouen, 283, 332
Rouher papers, 162
Russell, Mr. Odo, afterwards Lord Ampthill, English representative at German headquarters, subsequently Ambassador in Berlin, 191, 196, 219, 229, 232, 244, 245, 285, 304, 314, 318, 327
———, Sir William Howard, correspondent of *Times*, 21, 48, 64, 118, 119, 121, 129, 156, 157
Russia, 131, 144, 169
———, Tsar Alexander II, 121, 128, 310, 319
———, Tsar Nicholas I, 14, 16

Saar, river, 48, 50
Saarbrücken, 20, 42
———, engagement at, 43, 48, 54
Saarburg, headquarters, 53
Saint-Cloud, 123, 137, 152, 154, 159, 162, 164, 189, 274, 289, 291, 301
Saint-Cyr, 146, 174
Saint-Denis, 116, 262, 278
Saint-Germain-en-Laye, 134, 137, 146, 159, 190
Saint-Germain l'Auxerrois, church in Paris, 121
Saint-Menges, 84, 85, 86, 88, 89
Saint-Pierremont, headquarters, 78, 79, 80
Saint-Privat, 64
Saint-Quentin, actions at, 265, 277, 278, 331
Saint-Remy, church of, at Reims, 107
——— ———, on the Lauter, 23
Saint-Sulpice, church in Paris on left bank, 257
Sainte-Marie aux Chênes, action at, 64
Sainte-Menehould, headquarters, 75
Sallbach, Major, of Prussian War Ministry, 245
Sandrart, Carl, Bavarian Lieut.-General, 23, 34, 39, 231, 274, 291
Sauerbach, 30, 33, 35, 36, 38
Saxony, troops, 63, 64, 208, 209
———, King Johann, 46, 202

Saxony, Crown Prince Albert, 68, 71, 73, 74, 75, 78, 80, 81, 83, 85, 88, 89, 98, 104, 109, 112, 116, 142, 169, 209, 264, 270, 325, 329, 337
———, Prince Georg, 142, 207, 208, 209, 270
Saxe-Altenburg, Duke Ernst, 270
———, Prince Albert, 68
Saxe-Coburg, Duke Ernst, 9, 19, 39, 63, 76, 92, 112, 139, 156, 178, 186, 222, 249, 270, 283
Saxe-Meiningen, Duke Georg, 18, 39, 68, 132, 270
———, Duchess Charlotte, 10, 39, 70
———, Hereditary Prince Bernhard, 18, 39, 68, 270
Saxe-Weimar, Grand Duke Karl Alexander, 92, 93, 112, 147, 242, 270, 296, 301
———, Hereditary Grand Duke Karl August, 92, 259, 270
Schachtmeyer, Frans von, Lieut.-General, 33, 109, 141
Schaefer, Pastor at Schweighofen, 29
Schaumburg-Lippe, Prince Adolf zu, 246, 270
Scheffer, Ary, painter, 111
Schenck, Hermann von, Colonel, 35
Scherbening, von, Colonel, 90
Schillbach, Professor, surgeon, 230
Schiller, "Wallensteins Lager," 13, 66
Schimmelmann, Gustav, von Lieutenant, 183, 194
Schirrlenhof, in Alsace, 16
Schleich, von, Major-General, 34
Schleinitz, Alexander Count von, Prussian Minister, 258, 261, 264, 268, 280,
Schleithal, near Weissenburg, 24
Schleswig-Holstein, Duke Friedrich, 12, 52, 67, 70, 92, 111, 152, 270
———, Prince Woldemar, 263, 277
Schlettstadt, 167
Schlotheim, Ludwig, Baron von, Saxon General, 104, 176
Schmettow, Count von, 113
Schmidt, Christoph von, Lieut.-General, 58, 291
Schneider, Louis, reader to King William I, 108, 147, 205
Schödler, chef of Crown Prince, 116
Schön, von, Colonel, 58
Schönfels, von, Major, on Staff of Cavalry Division, 87
Schulz, Major, 146
———, Major-General, 151, 190
Schwarzburg-Rudolstadt, Prince Georg von, 270
Schweigen, village near Weissenburg, 23

INDEX

Schweighofen, headquarters, 22, 29
Schwemler, von, Captain, 27
Schwetzingen, in Baden, 19
Seckendorf, Götz Count von, High Chamberlain, 36, 84, 85, 104, 157, 228
Sedan, 72, 79, 85, 112, 118
——, battle of, 82–96, 112
Senuc, headquarters, 76, 77, 78, 79
Sèvres, 126, 142, 207, 260
——, porcelain works, 300
Shee, Mr., head of an English ambulance, 187
Sheridan, Philip Henry, American General of Cavalry, 90 91
Siemon, Lieutenant, 26
Sigismund, Prince of Prussia, 10, 119
Simson, Martin Eduard von, President of Reichstag, 225, 226, 227
Skinner, Mr., correspondent of *Daily News*, 21, 48, 69, 150
Sohns-Sonnenwalde, Eberhard Count von, Prussian diplomatist, 52, 63, 178, 313
Sommerfeld, von, Captain, one of Crown Prince's A.D.C.'s, 33, 86
Sophie, Grand Duchess of Baden, mother of Grand Duke Friedrich, 17
——, Princess of Prussia, daughter of Crown Prince, 4, 10, 190, 334, 335
Sorbonne, 257
South Germany, population, 15, 19
—— ——, troops, 7, 40
Spicheren, battle of, 42
Spires, headquarters, 17, 18, 21, 133
Spitzemberg, Karl Baron von, Württemberg Ambassador in Berlin, 14
Starkloff, von, Major-General, 36
Stauffenberg, Wilhelm Baron von, Bavarian Captain of Horse, 25
Stein, von Kaminski, Col., Chief of General Staff, 36, 38
Steinmetz, Karl Friedrich von, General Field-Marshal, 7, 21, 56, 66, 70
Stern, Frankfurt banker, 157
——, Villa (Versailles), 157, 188, 207, 249
Stieber, Wilhelm, Director of Field Police, 147, 229
Stiehle, Gustav von, Colonel, later General, 3, 4
Stillfried-Rattonitz, Count von, Prussian High Master of Ceremonies, 261
Stockmar, Christian, Baron von, Belgian Royal Court Chamberlain, 168
Stoffel, Eugène Céleste, Baron de, French military attaché in Berlin, 8

Stolberg, Wilhelm, Count zu, Lieut.-General, 22, 100, 123
Stonne, hill, 78
Stosch, Albrecht von, Intendant-General of Army, 7, 35, 66, 71, 90, 109, 131, 157, 183, 201, 210, 217, 218, 298, 330
——, Colonel von, brother of above, 35
Strantz, von, Captain, 161
Strasburg, 11, 20, 25, 49, 60, 105, 124, 129, 132, 138, 145, 252
Strauss, Dr., Military Chaplain, Potsdam, 7, 149
Stülpuagel, von, Major-General, 146
——, Lieutenant, 34
Stuttgart, 10, 11, 13, 14, 142
Suckow, Albert von, Württemberg War Minister, 186
Sulz, headquarters, 29, 30, 31, 32, 42
Sulzbach, 16
Sweden, Queen of, née Princess Viktoria of Baden, 17, 71

Tann-Rathsamhausen, Ludwig Baron von and zu (von der Tann), Bavarian General, 33, 34, 36, 71, 78, 83, 85, 89, 109, 149, 152, 153, 158, 159, 162, 178, 183, 185, 186, 187, 188, 200, 209, 217, 235, 339
Tascher de la Pagerie, Louis Comte, Senator, 30
——, Sophie Comtesse, 5
——, Stéphanie Comtesse, 30
Thiers, Adolphe, statesman, 148, 167, 169, 170, 174, 175, 176, 177, 178, 179, 181, 183, 216, 303, 307, 308, 309, 310, 311, 313, 314, 315, 316, 318
Thile, Hermann von, Secretary of State, 3, 6, 171
Times, 20, 21, 48, 67, 69, 178, 121, 156, 195, 299, 330
Torre, Marchesa della, 162
Toul, 57, 61, 62, 68, 115, 132, 145
Touraine, 307
Tours, 68, 118, 151, 178, 195, 217, 277, 306
Treskow, Hermann von, General, Chief of Military Cabinet, 96, 173, 180, 182, 194, 331
Treuenfels, von, Captain, 85
Trianon, Le Grand-, Park of Versailles, 213, 222
——, Le Petit-, Park of Versailles, 133, 223
Trochu, Louis Jules, French General, 108, 113, 131, 159, 162, 172, 179, 180, 181, 182, 188, 199, 215, 216, 221, 223, 227, 240, 260, 276, 277, 281, 284, 296, 297
Tümpling, Wilhelm von, 130, 290

A A   EMP. FRED.

Türckheim, Countess, 42
Turkos, 25, 28, 36, 42, 45, 46, 153, 178
Uhlans, Prussian, 178
Ulm, 13
Ultramontanism, 13, 106, 116, 287
Unification of Germany, 114, 186, 194, 200, 213, 225, 242, 280, 287
Unruh, von, Major, 27
Usedom, Guido Count von, Prussian Ambassador at Florence, 13
Uslar, von, Lieutenant, 286

Val-de-Grâce, Paris military hospital, 257
Valérien, Mont, 132, 134, 136, 144, 148, 149, 154, 164, 218, 227, 229, 236, 274, 275, 288, 289, 304
Vallandray, Château, 307
Valmy, 75, 76
Vanves, fort, 252, 290
Varnbüler, Karl Baron von, Württemberg Minister, 14
——, Konrad Baron von, Württemberg Ambassador in Paris, 14
Vaucouleurs, 115
——, headquarters, 64, 65, 66, 67
Vaucresson, Hospice, 274, 276
Velde, van der, Dutch ambulance, 152
Vendresse, Marquise de, 119
Verdun, 74, 184
Verdy, du Vernois, Julius von, Lieut.-Colonel, later Minister of War, 21
Versailles, 123, 162, 164, 174, 294, 297, 299
——, headquarters, 127-304 307-328
——, inhabitants, 126, 128, 177, 229, 264, 273, 274
——, town, palace, park, 127, 128, 129, 132, 134, 135, 136, 147, 148, 172
Veuve Clicquot, 107, 114, 115
Victoria, Queen, v, 137, 144, 157, 262, 303, 341
——, Crown Princess of Prussia, v, 10, 62, 70, 115, 147, 196, 198, 201, 220, 222, 230, 236, 238, 248, 271, 307, 332, 334, 335, 340
Viebahn, von, on General Staff of IIIrd Army, 216
Viktoria, Princess of Prussia, daughter of Crown Prince, 11, 198, 205, 235, 292
——, Princess of Baden, afterwards Queen of Sweden, 17, 71
Villejuif, entrenchment at, 128, 129, 132, 140, 157, 290
Villiers, engagement at, 206, 207, 208, 214

Vinoy, French General, 214, 281, 283, 284, 321
Vionville, battle of, 58
Virchow, Professor, 303
Voigts-Rhetz, Wilhelm von, Major-General, 24, 39, 126, 127
Volkszeitung, Berlin newspaper, 110, 114, 190
Vosges, 29, 45, 57, 255, 256, 257, 259, 260

Waghäusel, in Baden, 17
Waldau, French General, 321
Waldemar, Prince of Prussia, 146, 152, 153, 205
Waldersee, Georg Count von, Colonel, 27, 176
——, Rudolf Count von, Major, 174
Wales, Edward Prince of, 18, 119, 197
Walther-Monbary, von, Major-General, 29, 34, 85
Warmeriville, headquarters, 106
Wegner, Dr., physician, 152
Weimar, 334
Weissenburg, battle of, 22-29
Werder, August Count von, General, 11, 21, 29, 35, 43, 138, 176, 235, 236, 243, 251, 254, 256, 257, 258, 259, 260, 262, 264, 269, 276, 283, 284, 333
Werlé family, 107
Wesdehlen, Georg Count von, Captain of Horse, 61
Westarp, Ludwig Count von, Captain of Horse, 61
Wilhelm, Duke of Mecklenburg-Schwerin, brother of Friedrich Franz, Grand Duke, 87, 144
—— (elder), Prince of Prussia, 270
——, Prince of Württemberg, 14, 34, 92, 207, 270
Wilhelmshöhe, near Cassel, 97, 98, 104, 121, 176, 340
William I, King of Prussia, afterwards Emperor, 5, 6, 7, 8, 9, 10, 17, 18, 19, 37, 49, 57, 58, 62, 63, 64, 65, 71, 72, 73, 85, 88, 90, 92, 94, 95, 97, 98, 99, 100, 101, 112, 139, 140, 142, 146, 147, 148, 162, 163, 171, 176, 180, 190, 191, 193, 194, 212, 219, 221, 224, 242, 249, 251, 256, 259, 263, 265, 266, 267, 268, 269, 270, 272, 276, 277, 279, 290, 296, 298, 308, 313, 318, 320, 322, 324, 329, 331, 335, 336
—— (II), Prince of Prussia, subsequently Emperor (the " ex-Kaiser "), v, vi, 285, 292, 334, 337
—— (II), Prince (King) of Württemberg, 14, 34, 92, 207

INDEX

Wilms, Dr., army doctor, 115, 143, 248
Wimpffen, Félix Baron de, French General, 95, 97, 103
Winckelstein, domestic of Crown Prince, 51
Winsloe, Lieutenant, 16
Winterfeld, Hugo von, on General Staff of Royal headquarters, 54, 92, 304
——, Wilhelm von, Lieut.-Colonel, 54
Winterhalter, François Xavier, portrait painter, 198
Wittenberg, town of, 11
Wittgenstein, Peter Prince, Russian military plenipotentiary in Paris, 148, 221, 223
Wittich, Ludwig, Lieut.-General, 187, 302
Wodehouse, Mr., Secretary English Embassy in Paris, brother of Earl Kimberley, 191

Woldemar, Prince of Schleswig-Holstein, Prussian General, Governor of Mainz, 263, 277
Wörth, 30, 43, 44, 46, 53, 68, 71
——, battle of, 31, 42
Württemberg, Constitution, 14
——, King Karl, 10, 14, 15, 202
——, Queen Olga, 14, 15
——, Prince August, 270, 331
——, Prince Max, 134
——, —— Wilhelm, 14, 34, 92, 207, 270
——, Duke Eugen (elder), 270
——, —— —— (younger), 259, 270

Xylander, von, Captain of Horse, attached General Staff of Crown Prince, 33, 86

Zaluskowski, von, Major, 175, 176
Zastrow, von, General, 235, 236, 243
Zeppelin, Ferdinand von, Captain, 16
Zouaves, 35, 42, 47, 48, 49, 82, 89, 100, 129, 131, 153